MW00848564

DEEP RIVER

30150   020464514

NEW AMERICANISTS

A Series Edited by Donald E. Pease

DEEP RIVER

Music and Memory in

Harlem Renaissance Thought

PAUL ALLEN ANDERSON

Duke University Press Durham & London 2001

© 2001 DUKE UNIVERSITY PRESS

All rights reserved

Printed in the United States of America

on acid-free paper ∞

Designed by Amy Ruth Buchanan

Typeset in Carter and Cone Galliard by

Wilsted & Taylor Publishing Services

Library of Congress Cataloging-in-Publication

Data appear on the last printed page of this book.

To Gilbert and Lucille Anderson

CONTENTS

ACKNOWLEDGMENTS

It would be impossible to thank everyone who assisted this project through the gifts of inspiration, support, and dialogue. Larry Moore, Dominick LaCapra, and Joel Porte were generous with their expertise and time throughout my graduate education. They encouraged an unusual history dissertation that was always in danger of sliding through the disciplinary cracks. I must especially thank Larry Moore for being such an intellectually stimulating and supportive teacher and adviser over the years. He offered a critical and demanding reading of everything I gave him, and he patiently shepherded me through the long process. While at Cornell, I studied under a number of others who influenced the project early on, including Michael Kammen, Michael Steinberg, Henry Louis Gates Jr., Kenneth McClane, and Hal Foster. I thank them all for the education they imparted and the encouragement they gave to the various pieces that made up the project.

Extra-special thanks go to the friends and colleagues who read and commented on parts of the manuscript or the whole of it. While a complete list of their names is impossible, thanks go to Tony Nassar, Charles Reeve, Todd DePastino, Michael Slind, Blake Stimson, Jeff Stimmel, Michael Szalay, James Boyd White, Adam Smith, Laura Swartzbaugh, Robert Self, Oz Frankel, Eric Guthey, Richard Candida-Smith, Jonathan Freedman, Jim McIntosh, Tamar Barzel, Travis Jackson, and George Hutchinson. The two anonymous readers for Duke University Press extended detailed critiques of early versions and prodded me to write a better book. The diplomacy of Valerie Milholland and Miriam Angress of Duke Press ensured that the manuscript reached its destination. For permission to reprint photographs, special thanks to Bruce Kellner, Executor, Carl Van Vechten Estate. For photographic reproductions, thanks to the Library of Congress, Photoduplication Service, and the Yale Collection of

American Literature, Beinecke Rare Book and Manuscript Library, Yale University.

I am grateful to Bruce Boyd Raeburn for his early enthusiasm about the project and his knowledge of early jazz and the resources of the Hogan Ransom Jazz Archive at Tulane University. Thanks are also due the staffs of the Moorland Spingarn Research Center at Howard University, the Schomburg Center for the Study of Black Culture, the New York Public Library, Olin Library at Cornell University, and the Hatcher Library of the University of Michigan. The manuscript improved immeasurably because of the financial support and intellectual camaraderie of the Michigan Society of Fellows. During a year of research and writing, I enjoyed the financial support of a Mellon Foundation Fellowship; the Mellon Foundation bears no responsibility for the book's content. Finally, Alaina Lemon provided challenging criticisms along the way, and always gave me someone to sing with.

INTRODUCTION

Deep River, my home is over Jordan;
Deep River, my home is over Jordan.
O don't you want to go to that Gospel Feast
That Promised Land where all is Peace?
Deep River, I want to cross over into camp
ground.
—traditional African American spiritual[1]

The migrant masses, shifting from countryside to city, hurdle several generations of experience at a leap, but more important, the same
thing happens spiritually in the life-attitudes
and self-expression of the Young Negro. . . .
The wash and rush of this human tide on the
beach line of the northern city centers is to be
explained primarily in terms of a new vision
of opportunity, of social and economic freedom, of a spirit to seize, even in the face of an
extortionate and heavy toll, a chance for the
improvement of conditions. With each suc-
cessive wave of it, the movement of the Negro
becomes more and more a mass movement
toward the larger and the more democratic
chance—in the Negro's case a deliberate flight
not only from countryside to city, but from
medieval America to modern.
—Alain Locke[2]

Alain Locke's introduction to *The New Negro* (1925) recognized the ongoing black migration to "northern city centers" as a turning point in American history. World War I had sparked new industrial labor demands, thus aiding the exodus of African Americans eager to escape rural peonage and nakedly enforced white supremacy in the South. However, as the explosive antiblack violence of 1919 made clear, Northern cities remained a distant cry from the "Promised Land where all is Peace." The persistence of white hostility and economic inequality in the North demonstrated to black migrants that their hopes for democracy in the United States would not be fulfilled any time soon. As editor of the landmark *The New Negro* anthology, Locke optimistically set his sights on a "new vision of opportunity" appropriate to his sense of the New Negro's demands for equal rights, cultural recognition, and uninhibited social mobility.

Locke insisted that the forthright self-possession of America's New Negro was already having worldwide consequences; the New Negro had "the consciousness of acting as the advance-guard of the African peoples in their contact with Twentieth Century civilization."[3] The Howard University professor of philosophy savored an image of breakneck modernization where black migrants hurdled "several generations of experience at a leap" in a "deliberate flight not only from countryside to city, but from medieval America to modern." Cultural inheritances from the past merged with modernist dreams for a transformed future in the turn from false and externally enforced images of the "Old Negro" to a "New Negro" agenda of unlimited opportunity. *The New Negro* anthology, like the mid-1920s Renaissance movement it helped define, explored what it meant to be an American Negro reaching for "the more democratic chance" of individual and collective self-definition.

Many artists and critics associated with the Harlem Renaissance or Negro Renaissance agreed that the exploration of deep streams of black social memory and expressive practice would only aid black advancement in the modern world. (In accordance with the preferred usage of Alain Locke and his eminent colleague at Howard, Sterling Brown, this book will characteristically refer to the broader interwar moment as the Negro Renaissance.) The progress of the New Negro depended on a successful recuperation and elucidation of the long-maligned black cultural inheritance. Arthur Schomburg, a West Indian immigrant, scholar, and archivist, gracefully captured the point in "The Negro Digs Up His Past," his essay for *The New Negro*. "The American Negro," Schomburg wrote, "must remake his past in order to make his future. History must restore what slavery took away."[4] The reconstruction of black history and social memory that Schomburg advocated was neither a connoisseurial nor an antiquarian project. Instead, a recuperated black inheritance would give voice to a daring "advance-guard" project of liberation barely imaginable in the racist world of 1920s America. Fixing the ideal equation for the relationship between African American political action, institution-building, and art-making was, however, a subject of intense debate in the interwar years. Indeed, the artistic and political successes and failures of the Renaissance era remain topics of the most vigorous debate to this day.

The black folk music inheritance played a central role in Negro Renaissance debates about history, social memory, and cultural transmission. The present book, *Deep River*, offers a window into those debates. "The Harlem Renaissance has been treated primarily as a literary movement," the musicologist Samuel Floyd has noted, "with occasional asides, contributed as musical spice, about the jazz age and performances of concert artists. But music's role was much more basic and important to the movement."[5] To agree with Floyd as heartily as I do is to anticipate a whole series of historical and critical treatments of music's role in the Renaissance. *Deep River* does not aspire to a panoramic synthesis but instead trains its sights on reconstructing and elaborating a set of critical turns in Renaissance debates about the folk music inheritance, black nationalism, and the cosmopolitanism of the New Negro. The book approaches its goal through a series of intellectual portraits that focus attention on no more than a dozen figures. Needless to say, the selection of a cast of characters in a project like this one—where the historian or critic could have focused attention on another dozen or more important figures—has everything to do with whatever claims to representativeness the book's arguments can aspire to make. Readers already conversant with the intersection of literary, historical, and musicological approaches to the Harlem Renaissance comprise only one intended audience. Readers new to the Harlem Renaissance might also find this book a useful introduction to intellectual life in the period and to broader American debates about music, culture, and racial ideologies in the first half of the twentieth century.

By necessity, digging up the African American past is an interminable and unavoidably controversial project, for reasons Arthur Schomburg knew well; eager to share his resources, Schomburg donated his vast book collection to the Harlem branch of the New York Public Library at 103 West 135th Street. Many of the questions addressed here about the intersection of class stratification and ideologies of racial and ethnic difference are ones that continue to haunt our society at an everyday level. This book aspires to present a fresh understanding of certain cultural dynamics in the interwar years and, it might be hoped, a renewed kind of enthusiasm for digging up the musical past—not least for the sake of making, and remaking, the future. It is a truism to say that our present is haunted by the past or ideas of the past in ways we can only begin to recognize. Repeated to the point of meaninglessness, the truism is a blunt commonplace in our therapeutic culture; its hard kernel of truth, however, remains no easier to master or overcome. For many of the African American intellectuals and artists encountered in this book, the half-understood haunting of the present by the racial traumas of the recent past was a reality too deeply felt to be considered banal. With that in mind, this book explores how musical performances (and literary evocations of them) provided especially haunting and portable sites for the staging of social memory. In the case of music—which may be the expressive form most frequently associated with experiences of spirit possession, contemplative reverie, and wistul or violent nostalgia—our most striking experiences often take place at moments of half-understood hauntedness. Therefore, the intersection of music and social memory constitutes an especially propitious site for cultural analysis, not least in the study of Harlem Renaissance intellectual life.

Alain Locke's essay on the "Negro spirituals" in *The New Negro* addressed the slave spirituals as representative fragments of a rural folk culture quickly fading into obsolescence. He encouraged the hybridization of classic folk spirituals into formal art songs and long-form, scored-through concert music. Black folk song, he argued, could undergo, "without breaking its own boundaries, intricate and original development in directions already the line of advance in modernistic music."[6] Idiomatic evolution struck Locke as a fitting musical analogue to the "advance-guard" responsibilities of the elite New Negro and to the black migrants' modernizing flight away "from medieval America." Locke's call to transform black folk music materials into formal art music crystallized his vision of elite cosmopolitanism as the highest measure of New Negro cultural progress. "Negro folk song is not midway its artistic career yet," he argued, "and while the preservation of the original folk forms is for the moment the most pressing necessity, an inevitable art development awaits them, as in the past it has awaited all other great folk music."[7]

William Edward Burghardt Du Bois, the leading senior voice of black intellectual life in the interwar era, had long supported the folk spirituals' canonization as central monuments of African American culture. His influential essay on the "sorrow songs" in *The Souls of Black Folk* (1903) went far in foreshadowing the ideological terrain of the Renaissance debate about the spirituals. Du Bois's and Locke's perspectives on the spirituals as vessels of black social memory were not identical on many details. Nevertheless, their conceptions of music and African American cosmopolitanism faced related criticisms in the 1920s and 1930s. As we shall see, the terrain of the debate over the spirituals stretched beyond specifically musical concerns to broader social questions about the tempo and consequences of African American cultural modernization and the cosmopolitan leadership of an educated "advance-guard."

The first chapter, "Unvoiced Longings," explores the uses of music in Du Bois's *The Souls of Black Folk* in the context of broader philosophical commitments explicated there and elsewhere in his early black nationalist thought. The "sorrow songs" figure prominently in *The Souls of Black Folk* as haunting and prophetic monuments of the black folk inheritance. As such, the songs bear directly on Du Bois's call for black liberation. His approach to music and folk culture wedded a late Victorian ideology of aesthetic idealism and a romantic, quasi-Hegelian strain of black nationalist thought. Du Bois's legendary depiction of alienation and disalienation in black "double-consciousness" crystallized his intellectual and existential aspiration to dialectically reconcile a number of contradictory impulses. On the one hand, his romanticization of the "sorrow songs" reinforced ideas of unmediated expressivity and emotional sublimity as characteristics of authentic folk music. On the other hand, Du Bois upheld ideals about cultural evolution—where Western European high culture figured as a leading model of advanced civilization—as appropriate to African Americans and other "colored" peoples. His application of evolutionary civilizationist ideals to African Americans combated white racist prejudices about black culture as immutably undeveloped, imitative, and inferior. There had been great black civilizations in the past, he later argued, and there would be again in a liberated future. The elevation of the "sorrow songs" through cosmopolitan practices of formalization spoke to the folk romanticism in Du Bois's black nationalism as well as his urgency about pushing African American culture further along toward his developmental goals of high civilization. He imagined this double agenda not as self-contradictory but as reconcilable through a transformative synthesis. Music offered itself to Du Bois's imagination as not only a haunted site of memory but as an energizing site of utopian anticipation. Du Bois's primary concerns as an intellectual were always political rather than aesthetic. My analyses look to broader ideological contexts of Du Bois's aesthetic and philosophical thought but also attempt to delineate some of the surprisingly idealistic philosophical implications of his explicitly political and this-worldly agenda as an intellectual and social activist.

Du Bois's formulations about the folk roots of the "sorrow songs" and his idealism about the elite "kingdom of culture" called for a dynamic musical synthesis of folk-based black nationalist content and idealist European forms. His interpretation of the "sorrow songs" as vessels for transmitting black social memory paralleled the logic of dialectical overcoming active in his notion of black "double-consciousness." First, the cancellation of racial hierarchy, its alienating consequences, and the merely contingent residue of so-called black "backwardness"; second, the preservation of certain essential cultural differences; and, finally, the elevation of a hybridized African American identity. "In this merging," Du Bois wrote, the American Negro "wishes neither of the older selves to be lost. . . . He simply wishes to make it possible for a man to be both a Negro and an American, without being cursed and spit upon by his fellows, without having the doors of Opportunity closed roughly in his face."[8] Du Bois's approach to the social function of art and the meaning of cultural evolution came under tremendous pressure in the 1920s Jazz Age milieu of the "Negro vogue," interracial modernism, newly glamorized notions of the primitive, and the mixed blessings of increased white patronage toward black writers and artists.

Deep River's second chapter, "Swan Songs and Art Songs," focuses on several careers in the 1920s that unfolded within the long shadow of Du Bois's interpretation of the "sorrow songs." Jean Toomer's literary experiment *Cane* (1923), a book Toomer referred to as a "swan song" to African American folk culture, contributed an arresting modernist vision of ruptured continuity, cultural disenchantment, and deracination. "The folk-spirit," Toomer wrote, "was walking in to die on the modern desert. . . . Its death was so tragic."[9] Toomer admired the African American folk spirituals tremendously, but he rejected Du Bois's ideal of a hybridic "double-consciousness." Instead, Toomer interpreted black modernization as a fundamentally traumatic and irreparable rupture between traditional folk culture and modern urban culture. His artistic and personal response to the fate of black culture in twentieth-century modernity was utterly distinct from Du Bois's frankly "propagandistic" sense of art's liberatory function and Locke's more formalist vision of steady cosmopolitan evolution and developmental continuity.

The second chapter's contrasting "art song" narrative emerges in a discussion of the pioneering African American concert singer Roland Hayes. Hayes attended Fisk University in the first decade of the twentieth century and toured with the Fisk Jubilee Singers. By the 1920s, he was widely appreciated as a solo concert performer of European art songs. Hayes added another dimension to his solo concerts by programming several spirituals along with his traditional concert repertoire. "Before my time," he noted in his 1942 autobiography, "white singers had often been in the habit of burlesquing the spirituals with rolling eyes and heaving breast and shuffling feet. . . . It pleased me to believe that I was restoring the music of my race to the serious atmosphere of its origins, and helping to redeem it for the national culture."[10] Du Bois, Locke, and many others championed Hayes as an icon of artistic cosmopolitanism and racial pride. Nevertheless, Hayes's comparatively Europeanized renditions of the spirituals inspired skeptics to fault his interpretations as inauthentic and untrue to the very folk practices he intended to commemorate.

Such criticisms expanded at times into a broader skepticism about musical syntheses of black folk idioms and European-based formal idioms. The mixed reception of Hayes's cosmopolitanism and concert spirituals replayed some of the conflicting, if not contradictory, impulses of Du Boisian "double-consciousness." How was folk authenticity to be preserved in the concert spirituals and simultaneously reconciled with European techniques of formal art music? The aesthetic debate found its solo concert exemplars in the contrasting styles of Hayes and Paul Robeson. One of Robeson's most influential patrons in the mid-1920s was Carl Van Vechten, a white associate and patron of many African American artists. Van Vechten's involvement in the "Negro vogue" and the Harlem Renaissance may have been as indispensable as it was controversial. Van Vechten's championing of Robeson's "traditional, evangelical renderings" of the spirituals over Hayes's "more refined performances" offers an occasion for reconsidering the cultural politics of racial authenticity, exoticism, and patronage in an era "when the Negro was in vogue" (to quote Van Vechten's friend Langston Hughes).[11] Du Bois's famous condemnation of Van Vechten's best-selling novel *Nigger Heaven* (1926) made public his long-simmering worries about the "decadent" and counterprogressive influences of racial exoticism and aestheticism in a politically suspect "Negro vogue." Nevertheless, some other African American writers and artists welcomed Van Vechten's celebration of jazz and the blues and his "bohemian" willingness to fly in the face of black and white bourgeois expectations for morally instructive and idealistic art. The debate over Van Vechten's patronage exposed some of the definitive generational, political, and temperamental fissures marking the African American intelligentsia of the interwar period.

Chapter 3 of *Deep River* tracks "the key of paradox" in Alain Locke's writings about music and culture.[12] One of Locke's central goals as a theorist of black art was to resist static or antihybridic notions of black cultural difference and the assimilatory pull of traditional European cosmopolitanism. The best New Negro art, he argued, brilliantly fused black particulars with cosmopolitan universals, thereby merging and expanding multiple horizons of aesthetic possibility. Locke championed many modernist developments in African American music, literature, and visual art through a synthesis of cosmopolitanism and pluralism that shared traits with Du Bois's dialectical ideal of disalienated black "double-consciousness." Locke wrote of himself as a "philosophical mid-wife to a generation of younger Negro poets, writers, [and] artists," and he rationalized his aesthetic vision as that of "a cultural cosmopolitan, but perforce an advocate of cultural racialism as a defensive counter-move for the American Negro."[13] His music criticism espoused folk nationalism in African American concert music as the ideal reconciliatory glue for a synthesis of the local and vernacular with the universal and classical.

Locke contended that jazz began as a folk music whose "often wholly illiterate" originators were "humble troubadours [who] knew nothing about written music or composition." In the 1920s, however, jazz had begun to develop into something else entirely, especially through the vaguely defined concert idiom of "symphonic jazz." No longer a folk music of the "Mississippi headwaters," jazz had become a cosmopolitan and multiracial affair. A music, according to Locke, rooted in folk spirituals like "Deep River" had met its cosmopolitan destiny by enlarging itself to meet the full dimensions of an "international ocean."[14] At the same time, many white intellectuals and artists of the Jazz Age endowed the new popular music with a countercultural aura of erotic liberation. The exoticism of the "Negro vogue" provided a modernist gloss to old habits of romantic racism, habits that stereotyped black musicians as racially characteristic ciphers of desublimated expressivity. Locke argued in response that "the Negro, strictly speaking, never had a jazz age."[15] He chose not to celebrate jazz, or any musical idiom, as a therapeutic refuge from aesthetic or psychic discipline or the developmental challenges of musical formalization. Instead, Locke elaborated the centrality of sublimation in advanced cultural production and contested interpretations of black music that implicitly or explicitly enforced a racial double standard.

The reigning double standard especially neglected or denied the hard-won advances and vindicating potential of black concert music. On the one hand, the popular music marketplace too often cultivated the lowest common denominator in musical production, according to Locke, and reinforced racial stereotypes anathema to Locke's New Negro agenda. Racial vindication, he believed, would emerge instead in more elite realms of cultural production, hence the symbolic importance of the concert spiritual idiom. On the other hand, institutionalized racism blocked African American progress in the elite realms of fine arts and concert music. One reason why Roland Hayes became famous as a solo performer was his inability to find employment in white opera companies in the United States. Likewise, Marian Anderson, the world-acclaimed African American contralto, did not win passage onto the stage of the Metropolitan Opera House until 1955 at the age of fifty-seven. Facing the grim barriers blocking the development of black musical freedom, Locke clung to New Negro cosmopolitanism as a "new vision of opportunity, of social and economic freedom."

Dissenters challenged many of Du Bois's and Locke's ideas about folk-to-formal musical development and the "advance-guard" responsibilities and privileges of the black middle-class elite. Chapter 4 of *Deep River*, "Beneath the Seeming Informality," focuses on the revisionist agendas of Langston Hughes and Zora Neale Hurston regarding the blues, spirituals, and vernacular strategies of formalization. Hughes and Hurston challenged dominant cosmopolitan assumptions in the interwar years about long-form concert music as the ideal toward which all music should aspire. In contrast to Du Bois and Locke, Hughes pointed out limitations of evolutionist schemes that rigidly stratified elite and popular musical idioms. Thus, he explicated the easily overlooked sophistication of expert blues singers and musicians and demonstrated the poetic force of the blues idiom. Hughes also parted from curatorial and folkloric approaches toward the "sorrow songs" as vessels of black folk memory. He emphasized instead the poetic and musical power of the blues, a genre he regarded as both an urban folk music and a proletarian art form rich in political implications. Hughes's blues advocacy, especially during the 1930s, eschewed Du Bois's folk romanticism and directed attention instead to the social significance of contemporary vernacular forms.

Zora Neale Hurston interpreted the formal concert spirituals of Ro-

land Hayes, Marian Anderson, and other classically trained concert singers as assimilationist and untrue to the authentic values of the black folk
inheritance. She instead celebrated the pleasures and overlooked sophistication of vernacular practices among black folk in the South. Hurston's
polarizing revisionism about the spirituals indicted Du Bois's depiction
of the "sorrow songs" as a corollary to his elite black nationalist vision of
overcoming alienation and injustice through racial solidarity and collective action. Hurston charged that the "idea that the whole body of spirituals are 'sorrow-songs' is ridiculous. They cover a wide range of subjects
from a peeve at gossipers to Death and Judgment."[16] Hurston pushed sorrow away from the center of the spirituals' legacy and likewise decentered
themes of bitterness and alienation in her interpretation of black folk culture. She elaborated an alternative to the developmental dialectic under-
girding Du Bois's aesthetic and social thought. Hurston's challenge to Du
Bois refigured the hybridizing aesthetic of "double-consciousness" and
black musical cosmopolitanism according to a nondialectical model that
preserved rather than resolved tensions between disparate elements and
expectations in a musical performance or composition. The latter-day influence of Hughes and Hurston's New Negro revisionism is hard to over-
estimate. Hurston, for example, inspired prominent postmodernist elaborations of black vernacular practices with her often-cited discussion of
the "will to adorn" in "Characteristics of Negro Expression" (1934). The
analysis in chapter 4 suggests that the ideal of a truly pluralistic cosmopolitanism might only be approached when residual Eurocentric assumptions
about scored-through concert music and the intellectual trap of overvalu-
ing the mercurial quality referred to as folk authenticity are brought to
light and overcome.

The fifth and final chapter of *Deep River* approaches the history of African American musical cosmopolitanism from a comparative perspective.
"Saving Jazz from Its Friends" crosses over from the Harlem Renaissance
debate about the spirituals and the folk inheritance to implicit refractions
of that debate in jazz criticism during the Swing Era. Sympathetic white
partisans variously interpreted jazz as a blissful escape from the sobering
realities of the Depression and war, a symptomatic interracial battleground of industrialized cultural production, or a fragile vessel of social
memory and "premodern" authenticity threatened by commercialization
and misplaced artistic ambitions. John Hammond's 1938 "From Spirituals
to Swing" concert is used in chapter 5 as a perch from which to compare
Hammond's celebratory narrative of jazz's development against the less

jazz-focused narratives of Locke and Du Bois. Hammond's was the central voice of American jazz criticism in the 1930s, and "From Spirituals to Swing" reinforced his sense of developmental continuity and folk artistic legitimacy in jazz. The radical magazine *New Masses* sponsored Hammond's first "From Spirituals to Swing" concert, which contributed to the magazine's Popular Front project of constructing narratives of American folk music as proletarian harbingers of social democracy and multiracial pluralism in American life. This chapter also discusses Roger Pryor Dodge's classicist theories of improvisation and long-form development in "hot jazz." The golden age of jazz, Dodge argued, preceded a profound aesthetic decline into symphonic jazz, commercial swing music, and the modern jazz of the 1940s. Hammond came to share aspects of Dodge's elegiac swan song narrative of decline in jazz.

Deep River concludes with an overview of early reactions to the formal concert ambitions of Edward Kennedy Ellington. Duke Ellington's achievements as a composer, bandleader, pianist, and public figure encompassed key tenets of New Negro thought regarding concert music and the commemoration of the folk inheritance. "We are not interested primarily in the playing of jazz or swing music," Ellington once explained, "but in producing musically a genuine contribution from our race. . . . We try to complete a cycle."[17] Although they admired Ellington's genius, Hammond and Dodge were among the most vociferous critics of Ellington's longer compositions in the 1930s and 1940s, particularly "Reminiscing in Tempo" and *Black, Brown and Beige*. Unfortunately, Hammond, Dodge, and like-minded hot jazz partisans reinforced debilitating double standards about black musical ambition, even as they attempted to shore up the general public's appreciation of virtuosic artistry in jazz. The Swing Era music and commentary of Duke Ellington suggested a jazz composer's revision of the folk nationalist concert ideal propagated by Du Bois and Locke. Ellington's 1943 concert suite, *Black, Brown and Beige*—in which an original spiritual "Come Sunday" was a high point—brings the cycle of music and ideas investigated here to a close. The dramatic rise of modern jazz in the 1940s, simultaneous transformations in the worlds of popular music and concert music, and new visions of African American cosmopolitanism and black nationalism offered fresh challenges to imagining the traces of social memory in music.

Many contemporary artists, scholars, and scientists are interested in how the felt realities of individual memories are transmuted into, experienced as, or misrecognized as collectively shared or social memories. As a work of intellectual history, this book makes no strong reality claims for the musicalized traces of social memory that captured the imaginations of many Harlem Renaissance figures. Neither does it pursue a critical or philosophical agenda of thoroughgoing disenchantment with and de-idealization toward notions of social memory and claims about music as a site of social memory. My more basic goal is to understand how certain intellectuals, writers, and musicians of the Harlem Renaissance period pieced together, suggested, asserted, and argued for distinctive interpretations of music and social memory. That said, it seems to me that we can neither resurrect nor exorcise the recent past. We might instead work to recognize its simultaneous distance and proximity to us and consider its bearing on the present and on the possible futures we allow ourselves to imagine. In other words, more than a few of the questions addressed by the figures of the Harlem Renaissance remain with us.

ONE

"Unvoiced Longings": Du Bois
and the "Sorrow Songs"

The price of culture is a Lie.
—W. E. B. Du Bois[1]

The authentic utopia is grounded in recollec-
tion. "All reification is a forgetting." Art fights
reification by making the petrified world
speak, sing, perhaps dance.
—Herbert Marcuse[2]

In 1933, Olin Downes noted a recent Fisk University Choir concert at Carnegie Hall. The music critic for the *New York Times* found the concert a
disappointment and compared it unfavorably to the performances of African American singers in Broadway's *Porgy* or the Hall Johnson Choir's
work in *Green Pastures*. Downes recommended that readers contrast the
restrained Fisk concert with an event guaranteed to be out of the ordinary,
"a real religious revival in Harlem, as the writer has done." Describing the
peculiar charms of the experience, he explained that a visitor "will hear
hymns and spirituals, but they will have an emotion that was not to be felt
last night. That was one thing. Quite another thing is the wildness, the
melancholy, the intense religious feeling communicated when Negroes
sing in the sacred spirit and the uncorrupted manner of their race."

Downes's comments on black performance reinforced stereotypical assumptions about the "uncorrupted manner" of informal black musical expression, whether secular or religious. His remarks on the Fisk University
Choir led W. E. B. Du Bois to respond by critiquing a latent agenda of
those critics who held forth on the hazards of formal African American

musical aspiration. Insulted by Downes's comments, Du Bois wrote in the NAACP journal, the *Crisis*, that what Downes's assessment

> really means is that Negroes must not be allowed to attempt anything more than the frenzy of the primitive, religious revival. "Listen to the Lambs" according to Dett, or "Deep River," as translated by Burleigh, or any attempt to sing Italian music or German, in some inexplicable manner, leads them off their preserves and is not "natural." To which the answer is, Art is not natural and is not supposed to be natural. And just because it is not natural, it may be great Art. The Negro chorus has a right to sing music of any sort it likes and to be judged by its accomplishment rather than by what foolish critics think that it ought to be doing.[3]

The Fisk University Choir disappointed Downes's expectation of African American music delivered with "the wildness, the melancholy, the intense religious feeling . . . of their race"—music in other words, foreign to formal concert venues. The musicologist Jon Michael Spencer has repeated Du Bois's charge in arguing that Downes's conclusion "repudiated renditions of the spirituals that did not reflect the 'real' Negro with his 'natural' emotivity, sensuality, and inferiority."[4] Du Bois used the occasion to express his frustration with a tradition of criticism favoring informal and "primitive" black musical expression. It was a tradition, he insisted, that continued to have a debilitating effect on the careers of African American musicians and composers, including Harry Burleigh and Nathaniel Dett, both of whom had become prominent for their formal arrangements of spirituals.

If Downes preferred the black "frenzy of the primitive, religious revival," Du Bois countered that the Fisk University Choir had performed a program of carefully rehearsed music and not a concert facsimile of sanctified church styles. "Art is not natural and is not supposed to be natural," he stressed. "And just because it is not natural, it may be great Art." The abstract formulation implied that the naturalness of folk expression was altogether different from the artfulness of formal concert music. Downes, however, had found the music of a "primitive, religious revival" aesthetically superior to that of the Fisk University Choir. His comment on the "uncorrupted manner" of Harlem church singing reinforced dubious assumptions about naturalness or unself-consciousness in black musical performance. The basic problem, as Du Bois saw it, was that Downes seemed to imagine African American vernacular music as wholly other in its folk authenticity and black formal ambition as tantamount to racial corrup-

1. W. E. B. Du Bois, 1946. Photo by Carl Van Vechten. Courtesy of Carl Van Vechten Trust.

tion. Du Bois responded as he did because Downes's insinuating charge against the Fisk group—namely, the charge of betraying "the uncorrupted manner of their race"—was far from unprecedented.

Many reviewers of Fisk University's various touring singers had reacted to performances in ways that raised troubling questions about the ideological markers of racial difference and the shifting aesthetic borders between presumably natural and artistic expression. These reviewers reinforced an ambivalently complimentary tradition of romantic racialism found, among other places, in abolitionist commentaries on the slave songs in the antebellum era.[5] Such ambivalence informed many friendly reactions to Fisk University's first and most famous troupe during its historic American and European tours in the 1870s. As we shall see, the brief comments of Downes and Du Bois carried with them a century's worth of implications about African American musical performance and much else besides.

To appreciate the force of Du Bois's rejoinder that "art is not natural and is not supposed to be natural" one needs a clear sense of how the nature/art binary operated in his thought. His polemical riposte to Downes notwithstanding, Du Bois more often treated the relationship between nature and art as dynamic, indeed dialectical, rather than polar and absolute. His early writings reveal how he married a romantic theory of black folk expressivity as unself-conscious (and revelatory of black identity's authentic core) to an elite developmental ideal of formal self-consciousness in art. On the one hand, the polarizing distinction that Du Bois made between nature and art in 1933 privileged art as self-conscious artifice over the supposed naturalness of romanticized folk expressivity. On the other hand, *The Souls of Black Folk*, published when Du Bois was thirty-five years old, anticipated a dialectical reconciliation of art and nature. The prospective reconciliation of black "nature" with cosmopolitan art constituted a tacit aesthetic corollary to Du Bois's intertwining of high cultural idealism and folk romanticism throughout *The Souls of Black Folk*. Both anticipations of reconciliation resonated with that book's influential notion of black "double-consciousness."

The folk legacy of the "sorrow songs," according to Du Bois, would provide a passage into the "kingdom of culture" where distinctively black expressive content might find sympathetic expression in idealist cosmopolitan forms. Alain Locke and others among a younger generation of New Negro commentators elaborated variations of Du Bois's perspective, although they would not always earn Du Bois's full approval. Du Bois maintained a very brisk rate of scholarship and public writing throughout the decades between the world wars and closely monitored cultural trends as the chief editor of the *Crisis* during most of that period. Newer trends in the interwar years threatened his aesthetic vision with obsolescence as assorted modernist and populist challenges in intellectual discourse echoed transformations in popular culture. Some of the most striking alternatives to Du Bois's aesthetic vision decisively turned away from his synthesis of cultural idealism and folk romanticism. Among the most important symptoms of interwar cultural and intellectual change was the vast public appetite for jazz—including the "hot jazz" made famous by African American musicians—which spread like wildfire across the commercial circuits of the industrialized world.

The analysis offered here approaches Du Bois's views on music and aesthetic thought during the Harlem Renaissance through the formative contexts of *The Souls of Black Folk* and related early writings. These texts allow us to trace how he appropriated the Fisk Singers' legacy in terms of its relevance to his black nationalism and his cosmopolitan dialectic of "double-consciousness." A short survey of reactions to the original Fisk singing tours provides a backdrop for an inquiry into Du Bois's representation of the "sorrow songs." Du Bois's elaboration of the "sorrow songs" concept brought together his ideas about the relationship between formal art, folk expression, and social memory.

The "Puzzle" of the Fisk Jubilee Singers

Various distinctions between nature and art animate J. B. T. Marsh's *The Story of the Jubilee Singers* (1880), the most prominent account of the singing group's early tours. Marsh's discussion of the singers' critical reception highlights their evangelical religious appeal. The book recounts the uplifting success story of the group's tours in the early 1870s and its initial project of raising $20,000 for Fisk, a freedman's school founded by the American Missionary Association in 1866. Marsh notes in the course of his celebratory narrative that the group's music "was more or less of a puzzle to the critics; and even among those who sympathized with their mission, there was no little difference of opinion as to the artistic merit of their entertainments."[6] The singing group raised more than $100,000 in three years and endured any number of racial humiliations and insults along the way. Although they usually sang in churches or concert halls, some in the audience expected comedic minstrelsy entertainment and ridiculed the college students for refusing to gratify white expectations for black self-mockery. As the music historian Eileen Southern explains: "The students were not minstrel singers; their program included no jokes, no dances, no catchy tunes. . . . The format of the Fisk Jubilee Singers' concerts was similar to that of concerts presented by white artists of the time, except that a large number of spirituals were included."[7] Not least on account of the group's novel concept, the singers' presentations inspired various reactions. One could map these reactions across a broad discursive terrain: The Fisk Jubilee Singers' performances could be interpreted as informal, blessedly innocent of artifice, natural, formal, stiff, pretentious, self-consciously artistic, or refined to the point of a higher naturalism. Evading the question of musical value altogether, at least one critic simply dismissed them as a Barnumesque "humbug," a popular entertainment precisely aimed at puzzling audiences through elaborate fictions.[8] The "puzzle to the critics" who at least heard the singers as *musicians* was about how and where their music intersected with prevailing aesthetic categories. Upon which scale of value was their music to be measured?

On its first trip outside Nashville in October 1871, the student group of five women and four men (originally named "The Colored Christian Singers") and George White (Fisk's white treasurer and choir leader) dealt with basic issues of repertoire and style. The group adjusted its repertoire over time, based on the reactions of audiences. Singing the spirituals before predominately white and uninitiated audiences of outsiders raised concerns about what kind of framing procedures and concert-oriented refinements should be made to the folk songs. Above all, the group wanted to distinguish its mission of university development and religious and aesthetic edification from demeaning minstrel entertainment. It therefore took the route of self-conscious refinement and worked to burnish the "dirty" tonality and improvised arrangements of the folk songs to match the polished, round-toned style cultivated in formal European vocal music. An early white account identified the group as "a band of negro minstrels . . . genuine negroes," while one newspaper headline described their innovative presentation as "NEGRO MINSTRELSY IN CHURCH — NOVEL RELIGIOUS EXERCISE."[9] The early months of the Fisk group's first tour were not financially successful; however, the tour took on a remarkable second wind during a five-week stay in the New York City area in December 1871.

After receiving a letter from his brother praising the college group, Henry Ward Beecher, the nation's best-known clergyman, became a proud supporter of the Fisk Jubilee Singers and their school's affiliation with the American Missionary Association. Beecher sponsored a large benefit concert by and for the singing group in his Brooklyn church. The event's success and Beecher's connections led to a month of engagements in the metropolitan New York area and to important contacts for the group's later European tour. Beecher once explained the students' grisly qualifications for singing the spirituals with full emotional authenticity: "only they can sing them who know how to keep time to a master's whip."[10] The novelty of the spirituals became the group's calling card and its claim to fame. Theodore Seward's notes for a collection of transcriptions likewise suggests that "the excellent rendering of the Jubilee Band is made more effective and the interest is intensified by the comparison of their former state of slavery and degradation with the present prospects and hopes of their race, which crowd upon every listener's mind during the singing of their songs."[11]

According to the Reverend Theodore Cuyler's report to the New York *Tribune* about the group's effect on his Brooklyn congregation, "the wild melodies of these emancipated slaves touched the fount of tears, and gray-haired men wept like little children." The group, in this view, was tremendously affecting, utterly sincere, and free of artifice. Their repertoire included "a fresh collection of the most weird and plaintive hymns sung in the plantation cabins in the dark days of bondage." Such music was "the very embodiment of African heart music." "The harmony of these children of nature and their musical execution," Cuyler exclaimed, "were beyond the reach of art."[12] The Fisk Jubilee Singers' music, it would seem, "touched the fount of tears" and could generate in sensitive listeners foreign to the personal experience of chattel slavery a queer mixture of pain and rapturous pleasure. Both "weird and plaintive," the execution of the native songs of "these children of nature" transcended the confines of ordinary hymn singing and moved to a rarer destination "beyond the reach of art."[13] Cuyler's evaluation bore witness to impressions of an overpowering, indeed sublime, listening experience at a performance perceived as raw to the point of naturalness and thus "the very embodiment of African heart music." As the musicologist Ronald Radano explains, "only rarely did writers depict the spirituals according to conventional musical images of perceptible beauty. Rather, the songs seemed to test the limits of white comprehension, expressing a transcendent musical perfection born out of some uncharted realm."[14] Generalizations about emotionally affecting music as sublime or as inducing an experience of the sublime, though intended as high praise, could also turn into a trap of racial exoticism in the case of folk musics judged in terms of their unself-conscious authenticity. How, after all, was one to distinguish musical expression (especially when outside the frameworks of European concert music) that went *beyond* art from that which took place *below* art? Deep stereotypes fueled debilitating judgments about black culture in general, even when the performances of prominent black musicians were romanticized and interpreted as taking place outside the reach of self-conscious artistry. Du Bois's retort to Olin Downes in 1933 was, in short, a protest against an interpretive tradition that celebrated black musical performances as emotionally transparent and without artifice.

The Fisk Jubilee Singers had to adjust their original repertoire in order to showcase "Go Down, Moses" and other spirituals that Cuyler referred to as "the most weird and plaintive hymns sung in the plantation cabins." Those distinctive songs generated the most enthusiastic audience reactions. But in contrast to Cuyler's gushing comments that the music constituted something "free of artifice" and therefore was "beyond the reach of art," hostile reactions suggested an entirely different assessment of what the singers and their "wild melodies" were up against. The *New York Herald*'s reviewer reduced the group's performances to the comedic genre of minstrelsy: "BEECHER'S NEGRO MINSTRELS . . . THE GREAT PLYMOUTH PREACHER AS AN END MAN . . . A FULL TROUPE OF REAL LIVE DARKIES IN THE TABERNACLE OF THE LORD." The reviewer also lampooned white audiences as "people of a superior race, or [people that] fancy they belong to a superior race, who like to patronize those whom they fancy to be of an inferior or docile race." A reviewer for the *New York World* derided the group's mixed repertoire of hymns, spirituals, and art songs and insisted that "this amateur group of Negro Minstrels should sing camp meeting and nigger melodies rather than opera."[15] Sixty years later, Du Bois interpreted Olin Downes's critique of the Fisk Choir as belonging to this tradition of exoticism and limitation. As Du Bois ventriloquized the discourse: "Negroes must not be allowed to attempt anything more than the frenzy of the primitive, religious revival." The Jubilee Singers' mixed reviews demonstrated that the college students won neither universal praise nor universal respect. Nevertheless, the group's American and European tours during the hopeful era of Reconstruction raised an unexpectedly large amount of money for their school. Latter-day commentators, Du Bois not least among them, would memorialize the early tours as vindicating triumphs.

The European tour of 1873 and 1874 constitutes the high point of Marsh's *Story of the Jubilee Singers*. In contrast to the blatant indignities of American racist customs, elite European hosts and audiences offered more respectful recognition to the visiting artists. Marsh relishes the chance to count among the group's audiences the highest political and social leaders. In a private performance for Queen Victoria, they sang the spirituals "Go Down, Moses" and "Steal Away to Jesus" and chanted the Lord's Prayer. A polite breakfast with Britain's Prime Minister William Gladstone, according to Marsh, constituted nothing less than a "rebuke to the caste spirit of America."[16] The sociologist Paul Gilroy suggests that seeing and hearing the Fisk Jubilee Singers presented liberal British patrons an "opportunity to feel closer to God and to redemption." At the same time, "the memory of slavery recovered by [the singers'] performances entrenched the feelings of moral rectitude that flowed from the commitment to political reform for which the imagery of elevation from slavery was emblematic long after emancipation."[17] The Jubilee Singers' performances inspired feelings of righteous vindication for both the visiting African Americans and their hosts, though the groups' feelings were hardly interchangeable. The same had undoubtedly been true in the United States with sympathetic whites who aligned the singing group with the American Missionary Association and its controversial project of black education and evangelical uplift in the South.

Marsh notes the appraisal of Colin Brown, a Glasgow music professor, as an especially insightful commentary. After enjoying a local performance, Brown argued that the Fisk Singers' greatness resided in their attainment of a quality of seamless naturalness that only results from extraordinary discipline and rehearsal. "The highest triumph of art," Brown wrote, "is to be natural." "The singing of these strangers is so natural," he continued, "that it does not at once strike us how much of true art is in it, and how careful and discriminating has been the training bestowed upon them by their accomplished instructor and leader, who, though retiring from public notice, deserves great praise." Any simple distinction between art and nature would not do, regardless of whether George White or the singers deserved the greater share of praise. The singers' triumphant performances only became natural, Brown was suggesting, through the elevating mediations of stylization and artifice. The Scottish commentator thus eschewed the typical remarks about emotional sublimity and naturalness in analyzing the singers' effectiveness. His review instead emphasized that only painstaking practice made the breakthrough into seemingly transparent expressivity and artlessness possible. Brown rounded out his assessment by reminding readers that the singers' "careful and discriminating" mastery of artifice in their production of naturalness was hardly their only laudable attribute. The evangelical message at the heart of the singers' precisely modulated performances also commanded attention: "how strange it is that these unpretending singers should come over here to teach us what is the true refinement of music, make us feel its moral and religious power."[18] The greatness of "these unpretending singers" rested not only in a calibrated replication of the presumably unself-conscious attributes of folk singing but in a capacity for grand "moral and religious power."[19] The labor of artifice, the aura of folk authenticity, and an "unpretending" moral sincerity worked together (however paradoxically) to elevate the performance's power, according to Brown.

Evidencing the ongoing "puzzle to the critics," a German minister opined that "these are not concerts which the negroes give; they are meetings for edification, which they sustain with irresistible power."[20] Marsh notes the Fisk group's humble background and reports how in Germany "thoughtful people said with surprise, 'We could not take even our German peasantry and reach such results in art, and conduct, and character, in generations of culture, as appear in those freed slaves.' "[21] The comparison, juxtaposing the musical inheritances and social manners of the "freed slaves" and the "German peasantry," reveals another layer of the "puzzle to the critics." A comment attributed to "thoughtful people" in Germany suggests how strangers to the African American spirituals and to their performance could interpret them through general preconceptions about folk cultural practices. Johann Gottfried von Herder's influential writings from the late eighteenth century constituted one context for reactions in Germany and elsewhere, including the United States, to the aura of folk authenticity in the Fisk Jubilee Singers' performances. According to Herder, a pioneering German folklorist and former student of Immanuel Kant, the communal expressive forms of the peasantry (music and language most especially) promised powerful seed material for national cultural expression and icons of organic communal creativity.[22] Herder was responding to the limitations of a French-dominated model of universal cosmopolitanism. Each "nation," Herder contended, was to find its unique expressive identity in the humble and peaceable roots of its native folk culture. The purest voice of music was also "the voice of nature" and thus "the power of tone, the cry of the passions, belongs sympathetically to the whole species, to its bodily and mental constitution."[23] Herder's romantic and nationalist conception of folk poetry and music sheds light on the Fisk Singers' reception and on considerations of music and social memory in the work of Du Bois and others:

> But Nature has conferred another beneficent gift on our species, in leaving to such of it's [*sic*] members as are least stored with ideas the first germe [*sic*] of superior sense, exhilarating music. Before the child can speak, he is capable of song, or at least of being affected by musical tones; and among the most uncultivated nations music is the first of the fine arts, by which the mind is moved. The pictures, which Nature exhibits to the eye, are so various, changeable, and extensive, that imitative taste must long grope about, and seek the striking in wild and monstrous productions, ere it learns justness of proportion. But music, however, rude and simple, speaks to every human heart; and this, with the dance, constitutes Nature's general festival throughout the Earth. Pity it is, that most travellers, from too refined a taste, conceal from us these infantile tones of foreign nations. Useless as they may be to the musician, they are instructive to the investigator of man; for the music of a nation, in it's [*sic*] most imperfect form, and favourite tunes, displays the internal character of the people, that is to say, the proper tone of their sensations, much more truly and profoundly, than the most copious description of external contingencies.[24]

Music and cultural expression in general, according to Herder's organicist model, can be measured comparatively and developmentally in terms of group maturation and national distinctiveness.[25] More specifically, particular forms of music express the soul of a people qua nation: "the music of a nation, in its most imperfect form, and favourite tunes, displays the internal character of the people." Nature had granted those "most uncultivated nations" that were "least stored with ideas"—among whom Herder counted sub-Saharan Africans—a compensatory developmental gift for song: an immature nation's "infantile tones" would necessarily "seek the striking in wild and monstrous productions, ere it learns justness of proportion." The values of poise, balance, and a formal "justness of proportion" always came late in artistic development.

If audiences appreciated the Fisk Jubilee Singers' music for its "rude and simple" qualities, the precepts of Herder's 1784 book *Outline of a Philosophy of the History of Man* implored them to understand "that imitative taste must long grope about" before it reaches modern European ideals of classic beauty. Thus, "wild" and sublime musical artifacts developmentally predated mature attainments of aesthetic rigor. Additionally, if audiences heard in the Fisk Jubilee Singers "the infantile tones" of a different nation, they may have imagined the "music of a nation" that was black. Some fifteen years later, W. E. B. Du Bois heard the stirrings of self-conscious black nationhood in the legacy of the Fisk Jubilee Singers.

In his 1888 graduating address at Fisk University, Du Bois celebrated the autocratic German Chancellor Otto von Bismarck for making a nation "out of bickering peoples." Du Bois's prophetic and implicitly self-referential address explained that "the life of this powerful Chancellor illustrates the power and purpose, the force of an idea."[26] The relevant political idea in question was, of course, modern nationalism. It would be inaccurate and misleading to conflate the altogether distinct nationalist agendas of Herder and Bismarck, but for a college-age Du Bois an interwoven conception of an underdeveloped "folk" with a rising "nation" proved irresistible: "American Negroes" also needed to march "forth with strength and determination under trained leadership."[27] The puzzle of the Fisk Jubilee Singers occasioned questions among some listeners about emotional sublimity, Christian edification, and moments of naturalistic expression that transcended "the reach of art." For Du Bois, the Fisk Singers and their legacy raised political questions as well. Although far from the first black nationalist intellectual in the United States, Du Bois adapted Herderian folk nationalist themes to his intraracial aspirations for top-down Bismarckian leadership. As the literary scholar Arnold Rampersad notes: "Du Bois accepted Herder's basic terms for the evolution of culture." "But beyond his deep admiration for the religious songs," Rampersad continues, "Du Bois was no champion of folk expression. . . . His definition of 'folk' is primarily a political one and should be understood as interchangeable with the more daring term 'nation.'"[28]

We can now turn to how the impulses to aestheticize "nation" and "race" and to politicize the concept of the "black folk" energized Du Bois's thought in the late nineteenth century. A driving question for Du Bois was how to rethink black cultural riches inherited from slavery and earlier in relation to black longings for liberation and recognition. Scholars have long recognized that black nationalism and folk romanticism informed his reading of the "sorrow songs." Some historians and literary scholars have argued further that a dialectical and quasi-Hegelian interpretation of "double-consciousness" helps to explain the developmental and "civiliza-tionist" logic of *The Souls of Black Folk* and other early Du Bois texts. A general difference between the views of Herder and Hegel on the philoso-phy of culture, it should be noted, is the distinction between Herder's plu-ralistic views on the desirability of cultural differences and the universal scope of the World Spirit's dialectical unfolding in Hegel's thought. "Uni-versal history," according to Hegel's 1822 lectures on world history, "shows the development of the consciousness of Freedom on the part of Spirit, and of the consequent realization of that Freedom. This development im-plies a gradation—a series of increasingly adequate expressions or manifes-tations of Freedom, which results from its Idea."[29] Du Bois was never an orthodox Hegelian and, indeed, one has trouble finding direct references to Hegel in Du Bois's work. Hegel insisted that the Negro peoples lacked all historical self-consciousness and had no role to play in the otherwise universal drama of the self-realization of Spirit. On that point, Du Bois obviously disagreed. But on many other points Du Bois found the dialecti-cal approach to the "development of the consciousness of Freedom on the part of Spirit" quite appealing.

The pluralistic and the universalizing moments in Du Bois's early thought coiled around one another in a dialectical vision of moderniza-tion and the prophetic destiny of black self-consciousness. Du Bois's lec-ture on "The Spirit of Modern Europe" (c. 1900) gives an example of his sense of national development as a dialectical process of collective self-overcoming. The lecture, presented to a black audience in Louisville, Ken-tucky, outlines the ascent of nationalist ideology as modern Europe's most important social phenomenon. Du Bois interprets nationalism as a progression from liberal eighteenth-century notions of individualism to newer ideas about the nation as an organic community—a modern com-munity paradoxically presumed to be of archaic origins. He argues that the inherent flaws of modern individualism can be sublated or dialectically overcome through nationalism's sense of collective purpose, even as the liberatory promises of individualism are preserved and redoubled. The "spirit of the 20th century is not a negation of the individual," Du Bois contends, "but a heightening of his significance; he is regarded not as his own end and object, but chiefly as related to his fellow-men, as one link in a chain which is daily holding vaster weight."[30] Modern nationalism pro-vided new links between individuals, thus strengthening each individual in the process. Modern European individualism was not being demol-ished but perfected and refined; nationalism took the experience of post-

Enlightenment individuality to a higher level of spiritual development through the broadening and humanizing impact of national belonging.

Du Bois argued that these European developments were of profound relevance for African Americans in Kentucky and elsewhere. Only through a careful study of the world's historic civilizations and the shifting centers of European power could Du Bois's black audience come to self-consciousness about its own place in the world and its duty to a reemerging black civilization. Thus he guided the Louisville audience through an imagined tour across the European continent and likened Poland's nascent nationalism to that of the "black nation." The invaluable lesson of recent Polish accomplishments in literature, language, and spirit was that "all this is not organization—Poland is not a State, but she represents the disembodied idea of statehood—of race ideal, of organized striving which some day must tell." Insurgent national self-consciousness in the realm of culture represented, according to Du Bois's telling notion, "the disembodied idea of statehood." "In a day when the battle of humanity is being fought with unprecedented fierceness," he noted, "and when the brunt of that battle is about to fall upon the shoulders of a black nation which though larger than the Greek State is half shrinking from its high mission to dabble in the mud of selfishness, it is well to pause in our perplexity and critically study the path before us." Du Bois's conclusion that the nascent "black nation" was moving slowly toward its "high mission" returned in *The Souls of Black Folk* along with frequent references to the widespread moral damage wrought by slavery and the materialistic and short-sighted "Gospel of Wealth" in the post-Reconstruction period. While "the Spirit of Modern Europe" calls for African American leadership, the vaguely defined black nation sketched there transcends the particularities of African America.[31]

A powerful unified Germany embodied one nationalistic ideal toward which Du Bois aimed his black Louisville audience. The chastening lecture echoed Du Bois's Fisk commencement address with the assertion that German leaders "form an example of human pluck and perseverance, dogged determination and royal service." Du Bois underscored how the "disembodied idea" of a united Germany had long been perceived as unrealizable. The German people had nevertheless "struggled on led by hero hands, fed by master minds and idealized by one Vast Ideal till it accomplished what men called impossible."[32] "The principle of authority," Du Bois explained in one of his occasional expressions of jarring authoritarianism, "declares that in the limited range of special ability or training men should be rendered implicit obedience by their fellow men; that we should bow to the rule of rulers." True or positive freedom, then, is a matter of "slavery to an Ideal which through the Truth shall make you free," while true justice demands the abolition of prejudice and discrimination. Regarding "systemic knowledge," Du Bois upheld the search for Truth, Beauty, and Goodness as "the only way in which the world can advance to higher culture, to more eternal Life, to more unquestioned authority."[33] The modern cosmopolis of Vienna figured for him as the very embodiment of "the spirit of Knowing," an exemplar of the urban imperative of civilizational evolution. Du Bois's lecture lays bare the cosmopolitan orientation beneath his idealizing forays into folk romanticism. He signaled his distance from the perspective of Booker T. Washington by announcing that "the riddle of human life is better answered in cities. Knowledge of human affairs is broader and deeper—the world instead of being bounded by bare hills and petty gossip spreads from sea to sea, leaps the ocean, sweeps the world and yet rests upon our breakfast tables!" World cities like Vienna, Paris, and Berlin (Du Bois had, of course, traveled broadly as a visiting scholar in Berlin) supply the essential "pulse of cosmopolitan life."[34]

Du Bois later came to regret his youthful affirmation of Bismarckian nationalism. Despite an early fascination with German power and authoritarian nationalism, he rejected the necessity of national aggression and imperialism in the 1900 lecture. The future of each race must, in the end, be put "in the hands of that race" so that it might "work out its own peculiar civilization," he asserted. The point echoes Herder's eighteenth-century fear that aggression in the name of nationalism would crush the idealistic prospects of pluralism. Du Bois put forth his own version of Herder's nonaggressive pluralism: "the national and Race ideal has been set before the world in a new light—not as meaning subtraction but addition, not as division but multiplication—not to narrow humanity to petty selfish ends, but to point out a practical open road to the realization in all the earth of a humanity broad as God's blue heavens and deep as the deepest human heart." Truly enlightened social development would lead to reduced antagonism in the world through increased knowledge and acceptance of national diversity. A pluralist's optimism resounded in Du Bois's explanation that "Races and Nations represent organized Human effort, striving each [in] its own way, each in its own time to realize for mankind the Good, the Beautiful, and the True. The German unites and strives in *his* way, and so long as they [*sic*] strive not *against*, but along *with* each other the results blend and harmonize into [the] vast striving of *one hu-*

manity.[35] The universal striving of humanity, in other words, demanded the particularistic endeavors of its constitutive or nascent nations. As Du Bois argued in his early nationalist manifesto, "The Conservation of Races" (1897), only Negro unity could make possible "the realization of that broader humanity which freely recognizes differences in men, but sternly deprecates inequality."[36]

Above all, Du Bois's Louisville audience was to see in itself the leadership of a "new race" of African people. The "new race" existed at present only in a fragmented and unrealized form. "The African people sweep over the birth place of human civilization," Du Bois explained, "they dot the islands of the sea, they swarm in South America, they teem in our own land." His audience needed to reconstruct its identity as "the advance guard of the new people." European nationalist ideals presented models to those African Americans responsible for bringing the "black nation" or "new race" to self-consciousness about its destiny on the stage of history. Du Bois referred to college-educated African Americans as a potential "aristocracy of learning and talent." They were "not to be trained for their own sakes alone but to be the guides and servants of the vast unmoved masses who are to be led out of poverty, out of disease and out of crime."[37] Du Bois's *The Philadelphia Negro* (1899) gave a full-scale sociological diagnosis of the "vast unmoved masses" and the city's other black social strata along with prescriptions for uplift ideology and self-conscious leadership among the black bourgeoisie.

Du Bois wrote of the "sorrow songs" in a Herderian manner as the "music of a nation," but he did so without explicit reference to Herder. The historian Wilson Moses suggests that "the relationship between black nationalism and German nationalism . . . is one of cognates and analogues, not necessarily one of direct influences." Moses adds that "Du Bois, like most African American nationalists, expressed ideas congruent with those of Herder, which may or may not have had anything to do with his German education."[38] These caveats on "cognates and analogues" should be kept in mind even as we approach some of Du Bois's ideas in the light of Herder's formulations. Du Bois's vision of the "sorrow songs," I am arguing, more than faintly reinscribed what Herder called "the internal character of the people, that is to say, the proper tone of their sensations." The black nation's not yet fully realized "internal character" was crystallized for Du Bois in this folk music, interpreted as a repository or archive of social memory. Nonetheless, the tragic specificities of slavery and geographic dislocation that gave rise to the "sorrow songs" and to Du Bois's formulations about diasporic black identity forestalled, or at least problematized, any nostalgic vision of integrated folk purity. Du Bois evoked the "internal character" of the black folk for the sake of a forward-looking vision of a "new nation." Thus, the Fisk Jubilee Singers' success performed a double service in helping to build a university for training black leaders. Their music and message also contributed a unifying voice for a large, dispersed, and heterogeneous minority population in the United States. Their example materialized in sound, performance, and musical transcription a "disembodied idea of statehood." As we shall see, Du Bois used his appreciation of the Fisk Singers and the "weird old songs in which the soul of the black slave spoke to me" to underwrite his inheritance claims on the imagined homogeneity or "unisonance" of black national memory.[39]

The Politics of "Wild Sweet Melodies"

Du Bois appropriated the "sorrow songs" in The Souls of Black Folk as conceptual tools with which to burrow into the Southern past and the "soul of the black slave." The songs' symbolic power animated a usable past essential to his early vision of black liberation, a liberation that would include artistic self-possession as "co-workers in the kingdom of culture." Decades later, Alain Locke favorably compared the epochal impact of Du Bois's 1903 book upon the African American intelligentsia to the more broadly inspirational work of the original Fisk Jubilee Singers. James Weldon Johnson similarly regarded The Souls of Black Folk as "a work which, I think, has had a greater effect upon and within the Negro race in America than any other single book published in this country since Uncle Tom's Cabin."[40] Johnson's significant 1912 novel about a black man's thwarted formal musical ambition, The Autobiography of an Ex-Colored Man, played out a racial and musical drama readily legible along the lines of Du Boisian "double-consciousness." Movement toward the ideal of disalienated "double-consciousness" is blocked in Johnson's narrative. Having chosen to "pass" into the white world, the ex-colored man's "double-consciousness" retreats from the burdens and opportunities of a black cosmopolitan identity. The protagonist ultimately finds himself in a melancholic state, alienated from his highest musical ideals and the cosmopolitan promise of the legacy of the "sorrow songs."[41] According to the literary critic Robert Stepto, "the hallowed dialectic between race and music which yields the most revered expressions of the Afro-American *genius loci* in much of the literature preceding and following *The Autobiography* is an alien idea for the Ex-Coloured Man."[42]

Du Bois's discussion of the spirituals in *The Souls of Black Folk* confronted dominant ideas about the African American cultural inheritance by countering that "there is no true American music but the wild sweet melodies of the Negro slave." He further asserted that "we black men seem the sole oasis of simple faith and reverence in a dusty desert of dollars and smartness." The "sorrow songs," a folk music rooted in rural slavery and thus generically distant from urban industrial society, offered a refuge, Du Bois argued, from the materialistic "Gospel of Wealth" and the expanding desert of "vulgar music." The songs had outlived legalized slavery as a beacon signaling the ongoing necessity of black liberation. A plea for uplift and regeneration rhetorically asked whether America will "be poorer if she replace . . . her vulgar music with the soul of the Sorrow Songs?"[43] In a book dedicated to exploring the inner life of African America behind the veil of racial misunderstanding and separation, the proprietorship of the "sorrow songs" was clear. Nevertheless, Du Bois made sure to extend the "sorrow songs" as a gift to the dominant culture in a gesture of reconciliation. The humblest of Americans had supplied the nation with its greatest musical idiom and a most challenging test to its democratic promises.

Du Bois had heard the "sorrow songs" since childhood in western Massachusetts and had always been moved by them without fully understanding their origin or meaning. "Then in after years when I came to Nashville I saw the great temple builded [*sic*] of these songs towering over the pale city. To me Jubilee Hall seemed ever made of the songs themselves, and its bricks were red with the blood and dust of toil."[44] The edifice of uplift and refinement that was Fisk University had been built, at least in part, from the life-giving raw materials of black folk culture. Moreover, the concert presentation of the "sorrow songs" as performed by college singers had since become a fund-raising strategy for other black colleges, including Booker T. Washington's Tuskegee Institute and, even earlier, Hampton Institute in Virginia. The legacy of the spirituals was a non-threatening weapon for schools situated in the midst of white populations hostile to the mission of racial regeneration through black higher education. Du Bois cherished the cultural mission of concert presentations and condemned unworthy imitations of the special idiom as corrosively superficial and alien to the uplifting legacy of the "sorrow songs." The Reconstruction-era history of the original Fisk Jubilee Singers foreshadowed Du Bois's own aesthetic ideal of a black national art grounded in folk materials and reaching out toward an unrestricted future in the cosmopolitan "kingdom of culture." He pointed to the original singers' immediate relation to slavery and folk culture and asked readers to transfer their sympathies to the mission of liberal arts education for African Americans. Like the singers, the black colleges had been misunderstood, ridiculed, and received with hostility.

Du Bois stated without qualification that the colleges' long-term efficacy and quality promised to become as self-evident as the Jubilee Singers and the legacy of the "sorrow songs." His discussion went further and linked the Jubilee Singers as bearers of the true meaning of the "sorrow songs" to his own agenda for civil rights agitation under "talented-tenth" leadership. Du Bois cannily enlisted the spirituals qua "sorrow songs" as musical sites of black social memory in his polemic against the authority of Tuskegee's Booker T. Washington, the most powerful African American of the period. Washington also encouraged concert presentations of the spirituals, but his interpretation of the folk legacy did not share Du Bois's confrontational public critique of white American racism. The literary scholar Eric Sundquist cogently interprets Du Bois's rhetorical strategy as a "seizure and celebration of indigenous African American culture that allowed [him] rebelliously to sweep away Washington's populist advantage, replacing his philosophy of the toothbrush with a philosophy of black soul and transfiguring the narrow conception of labor and nation building in Washington's program into a broad, exhilarating call for the labor necessary to construct a black American wing in the 'kingdom of culture.'"[45]

Du Bois's interpretation of the "sorrow songs" wove together a vision of the black past with one of the future. By now it is a commonplace to state that communal musical performance played a central role in shaping a ritualized space for African American solidarity and resistance in the midst of close surveillance during bondage. Du Bois's ambitious interpretation of the "sorrow songs" helped lay the groundwork for later scholarship on music's role in community-building and social memorialization among African Americans. Indeed, the multi-tiered thematization of music in *The Souls of Black Folk* would have a profound impact on generations of readers. Paul Gilroy suggests that Du Bois's text "sensitised blacks to the significance of the vernacular cultures that arose to mediate the enduring effects of terror. The book endorsed this suggestion through its use of black music as a cipher for the ineffable, sublime, pre-discursive and anti-discursive elements in black expressive cultures." Although many differences separate the two, Gilroy's dialectically inflected contributions to critical theory are clearly in the Du Boisian tradition and exemplify how "music has been regularly employed since *The Souls* to provide a symbol for various different conceptions of black commonality."[46]

Du Bois bound the "sorrow songs" to the recent American past as well as to older African expressive survivals. Thus he noted an ancestral lullaby passed on for generations (although the meanings of its words remained unknown) and claimed about the "sorrow songs" that "the music is far more ancient than the words."[47] The melodic fragments of the "sorrow songs"—represented through musical staff notation (rather than through their lyrics) in the epigraphs that precede each chapter of *The Souls of Black Folk*—reinforced Du Bois's point about African origins and his championing of an empowering "double-consciousness." The music's presence on the written page of his book also combated racist commonplaces about African Americans as bereft of collective memory and doomed to imitate their supposed racial superiors in all things. Du Bois countered that white strategies of dehumanization through a forced erasure of African traditions had failed in the long epoch of slavery and in the decades following Reconstruction. He used the concept of the "sorrow song" to narrow his musical focus (if not his generalizing cultural claims) to a very particular genre of sacred folk music. The "sorrow song" defined the genre that best provided anthems, at once elegiac and uplifting, for Du Bois's largely secular vision of black nationalism. He negatively remarked on the genres of black sacred and secular music that did not approximate his ideals of elegant militance and "masculine" emotional restraint.

Du Bois sketched black musical development in order to overturn ideas about the static character of African American musical forms. His four-stage developmental outline for African music in the United States deliberately focuses on the values of "growth" and "development." African music inhabits the first stage, exemplified by the sweet ancestral lullaby sung at home to Du Bois in an African language unknown to his family. For the second stage, labeled "Afro-American," Du Bois singles out the music of South Carolina's Sea Islands, where the black population shaped a distinctive culture in near-isolation from white influence. The Sea Islands, as Du Bois explained, "were filled with a black folk of primitive type, touched and moulded less by the world about them than any others outside the Black Belt. . . . their hearts were human and their singing stirred men with a mighty power." The folk songs of such people occupied a privileged crossroads in black musical development. Du Bois associates the "discovery" of the Sea Island songs by sympathetic white outsiders in the 1860s to subsequent efforts of memorializing the folk music legacy. Most important among white efforts was the work of former abolitionists Lucy McKim, William Francis Allen, and Charles Pickard White, who collected and transcribed the songs published in the 1867 collection *Slave Songs of the United States*. Du Bois adds that "the world listened only half credulously until the Fisk Jubilee Singers sang the slave songs so deeply into the world's heart that it can never wholly forget them again." Du Bois here identifies the folk spirituals sung by the Fisk Jubilee Singers in the 1870s as "slave songs." The label deserves notice as it reveals Du Bois's tendency (a tendency he shared with the romantic folklorism that animates *Slave Songs of the United States*) to treat African American folk materials as survivals from the slave past. If these folk resources belonged to the American slave past, then cultural custodians, including Du Bois's prospective corps of cosmopolitan black leadership, could imagine for themselves the responsibility of choosing which remnants to value most positively and thereby salvage, resuscitate, and memorialize. Similarly, they could imagine for themselves which resources to value negatively and thereby discard or forget. Du Bois rendered far less of the African American and African cultural inheritance obsolete than many of his elite predecessors and contemporaries, in part because of his romantic folk nationalism.

The third stage of African-influenced music in America, according to Du Bois, is the blending of Negro music "with the music heard in the foster land." "The result is still distinctively Negro and the method of blending original," Du Bois notes, "but the elements are both Negro and Caucasian." Black appropriations and variations on white materials, in short, were original rather than passively imitative. Peoples of African origin in North America absorbed, reconfigured, and virtually reinvented white forms, while white musicians creatively interacted with black musical materials. Du Bois's fourth stage consists of white American musical idioms "distinctively influenced by the slave songs or [which] have incorporated whole phrases of Negro melody." His point was not to privilege white music as central to the American national experience but rather to render as explicitly as possible black music's shaping influence on white music in the United States. Du Bois excluded what he regarded as degraded musical styles in his brief sketch of black music and American musical "growth" and "development" overall. "Side by side, too, with the growth has gone the debasements and imitations—the Negro 'minstrel' songs, many of the 'gospel' hymns, and some of the contemporary 'coon' songs,—a mass of music in which the novice may easily lose himself and never find the real Negro melodies."[48] These excluded genres help clarify Du Bois's canonizing strictures on building a usable past out of African American musical forms. As Ronald Radano notes, "for Du Bois, the Fisk song-texts were both a marker of a profound moment of chance and a harbinger of the new black civilization, of a fully realized consciousness of vast critical potential, clearly distinguished from, and more powerful than, the separate and pure semi-consciousness of an uncompleted black folk."[49] Du Bois was not interested in musics that lacked "critical potential." Elsewhere, Du Bois recorded his distrust of gospel hymns as sacred songs that captured "the body but not the soul" of the Jubilee songs.[50] Such music struck him as dialectically inert. The "soul" or philosophical content of the "sorrow songs" was his primary interest. Not all song genres provided reliable access to the energizing "inner" musical content that Du Bois wanted to publicize.

Du Bois specified sadness and disappointment along with joyful millenial expectation as key components of the authentic "sorrow songs." "They are the music of an unhappy people," his chapter contends, "of the children of disappointment; they tell of death and suffering and unvoiced longing toward a truer world, of misty wanderings and hidden ways." Du Bois's formulations directly contradict stereotypes about slaves enjoying the civilizing process at the benevolent hand of whites. The "sorrow songs" undermined false images of bondage and racial hierarchy and instead revealed the most somber feelings of slaves. The songs demonstrated the slaves' masked and "unvoiced longings" through subtle shifts between secular and spiritual imagery and self-referential invocations of the ancient Israelites' bondage in songs like "Go Down, Moses" or of Christ's passion in "Were You There When They Crucified My Lord." The deepest meaning of the songs would not be obvious to strangers, but instead "naturally veiled and half articulate."[51] That the "sorrow songs" expressed a critical and prophetic interpretation of slavery offers one reason why Du Bois was so adamant to distinguish them from various imitations and related sacred and secular genres. His assumption of the intimate association between the musical form and its "soul" or critical content motivated the complaint that "caricature has sought to spoil the quaint beauty of the music, and has filled the air with many debased melodies which vulgar ears scarce know from the real."[52] Both before and after the 1870s vogue of the Fisk Jubilee Singers, the spirituals had inspired crude and often unflattering imitations damaging to the appropriate memorialization of the music's social message. Far more than a musical disappointment, "debased" imitations obscured the multiple cultural functions of the "sorrow songs." The flood of "debased melodies" contributed to the intensified racism of the post-Reconstruction United States by giving the impression that African Americans were childlike, impulsive, and otherwise ill-suited for higher education, civil rights, or political responsibility.

Du Bois's treatment of the "longing toward a truer world, of misty wanderings and hidden ways" in the "sorrow songs" also countered interpretations of the songs as signs of unilinear assimilation to the white "surrounding world" and its religious worldview. Rather than emphasize biblical references and the context of Christian eschatology in the "sorrow songs," Du Bois held not only that the music was "far more ancient than the words" but that Christianity was a "dimly understood theology" among slaves. His theologically imprecise interpretation of the "sorrow songs" contrasted with the evangelical Protestant context of the Fisk Jubilee Singers' church performances in the United States and their participation in Moody and Sankey religious revivals. Though many had applauded the Fisk Jubilee Singers in terms of theological familiarity, Du Bois read signs of difference all through the legacy of the "sorrow songs." He refrained from mentioning heaven by name, for example, in his discussion of the religious songs, perhaps refusing to underwrite religious orthodoxy. Du Bois had grown up in the African Methodist Episcopal Church and the Congregational Church in Great Barrington, Massachusetts. By the time he wrote *The Souls of Black Folk*, however, he was a freethinker leaning toward the reformist and this-worldly impulses behind the Protestant Social Gospel movement.[53] His interpretation of the "sorrow songs" did not rest on otherworldly formulations. He eschewed theological self-certainty and instead wondered aloud about the possibility of racial harmony within human history.

> Through all the sorrow of the Sorrow Songs there breathes a hope—a faith in the ultimate justice of things. The minor cadences of despair change often to triumph and calm confidence. Sometimes it is faith in life, sometimes a faith in death, sometimes assurance of boundless justice in some fair world beyond. But whichever it is, the meaning is always clear: that sometime, somewhere, men will judge men by their souls and not by their skins. Is such a hope justified? Do the Sorrow Songs sing true?[54]

The passage modulates between "calm confidence" and uncertainty as it lays out Du Bois's ultimate claim upon the "sorrow songs." *The Souls of Black Folk* intertwines the spirituals with the threats of black fatalism and moral anarchism, the social viciousness of American racism, and the radical demand for an elimination of the "color-line." The passage above, like the chapter in which it appears, also signals Du Bois's aspiration to prophetic authority as a philosophical bard of black social memory, a keeper of the "sorrow songs" in the hallowed Fisk tradition.

Du Bois cherished the moral wisdom and fortitude of the "primitive" folk even as he called for modernization in the overcoming of black and white "backwardness," most especially among the lower classes.[55] He assumed the necessity of top-down social leadership. "Under the lax moral life of the plantation, where marriage was a farce, laziness a virtue, and property a theft, a religion of resignation and submission degenerated easily, in less strenuous minds, into a philosophy of indulgence and crime," Du Bois lamented. "Many of the worst characteristics of the Negro masses of to-day," he continued, "had their seed in this period of the slave's ethical growth."[56] The kernel of the "sorrow songs" legacy presented an alternative to resignation, submission, indulgence, and moral weakness, according to Du Bois. His analysis of evangelical revivalism in *The Souls of Black Folk* revealed a profound fascination and an equally strong discomfort with religious styles that courted "a pythian madness, a demoniac possession, that lent terrible reality to song and word."[57] The "talented tenth's" leadership over an only vaguely self-aware black nation in the United States required a deep reservoir of self-restraint, a thorough education in the history of civilizations, and a far more extensive program of scholarship and social research than Booker T. Washington advocated.

The conclusions that Du Bois reached about the dangerous impurities of "backwardness" and slavery's moral legacies betray the contradictions of his folk romanticism. To cultivate and memorialize an idealistic image of the folk legacy and of folk expression, a romantic nationalist must spend considerable imaginative energy in protecting that image from contamination. Romantic images of "the folk" (regardless of ethnicity or nationality) need to be set apart and above from the vicissitudes of historical change in a preserve of purified cultural difference.[58] The ideological operations at work in Du Bois's conceptualization of the black folk were, in short, hardly exclusive to his nationalist vision. An impulse to idealize the folk energized his appreciation of the "primitive" character of the "sorrow songs" as a music whose "quaint beauty" evidenced the imagined folk's charming "nearness to nature." His romanticism about folk music thus reinforced pieces of the critical puzzle summoned by the original Fisk Jubilee Singers in the 1870s. While white audiences, especially, may have been unaware or unaccepting of the fact, Du Bois understood that the Fisk Jubilee Singers were neither folksingers unself-consciously sharing their traditional music nor practitioners of deceptive "humbuggery." They were formally trained singers publicizing a specific image of African American humanity through music for the sake of underwriting black higher education. For the romanticist Du Bois, a strong quotient of folk authenticity could be preserved even in self-consciously formal performances and arrangements alien to most folk performance practices. Formal training did not render black music inauthentic. Instead, the refinement of folk music materials could signal a concentration of the music's "soul" or expressive content and, thus, heightened power rather than dilution.

Du Bois wanted African American musical development to follow a logic of "double-consciousness" and ultimately overcome the apparent contradictions between folk and formal music. In other words, cosmopolitan refinement and the "primitive" authenticity of black racial expression would be developmentally reconciled. Black cultural inertia, according to Du Bois, and the distorting impact of deep stereotypes and institutionalized racism conspired to thwart the actualization of his developmental ideal. The painful distance between the fledgling "aristocracy of learning and talent" and the "vast unmoved masses" provides the subject for "Of the Coming of John," the one short story included in *The Souls of Black Folk*. The metaphysical function of Wagnerian opera in the story sheds light on Du Bois's calibration of a dialectic between folk romanticism and cultural idealism, an aesthetic calibration crucial to his subsequent resistance to cultural transformations for which the spread of jazz music was symptomatic.

The Chasm Between Two Worlds

In "Of the Coming of John," a young black man from a small town in southeastern Georgia journeys alone to the North for a college education. John Jones learns that he will never be welcome as an equal among whites, Northern or otherwise, and returns to his hometown. Teaching in the local black school makes him only more impatient with what strikes him as rural black passivity, provincialism, and backward religiosity. Having familiarized himself with a wider world of cosmopolitan literature and culture, John's critical intellectual sensibility positions him as a threat to a segregationist regime where the constant threat of reprisal and violence underwrites white privilege. John kills a white childhood friend after the white man makes sexual advances upon his younger sister. A white vigilante mob murders him in revenge or leads him to a heroic suicide.

One is left to conclude from Du Bois's nightmare that John Jones's cosmopolitan transformation amounted to a dangerous exercise in social frustration and spiritual exile. The protagonist's rapturous enjoyment of Wagnerian opera in the midst of an otherwise all-white concert audience in Manhattan precipitates his fate. While enjoying *Lohengrin* in the ritual context of Euro-American high culture, John undergoes a negative epiphany: the white racists surrounding him would always impugn his dignity and there would be no escape or refuge. Even the highest realms of artistic performance (or perhaps especially those realms) offered little solace against racial injustice and humiliation. Reflecting the story's uncanny mood, John's childhood playmate from the South is also present at the opera, as if shadowing John's development. John's presence in a social ritual of elite culture unnerves the spoiled white doppelganger (also named John), and the former black friend is ejected from the theater. John is forced from a treasured cosmopolitan milieu and thus denied access to aesthetic bliss and public acceptance alike. Only then will he reluctantly return to his Southern home as a teacher. Du Bois details John's all too brief operatic epiphany:

> [John] sat in a half-maze minding the scene about him; the delicate beauty of the hall, the faint perfume, the moving myriad of men, the rich clothing and low hum of talking seemed all a part of a world so different from his, so strangely more beautiful than anything he had known, that he sat in dreamland, and started when, after a hush, rose high and clear the music of Lohengrin's swan. The infinite beauty of the wail lingered and swept through every muscle of his frame, and put it all a-tune. He closed his eyes and grasped the elbows of the chair, touching unwittingly the lady's arm. And the lady drew away. A deep longing swelled in all his heart to rise with that clear music out of the dirt and dust of that low life that held him prisoned and befouled. If he could only live up in the free air where birds sang and setting suns

had no touch of blood! Who had called him to be the slave and butt of all? And if he had called, what right had he to call when a work like this lay open before men?

Then the movement changed, and fuller, mightier harmony swelled away. He looked thoughtfully across the hall, and wondered why the beautiful gray-haired woman looked so listless, and what the little man could be whispering about. He would not like to be listless and idle, he thought, for he felt with the music the movement of power within him. If he but had some master-work, some life-service, hard,—aye, bitter hard, but without the cringing and sickening servility, without the cruel heart that hardened his heart and soul. When at last a soft sorrow crept across the violins, there came to him the vision of a far-off home, the great eyes of his sister, and the dark drawn face of his mother. And his heart sank below the waters, even as the sea-sand sinks by the shores of Altamaha, only to be lifted aloft again with that last ethereal wail of the swan that quivered and faded away into the sky.

It left John sitting so silent and rapt that he did not for some time notice the usher tapping him lightly on the shoulder and saying politely, "Will you step this way, please, sir?"[59]

The story's despairing drama of cosmopolitan desire and racial isolation illuminates wounds well known to the Du Boisian intellectual type, the ambivalently Europeanized "black man of culture."[60] The literary scholar Arnold Rampersad astutely argues that the story "turns on the savage irony that, for the black man in a racist world, the acquisition of culture is a dangerous and often destructive process. . . . Neither a hypocrite nor a rebel, [John] stands between two worlds, isolated from everything but his capacity to dream."[61] John's operatic epiphany takes on additional significance in the context of nonfictional episodes recorded elsewhere in *The Souls of Black Folk* and an awareness that Wagner was a composer to whom Du Bois always felt a profound spiritual kinship. First staged in Weimar in 1850, *Lohengrin* had its American premiere in 1871 at the Stadttheater in the Bowery. A great success, it would become one of the most frequently staged Wagner spectacles, at least until the decline of Wagner's popularity in America during World War I. Moreover, *Lohengrin* was Du Bois's favorite opera; as of 1936, he had heard "it six or eight times, under many circumstances, in different languages and lands."[62] Indeed, one can superimpose Rampersad's insight about John as a man standing "between two worlds" onto the general predicament of Du Boisian "double-consciousness." As we shall see, Du Bois worked hard to formulate an intellectually convincing and emotionally resonant response to John's melancholic and ultimately fatal predicament.

Du Bois marks "double-consciousness" in the first chapter of *The Souls of Black Folk* as a basic characteristic of African American cultural identity. Sometimes characterized as an interminable malady of self-doubt inflicted on Du Bois by racism, his figure of "double-consciousness" did not signal an incurable threat to a healthy, integrated identity. Instead, he referenced a parade of world civilizations in order to illustrate contemporary African American self-consciousness.

> After the Egyptian and Indian, the Greek and Roman, the Teuton and Mongolian, the Negro is a sort of seventh son, born with a veil, and gifted with second-sight in this American world,—a world which yields him no true self-consciousness, but only lets him see himself through the revelation of the other world. It is a peculiar sensation, this double-consciousness, this sense of always looking at one's self through the eyes of others, of measuring one's soul by the tape of a world that looks on in amused contempt and pity. . . . The history of the American Negro is the history of this strife,—this longing to attain self-conscious manhood, to merge his double self into a better and truer self. In this merging he wishes neither of the older selves to be lost. . . . He simply wishes to make it possible for a man to be both a Negro and an American, without being cursed and spit upon by his fellows, without having the doors of Opportunity closed roughly in his face.[63]

Membership in the "kingdom of culture" called for the African American to reach "self-conscious manhood, to merge his double self into a better and truer self." The developmental process of "double-consciousness" therefore demanded a reconciliation and a dialectical overcoming of contrasting realities—a shift from the painful split or scission of "second-sight" to a higher, disalienated doubleness.[64]

The anxiety of "double-consciousness" signifies only a temporary lack. In the case of the fictional John, a thwarted and musically induced identification with the promise of an ideal world (as revealed in Wagner's metaphysical opera) leaves him in a solipsistic state of melancholia. One philosophical valence of this condition might be approached through Hegel's notion of "the unhappy consciousness." Du Bois studied Hegel with the philosopher George Santayana during the 1889–90 school year at Harvard and encountered the German philosopher's mythic depiction of human history as a unified narrative legible in terms of the development of humanity's self-consciousness.[65] Although Du Bois studied forensics rather than philosophy with the idealist philosopher Josiah Royce (who introduced Hegel's dialectical style to Santayana), Royce's characterization of Hegel's "unhappy consciousness" resonates well with Du Bois's characteristically masculinist framing of "double-consciousness" as the pursuit of "self-conscious manhood."[66] "The dialectic situation depends upon the pathetic fact that the unhappy consciousness always actually has its salvation close at hand," Royce wrote, "but is still forbidden by its own presuppositions to accept that salvation. What it seeks is nothing whatever but an inner self-confidence, which it apparently ought to win by a mere resolution—an act of manly will. Yet . . . it is estranged from every resolute inner self-consciousness, since it conceives all good as belonging to its object, the Changeless."[67] Du Bois's seeming transformation of the Hegelian "unhappy consciousness" into the dilemma of black "double-consciousness" proposed a developmental vision of progress and reconciliation through the satisfying "master-work" or "life-service" that John never believed he had found.[68]

The protagonist in "Of the Coming of John" is caught between an ethereal "dreamland" of individual bliss and the "talented tenth's" collective burden of enlightening and motivating the "vast unmoved masses." John's condition recapitulates a tension that energizes *The Souls of Black Folk*—the existential impact of racial hierarchy and segregation on the "black man of culture" most sensitized to the highest cosmopolitan promise of "double-consciousness." Du Bois wrote elsewhere in the book about how "in the higher walks of life, in all the higher striving for the good and noble and true, the color-line comes to separate natural friends and co-workers." Meanwhile, "at the bottom of the social group, in the saloon, the gambling-hall, and the brothel, that same line wavers and disappears."[69] John Jones was denied sustained access to Wagner's artistic ambition of giving voice to German Romantic nationalism. The "dreamland" that Wagner's mythic opera briefly opens to John evokes Du Bois's depiction elsewhere of a realm above the veil separating the white and black worlds. For Du Bois and the fictional John, to rise above the veil would mean transcending provincial limitations and the misrecognitions projected and enforced by white racial ideology in the United States. Fleeting epiphanies

and solo flights above the veil, when they could be experienced, hardly fulfilled the social function of the black "aristocracy of learning and talent"
to lead a "new people" into national self-consciousness. Du Bois's point
was not merely that racist prejudice could thwart the apparently private
epiphanies of the black cosmopolitan. The pleasures of aesthetic contemplation and self-culture (*Bildung*) also were political issues for him. In
other words, he too "felt with the music the movement of power within
him." As the literary critic Ross Posnock notes, "aesthetic bliss and the erasure of the color line would forever be fused" in Du Bois's thought.[70]

The pure air of Wagner's "dreamland" and the most idealistic of cosmopolitan aesthetic experiences could not be detached from dominant American ideologies of racialized embodiment and social stratification. This is
one context in which to appreciate Du Bois's statement that "the price of
culture is a Lie." By withholding access to high culture, the dominant culture deliberately withheld materials essential to the anxious subjects of
"double-consciousness" as they struggled toward a self-confident and disalienated black cosmopolitanism. The message of racist exclusion from
high culture was clear: "Be content to be servants, and nothing more;
what need of higher culture for half-men?"[71] Thus Du Bois argued that
Booker T. Washington's advocacy of industrial education over liberal arts
education was in effect an emasculating acceptance of the white view of
black manhood's limited potential. Du Bois insisted on the masculinizing
benefits of black access to liberal arts education and training in the aesthetic contemplation of an ethereal space above the veil. He writes of the
veil in *The Souls of Black Folk* and about how, even as a child, he intuited the
special space above it.

> Then it dawned upon me with a certain suddenness that I was differ-
> ent from the others; or like, mayhap, in heart and life and longing, but
> shut out from their world by a vast veil. I had thereafter no desire to
> tear down that veil, to creep through; I held all beyond it in common
> contempt, and lived above it in a region of blue sky and great wander-
> ing shadows. That sky was bluest when I could beat my mates at exam-
> ination. . . . Alas, with the years all this fine contempt began to fade;
> for the worlds I longed for, and all their dazzling opportunities, were
> theirs, not mine. But they should not keep these prizes, I said; some,
> all, I would wrest from them.[72]

The "region of blue sky and great wandering shadows," a soaring "dreamland" of disembodied freedom, reappeared in John's interrupted epiph-

any above the veil. A musically induced flight above the veil forces the conscience-ridden character to confront his familial loyalties as a challenge to his solitary pursuit of cosmopolitan pleasures such as European opera.[73] The dilemma is solved for him by his forced ejection from the concert hall. John's attempt to "creep through" the veil and live above others in "common contempt" fails. He will reluctantly return home to his rural community and work from there to "tear down that veil."

Du Bois's portrayal of John's operatic epiphany suggests a metaphysical sense of idealism and a promise of experiences that taste a higher spiritual realm. In this context, one might consider an intuition of the philosopher Stanley Cavell about opera as a site for "the intervention or supervening of music into the world as revelatory of a realm of significance that either transcends our ordinary realm of experience or reveals ours under transfiguration." "The invocation of Kant's vision of the human being as living in two worlds, or capable, as he famously expresses it, of taking two standpoints toward human existence," Cavell continues, allows us "to pursue the intuition of opera as opening the question of the passage between these worlds."[74] John imagines himself at such a threshold separating the material world from an immaterial one, only to have the passageway of operatic rapture—and the idea that this passageway is available to him—slammed shut by white racists. As Du Bois recalls about his youth, "the worlds I longed for, and all their dazzling opportunities were theirs, not mine." Wagner's "dreamland" is an immaterial realm of disembodiment, a place without a "touch of blood." As such, it speaks to the "deep longing . . . to rise . . . out of the dirt and dust of the low life that held [John] prisoned and befouled." The goal of the African American "co-worker in the kingdom of culture," one reads elsewhere in *The Souls of Black Folk*, is "to escape both death and isolation, to husband and use his best powers and his latent genius."[75] Wagnerian opera suggests that the low world of the flesh—"of the dirt and dust of the low life"—can be escaped, if only fleetingly. Du Bois, in turn, intuited a transcendence of the veil of racial division through musicalized incantations of "the free air where birds sang and setting suns had no touch of blood."

Friedrich Nietzsche, after rejecting Wagner's "opera of redemption" as the apotheosis of Christian asceticism, denounced the composer as a decadent metaphysician and a true "*heir of Hegel*." "The same human type that raved about Hegel," Nietzsche wrote in 1888, "today raves about Wagner."[76] Du Bois recalled in his 1940 autobiography that he "came to know Beethoven's symphonies and Wagner's Ring" while a graduate student in Germany in the early 1890s: "I had been before, above all, in a hurry. I wanted a world, hard, smooth, and swift, and had no time for rounded corners and ornament, for unhurried thought and slow contemplation. Now at times I sat still."[77] Du Bois's abiding love for the high drama and metaphysical flavor of Wagner remained undiminished even in the 1930s. "Wagner's 'fancies' were of the highest importance for music and for the modern world," Du Bois wrote after enjoying a cycle of Wagner operas at the Bayreuth Festival in 1936. "He looked upon the opera not as a recreation for tired business men . . . but as a serious form of Art, calling for preparation, thought and knowledge on the part of the listener."[78] Du Bois took pains to underscore that "there has been no tragedy in modern times equal in its awful effects to the fight on the Jew in Germany," and he abhorred how the Nazi Party had adopted Wagner as a prophet of fascism.[79] Wagner's most enduring spiritual message, Du Bois maintained, was not his anti-Semitism but his socialism and his idealistic denunciation of all "ignorance that thinks that Clothes and Show and Extravagance spell Life."[80] Du Bois expected incomprehending reactions from many readers of the African American daily, the *Pittsburgh Courier*. He raised an already high rhetorical pitch a bit further and informed readers that the "whole meaning and end of my earlier teaching was to stress" the relevance of "Bayreuth and opera" for "starving Negro farm tenants in Arkansas or black college graduates searching New York for a job."[81]

Rampersad's reference to the protagonist in "Of the Coming of John" as trapped "between two worlds" can be extended to register a vertical axis of spirit (low/high; embodied/disembodied; beneath the veil/above the veil) as well as a horizontal axis of place (rural Southern/urban Northern). The "color line" inflects these paired axes, and it divides John from his inaccessible cosmopolitan dream. Morbidly stretched to the breaking point between two opposing worlds, the chasm between and beneath the worlds swallows and destroys John. Du Bois staged his cosmopolitan nightmare at the charged site of Wagnerian opera to dramatize the life-preserving necessities of idealistic culture and a bridge between opposing worlds. Thus the succeeding chapter of *The Souls of Black Folk* responds to the story's tragic conclusion with a redemptive interpretation of the folk-rooted "sorrow songs" that would bind together Du Bois's aspirations to black national self-consciousness, equality in the "kingdom of culture," and free access to the "dreamland" of idealistic culture. His "sorrow songs" discussion needed to bridge the cultural chasm that generated the fictional John's frustration and despair.

Du Bois wove the prescription of the "sorrow songs" throughout *The Souls of Black Folk* as an antidote to African American rage, hopelessness, and resignation. John's tragedy illuminated a chasm between two worlds; Du Bois's interpretation of the "sorrow songs" sketched a bridge built from the resources of African American folk culture and social memory. The dialectical machinery of a post-Kantian "objectification of metaphysics" (as evidenced in a musicalized "materialization of the invisible" world) and the promise of historical transformation suggested how a "double self" could be merged "into a better a truer self."[82] To feel "with the music the movement of power" was to overcome the lie of racist culture and to imagine the historical project of reconciling the real and the ideal. "Men continually try to think that life is hard fact; that education is the learning of Truth. But education is far more than this. . . . Life is not simply fact, but the thought of fact, the impression made by facts, the dreams and ideals that facts give birth to," Du Bois later rhapsodized under the inspiration of Wagnerian opera at Bayreuth. Facts and empirical sensations gave rise to impressions and "dreams and ideals"; desires for the empirical realization or objectification of immaterial notions in turn fueled projects for transforming the world of sensation. There was far more to education than today's hard facts, Du Bois explained, because the dreams of one day could become the facts of the next. "So it is that the poet and musician, the dreamer and the prophet must all be known and consulted by those who seek real education—who wish in truth to know Life."[83]

These philosophical considerations aid us in understanding why each chapter of *The Souls of Black Folk* opens with paired quotations from white European or European-American poetry (with several exceptions) and musically notated melodies from African American spirituals.[84] The gesture speaks to Du Bois's concern with reconciliation in the "kingdom of culture." Eric Sundquist has contended that Du Bois's pairings undermined the hierarchical ordering of cultural expression that accompanied white supremacist discourses on the scientific ordering of races. Parity rather than stratification was the message of the epigraphic juxtapositions. "Indeed, because Du Bois refused to accept as necessary the contradiction between elite and folk culture," Sundquist argues in the course of a lucid close reading, "his use of the spirituals was itself an example of this belief in action."[85] More precisely, the pairings underscored Du Bois's regard for the "sorrow songs" and suggested the congruity of their ennobling sensibility with, for example, elite English poetry. The traditional stratification of cultural artifacts, by contrast, allowed only formal elite artifacts the status of legitimate art in the "kingdom of culture." Du Bois's vision of the "kingdom of culture" carried pluralistic, even relativistic, conclusions, according to Sundquist, who emphasizes passages in Du Bois's text that define "a world in which the alternative epigraphs would be in communion, not in conflict, in which the Western and African traditions might harmoniously coexist."[86] The prospective sense of "might" and "would be," however, connotes a present lack of parity. Du Bois's demand for the full development of African American aspirations to the "kingdom of culture," I would argue, was part of a vision of prospective parity that operated according to a European standard of cultural maturity and evolution. Du Bois's perspective did not, according to Sundquist's interpretation, privilege European achievements (such as the Wagnerian opera that delivers up great masculinizing "clouds of bliss") as a normative basis for comparisons.[87] The dialectic of "double-consciousness," one might counter, called for a transformed black role in the "kingdom of culture" and the cleansing of supposed impurities from the legacy of the "sorrow songs" and the black folk inheritance. Du Bois's enthusiasm for cultural transformation and the "movement of power" in the dialectic of "double-consciousness" distanced him from the more fixed pluralism toward which Sundquist's interpretation begins to move.

Du Bois's analysis must also be set apart from any nostalgic aversion to folk-formal hybridization as corruption.[88] Hybridity and purity were not in conflict in his vision of an empowered "double-consciousness." Du Bois's epigraphic pairings certainly direct readers to points of convergence between the "sorrow songs" and elite white poetry. The pairings thus argue for the thematic congruity of African American folk expression with the poetry of Schiller, Byron, James Russell Lowell, and others. The bold epigraphic gesture exacted a high price, however, in its implicit repudiation of the intermediary cultural territory between romanticized folk and idealized elite forms. The vast majority of black expressive forms were excluded from Du Bois's conditions for dignified black self-representation; the silenced forms occupied the intermediate territory between the purer, uncommercial worlds of folk and formal music. Sundquist's interpretation, for example, adjusts the texture of Du Bois's argument somewhat by drawing attention away from Du Bois's contrast between the "sorrow songs," the "debased melodies which vulgar ears scarce know from the real" folk songs, and the playfulness of much ragtime and other popular secular music. Blissful imaginings of disembodiment in John's operatic epiphany and Du Bois's reports of the "blue regions" above the veil suggest that the demands of idealism conflicted with popular secular music as well as the "debased" reworkings of the spirituals that Du Bois found so repugnant.[89] Du Bois's hope was that "the true Negro folk-song still lives in the hearts of those who have heard them truly sung and in the hearts of the Negro people."[90]

"Art is not natural," Du Bois later wrote. One might interpret this to mean that without the promise of a transformed nature in a truly free society, the truth content of art could not reach its final destination. Pleasure, whether imagined as embodied or disembodied, remained a political question whenever Du Bois took on the responsibilities of the social reformer. "Proper amusement," he explained in 1897, was a "nice adjustment between repression and excess."[91] Too much moral repression or religious asceticism only inspired an inevitable backlash and a corresponding "excess of pleasure." An appropriate balance of "inspiration and amusement" was essential; excess work destroyed vigor while excess amusement caused dissipation. The proper reconciliation of work and amusement, he concluded, came through the "divine institution" of play. Play, according to Du Bois's Schillerian image of the reconciliation of work and amusement and man and nature, "ever has and ever will go hand in hand with work."[92] Du Bois's readings in German idealism during his 1892 fellowship at the University of Berlin included Schiller. Returning home, he brought his recondite education to bear on his moral prescriptions for African American readers. "Instead of warning young people so constantly against excess of pleasure," Du Bois implored, "let us rather inspire them to unselfish work, and show them that amusement and recreation are the legitimate and necessary accompaniments of work, and that we get the maximum of enjoyment from them when they strengthen and inspire us for renewed effort in a great cause." The young Du Bois, hardly an ascetic in his personal life or the fantasy life he later projected into novels like *Dark Princess* (1928), campaigned in particular to rescue the bodily pleasures of social dancing as a "pleasant, innocent, and natural" amusement "from its evil associations and conditions." Pleasure and amusement had their places in Du Bois's black nationalist program for social transformation, but always within very carefully circumscribed limits.[93] His imagined equilibrium of work and pleasure at the turn of the century served a restricted economy of racial uplift through moral progress and "the development of Negro character to its highest and holiest possibilities."[94] The challenges of unregulated, excessive, or "surplus passion" rose as a political and personal problem for Du Bois. "In order for eroticism to fuel political change," the literary critic Claudia Tate writes about Du Bois's perspective, "it must remain sublimated (or subsumed) within social activism." "If the eroticism does not remain submerged within the political objective," Tate continues, "its drive for pleasure becomes overly personalized, and its preoccupation with individual gratification subverts the collective goal."[95] Tate's critical work effectively demonstrates how the disequilibriating force and incomplete sublimation of Du Bois's own fantasies and "surplus passion" erupted in his critical and creative writings.

One of the aspirations behind Du Bois's 1903 vision of "double-consciousness" was to dialectically overcome the contradictions between an idealistic orientation toward an invisible, supersensible realm (the space above the veil) and the social focus of his African American exceptionalism (the specificity of "the true Negro folk-song"). The marriage of "disembodied spirit" and the aesthetic idealism of Wagner and Beethoven, on the one hand, and the "Song of Emancipation" in the particularist legacy of "Go Down, Moses," on the other hand, found its ultimate imaginative consummation in Du Bois's revealing international romance *Dark Princess*.[96] Throughout his comments on music, he focused on cultural purity and progressive hybridizing development and criticized the unregulated pleasures of unproductive entertainment. He located unproductive or dialectically inert genres in *The Souls of Black Folk* at locations between the "sorrow songs" context (the romanticized rural folk's nearness to "Nature's heart") and the uplifting path toward the "Kingdom of Culture." "Debased" stages and pleasures, Du Bois implied, only hindered a dialectical unfolding of history that would make the black folk into the self-conscious and objectively "new nation" or "new race" they were destined to become. Excessively amusing, even decadent forms of expressive culture did not inspire effective antiracist political activity or aid black participation in the "kingdom of culture."[97] Thus, it was deeply discomforting for Du Bois to see the color line dissolving most often where the veil was set aside for the sake of racially shared degradation and license. "Debased" racial interaction took place in the least dignified and productive environs, social spaces like Storyville, the fabled New Orleans zone of ragtime and legalized prostitution from 1897 to 1917. Blues, ragtime, and jazz—the music identified with these compromised social spaces of potentially unregulated pleasure—frustrated Du Bois's cultural and political program when he wanted African Americans to break the color barrier and rend "the veil" at the most refined and uplifting points of cultural contact. From Du Bois's perspective, the socially progressive consequences of the 1920s urban Jazz Age revolt against Victorian culture were far from obvious.

"The Romance of This World Did Not Die"

This chapter began with Du Bois's bitter response to Olin Downes's comparison of a 1933 Fisk University Choir performance with the "uncorrupted" music offered at an evangelical church service in Harlem. Du Bois did not see the black expressivity of sanctified singing or "shouting"—or so-called "hot jazz," for that matter—as culturally liberating or conducive to moral self-control. His disparaging comments in *The Souls of Black Folk* on culture and musical genres at the lower reaches of the veil aptly foreshadowed his skepticism toward certain strains of interracial modernism and the "Negro vogue" of the 1920s. According to Du Bois, the Jazz Age fad of high-spirited white slumming fetishized black racial difference through a fascination with the most ribald and seamy side of African American life.[98] Imagining the secret pleasures of black popular culture as keys to unlocking repressed bourgeois needs for transgression and unmediated "natural" pleasures, the logic of slumming precisely emphasized those social and moral zones where "higher strivings for the good and noble and true" were least evident.

In contrast to J. B. T. Marsh's reference to a "puzzle to the critics" regarding the 1870s Fisk Jubilee Singers, the "Negro vogue" of the Jazz Age set up a different, but not unrelated, puzzle. How was psychic liberation to be imagined in jazz performance and participatory dancing, apparently anarchic and unrepressed cultural forms that were often carefully rehearsed and laden with formal expectations? Ideologies of romantic racialism and primitivism were, of course, not new in the 1920s; the prominence of black creative figures who appropriated images of unrepressed sublimity in black expressivity for their own strategic purposes, however, was a striking development. The Jazz Age discourse of expressive individuality under the banner of anti-Victorian psychic and sexual freedom often collided with the dominant Negro Renaissance discourse (espoused by Charles Johnson, James Weldon Johnson, Alain Locke, and others) of racial vindication under the banner of bourgeois refinement and formal cosmopolitanism. Du Bois articulated his sense of a proper Negro Renaissance by positioning himself against the Jazz Age current of anti-Victorian desublimation.

Some whites spoke out in the 1920s and 1930s against racism in the music and entertainment business and against white condescension toward African American cultural achievement. Unfortunately, white publicity about and patronage of black music too often bolstered stereotypes of authentic black expressivity as unrefined and "natural." Double-edged flattery reinforced old barriers against black aspiration, most especially in the realm of formal concert music. Du Bois's reaction to Olin Downes can be paired with his more famous protest against Carl Van Vechten, the era's foremost white patron of black music and literature. Du Bois bitterly opposed the prominence of modernist primitivism in Van Vechten's novel *Nigger Heaven* (1926). Remarking on the disjunction between a much-needed realistic portrayal of Harlem and the controversial novel's vision of racial difference, Du Bois thundered against the "theory of Harlem" in *Nigger Heaven* and its representation of "low-down" Harlem cabaret culture. For Van Vechten, according to Du Bois, "the black cabaret is Harlem; around it all his characters gravitate. Here is their stage of action. Such a theory of Harlem is nonsense. The overwhelming majority of black folk there never go to cabarets. The average colored man in Harlem is an everyday laborer, attending church, lodge and movie and as conservative and conventional as ordinary working folk everywhere."[99]

At least for Du Bois, the "theory of Harlem" in *Nigger Heaven* was a racial fantasy designed to fulfill white desires for racial transgression. The interracial artistic movement that Van Vechten participated in aimed to topple an older moral and metaphysical idealism inherited from Victorian culture and the "genteel" literary tradition. Romantic primitivism was only one of the weapons that Van Vechten and others used in their generational struggle. The literary critic Michael North has argued that the socially progressive promises of modernist interracialism largely failed in the period between the world wars. The racial emphases of modernist primitivism and the vastly unequal institutional power of black and white artists played key roles in the shortcomings of the avant-garde:

> the generational conflict between the older critics clustered between the American Academy's walls and the younger writers outside was fought over the body of a third figure, a black one. . . . Modernism became another form of mongrelization. . . . The figure in the midst

of all this, the racial alien, is, of course, a cipher, and yet it actually represents the one point of agreement in the battle of literary generations. Both sides tend to see this figure as natural, primitive, life-affirming, and impatient of restraint.[100]

The details of North's biographical and institutional claims strongly contrast with other, more positive, perspectives on modernist interracialism in scholarship of recent years, including George Hutchinson's *The Harlem Renaissance in Black and White* and Ann Douglas's *Terrible Honesty*. It is worth noting that North's critique of primitivist motifs and power imbalances in the literary world coheres with Du Bois's skepticism, though North does not share Du Bois's positive aesthetic. When the mongrelizing white avant-garde rebelled against "genteel" artistic ideals and whiteness as hegemonic signs of civilization and cultural superiority, it summoned a "double-consciousness" that in some senses reversed Du Bois's desired synthesis. White mongrelization could appear critical and transgressive while it contradicted and disrupted dominant images of whiteness; at the same time, it could reinscribe with equal strenuousness a stereotypical counterimage of blackness. The traffic in this logic of subcultural appropriation consistently moved in one direction: from low to high and black to white.[101] An imagined surfeit of burdensome elite culture inheritances inspired elite white mongrelization and the transfusion of black-coded authenticity, rawness, and vernacular creativity. The cross-racial transfusions too often tended toward cultural vampirism: it was fitting that some of Van Vechten's contemporaries pictured him as vampiristic in appearance. Du Bois winced at the condescending irony of white "double-consciousness" and its "deracinated" complaints about overcivilization and an overdeveloped European cultural inheritance.

Maintaining his idealistic commitment to an aesthetic of Beauty, Truth, and Goodness, Du Bois feared that an encroaching aesthetic of decadence—most especially among the "talented tenth"—might derail black art from its role in the broader struggle for racial liberation. "We have with this generation," he wrote in 1925, "just come to the time where there is a very small but very real group of American Negroes with minds enlightened enough and with sufficient fine carelessness concerning their mere bread and butter to be about to be real artists."[102] Du Bois's understanding of "real artistry" included assumptions about appropriate racial representation despite his embrace of "sufficient fine carelessness" as a prerequisite for young artists. The challenging memory of the "sorrow songs" and the requirement of seeing "the Eternal Beauty that shines through all Truth" demanded both politically responsible expression and artistry of the highest quality.[103] Satisfying this twin demand was not to be taken lightly. Du Bois's generally favorable review of Alain Locke's anthology *The New Negro* (which included a Du Bois essay, "Worlds of Color") issued a stern warning: "It is the fight for Life and Liberty that is giving birth to Negro literature and art today and when, turning from this fight or ignoring it, the young Negro tries to do pretty things or things that catch the passing fancy of the really unimportant critics and publishers about him, he will find that he has killed the soul of Beauty in his Art."[104] Black art was crippled, Du Bois insisted, when artists (left unnamed) directed their work to attracting white patrons, publishers, and audiences more comfortable with apolitical aestheticism or unthreatening stereotypes than with politically challenging renderings of America's multiracial civilization. As later chapters detail, prominent younger black artists and critics in the 1920s chafed at Du Bois's analysis of the literary marketplace, his undisguised class and cultural elitism, and the metaphysical assumptions behind his cultural idealism.

Along with other factors, frustration with the progress and recognition of African American art encouraged Du Bois's shift toward a political agenda of voluntary self-segregation and explicit socialism in the mid-1930s. Walter White pushed the increasingly radical Du Bois to resign, if temporarily, from the NAACP. Du Bois's frustration with the liberal integrationists at the NAACP and his calls for voluntary black separatism clarified his understanding of African American progress into the "kingdom of culture." He made the case in 1939 in an apparent rebuff to recent essays by Alain Locke (such as "A Contribution to American Culture" and "The Negro's Contribution to American Culture"). "Our Art can make black beautiful," Du Bois countered. "It can be, not simply a 'contribution to American culture,' but a contribution to our own culture, which is and long will be a thing largely segregated and apart, despite all we think or do." Du Bois used the occasion to emphasize the intense limitations of liberal interracialism in white-dominated institutional settings. He asked "why not see Negro literature in terms of the Negro audience; as a means of expression of their feelings and aspiration; as a picture painted for their own enlightenment of the vast tragedy of their life, and the comedy of their very frustrations." Du Bois's turn away from interracialism did not, however, mean a turning away from the broader teleological ideals of universal cosmopolitanism. "In the end," he reminded, "such literature and only such will be authentic and true enough to join the Art Universal."[105] An indiscriminate embrace of interracialism as a cosmopolitan ideal, in other words, could squelch the historically essential cultivation of black distinctiveness and the ultimate cosmopolitan goals of the "Art Universal." In "Of the Coming of John," John desires sustained access to the elite white institutions that conjure the "dreamland" of Wagnerian opera. By contrast, a chief concern of Du Bois's 1939 essay on "The Position of the Negro in the American Social Order" was the development of the African American audience for advanced art and a strong infrastructure for cultural innovation. Here one finds Du Bois, the lifelong Wagnerian, criticizing the optimistic "contributionism" of New Negro integrationists. He pointed beyond liberal interracialism toward independent black cultural institutions, but he implored his black readers to familiarize themselves with the landmarks of European high culture and with the Russian and French Revolutions. These disparate motifs in Du Bois's oeuvre appear less contradictory when one allows the distinctive dialectical rhythm of his thought to come into view.

Significant aesthetic and political differences distinguished Du Bois's early black nationalism and his evolving pan-Africanism from prominent articulations of the "black aesthetic" made by Amiri Baraka, Larry Neal, Hoyt Fuller, and others in the 1960s.[106] As we have seen, Du Bois's selective synthesis of black folk romanticism and Victorian cultural idealism included little sympathy for the expressive style of "pythian madness" he found in the nonelite black church, nor for most of the expressive styles he encountered in ragtime, blues, and jazz. Baraka's *Black Music* (1967), by contrast, celebrated the revolutionary power of the "new music" of the jazz avant-garde precisely through its recuperative populist links to the "shouts" and "hollers" of the "Sanctified or Holy Roller church (the blacker churches)."[107] Du Bois and Baraka pursued the legacies of the "sorrow songs" and the "shouts" for decidedly different projects of cultural recovery. Some of the most challenging African American jazz of the 1960s (like that of Albert Ayler and John Coltrane), Baraka argued, gave voice to the oldest and most authentically black expressive impulses in African American sacred music. Baraka's dialectically-inflected aesthetic of black nationalism in music hoped to unleash the disruptive antibourgeois power of the "surplus passion" that Du Bois wanted to rationally control and carefully sublimate. From this perspective, the burdens of Western

rationalism, the Protestant work ethic, and a disabling trust in sublimation restricted Du Bois's capacity to feel "with the music the movement of
power within him."

Du Bois's comments on interwar innovations among African American
writers often restated his expectation for the copresence of aesthetic perfection (Beauty), transformative knowledge (Truth), and ethical rigor (the
Good). His aesthetic paradigm seemed to be on the verge of obsolescence
even as his politics became more radical. Du Bois's perspective ran counter
to new fashions for "realistic" and plain-spoken literature and for concert
music less wedded to metaphysical justifications of art's moral purpo-
siveness. In *The Souls of Black Folk*, the legacy of the "sorrow songs" promised a reconciling bridge between separate worlds, between the folk's
primitive "nearness to nature" and the uplifting, cosmopolitan "kingdom
of culture." In a manner reminiscent of that celebration of the "sorrow
songs," Du Bois applauded the historical writings of Carter Woodson in
1926. Du Bois explained that Woodson, who founded the Association for
the Study of Negro Life and History in 1915, allowed the hidden truths
and hitherto submerged memories of the black past to illuminate contemporary ideals and the race's grand future:

> What has this Beauty to do with the world? What has Beauty to do
> with Truth and Goodness—with the facts of the world and the right
> actions of men? "Nothing," the artists rush to answer. They may be
> right. I am but an humble disciple of art and cannot presume to say. I
> am one who tells the truth and exposes evil and seeks with Beauty and
> for Beauty to set the world right. That somehow, somewhere eternal
> and perfect Beauty sits above Truth and Right I can conceive, but here
> and now and in the world in which I work they are for me unseparated
> and inseparable.
>
> This is brought to us peculiarly when as artists we face our own
> past as a people. There has come to us—and it has come especially
> through the man we are going to honor tonight [Carter Godwin
> Woodson, twelfth Spingarn Medallist]—a realization of that past, of
> which for long years we have been ashamed, for which we have apolo-
> gized. We thought nothing could come out of that past which we
> wanted to remember; which we wanted to hand down to our chil-
> dren. Suddenly, this past is taking on form, color and reality, and in
> a half shame-faced way we are beginning to be proud of it. We are

remembering that the romance of the world did not die and lie forgotten in the Middle Ages; that if you want romance to deal with you must have it here and now and in your own hands.[108]

Du Bois's "romance of the world" implied the penetration of an immaterial realm of Beauty, Goodness, and Truth into the messy, impure world of secular history. No small part of the creative and social power of jazz, on the other hand, resided in an aesthetic of tonal impurity and the adjacent ideological implications of a sensuous materialism seemingly detached from Du Bois's idealism and his trust in the preternatural unity of virtue. He allowed that "somehow, somewhere eternal and perfect Beauty" might sit "above Truth and Right," but he confessed a commitment to believing that "here and now and in the world in which I work they are for me unseparated and inseparable." Du Bois's pointed comments responded not only to specific ideological dissents voiced by Alain Locke, Langston Hughes, and others, but to broader transformations sweeping folk, commercial, and elite culture alike.

The emergent popular music of the Jazz Age had a great capacity for exciting formal hybridization. Such hybridization aided the music's rapid ascent through various strata of cultural life throughout the industrialized world. In contrast to Du Bois's model of rural folk romanticism, jazz music climbed upward from a birthplace less in the souls of rural folk close to "Nature's heart" than at the edges of an urban working-class milieu. Du Bois's stern moralism about entertainment and the Jazz Age was, of course, hardly unique. Many black and white commentators interpreted the popularity of jazz recordings and related African American dance styles as symptomatic of a post-Victorian transformation; new ideals of commercialized secular pleasure and an unapologetically materialistic sense of popular music's function were revising the aesthetic "romance of the world." Commentaries on jazz as a symptom of breakneck modernization and cultural disruption were ubiquitous in the 1920s. A *Vanity Fair* commentator offered a vulgarized Freudian interpretation of the Jazz Age in a tone worlds away from Du Bois's cultural vision:

> Men and women no longer tolerate the repression of their emotional responses. . . . When the dance is plastic and classical, it reveals the mind's response to beauty; when it is "jazzed" it reveals the body's response to rhythmical stimulation: in both cases it is an expression of one's self, a reaching toward a more idealized form of life. . . . The

dance "mania" is one of the symptoms of our national disease: adult-infantilism. We are like children in our emotions and we have no capacity for measure. Our immaturity is displayed most conspicuously in the management of our fundamental urges. They will not be standardized and they resent repression. When the most potent of them is repressed it finds an avenue of escape. Dancing is one of them, and not the worst by any means.[109]

For the commentator, the "dance 'mania'"—a regressive mismanagement of "fundamental urges" in the service of a new "idealized form of life"—took place as a revolt against older, European-derived formal dance styles and their restrictive classicism. The comment that when dance "is 'jazzed' it reveals the body's response to rhythmical stimulation" alluded to the novelty of particular kinds of "rhythmical stimulation" captured in eroticized popular dance styles. Locating the secret of a supposedly liberatory desublimation within the puzzle of black expressive sublimity —despite the fact that the latter was a product of stylization—revealed a racialized misrecognition about African American culture. One can understand Du Bois's frustrations with Van Vechten's "theory of Harlem" and Downes's taste for music performed in the "uncorrupted manner of their race" in the context of Du Bois's critique of a logic of cultural desublimation that only disabled social progress, at least as he understood it.

"Art does not imitate nature," Du Bois wrote in the early 1890s, "but nature imitates art. Or to put it better both strive toward one vast Ideal, the infinite beauty of the other world."[110] We are left to confront Du Bois's romantic implication that art, properly understood, was not the antithesis of nature, but instead a redemptive vehicle for nature's transformation and an intelligent aid to the antiracist goals of political and social transformation. One must juxtapose against the popular image of the Jazz Age Du Bois's earlier hope of replacing America's "vulgar music with the soul of the sorrow songs." Aspects of the black cultural inheritance had been transformed into urban and commercialized leisure projects in the 1920s. The vaunted authenticity and electrically charged sublimity of these cultural artifacts, at least for some consumers, depended on their association with a folk's closeness to the processes and rhythms of nature. Vernacular materials fed popular music, secular and sacred, as well as the self-conscious art music that Du Bois preferred, including the refined New Negro music most congenial to his idealistic values.

Chapter 2 turns to several artists' negotiations of the "sorrow songs" legacy as it intersected with the demands of 1920s modernity, secular cosmopolitanism, and the promise of an interracial avant-garde. "We thought nothing could come out of that past which we wanted to remember," Du Bois recalled in 1926. "Suddenly this past is taking on form, color, and reality." But what form, which colors, and whose reality was the remembered black past taking on in the mid-1920s? As a cultural marker of the Great Migration, the Renaissance itself turned on a perplexity of historical dimensions: what happens in the realm of culture when a previously rural minority population becomes part of the modern urban masses almost overnight? In the context of that question, the legacy of the spirituals remained a central site of memory and contestation among African Americans, including a rising generation of writers, musicians, and artists.

TWO

Swan Songs and Art Songs:

The Spirituals and the

"New Negro" in the 1920s

Music is an almost instantaneous evocator of inner-experiences not being had, not being thought of as possible, until the music begins. Add music, and you can instantly transport yourself, through inner-experience, into a different world. . . . Music, however, though able to transport you into a different world, cannot keep you in that different world—no, not even if you yourself are a musician. Once it is over for the time being, you slide back into this world.
—Jean Toomer[1]

Like performance, memory operates as both quotation and invention, an improvisation on borrowed themes, with claims on the future as well as the past.
—Joseph Roach[2]

"The aesthetic of the machine [and] the artistic acceptance of what is undeniably dominant in our age" energized Jean Toomer's modernist vision in the early 1920s. His ideal was "the artist creatively adapting himself to angular, to dynamic, to mass forms," to the things with "life and vitality in them." "I think my own contribution," Toomer predicted, "will curiously blend the rhythm of peasanty [*sic*] with the rhythm of machines." It would be a "syncopation, a slow jazz, a sharp intense motion, subtilized, fused to a terse lyricism."[3] Toomer's poems and stories, many of which he included in his landmark 1923 text *Cane*, were heralded in white modernist periodicals of the 1920s as well as in the NAACP's *Crisis* (edited by W. E. B. Du Bois) and the National Urban League's ambitious new monthly, *Opportunity: A Journal of Negro Life*. Toomer's disparate groups of fans ranged from Claude McKay (who published Toomer in the *Liberator*) to William Stanley Braithwaite to Max Eastman to the Southern Fugitive Allen Tate. Tate, for example, recognized Toomer's *Cane* as "highly important for literature" in a review for the *Nashville Tennessean*.[4]

A cycle of poems and stories in three sections, *Cane* dramatizes a black modernist's search for a literary voice capable of reconciling the antinomies of American life. One of Toomer's strategies was to "curiously blend" the slower diurnal rhythms of rural life with the faster mechanical rhythms of the industrial city. The critic and anthologist William Stanley Braithwaite was of an older generation of black literary figures, but he nevertheless singled out Toomer in the *Crisis* as "the very first artist in his Race who, with all an artist's passion and sympathy for life, its hurts, its sympathies, its desires, its joys, its defeats, and strange yearnings, can write about the Negro without the surrender or compromise of the artist's vision."[5] The original publication of *Cane* yielded many glowing reviews and few sales. Moreover, its "terse lyricism" was so effective in defining Toomer's reputation that he would ever after attempt to elude and overcome the book's impact. While his later life and published works sank into obscurity, the importance of *Cane* for the black modernist tradition only grew with each passing generation.

Roland Hayes, Toomer's elder by seven years, performed the vocal repertoire of the European classical tradition. Born in 1887 and raised on a farm in rural Georgia, Hayes began his higher education at Fisk University in 1905. He sang there with the Jubilee Singers and later toured with the group. Among other musical projects, Hayes performed duets with composer and baritone Harry T. Burleigh on a Booker T. Washington lecture tour in 1914.[6] "With Dvořák's encouragement," Hayes wrote, "Burleigh had jotted down traditional musical settings for some of our Afro-American songs. Traveling along with him, I felt close to the inspired sources of our native music."[7] Washington died the following year, but the tour turned Hayes into a longtime devotee of what he called Washington's "democratic realism." "Some of us," Hayes later wrote, "must advance be-

2. Roland Hayes, 1954. Photo by Carl Van Vechten. Courtesy of Carl Van Vechten Trust.

yond the rudiments, as Du Bois believes and teaches; but our racial culture ought to rest on the solid foundation of skill in factory and field. I may be old-fashioned, but I like to think that I am a better singer for having learned to plow a straight furrow when I was a boy in the Flatwoods."[8] Nevertheless, Hayes's musical ambitions followed the contours of Du Boisian cosmopolitanism quite closely. A 1917 triumph at Boston's Symphony Hall advanced Hayes toward widespread acclaim. The concert left him with a hefty profit of $2,000 and made possible a trip to Europe for vocal instruction and concerts in London, Paris, and Vienna in the early 1920s.[9] Hayes returned triumphantly to the United States in 1923 and enjoyed star status in New York City and Boston: "For several years following I was one of a small group of three or four artists—I believe I am right in saying this—who could fill both Carnegie Hall and Symphony Hall three times every winter."[10]

Hayes later reflected that "when I began my career I realized that if I would speak to all men, I must learn the language and the way of thought of all men. What good could I do if I knew only my own ways and the thoughts of my own people? So I learned to sing the songs of all people."[11] Hayes's success helped to soften the barriers of segregation and discrimination in the American concert music world. The NAACP bestowed its highest honor upon him in 1924, the Spingarn Medal for personal achievement, to celebrate his racially vindicating artistry. He collected similar honors throughout a long career as a singer and teacher that lasted until his death in 1976. During the 1920s vogue for Negro spirituals, Hayes enjoyed a reputation as the foremost African American master of both the European art song repertoire and the solo concert spiritual. A 1925 *Opportunity* editorial sketched an ongoing debate about the concert spiritual in terms of two contending "schools of thought." On the one side were "those who insist that the songs should be preserved in all their native simplicity." On the other were "those who believe that the original tunes should be used as the basis for the limitless development of a new music which would, of course, preserve the distinguishing characteristics of the original."[12] The editorialist, like Hayes, the composers Nathaniel Dett and Harry Burleigh, and others, belonged to the second camp. Among those who wrote in favor of the first view, Carl Van Vechten preferred Paul Robeson's "more natural" (Van Vechten's term) low baritone over Hayes's delicate tenor. Robeson, a recent graduate of Columbia Law School, had just made a stir on the New York stage with performances in two plays on black topics by Eugene O'Neill, *All God's Chillun Got Wings* and *Emperor*

Jones. Accompanied by Hayes's former pianist, Lawrence Brown, Robeson gave a successful series of New York recitals in 1925, consisting entirely of African American spirituals. The all-spirituals format and Robeson's charismatic performances made a powerful impression on many in the audience. "To those who are accustomed to hear Negro Spirituals delivered in a sanctimonious, lugubrious manner, or yet worse, with the pseudo-refinement of the typical concert singer," Van Vechten crowed, "the evangelical, true Negro rendering of Paul Robeson and Lawrence Brown will come as a delightful surprise."[13]

Hayes, unlike Robeson, was never motivated to perform an all-spirituals concert, even during the height of the 1920s spiritual vogue. He chose instead to program a few spirituals in his formal recitals of classical European repertoire. Hayes's 1942 autobiography accounts for his perspective and details his technical and intellectual influences along with the racial barriers he confronted while a music student in Nashville, Boston, and London. A Washingtonian narrative of self-discovery and racial uplift shapes the autobiography. Hayes admits that he worried about the presumed racial characteristics of his voice and style long before Van Vechten and others contrasted his style against Robeson's. A climactic scene between Hayes and his mother illustrates how his vocal apparatus struck him in the late 1910s after more than a decade of formal training in the European tradition:

> "Do you suppose," I said, "that I have been trying to turn myself into a white artist, instead of making the most of what I was born with?"
>
> "I am glad you are finding yourself out, son," said my mother. "I knowed what was what all the time, but I wasn't going to tell you. Now go ahead and work hard and be your own man." . . .
>
> . . . In the midst of my studies in Boston I had not, thank God, lost my respect for my racial origins. I had simply added a new culture to an old one. But I was breaking ground, I had no pattern to follow, and I had been suffering from a racial habit of imitation. I had been working in a cloud of depression because my voice had not come out as "white" as, in the beginning, I must have hoped it would. Now I swore I would use the "rich purplish red" voice that Nature had given me. I felt a great release from nervous tension, and at the same time a kind of exaltation. I felt I could be what no white artist could ever be: I could be myself, sole, personal, unique. . . . I felt I had found a motto for my career: to understand the beauty of a black voice.[14]

3. Paul Robeson, 1933. Photo by Carl Van Vechten. Courtesy of Carl Van Vechten Trust.

Both Roland Hayes and Jean Toomer undertook groundbreaking journeys as they struggled to capture the distinctive "beauty of a black voice." Their respective accounts of this struggle illuminate the aesthetic currency of race in circulation throughout elite New Negro cultural production in the 1920s. The concert spirituals functioned in this discourse as sites of memory where the aesthetic terms of New Negro identity were contested. Toomer's *Cane* and the debate over spirituals both illustrate Joseph Roach's insight about how social "memory operates as both quotation and invention, an improvisation on borrowed themes, with claims on the future as well as the past." Indeed, the spirituals debate was about imagining the future through selectively recuperating the past. Toomer's characterization of *Cane* as a "swan song" portrayed American modernity in terms of the disenchanting erosion of spiritually integrated folk cultures and traditions.[15] A modernist swan song could be elaborated positively through an optimistic promise of democratic individualism, social mobility, and technological innovation, or negatively as an entropic decline into anomic rootlessness, historical amnesia, and empty homogenization. Different aspects of Toomer's life and work allowed for both interpretations.

This chapter employs the trope of the art song not only in reference to Hayes's musical repertoire but also to the model of cultural evolution articulated by Alain Locke and like-minded New Negro publicists. Some of Toomer's poetry appeared in Locke's special March 1925 issue of *Survey Graphic*, republished in book form as *The New Negro* by Albert & Charles Boni, Inc. Locke's essay on "The Negro Spirituals" in *The New Negro* celebrated the efforts of Du Bois, Hayes, Robeson, and others on behalf of the folk spirituals' evolution to the stage of formal music. According to Locke's paradigm of New Negro aesthetics, Toomer's swan song of discontinuity and Hayes's art song of racial uplift through elite cultural vindication were more intertwined than antagonistic. These paired narratives came together with Locke's appropriation of a modernist swan song to reinforce his sense of an evolution from the African American folk inheritance to a 1920s Renaissance in league with modernist interracialism.

The predicament of black "double-consciousness" in the world of white Euro-American high culture prompted Locke's vision of reconciliation in the aesthetic sphere as a foreshadowing of democratic progress and racial reconciliation. The success of the concert spirituals, in other words, struck him as a solid down payment on the "more democratic chance." Skeptics, at the time and later, regarded the concert spirituals and the art song narrative of New Negro evolutionism as compromised by an assimilationist aesthetic. This chapter locates one version of that skeptical perspective in Carl Van Vechten's argument for Paul Robeson as a more legitimate heir of the folk spirituals than Roland Hayes. A related criticism faulted bourgeois New Negro publicists for evading contemporary black vernacular musics like blues and jazz and the social milieux from which they were emerging. That line of criticism will be touched on here but explored in greater depth in a later discussion of Langston Hughes and Zora Neale Hurston (see chapter 4).

The Swan Song of Jean Toomer

The rural folk culture of a "song-lit race of slaves," according to Jean Toomer, was fast moving toward obsolescence. Du Bois influenced many black intellectuals when he conceptualized the "sorrow songs" through the lens of folk romanticism. In Du Bois's refiguration of black cultural nationalism, the old folk songs seemed to render "the music of a nation" and give voice to the inner longings and millenial expectations of African America. Alain Locke reinforced Du Bois's conclusion and venerated the "Negro spirituals" as America's greatest "folk-gift," songs that stood "among the classic folk expressions in the whole world."[16] Locke returned again and again to the invaluable inheritance of the spirituals throughout the 1920s and 1930s in *The New Negro*, numerous essays for *Opportunity* and other periodicals, and in his monograph *The Negro and His Music* (1936). Toomer's poem "Song of the Son" must have had a profound ring of familiarity to Du Bois and Locke.

> Pour O pour that parting soul in song,
> O pour it in the sawdust glow of night,
> Into the velvet pine-smoke air to-night,
> And let the valley carry it along.
> And let the valley carry it along.
>
> O land and soil, red soil and sweet-gum tree,
> So scant of grass, so profligate of pines,
> Now just before an epoch's sun declines
> Thy son, in time, I have returned to thee,
> Thy son, I have in time returned to thee.
>
> In time for though the sun is setting on
> A song-lit race of slaves, it has not set;

Though late, O soil, it is not too late yet
To catch thy plaintive soul, leaving, soon gone,
Leaving, to catch thy plaintive soul soon gone.

O Negro slaves, dark purple ripened plums,
Squeezed, and bursting in the pine-wood air,
Passing, before they stripped the old tree bare
One plum was saved for me, one seed becomes

An everlasting song, a singing tree,
Caroling softly souls of slavery,
What they were, and what they are to me,
Caroling softly souls of slavery.

—Jean Toomer, "Song of the Son"[17]

Like many of the poems and stories in the first section of *Cane*, "Song
of the Son" evokes the plaintive tone and pacing of a mournful spiritual or
"sorrow song." The slow spirituals "Deep River," "My Lord, What a Morning," and "Go Down, Moses," all likely reference points for Toomer's
"Song of the Son," are alluded to elsewhere in *Cane*. The poem first appeared in the June 1922 issue of the NAACP monthly founded and edited
by Du Bois from 1910 until his temporary resignation in 1934. "Song of the
Son" appeared the following year in *Cane* and several years later in *The
New Negro*. Toomer's response to the spirituals and their function as sites
of social memory proceeded, however, according to a cultural logic notably different from the views of Du Bois and Locke.

In Toomer's poem, the refrains of an exhausted culture's "parting soul"
follow the cadence of a spiritual that echoes through a haunted rural
Southern valley. The fading culture's soul, the poem intimates, depended
on the folk's attachment to and immediate identification with its landscape of "red soil and sweet-gum tree, / So scant of grass, so profligate of
pines." The poem enacts an elegy for a dying folk culture as the epochal
Great Migration looms over a harsh and depleted Southern landscape. A
son who has "in time returned to thee" must strive to span the growing
distance between an urban life of constant acceleration and a residual folk
culture. Despite its lyric of loss, "Song of the Son" scarcely inspires sentimentalism about the folk culture in twilight. *Cane* replicates neither the
racist sentimentalism of the "plantation tradition" nor the antimodernist
critique of the present that is found in Eliot's modernist elegy, *The Waste
Land*.[18] The fading world of "Song of the Son" and other Southern seg-

ments of *Cane* is never pastoral; rural Georgia is instead portrayed as a brutal and bloodstained landscape. The novelist and literary critic Nathaniel Mackey points out that *"Cane* is fueled by an oppositional nostalgia." "A precarious vessel possessed of an eloquence coincident with loss," Mackey continues, Toomer's book "wants to reach or keep in touch with an alternate reality as that reality fades."[19]

A song drifts through the poem's Georgia valley, "[c]aroling softly souls of slavery." The song passes along memories of racial subjugation and terror (it depicts African Americans as "dark purple ripened plums, / Squeezed, and bursting in the pine-wood air"), but it also holds out the protective resources of a "song-lit race of slaves." Lamenting its own fragility and eroding beauty, the culture extends a saving remnant to a visiting son: "Passing, before they stripped the old tree bare / One plum was saved for me, One seed becomes / An everlasting song, a singing tree." The "everlasting song" appears to promise black cultural continuity in the face of renewed racial terror and abrupt modernization. Toomer's musicalized depiction of black social memory climaxes with the last-minute rescue and inheritance of the "everlasting song" as a representative kernel of the folk's soul. The song will retain its power and perhaps even be enhanced as a countercurrent of memory or "oppositional nostalgia" in the wake of migratory displacement.

Cane closes with "Kabnis," a similarly allegorical narrative about African American social memory with a musicalized and potentially redemptive denouement. Originally intended for the stage, the short story opens with the title character, a Northern mulatto teacher, alone at night in his rural Georgian cabin. "Night winds in Georgia are vagrant poets," and they whisper a haunting song to Ralph Kabnis.[20] Anxieties about "connecting" to the people and to the rural South as an ancestral land have left him sleepless. He pleads for "God Almighty" to "not torture [him] with beauty" he cannot touch or call his own. Rather than suffer the frustrating nearness of an inaccessible world of black beauty, Kabnis asks for "an ugly world." "Dear Jesus, do not chain me to myself," he cries, "and set these hills and valleys, heaving with folk-songs, so close to me that I cannot reach them."[21] Kabnis is a well-educated and painfully self-conscious young man, another distant son who has yet to experience the power of "an everlasting song" as an inheritance truly available to him. On the following morning, a Sunday, he sits with several neighbors and explains his distaste for the cathartic "shouting" and "moaning" in the town church and makes known his preference for more subdued church music and liturgy.

Kabnis is similar in many ways to Du Bois's unhappily educated protagonist in "Of the Coming of John." Both men suffer from "a promise of a soil-soaked beauty," as if "suspended a few feet above the soil whose touch would resurrect."[22] Kabnis loses his teaching position on the grounds of illegal drinking. Du Bois's John Jones loses his job after teaching the French Revolution and related "dangerous" ideas of egalitarian struggle to his black charges. Kabnis, unlike Du Bois's protagonist, begins what might be called a Southern vernacular apprenticeship in a tool shop of black locals. One night after work, a handful of young men and women descend into "the Hole" beneath the workshop for a drinking party. The cavernous setting simply overwhelms Lewis, a peer of Kabnis's. The gothic history of "the southern town descends on" Lewis all at once. He finds the town's pain "too intense" and runs "through the work-shop and out into the night."[23] Kabnis, however, stays in "the Hole" through the night and endures a dramatic existential trial. The symbolic device of "the Hole" represents not a simple absence or hole; it is a staging ground for a confrontation with what literary critic Houston Baker has referred to (in a different, but related, literary context) as "a subcultural (underground, marginal, or liminal) region in which a dominant, white culture's representations are squeezed to zero volume, producing a new expressive order." The "black hole" appears, then, as a space for a ritualized catharsis and, ultimately, a healing reconciliation with a traumatic racial past and its ancestral heritage. "Having passed the event horizon into the singularity of (W)holeness," Baker writes, "the initiand and his experience are irretrievably transformed."[24] Kabnis's ultimately successful passage warrants the inheritance of the "soil-soaked beauty" that will grant access to "the beauty of a black voice" and enable him to write.

Once Kabnis's acuity for ancestral remembrance is elevated, he can perceive two local women who also stayed through the night as "princesses in Africa going through the early-morning ablutions of their pagan prayers."[25] His most daunting task is to confront the totemic presence of an elderly character referred to by a local as "Father John." John directly memorializes the experience of slavery. After a long silence, he speaks to Kabnis in a halting and cryptic manner: "Th sin whats fixed . . . . upon the white folks—. . . . f tellin Jesus—lies. O th sin the white folks 'mitted when they made th Bible lie."[26] At first unmoved, Kabnis calls John an "old black

fakir." Playing the role of nurse, a woman holds Kabnis tenderly until he is
ready to climb the stairs. Having imagined the woman's embrace as the
soil's healing maternal touch, Kabnis rises from the hole/whole to encounter a sunrise that "sends a birth-song slanting down gray dust streets and
sleepy windows of the southern town."[27] The sunrise's "birth-song" clarifies Kabnis's spiritual awakening and the reconciliation of his agitated cosmopolitan intellect with the delivered "promise of a soil-soaked beauty."
One encounters a character fully prepared to act as the narrator and liberated racial amanuensis of "Song of the Son."

In the days leading up to his ritual passage through "the Hole," Kabnis
describes his difficulty in finding a literary voice appropriate to the rural
Georgia setting. He explains how he has been "shaping words t fit m soul.
. . . sometimes theyre beautiful an golden an have a taste that makes them
fine t roll over with y tongue." But more often the "form thats burned
int my soul is some twisted awful thing that crept in from a dream, a
godam nightmare, an wont stay still unless I feed it. An it lives on words.
Not beautiful words. God Almighty no. Misshapen, split-gut, tortured
words."[28] Like his fictional creation Kabnis, Toomer was not a native son
of the Deep South. He attended Dunbar High School and grew up within
Washington, D.C.'s, black elite as a grandson of P. B. S. Pinchback, a black
governor of Louisiana during Reconstruction. David Levering Lewis has
described Toomer's adult initiation into the rural Southern world of the
folk spirituals in terms comparable to Du Bois's rendering of his own
teaching experiences in rural Tennessee. In both accounts, a black cosmopolitan heavily burdened by "double-consciousness" descends into a rural
Southern world, uneasily confronts that unfamiliar environment, and
struggles toward a personal reconciliation with a folk world of black
difference. "In a cabin whose floor boards permitted the soil to come up
between them, listening to the old folk melodies that Negro women sang
at sun-down," Lewis suggests, "Jean Toomer came down to earth, into the
cotton and cane fields, for the first time in his life." "*Cane* was possible,"
Lewis concludes, "only because its author had been able to resolve his racial duality by affirming it—just for an instant."[29] Lewis's account of the
writing of *Cane* replays the scenario of "Kabnis" as Toomer's veiled autobiography. Toomer's own reflections on the text anticipated such readings
when he wrote to his friend Waldo Frank that "Kabnis is *Me*."[30]

Music, especially the spirituals at their slowest and most mournful,
figures centrally as symbol and site of cultural transmission in *Cane*. In

a Georgia valley "heaving with folk-songs," the folk inheritance is not readily available or explicable to outsiders. Instead, shards of incompletely repressed memories occasion traumatic revelations in dreams, haunting melodies, and the cathartic tumult of evangelical church services. Houston Baker argues that the trances, mediums, and spirituals in *Cane* reach out to make "contact with the numinous element of the universe." They represent "the history of the Afro-American *soul* in its tortuous striving to convert a *possessed* state of slavery into the liberating beauty of a freeing and, I think, deeply Afro-American religious song." The "tortuous striving" of African American memory—from being enslaved and possessed as human capital, to the momentary ecstasy of otherworldly possession in a spiritual trance, to the lasting grip of self-possession—is enabled through the unparalleled services of music. Father John and the church singers of "Kabnis," for example, act as "channels of passage" or "as interactive forces ensuring communication with benign ancestral spirits." "Such mediums," Baker concludes, "are agents and agencies, in a word, of the *breakthrough*. The gifts of their various descents are prophecy and advice—salvific wisdom."[31] The skeptical Kabnis only receives his lyric-making inheritance and "the soul whose touch would resurrect him" after his traumatic encounter with the living memory of slavery. Kabnis's breakthrough to intergenerational and intercultural racial communication turns the book's final pages away from melancholic dissociation as he passes through "the Hole" to a symbolic embrace of what Baker calls the "black whole." He might evade the forlorn path of circling around "the hole" in its alternate destiny as an "open wound" (to borrow Freud's famous image of melancholia). The quiet "birth-song" that concludes "Kabnis" helps account for the reputation of *Cane* as a milestone of black modernist art. As Henry Louis Gates has noted, the book's "thematization of the myth of the return . . . made *Cane* readable as a 'nationalist' text," not least in the revolutionary and essentialist circles of the 1960s.[32] If Kabnis *was* Toomer, then Kabnis's confrontation and apparent reconciliation with black social memory and sacred folk music forms encapsulate one of Toomer's agendas in *Cane*.

Any reassuring prognoses about the health of the "folk-spirit" hinted at in *Cane* contrast with Toomer's own accounts of the book's genesis. On the one hand, certain moments in *Cane* extend hope for racial continuity through an "everlasting song" and imply a transmission of intact ancestral memory. On the other hand, Toomer's correspondence and later writings about the *Cane* period articulated a different relationship between the black folk tradition and the individual artist. Looking back from the early 1930s, Toomer wrote of his reaction to rural Georgia:

The setting was crude in a way, but strangely rich and beautiful. I began feeling its effects despite my state, or, perhaps, just because of it. There was a valley, the valley of "Cane," with smoke-wreaths during the day and mist at night. A family of back-country Negroes had only recently moved into a shack not too far away. They sang. And this was the first time I'd ever heard the folk-songs and spirituals. They were very rich and sad and joyous and beautiful. But I learned that the Negroes of the town objected to them. They called them "shouting." They had victrolas and player-pianos. So, I realized with deep regret, that the spirituals, meeting ridicule, would be certain to die out. With Negroes also the trend was towards the small town and then towards the city—and industry and commerce and machines. The folk-spirit was walking in to die on the modern desert. That spirit was so beautiful. Its death was so tragic. Just this seemed to sum life for me. And this was the feeling I put into *Cane*. *Cane* was a swan-song. It was a song of an end. And why no one has seen and felt that, why people have expected me to write a second and third and a fourth book like "Cane," is one of the queer misunderstandings of my life.[33]

Toomer's two-month stay in Sparta, Georgia, in 1921 motivated his artistic grappling with the black folk inheritance. The folk culture that gave birth to the spirituals, he believed, "was walking in to die on the modern desert." *Cane* was published in New York by Horace Liveright, and when Toomer "returned his signed contract to Liveright," Michael North records, "he expressed his gratification at entering 'the fold' along with Eliot."[34] Liveright, it should be noted, published *The Waste Land* in 1922. Toomer's image of the "modern desert" echoed the antimodernist despair of Eliot's poem and its disenchanted vision of urban modernity as a fallen state of hollow secularism and materialism. Toomer explained to his friend Waldo Frank "that if anything comes up now, pure Negro, it will be a swansong. Dont [*sic*] let us fool ourselves, brother: the Negro of the folksong has all but passed away." "The supreme fact of mechanical civilization," Toomer concluded, "is that you become part of it, or get sloughed off (under). Negroes have no culture to resist it with (and if they had, their position would be identical to the Indians), hence industrialism the more readily transforms them." An involuntary demand to join "mechanical civilization," Toomer argued, transformed all those in its path. The melancholic tone of this swan song of cultural decline casts a shadow of inconsolability over the "everlasting song" extended in "Song of the Son." "A few generations from now," Toomer predicted, "the Negro will still be dark, and a portion of his psychology will spring from this fact, but in all else he will be a conformist to the general outlines of American civilization, or of American chaos."[35]

Toomer's personal reflections did not shape the immediate critical reception of *Cane*. Du Bois, for example, gave the work a demanding reading and immediately recognized its historical significance. Toomer's talent and originality greatly impressed Du Bois, but the *Crisis* editor could only compose an ambivalent review. Toomer's formal experimentalism and taste for psychoanalytic observation conflicted with Du Bois's aesthetic position, or at least Du Bois's "manifest narrative" of self-possessed rationality for the sake of racial uplift and "political demand."[36] Toomer's openness to the uncanny soundings of an ancestral spirit world, together with the apparent antirationalism of his fragmentary "split-gut, tortured words," also challenged Du Bois's idealism about the redemptive copresence of Truth, Beauty, and Goodness. The ultimate promise of the aesthetic realm, according to Du Bois's expansive formulations, was to provide anticipatory gestures of an ideal world for the sake of cultural elevation and progressive social critique. Toomer's commitment to the latter goals lacked the clarity that Du Bois preferred. Though appreciative of the mature sexual frankness of *Cane*, Du Bois responded with incomprehension to Toomer's abstractness and subjectivism. Toomer's "art carries much that is difficult or even impossible to understand," Du Bois wrote. "The artist, of course, has a right deliberately to make art a puzzle to the interpreter (the whole world is a puzzle) but on the other hand I am myself unduly irritated by this sort of thing." Du Bois frankly confessed to not being sure "that I know what 'Kabnis' is about."[37] Taken as a whole, the calculated modernist indeterminacy of Toomer's art imparted no philosophically coherent or politically legible message to Du Bois. We might conclude that Toomer's art, at once ancestralist and ultramodernist, offered a complex encryption of the spirituals as the "music of a nation" that both resonated and contrasted with Du Bois's formulations. "Music," Toomer later wrote, "is an almost instantaneous evocator of inner-experiences not being had, not being thought of as possible, until the music begins. Add music, and you can instantly transport yourself, through inner-experience, into a different world." Du Bois could hardly disagree. However, Du Bois's lack of enthusiasm for evangelical "shouting" and the religious practices of "pythian madness" and "demoniac madness" (as he put it in *The Souls of Black Folk*) separated him from the supersensible "agents and agencies" of spirit possession and antinomianism in *Cane*.

Du Bois alluded in *The Souls of Black Folk* to unhealthy forces threatening the integrity and developmental future of the "sorrow songs," especially at cultural locations where unrefined sacred and secular musics met and intermingled. If the larger audience understood the "sorrow songs" in the appropriate way, the music's uplifting call for liberation and black nationalist self-consciousness would be heard. Du Bois imagined himself eschewing assimilationism and Washingtonian accommodationism alike when he heard the "sorrow songs" as a call for enlightened human progress. For Toomer, the urban alienation from and rural disintegration of African American folk culture—the cultural death that "was so tragic"—found its source in general trends of modernization; the tragedy was a regrettable consequence of "industry and commerce and machines." The silencing of "back-country Negroes" and their evangelical "shouting" songs by their assimilationist superiors with "victrolas and player-pianos" was a symptom of modernization to Toomer. In this sense, those offended by the "shouting" spirituals were voicing predictable responses to urbanization, class stratification, and dissociation from residual folk patterns. "The modern world was uprooted," Toomer intoned dramatically, "the modern world was breaking down, *but we couldn't go back*. There was nothing to go back to. Besides, in our hasty leaps into the future we had burned our bridges."[38] The avant-gardist in Toomer preferred, at least in such formulations, not to encourage ameliorative narratives of cultural continuity between modern identity and the "pure Negro" ancestral legacy.

Returning several decades later to the importance of *Cane* for African American literature, Locke asserted that Toomer's text "raised a new summit, as it soared above the plane of propaganda and apologetics to a self-sufficient presentation of Negro life in its own idiom." Toomer's formal advance in creating a lyrically charged idiom at once fully "Negro" and fully modernist stirred Locke especially; he later ranked *Cane* as a literary work matched only by Richard Wright's *Native Son* and Ralph Ellison's *Invisible Man*. Nevertheless, Locke also had his share of difficulties with Toomer's perspective. Like other publicists of the Negro Renaissance, Locke dedicated himself to a narrative of continuity through steady evolution in African American social memory. The Lockean strand of New Negro thought turned away from Toomer's view that "we had burned our bridges" and his swan song of discontinuity and unbreachable rupture. According to Locke, a New Negro cultural infrastructure could bridge generations and varied African American populations and safely transport the precious folk inheritance. Otherwise, the predicament of Du Bois's "Of the Coming of John" threatened, with its cosmopolitan protagonist's melancholy about the intransigence of white domination and the black folk's supposed backwardness and passivity. Du Bois's frustrated hero died prematurely after either being lynched or jumping into a deep chasm. That fatal chasm materialized John's despair about the distance between the world that his unhappy consciousness inhabited and the ideal world that he imagined as unreachable. A melody from Wagner's *Lohengrin* momentarily transported John to the ideal world he dreamed of; a spiritual like "Go Down, Moses" (the hopeful anthem of Du Bois's major Renaissance era text, *Dark Princess*) could not. The scenario revealed not only the character's heroic stoicism but his distance from the black "promise of a soil-soaked beauty" depicted in *Cane* and what Hayes called "the beauty of a black voice."

Locke noted that despite the admiring critical reception of *Cane*, Toomer "chose not to continue" his efforts in a black modernist idiom of "terse lyricism."[39] The swan song depiction of African American modernization as an irresistible break with the past had a special personal meaning for Toomer. His particular hybridized lines of descent left him with a relatively light complexion, straight dark hair, and the visual cues necessary for racial "passing." *Cane* had signaled a very personal "song of an end." Having completed his swan song to the folk culture of black America, Toomer felt no personal identification with what he saw as a wholly different and new black urban culture. "Seventh Street is the song of crude new life," he explained to Waldo Frank. "Of a new people. Negro? Only in the boldness of its expression. In its healthy freedom. American."[40] Traditional identities were being plowed under and the 1920s modernist moment represented new possibilities for Toomer. He took up a prerogative of his appearance and chose no longer to identify himself as racially or culturally black. Toomer later contended that Locke had deceived him to obtain pieces from *Cane*, along with a freshly commissioned Winold Reiss portrait, for *The New Negro*: "Out of curiosity or vanity or whatever, I did sit for Reiss; and, so far as I knew, that was that. But when Locke's book, *The New Negro*, came out, there was the Reiss portrait, and there was a story from *Cane*, and there in an introduction, were words about me which have caused as much or more misunderstanding than Waldo Frank's." "For a short time after the appearance of Locke's book I was furious because I felt blocked," Toomer wrote. "My dear enemies," he explained, "those who liked to misrepresent me, would have echoed Horace Liveright and said at once, 'Toomer wants to deny race.'"[41] Toomer reaffirmed his disaffiliation when he declined James Weldon Johnson's request to include his poems in the revised 1930 edition of *The Book of American Negro Poetry*. One can hardly doubt that Johnson would have included "Song of the Son" as one of the canonical poems of the Renaissance. Michael North adds that "the writer who could most successfully have embodied Locke's hope for a dual renaissance, a confluence of Harlem and the moderns, had also abandoned all but a few of his friends in the avant-garde."[42]

Toomer did not interpret his actions in terms of "passing" for white. His policy was to claim neither a private black self nor a public or private white identity. Refusing the racial classifications of American law (which were only bearing down harder on the category of the mulatto at the time), Toomer aspired to be raceless or race-free in theory and practice. The death of the "folk-spirit" may have been tragic, but rather than suffer modernity as a personal crisis he reached for a re-enchanting transformation into an altogether new kind of American. Toomer continued to write fiction and nonfiction, but not on racialized subjects. His next major work, *Essentials* (1931), gathered together clusters of philosophical aphorisms emblematic of his discipleship to the religious teacher, Georgi Gurdjieff. Toomer gave a futuristic and mystical inflection to his postracial identity: "I am of no particular race, I am of the human race, a man at large in the human world, preparing a new race. I am of no specific region. I am of earth. I am of no particular class. I am of the human class, preparing a new class. I am neither male nor female nor in-between. I am of sex, with male differentiations. I am of no special field. I am of the field of being." Distinctions of racial identity, among other fixed and local forms of identity, were now precisely inessential for Toomer's dispersed and labile "field of being."[43] Henry Louis Gates has described Toomer's project as an attempt to invent "an entirely new discourse, an almost mythic discourse . . . in which irreconcilable opposites, sexual and racial differences were not so much reconciled as absent, unutterable, unthinkable, and hence unrepresentable."[44] Gates's formulation about Toomer might also be translated in light of the dialectic of Du Boisian "double-consciousness." If Du Boisian "double-consciousness" held out the prospect of a sublation of opposing identities—the merging of a "double self into a better and truer self"— Toomer may have preferred to dissolve the opposing terms of Du Bois's double self.[45] "There is a hope among people," Toomer later wrote, "that human beings can work out their salvation by some means less chaotic than a radical transformation of the human psyche. Of our many false hopes, this is the chief futility."[46] Toomer's mystical individualism sought to evade the collective predicament of "double-consciousness" and positive racial reinscription that framed the interwar Renaissance.

Alain Locke's public view of the particular newness of the New Negro differed severely from Toomer's sense of black transformation. While Toomer lamented the death of black folk culture under the pressure of migration and modernization, Locke imagined firmer bonds of continuity between traditional and modern African American culture. Against Toomer's rhetoric of an unbridgeable rural/urban rupture, Locke posed the satisfying communicability of the folk inheritance. It was inevitable, as Locke read the situation, for basic aspects of a traditionally rural culture to dissipate under the force of urban migration and concomitant cultural changes. Nevertheless, Locke's formulations differed markedly from the sense of rupture captured in Toomer's "song of an end." Indeed, Locke imagined far more than the basic preservation of folklore; he instead saw himself aiding the maturation of African American artistic culture in accordance with an evolutionary path from unself-conscious folk forms to self-consciously formal idioms. As Locke understood it, the evolution from folk spiritual to art song taking place in the realm of bourgeois art was immeasurably aiding black aspirations to a truly cosmopolitan "kingdom of culture." The benefits of the cultural vanguard's progress, Locke insisted in the 1920s, would trickle down to the general black population and serve the causes of antiracism and the progressive struggle for social justice and equality. Criticisms of this top-down strategy of cultural vindication were not hard to find.

"The Beauty of a Black Voice"

The tradition of the Fisk Jubilee Singers demonstrated to Du Bois's satisfaction that higher education and concert formalization did not endanger the essence of the "sorrow songs." The Jubilee Singers had not, however, been associated with Fisk's official program of music education. The history of music education at Fisk University, which Du Bois attended from

1885 to 1888, suggested some of the challenges facing the folk inheritance's formal musical memorialization. Fisk's all-white music faculty pursued a traditional curriculum and paid little attention to non-European folk and popular music. The music teachers, according to Du Bois, "were strange to the Negro music. Most of them did not understand it, some of them positively disliked it." Singling out a particular music instructor, Du Bois noted that "Jennie Robinson . . . said frankly that she 'could not abide the Negro music.'" He lamented that "the Fisk Conservatory which was being built up and which was sending out colored music teachers all over the South, and even the North, was being built up without its chief cornerstone."[47] The missing "cornerstone," of course, was the legacy of "sorrow songs." "So many spurious groups appeared in imitation of the Fisk Singers," the music historian Eileen Southern explains, "that Fisk University gave up its promotion of concert tours in 1878."[48]

Du Bois sang with the Mozart Society while a student at Fisk and for a while managed a glee club quartet there. John Wesley Work II, a black instructor at Fisk in Latin and history, took the lead at the turn of the century in preserving the old spirituals. The historian Michael Harris recounts in *The Rise of Gospel Blues* (1992) that Work "is credited with being the first black American to collect extensively and arrange black folk music. In 1901 the Work brothers [John and Frederick] published *New Jubilee Songs*, followed in 1907 by *Folk Songs of the American Negro*." John Work also "revived the defunct Fisk Jubilee Singers and led them on concert tours throughout the United States until 1915." Against those at Fisk who found no lasting merit in the slave spirituals, Work stood for the transformation of the folk songs into art songs. Harris writes about the art song spirituals and the controversy they generated: one "side seemed to want to make the spiritual an art song, to have it appreciated with minimal reference to the experience and feelings out of which it had originated. The other side argued that the spiritual belonged within the context of the traditional black religious experience—especially since emotional performance and equally emotional response were intrinsic to black worship." Harris's formulation implies that the options of elite formalization and traditional sacred performance were polarizing to the point of mutual exclusivity; in turn, he sympathizes most with those who preferred the traditional treatment of spirituals over bourgeois formal stylizations. "Work's purpose," Harris explains, "was to make the spirituals the music of 'educated Negroes,' by shaping it into a form befitting their advancement. For this reason he encouraged and praised the study of these songs at black colleges."[49]

Harris deftly analyzes African American church music and liturgy as a locus of barely sublimated class conflict, and he highlights anxious assimilationism in the "old-line" Northern black churches and within the black bourgeoisie. The chastening point about intraracial class stratification is incisive, even if one looks for some nonassimilationist motivations behind Work's dedication to folk song collecting and the concert spiritual tradition. Those educated at Fisk and other black Southern colleges might have been encouraged to simply absorb the exclusively white European tastes of music teachers like Jennie Robinson, were it not for partisans like Work. Work strongly criticized white authors (such as George Pullen Jackson and Guy Johnson) who challenged the black provenance of "Negro folk songs," and he wrote in 1923 "the Negro Folk Song is the only American Folk Music that meets the scientific definition of Folk Song." It was, therefore, "the only natural basis and inspiration for American National Music." Both claims resonated with Antonin Dvořák's controversial advocacy of African American folk music in the 1890s—advocacy spurred on by Dvořák's star black student Harry Burleigh—as a resource for a nationalist school of American music. "That these Folk Songs have the possibility of Art Music development," Work expounded, "has been clearly demonstrated by Dvorak, Chadwick, Schoenefeld, Burleigh, F. J. Work, Dett, and Coleridge-Taylor." "In the building of her National Music," Work proclaimed, "America will surely follow Nature and Truth."[50] Work's views echoed Du Bois's antiracist, but inescapably elitist, jeremiad in *The Souls of Black Folk*. Harris has good reasons to take aim at liberal New Negro integrationism and its aspirations for idiomatic formalization through the class-specific sphere of bourgeois artistic culture.

John Work left Fisk after falling victim to institutional pressures against the preservation and concert performance of the folk songs. Nathaniel Dett, the pioneering black folk nationalist composer and arranger of art song spirituals, would be forced to resign from Hampton Institute under similar circumstances in 1931. Jon Michael Spencer argues that "the handling of Dett and Work, both Renaissance artists responsible for the choral debut of the New Negro, reminds us of the perniciousness and the power of the whites who upheld the status quo Jim Crow and how difficult yet necessary it was for them to find a voice in those tight places."[51] Harris's and Spencer's contrasting approaches to John Work hint at broader debates in current scholarship about interwar strategies for African American social progress. On the one hand, Spencer highlights the struggles and racially vindicating musicianship of New Negro formal musicians amid a toxic atmosphere of white racism. He defends the black cultural nationalism of Work, Burleigh, Dett, and others against charges of assimilationism. On the other hand, Harris stresses how Work and leaders in old-line black churches in the North purveyed the "tasteful sermon and denatured spiritual" as "placebos administered to ease the pain of assimilation" experienced by newly urbanized migrants. "Migrants eagerly gulped down these doses of social and cultural medicine," Harris adds, "to the extent that they could be considered virtual co-conspirators in their deculturation."[52]

Spencer and Harris might share a perception of assimilation (to prevailing white bourgeois norms) as "deculturation," but they come to contradictory conclusions on the social function of the formal spirituals. We should recognize the continuity of this historiographical debate with Renaissance era debates about the spirituals and the distinctive but often interlocking valences of class and racial oppression. Was the color line the preeminent problem of the twentieth century, as Du Bois prophesied in 1903, or was it instead the more inclusive "distribution of wealth and knowledge," as William Colson contended in a 1920 article on Du Bois for the *Messenger*? "*Labor* will create a new world," Colson argued, "and in that new scheme the Negro must take his place, not as a Negro, but as an equal sharer of all opportunity among equal men."[53] In a 1926 article that appeared in the *Crisis* shortly after Work's death, Du Bois emphasized Work's heroism in resuscitating the Fisk Jubilee Singers despite rebukes from the school's music faculty and others who refused to take the black folk music inheritance so seriously (whether from feelings of shame or superiority). "As a teacher," Du Bois eulogized, Work "became a master of the music of his people and in his death he remains the one who began the restoration of the Negro Spiritual to the American people."[54] Work died a martyr, according to Du Bois, but he did not die in vain. Du Bois and others carried on the fight in an ultimately successful student and alumni movement for the ouster of Fayette McKenzie, Fisk's antireform president.

Roland Hayes's career emerged out of the contentious site of education and uplift that was Fisk University. He attended Fisk from 1905 until 1909 and sang with a revived version of the Jubilee Singers. Hayes later tied his troubles at Fisk to his ambitions to pursue music in both formal classes and extracurricular clubs. A rivalry existed between the two factions, and the more powerful music department held its competition in contempt. "It was suggested to me that in spending so much time with the Jubilee Singers," Hayes reminisced, "I had perhaps failed to do justice to my work in the department of music, which traditionally had nothing to do with the celebrated chorus; but I was never able to find out whether that was the case." Hayes remarked about Jennie Robinson that she "was an austere devotee of pure music. 'The composer's sentiment is written into his music,' she would say, 'and it is a vulgarity in the singer to add to the sentiment written into the notes.' Perhaps she thought the Jubilee standard was not so refined."[55] Despite being expelled from the school during his last term, Hayes continued to sing with the extracurricular group. When he performed at his class's commencement activities, a disgruntled Robinson walked out. She had been financially assisting Hayes without his prior knowledge while guiding him through the oratorios of Elgar, Haydn, Beethoven, and Mendelssohn.

Hayes joined the Fisk Jubilee Singers as lead tenor on a tour in 1911, and when the tour took the singers to Boston, he remained there to further his musical education. The subsequent tour with Booker T. Washington and Harry Burleigh inspired Robinson to reach out for an ultimately successful reconciliation with Hayes. The singer toured in 1915 under the banner of the Hayes Trio: "We wore stiff collars and flowing black ties, one-button black jackets, white flannel-trousers, and white-buckskin shoes. We sang Beethoven, Schubert, Rubinstein, and the obscure Venetian, Polani."[56] The following year, the duo of Hayes and pianist William Lawrence included on their programs vocal works by Will Marion Cook, J. Rosamond Johnson, Harry Burleigh, and Verdi and solo piano works by Chopin, Liszt, and Edward MacDowell. Hayes made recordings in 1918 of French and Italian arias as well as the spiritual "Swing Low, Sweet Chariot." In Hayes's rendering of the spiritual, according to F. W. Woolsey, "The voice is velvety and the enunciation is pure—too pure. The tenor seemed to be condescending to the spiritual and the result is quite unlike the rhythmic and idiomatic conviction he brought to Negro songs later."[57] In any case, Hayes received Fisk's first honorary doctor of music degree in April 1922, by then the most famous African American recitalist in the world.

Alain Locke argued that the great achievement of the black college singing groups under the direction of leaders like John Work at Fisk and Nathaniel Dett at Hampton Institute was that the old spirituals "were saved during that critical period in which any folk product is likely to be snuffed out by the false pride of the second generation."[58] Locke insisted that the proper attitude toward the African American past was not shame or a "false pride" determined to turn away from a traumatic past but instead a secure pride in the black past. The cultivation of this attitude was a driving force behind the anthology *The New Negro*. Locke contended there that the formal singers who inaugurated the practice of performing the spirituals in choral and solo concert settings "only anticipated the inevitable by a generation—for the folk that produced them is rapidly vanishing."[59] Like Du Bois, Locke preferred to hear the residues of slave culture in the spirituals—a distant call from the past. This strategy of surrogation through selective retrospection moved to circumvent the challenge of nonelite religious leaders, congregations, and musicians (including those involved in the new sanctified and "holiness" churches and the nonelite emergence of "gospel blues") who made alternative claims on the sacred music legacy. A mystifying conflation of black folk culture with an archaic slave culture, in other words, was sometimes used to underwrite Du Bois's and Locke's variants of New Negro aesthetic ideology.

Michael Harris's argument about music and intra-racial class stratification joins the work of several generations of critics and historians who have analyzed the Eurocentric cultural elitism, self-aggrandizing class biases, and petit bourgeois nationalism of such New Negro figures as Du Bois and Locke. "If the New Negroes of the Harlem Renaissance sought to erase their received racist image in the Western imagination," Henry Louis Gates has argued, "they also erased their racial selves, imitating those they least resembled in demonstrating the full intellectual potential of the black mind."[60] The most negative and radical analyses take a further step and declare the interwar Negro Renaissance and the more geographically focused Harlem Renaissance as outright failures, whether for aesthetic, social, or political reasons.[61] Intertwined in this complex skein of political and aesthetic debates is the critical reception of the concert spirituals tradition.

Some have moved to defend Renaissance era cultural work from any number (if not all) of the charges made against it. We have noted Jon Michael Spencer's apologia for New Negro concert music. Spencer mounts a spirited defense of the "two-tiered mastery of 'form and technique' and 'mood and spirit'" in his book *The New Negroes and Their Music: The Success of the Harlem Renaissance* (1997). Cultural nationalism and racial vindication in concert music were noble and necessary goals, Spencer insists, and the Renaissance artists' assault on both the "social" and the "essential-ist" color lines made an incalculable contribution to African American culture and the American pursuit of cultural democracy. Spencer borrows and reshapes the methodology of Houston Baker's *Modernism and the Harlem Renaissance* (1987) regarding the "mastery of form" and the "deformation of mastery" as essential twinned strategies in African American modernism. The controversial centerpiece of Baker's dazzling defense of the Harlem Renaissance is his theorization of the black "mastery of form" as a subversive (and often misread) strategy of faux assimilation. Baker's readings of assorted texts (especially Booker T. Washington's pre-Renaissance autobiography, *Up from Slavery*) aim to show how the "mastery of form" was a subtle mode of black self-defense and "Promethean appropriation" enacted through the techniques of concealment and mimicry, including the minstrel mask (literally and figuratively).[62] The "deformation of mastery" in African American modernist writing, by contrast, eschewed defensive mimicry and refused to submit to Eurocentric aesthetic norms. Instead it proudly advertised black cultural difference. Spencer argues that New Negro concert musicians and composers used both formal mastery and deformative creativity to extend the horizons of African American musical expression. Thus, Spencer concludes that the work of Hayes, Burleigh, Work, Dett, and others deserves full recognition as part of the "phenomenal accomplishment of the Negro Renaissance."[63] By contrast, other critics and historians (especially since the social and intellectual upheavals of the 1960s) have read the teleological thrust of New Negro evolutionism in music as too awestruck by the normative status of elite European models and too quick to reinforce generic class-based distinctions between "high" and "low" music.

Among historical accounts, *Uplifting the Race* (1996) by Kevin Gaines analyzes the liabilities of the "assimilationist cultural aesthetic of uplift ideology" with surgical precision.[64] Gaines's analysis of intraracial class and cultural conflict in the early twentieth century, like that of Michael Harris, details how an African American middle class, profoundly anxious about being identified (or misidentified) with less advantaged blacks, responded by adopting "racial uplift" and liberal integrationist variants of New Negro thought. In short, middle-class notions of racial improvement through cultural and moral elevation (notions publicized in the 1910s and 1920s by James Weldon Johnson, W. E. B. Du Bois, *Opportunity* editor Charles Johnson, and Alain Locke, to name just a few) reinforced severe and unfortunate divisions among African Americans. Gaines stresses how

middle-class African Americans, worried about securing their own tenu-
ous prosperity and social respectability vis-à-vis whites, often projected
racial stereotypes onto a black lower class already demonized by charges
of backwardness, sexual immorality, shiftlessness, and irresponsibility. In
particular, "the shift from race to culture, stressing self-help and seemingly
progressive in its contention that blacks, like immigrants, were assimilable
into the American body politic," Gaines contends, "represented a limited,
conditional claim to equality, citizenship, and human rights for African
Americans." Gaines argues that it "was precisely as an argument for black
humanity through evolutionary class differentiation that the black intelligentsia replicated the dehumanizing logic of racism. Still, however problematic, the bourgeois cultural values that came to stand for intraracial
class differences—social purity, thrift, chastity, and the patriarchal family—affirmed their sense of status and entitlement to citizenship."[65] The
explicitly antiuplift thrust of primitivist and "bohemian" rejections of
bourgeois respectability, by way of contrast, did little to overturn race and
class privileges and essentialist ideas when they exoticized subcultural idioms for the sake of transgressive elite art. Some New Negro writers in the
1920s and 1930s, including Langston Hughes, Sterling Brown, and Zora
Neale Hurston, made lasting contributions to the project of dismantling
the scapegoating divisiveness of "racial uplift" while also seeking to evade
the pitfalls of exoticism. Gaines is especially attentive to socialist and
left populist alternatives to uplift-oriented African American liberalism.
Spencer's defense of New Negro formal music, by contrast, focuses on the
external threat of white racism and does not concentrate attention on
intra-racial scapegoating or the manipulation of bourgeois art as a tool of
class hegemony.

One question from Renaissance era debates that continued to energize
African American artists and intellectuals radicalized during the Great
Depression was when, and according to what standards, could artworks
and performances be judged as useful to a progressive agenda of social
transformation? The question of social utility remains open for those who
confront judgments of the Harlem Renaissance as a failure, whether on
social or aesthetic grounds, or both. "To ask why the renaissance failed,"
Houston Baker posits, "is to agree, at the very outset, that the twenties did
not have profoundly beneficial effects for areas of Afro-American discourse that we have only recently begun to explore in depth. Willing compliance in a problematic of 'failure' is equivalent, I believe, to efforts of
historians—black and otherwise—who seek causal explanations for the

'failure' of the civil rights movement."[66] One might consider Baker's trenchant warning against "compliance in a problematic of 'failure'" through the Renaissance context of the "art versus propaganda" debate. Du Bois, for example, underscored the primacy of "propaganda" and socially effective results in his response to the Renaissance flowering of black literature and art; at the same time, few Renaissance figures held a more idealistic version of aesthetic ideology than Du Bois. We have already encountered Du Bois's comment in *The Souls of Black Folk* that "the price of culture is a Lie."[67] The aphorism might be approached through its resonances with an interpretation of art's "contradictory role" in bourgeois society associated with the Marxist critical theory of Theodor Adorno, Herbert Marcuse, and other Frankfurt School associates and acolytes. Peter Bürger aptly crystallizes the Frankfurt School thesis one might align with Du Bois's socially charged idealism: "In bourgeois society, art has a contradictory role: it projects the image of a better order and to that extent protests against the bad order that prevails. But by realizing the image of a better order in fiction, which is semblance (*Schein*) only, it relieves the existing society of the pressure of those forces that make for change."[68] For Du Bois, the lie of individual freedom in an antidemocratic and racist culture needed to be exposed, and the utopian promise of freedom in a "kingdom of culture" needed to be reinforced. Truly great occasions of artwork and performance fulfilled a simultaneously critical and anticipatory role, thus collapsing the apparent disjunction between art and propaganda.

On a great many other points, it would be inappropriate to align Du Bois's particular aesthetic judgments and antiracist agendas with the Eurocentric modernism of the Frankfurt School.[69] The juxtaposition pursued here, however, may allow us to appreciate how Du Bois, not least when he demanded propagandistic African American art, consistently held close a number of non-utilitarian assumptions about the promise of bourgeois art. Moreover, variations on this Du Boisian theme can be found in many other Renaissance era comments on aesthetics. "Hardly any art," NAACP field secretary William Pickens affirmed, "is as purposeless as a bird's song. The bird (but not men) may sing indeed just to get the song out of its throat, and it may sing although only the solitude listens. It sings best, however, to its mate. But men are not birds, they are purposeful beings, and their greatest efforts are inspired by purpose." Pickens adjusted Du Bois's view and charged that "propaganda is the subsoil out of which all art has grown,—religious, ethical, racial or classical. But (and here's what the near-artists stumble over) *it is the function of art to so conceal the propaganda as to make it more palatable to the average recipient, while yet not destroying its effect.*[70] But how, whether in the case of the 1920s Renaissance or elsewhere, is the scholar to measure the social impact or the relative successes and failures of artworks and performances elaborated according to similarly indirect and self-concealing strategies?

Alain Locke tended to defer conclusive judgments by interpreting black folk forms and New Negro achievements developmentally, and indeed teleologically, not merely for what they *were* but for what they might *become*. His 1923 "appreciation" of Roland Hayes's recent European concert tour amounted to a manifesto for New Negro concert music. Locke wrote that Hayes's addition of several spirituals to a program of European art songs did not always bring from his audiences "an admission of equal value— that could not be expected." Indeed, Locke would have regarded a conclusion of "equal value" as a hasty elision of differences between a folk form and a mature art form. Hayes's invitation to compare the African American spiritual to the European art song, Locke contended, elevated the concert audience's estimation of the spiritual. Respect and racial vindication for the spirituals met Hayes's "seriousness of purpose and mission and loyalty to self."[71] The singer's return to the United States in 1923 inaugurated a new concert vogue for the spirituals. The music critic and novelist Carl Van Vechten noted the connection: "Suddenly—perhaps the date coincides with Roland Hayes's return to this country, for it is certain that he has placed a group of Spirituals on his every program—they [the Negro spirituals] were not only appreciated, they achieved popularity, a popularity attested to by the flood of transcriptions issued by the music publishers."[72]

The spirituals' corruption in the form of antebellum and postbellum blackface minstrelsy and "coon songs" had long reinforced degrading racist stereotypes. As a result, the "false pride of the second generation" (to borrow Locke's phrase) tended to repress the public memorialization of slavery and the folk inheritance. Hayes's recital repertoire, by contrast, publicized the spirituals' transformation into art songs in the hands of New Negro composers like Dett and Burleigh. The singer's artistic and financial success paved the way for the comparable, and perhaps even greater, triumphs of Marian Anderson and bolstered Locke's enthusiasm for the cosmopolitan loyalty to multiple musical traditions. "Before my time," Hayes recalled, "white singers had often been in the habit of burlesquing the spirituals with rolling eyes and heaving breast and shuffling feet, on the blasphemous assumption that they were singing comic songs.

It pleased me to believe that I was restoring the music of my race to the serious atmosphere of its origins, and helping to redeem it for the national culture."[73] Hayes sought to demonstrate loyalty to his training in European formal music and to the separate African American folk inheritance. He did not interpret his loyalty to the spirituals as antithetical to the discipline of European concert music.

When Hayes turned his thoughts to politics he took an individualistic and Washingtonian approach to the struggle for racial equality. "Although I am not unsympathetic with pro-Negro lobbies," he wrote, "I do not expect that we shall be saved by law, I cannot believe that our most urgent need is the enactment of new laws by white legislators." Hayes imagined himself a patient missionary in the freedom struggle rather than a radical agitator for political, legal, or economic change. "In the back of every missionary's mind, there is a dream of bringing all the world to Christ, but in practice he goes after converts one by one. In the same way, we Negroes must reach the hearts of white folks singly."[74] "I feel $95^1/_2$ percent of the Negro-white problem is the responsibility of the Negro," he explained to a white interviewer in 1947. Hayes took pride in his distance from the political activism of the NAACP and those even further to the left, including Paul Robeson. "I could have fought prejudice in words and actions all my way, but how far would it have gotten me? I had to prove myself and my art as being worthy of what I sought."[75] Hayes recorded his Washingtonian understanding of racial vindication and self-sufficiency in a friendly 1924 letter to Locke. While touring in Vienna, Hayes wrote that "we must not be found guilty of the narrow and selfish (for me and my house) idea which those previous and during our time have and are practising. We are real MEN whose business it must become to refine and deliver our own wares along side those of other men. We must not want and ask alms for it is unbecoming to MEN, but it is helpful, noble, and kind to exchange wares."[76] Only the artistic refinement of multiple traditions could offer a working basis for a truly cosmopolitan ideal of reciprocal exchange. To approach the citadels of European high culture in the manner of a supplicant or a political radical was "unbecoming to MEN." Hayes's confident expectations of reciprocal exchange were no doubt emboldened by the European reception of his innovative recitals. "I am not pleased," he later wrote, "when I am told that my being black does not 'matter.' It does matter, it very much matters. I am black for some high purpose in the mind of the Spirit."[77]

Locke admired Hayes's artistry but held political views further to the political left than Hayes's individualistic approach to racial advancement. The *Opportunity* tribute that Locke wrote in the singer's honor addressed the pursuit of aesthetic reciprocity and hybridity in terms amenable to an image of strength in "double-consciousness." Locke accepted the "natural limitations" of Hayes's voice and noted that it had only "medium volume" and "would really be over-refined and two [*sic*] subtle except for the peculiarly fine rhapsodic flow which Mr. Hayes has taken over from the primitive race gift in the art of song." Hayes possessed Locke's ideal New Negro voice because his voice—"refined but unaffected, cultivated but still simple"—was a "voice of artistic paradoxes" with exceptional appeal and historic importance.[78] The paradoxical doubleness of Hayes's voice, Locke wrote, "has created a rare medium which satisfies the most critical and sophisticated, without losing the primary universal appeal of simplicity and directly apprehensible beauty." In short, Hayes's art reconciled the "primitive race gift" and "critical and sophisticated" formal development. The peculiar intensity of Hayes's refined solo treatments of the spirituals, Locke added, came "not so much from the techniques and discipline of art, but from the discipline of life itself, and most often from the side of it which we racially have so deeply tasted under the necessities of hardship."[79] The invocation of the "discipline of life itself . . . under the necessities of hardship" alluded to the commemorative function of the spirituals. Concert performances of arranged spirituals inaugurated a public tradition of African American memorialization at the juncture of a cosmopolitan "discipline of art" and a more specifically African American sense of "the discipline of life itself."

The New Negro formalization of the spirituals elaborated the work of black cultural transmission and the "three-sided relationship of memory, performance, and substitution" that Joseph Roach refers to as the contentious process of "surrogation." The process of surrogation, as Roach outlines it, "requires many trials and at least as many errors. The fit cannot be exact. The intended substitute either cannot fulfill expectations, creating a deficit, or actually exceeds them, creating a surplus."[80] Hayes's surrogation of the spirituals fulfilled Locke's expectations enough to embolden Locke's faith in a teleological narrative of cultural evolution. Nevertheless, Hayes's handling of the concert spiritual did not represent the final goal of African American musical development, according to Locke. Locke had grander plans for the surrogation of the folk inheritance in formal choir music. "For the moment," he contended, African American idioms are "caught in the transitional stage between a folk form and an art form."

While "an inevitable art development awaits them, as in the past it has awaited all other great folk music,"[81] the necessary institutional support for such evolution was not guaranteed a priori. The voluntarist character of cultural evolution necessitated leadership by a "cultured few" (Locke's term) foresighted enough to steer clear of the hidden perils of commercial success and the faddish vogues that threatened lasting artistic development. "The real damage of the popular vogue," Locke later insisted, "rests in the corruption and misguidance of the few rare talents that might otherwise make heroic and lasting contributions." A higher "constructive criticism and discriminating appreciation," essential for the sake of the "few rare talents," would "raise a standard far above the curb-stone values of the marketplace and far more exacting than the easy favor of the multitude."[82]

Locke approvingly quoted another critic's comment that Hayes "might have been a statue shaped by the hands of his own race through long centuries, for the ultimate purpose of transmitting the soul of the race."[83] It was not Hayes but Paul Robeson, however, who first received the invitation to pose for a larger-than-life nude sculpture. Finished in 1926, Antonio Salemmé's sculpture portrayed Robeson (who was a much larger man than the relatively diminutive Hayes) as an icon of empowered black manhood; it was titled "Negro Spiritual."[84] Locke defended Hayes's approach to the spirituals against Van Vechten, who championed Robeson's less-refined but more rhythmically propulsive style. Hayes's decades of formal training had created a surplus of Europeanized tonal purity and a consequent deficit of folk authenticity, according to Van Vechten, and an imperfect fit for the role of cosmopolitan surrogate to the folk inheritance. Van Vechten had overlooked "the fact that the folk itself has these same two styles of singing," Locke insisted, "and in most cases discriminates according to the mood, occasion and song type, between them. So long as the peculiar quality of Negro song is maintained, and the musical idiom kept unadulterated, there is and can be no set limitation." Van Vechten admired Hayes's artistry and Locke appreciated the need to retain authentic idiomatic qualities in the folk songs, but Locke refused to uphold Robeson's voice as the superior vessel for the folk inheritance. To the contrary, Locke insisted that "we must be careful not to confine this wonderfully potential music to the narrow confines of 'simple versions' and musically primitive molds."[85] To restrict the spirituals or any folk music to "the narrow confines of 'simple versions,'" according to Locke, was to stall a folk music's development at a crucial "transitional stage" and block movement toward the telos of "art development."

For an alternative to Locke's interpretation of Roland Hayes in *The New Negro*, one might turn to Sterling Brown's nonfiction entry to the first *Opportunity* literary contest in 1925. Brown, then teaching English at Virginia Seminary, won second prize for the essay. He was in estimable company, as the contest's other winners included E. Franklin Frazier (whose essay "Social Equality and the Negro" took first place), Zora Neale Hurston, Langston Hughes, and Countee Cullen. Brown's contest entry reflects on the meaning of a Hayes concert in Lynchburg, Virginia. It features a calm opening cadence that quickly breaks apart into a cacophony of discordant fragments. Brown's "essay" recalls the modernist style of Toomer's *Cane* (a book Brown found deeply inspiring) when Brown's feverish lyricism creates the impression of a repressed and agitated psychological subtext erupting and rushing to the surface of consciousness. Brown knew Toomer not only from *Cane* but also as a fellow graduate of Washington, D.C.'s Dunbar High School. True to the racial and psychological topography at work in *Cane*, Brown's *Opportunity* piece stages a return of the repressed in social memory when it moves back and forth between manifest and latent levels, between a visible concert scene and an invisible collective drama.

African Americans occupy the bleachers on one side of a high school gymnasium, whites sit on the other side, and Hayes stands between them. The singer's pioneering efforts on the concert stage included a refusal to play for segregated, whites-only audiences. The policy against performing for segregated audiences appeared in Hayes's contract beginning in 1923 on the occasion of his return from a European tour. "During the first year under that contract," according to one account, "Hayes sang thirty recitals. In his second year, he did 125, and southern managers had begun to complain that they had been left out. Soon he was singing in Birmingham, in Atlanta, and elsewhere across the South—always to unsegregated audiences."[86] White members of the audience, in Brown's account, pursue "their inalienable right to patronize" and take credit for Hayes's success in the concert music world: "On one side, kindly, curious contempt. More kindly to Roland, who has succeeded 'white folks' way,' and is the exception. On the other, self-conscious hostility to neighbors, curiosity, shy arrogation, half envy of Roland. And a feeling of difference to him."[87] The special intensity that Locke rooted in the "discipline of life itself" emerges in Brown's essay as the singer's "ecstatic despair." "Flawless, energetic, enrapturing beauty. Handel himself could not have grudged this interpreter.

... Roland Hayes gives himself to ecstatic despair, as if it were a long familiar thing. The beauty of it is troubled, and those who have not plumbed the deeps whence such beauty rises, even they are vaguely disturbed." Brown questions the taste of some of Hayes's song choices, holding whites accountable who "applaud the perky 'Would You Gain the Tender Creature.'" "Strange thing this, their love of artificial bric-a-brac," Brown adds. Brown's approach reverses Locke's ordering of Hayes's double loyalty and notes how some of the white European and Euro-American music was less musically challenging than styles of contemporary African American popular music: "A few more, some of the so-called 'classics' by which people mean easily followed harmony, not ragtime—but music." Unlike Locke or Du Bois, Brown was not one to presume the developmental immaturity or technical inferiority of a popular music like ragtime or the blues.

Hayes's concert concludes with the spirituals. His dignified stoicism dissolves racist stereotypes. Racial vindication and folk memorialization join together in his "energetic, enrapturing" performance and transport the audience to disturbing places. Both groups are forced to plumb "the deeps whence such beauty arises." Brown evokes Toomer's story "Box Seat" from *Cane* when Hayes's spirituals send the white audience into a silent panic. Hayes's masterful renditions of the spirituals unexpectedly force open a passageway into depths of social memory that are at once painful and rewarding:

> The Negroes brood; are stirred by something deep within, something as far away as all antiquity, as old as human wrong, as tragical as loss of worlds. What does he mean—and why are we so stirred—
>
>   ... required of us a song
>   And they that wasted us
>   Required of us mirth.
>
> And a thousand of our girls prostitute their voices singing jazz for a decadent white and black craving, and a number of lyricists turn off cheap little well-made bits of musical bric-a-brac, and Mose, having trundled a white man's fertilizer, walks wearily home, strumming a guitar. And a street car conductor jogs a black bricklayer to hear a comic monologue.
>
> How shall we sing the Lord's song in a strange land.
>   ... Roland Hayes sings. And as he sings, things drop away, the

uglier apparel of manhood slinks off, and the inescapable oneness of all becomes perceptible. Roland Hayes sings, and no centuries of fostered belief can change the brotherhood of white and black. Roland Hayes sings, and boundaries are but figments of imagination, and prejudice but insane mutterings. And what is real is a great fellowship of all in pain, a fellowship in hope. Roland Hayes sings, and for that singing moment, however brief, the world forgets its tyranny and its submissiveness.

> By the waters of Babylon, we sat down
>   and wept,
> Yea, we wept, when we remembered Zion.[88]

Hayes's performance makes "things drop away" as racial "boundaries" become "figments of imagination." The veil between black and white falls during a transfiguring "singing moment" when "what is real is a great fellowship of all in pain, a fellowship in hope." We are given pause to return to one of this chapter's epigraphs. "Music," Toomer once wrote, can "transport you into a different world," but it "cannot keep you in that different world." "Once it is over for the time being,'" he concluded, "you slide back into this world." In Brown's essay, the world that Hayes's audience returns to may look like the familiar one, but the audience has changed, if only momentarily. The eruption of memory imagined in Brown's essay also carries an echo of Du Bois's utopian interpretation of the "sorrow songs." Du Bois sought to transfer the engagement fueled by the songs' lyric of social memory, hardship, and the "fellowship in hope" into activism and social transformation. "How many of us realize the tremendous propaganda of Roland Hayes? . . . Think what it means to every black child in the world to have this black man singer," Du Bois wrote in the *Crisis*. "Let us crowd to hear his every performance."[89] Poems in the *Crisis* and *Opportunity* rhapsodized similarly. "He's coaxed and caught the pathos of all songs, / And then marched forth to halt and vanquish wrongs."[90] Likewise, Brown did not hear an elegiac swan song in Hayes's spirituals but a song of expectancy. The songs held out the promise that the world could forget "its tyranny and submissiveness" for more than a fleeting moment; the memories congealed in the old spirituals and revived in contemporary performance could serve the cause of collective liberation. But would varying performance styles determine the character of cultural transmission? Brown's reflection on Hayes's concert emphasized the expressive content and sincerity of Hayes's performance and did not measure Hayes's style against an ideal of folk authenticity. "Things drop away" when Hayes sings, Brown wrote, and extramusical concerns demanded more attention than idiomatic details.

Carl Van Vechten confessed to Alain Locke in 1925 that "I'm afraid we shall never agree on the subject of the Spirituals."[91] Van Vechten intended his involvement with Paul Robeson's landmark all-spirituals recitals that year to help correct a "problem" among black formal musicians: "too many colored singers . . . not only avoid the natural Negro inflections, but are inclined to avoid the dialect as well." The white critic confidently predicted "that many people will prefer the traditional, evangelical renderings of Paul Robeson, to the more refined performances of Roland Hayes."[92] Van Vechten's praise for Robeson's "natural Negro inflections" underscored an aspiration Robeson and Van Vechten shared: to legitimate the concert performances of black folk songs through vocal techniques distinguishable from formal European styles. Van Vechten was a prolific author and had published several volumes of music criticism based on his work as a New York music critic since 1906. He advocated the music of Mussorgsky, Rimsky-Korsakov, and other nineteenth-century Russian nationalist composers, and defended the controversial recent innovations of Richard Strauss, Debussy, Stravinsky, and Schoenberg. The modernist turn, Van Vechten argued, held vastly different valences for painting and concert music during the first decades of the twentieth century: "Picasso and Picabia have made us acquainted with a form of art which in its vague realization of representative values becomes almost as abstract an art as music was in the time of Beethoven, while such musicians as Strauss, Debussy, and Strawinsky [sic], have gradually widened the boundaries which have confined music, and have made it at times something very concrete."[93] Although modernist painters distanced themselves evermore from pictorial representation, advanced composers let their music become "more and more like nature, because natural sounds are not co-ordinated into symphonies with worked-out section and codas, first and second subjects, etc."

The best and most modern music, according to Van Vechten, was moving ahead by becoming less abstract and less bound to the architectonic rules of classical forms and hence more "concrete" and "natural." The escape from rule-bound idioms of classical abstraction in music accompanied, at least for Van Vechten, a retreat from a form of philosophical idealism that groped for a sublime transcendental realm. One finds in Van Vechten's thought a procedure that Hans Ulrich Gumbrecht labels "the absorption of Transcendence into Immanence" and an unintentionally

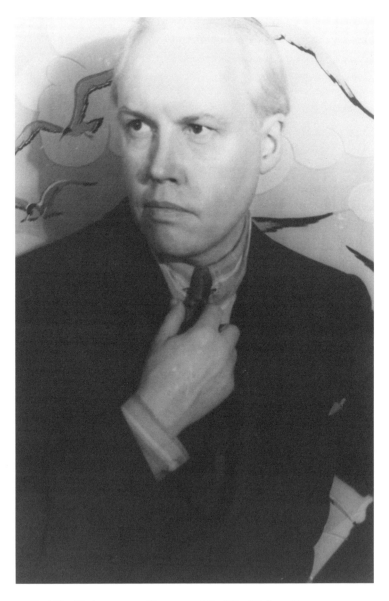

4. Carl Van Vechten, 1934. Courtesy of Carl Van Vechten Trust.

metaphysical valorization of the "natural" and the "concrete."[94] In other words, the modernist turn in elite music, as Van Vechten interpreted it, dovetailed with his enthusiasm for the more "concrete" pleasures of authentically rendered folk and popular music. "Spanish folk songs written down are pretty bare recollections of the real things," he asserted in 1916, "and when sung by singers who have no knowledge of the traditional manner of performing them they are likely to sound fairly banal. The same thing might be said of the negro folk-songs of America, or the folk-songs of Russia or Hungary, but with much less truth, for the folk-songs of these countries usually possess a melodic interest which is seldom inherent in the folk-songs of Spain." Van Vechten championed the concert presentation of folk styles and contemporary popular songs in the authentic or "traditional manner," and he selectively welcomed idiomatic hybridization of folk materials in scored-through composition. Hardly a purist about folk music, he was gratified that "it is not only folk-tunes but popular songs as well that fascinate Igor Strawinsky."[95] Thus, Van Vechten applauded the power of older spirituals and the best contemporary popular idioms, especially the blues, with equal enthusiasm.

Van Vechten critiqued imitative phrasing and tonal inflections identified with European classical music in concert spirituals. He insisted during the 1920s that less "refined" indigenous or folk styles constituted the richest starting point for further musical development; to emphasize folk authenticity single-mindedly, however, could discourage and inhibit formal development altogether. Exoticizing ideals of authenticity in black performance especially animated Van Vechten's *Vanity Fair* article "Prescription for the Negro Theatre" with its enthusiasm for the most "wild" and "hysterical" styles of black music and dance. Van Vechten's mischief-making taste for the shocking delights of primitivism animates the article's fantasy of a stage show populated by exotic icons of tribal sexuality:

> On the streets of Harlem this summer, or even on Broadway during the theatre hour, you may have encountered a crowd of pickaninny ragamuffins dancing the Charleston for backsheesh. . . . no sooner do they begin their exhibition of terpsichorean virtuosity than a large crowd collects. Has it occurred to any Negro producer that this scene on this stage would create a riot of enthusiasm in his auditorium? It has not. Nor has he arrived at the conclusion that an hysterical camp-meeting number with a chorus singing evangelical spirituals would probably cause so great a gathering to assemble before his box-office

that it would be necessary to call out the police reserves. . . . For the culmination of my imagined spectacle . . . I offer a wild pantomimic drama set in an African forest with the men and women as nearly nude as the law allows. There, in front of a background of orange-tinted banana fronds and amethyst palm leaves, silhouetted against a tropical blue sky divided by a silver moon, the bucks, their assegais stabbing the sky . . . and their lithe-limbed, brown doxies, meagrely tricked out in multi-hued feathers, would enact a fantastic, choreographic comedy of passion.[96]

The tonal contrast between Van Vechten's "imagined spectacle" of black music and dance and Sterling Brown's reverent account of a Roland Hayes concert could not be more severe. Brown, as we shall see, was not one to overlook the contrast. Van Vechten's hyper-erotic idealization of the "natural" also challenged Locke's evolutionist views about the developmental relationship between folk and formal expression and the "civilizing" effect of psychic sublimation in the fine arts. The *Vanity Fair* article lingered instead over a "hysterical camp-meeting number with a chorus singing evangelical spirituals." Robeson's all-spirituals concerts of 1925, it must be noted, fell far short of Van Vechten's primitivist fantasy, as Robeson did not include a "hysterical camp-meeting number." Van Vechten still found Robeson's performances with Lawrence Brown entirely rapturous. Robeson appreciated the attention. Martin Duberman, Robeson's biographer, writes that Robeson's "trust in Carlo [Van Vechten] on racial matters during the twenties (later to diminish) is exemplified in his reaction to Van Vechten's controversial novel. . . . Robeson telegraphed Carlo: 'Nigger Heaven amazing in its absolute understanding and deep sympathy. Thanks for such a book. Anxious to talk to you about it.' "[97]

Paul Robeson was neither a naïf fresh off the farm nor a vaudeville entertainer. He had sung in his father's New Jersey church and during his college years at Rutgers. Born in 1898, he was eleven years younger than Hayes. Du Bois had noted Robeson as a talented "baritone soloist" in 1918 when Robeson was a Rutgers undergraduate.[98] Robeson was a skilled musician, but he did not have years of European-style training behind him as Hayes did. Although he worked with several vocal teachers and coaches in the 1920s and 1930s, Robeson set his own schedule in learning the traditional European art song repertoire. He explained that "I am not an artist in the sense in which they [music critics] want me to be an artist and of which they could approve." Nevertheless, Van Vechten and other like-minded critics most certainly approved of the singer's unusual artistry. Robeson highlighted the differences between himself and Hayes, Marian Anderson, Dorothy Maynor, Jules Bledsoe, and other African American concert singers when he added, "I have no desire to interpret the vocal genius of half a dozen cultures which are really alien cultures to me. I have a far more important task to perform."[99] By contrast, Hayes's "artistic platform" in the 1920s was that "I will never sing spirituals without classics, or classics without spirituals, for properly interpreted they are classics."[100]

Locke detected a creeping skepticism in Van Vechten's praise for Robeson's "traditional evangelical renderings" and comparatively "natural" singing style. H. L. Mencken took up the theme in a glowing 1925 review of James Weldon and J. Rosamond Johnson's *The Book of American Negro Spirituals*. Mencken commented that "the spirituals are full of rhythms of the utmost delicacy, and when they are sung properly—not by white frauds or by high-toned dephlogisticated Negroes from Boston, but by black singers from the real south—they give immense pleasure to lovers of music."[101] Mencken presumably meant to ridicule the Boston-based Hayes as a "high toned dephlogisticated" singer bereft of true racial vitality. Carl Sandburg's harsher contrast between the "real thing" and Hayes's overschooled and "imitative" style all but foreclosed the possibility of formal art song development of the spirituals. "Hayes imitates white culture and uses methods from the white man's conservatories of music," Sandburg contended, "so that when he sings a Negro spiritual the audience remarks, 'What technic; what a remarkable musical education he must have had!' When Paul Robeson sings spirituals, the remark is: 'That is the real thing—he has kept of the best of himself and not allowed the schools to take it away from him!'"[102] Robeson, it should be noted, sang arrangements by Harry Burleigh even in his campaign to publicize more "natural" concert representations of black folk singing. In a 1925 article for the *Messenger*, Robeson opined: "today Roland Hayes is infinitely more of a racial asset than many who 'talk' at great length. Thousands of people hear him, see him, are moved by him, and are brought to a clearer understanding of human values. If I can do something of a like nature, I shall be happy."[103] Mencken, Van Vechten, and like-minded cultural modernists committed to ridiculing the "genteel" tradition as otherworldly and blandly idealistic seized on the symbolism of Robeson's "natural Negro" style. The polemical binary between imitative, "over-civilized" refinement and unschooled, "natural" authenticity reinforced a perilous aesthetic of racial essentialism, despite Robeson's efforts and the compromised antiracism of Mencken and Van Vechten.[104] More destructive still was the stereotypical counter-cultural equation of black authenticity with the absence of sexual repression and bourgeois moral hypocrisy. In short, a Van Vechtenite "absorption of Transcendence into Immanence" could inspire a reification of black music into the static function of a "natural" or "authentic" alternative to a bourgeois standard imagined as artificial and repressed. We have already encountered Du Bois's articulate riposte to the predicament of modernist primitivism.

Van Vechten's essays on performance and black culture displayed a provocateur's impulse toward hyperbole, to say the least. On the other hand, his writings often projected a degree of sympathy and admiration that separated his exoticizing gaze from simple racism. His formulations about Robeson's simultaneously formal and informal concert approach to the spirituals had a subtlety missing from many of his more outrageous statements about black performance. For example, Van Vechten stepped beyond the crude binary between "natural" and "refined" singing in his notes for Robeson's spring 1925 concerts in Greenwich Village. Robeson's "original primitive interpretation" of the spirituals was not unrefined, Van Vechten clarified, despite a "poignant simplicity." Van Vechten noted the similarities between Robeson's carefully rehearsed renderings of the spirituals and his recent performances in *Emperor Jones* and *All God's Chillun Got Wings*. Van Vechten understood the control and restraint required for Robeson's calibrated performances: "His postures and gestures and the volume of his voice are under such complete control and such studied discipline that he always suggests the possession of a great reserve voice." When singing the spirituals, Robeson's voice "retains its beautiful quality and the same sense of reserve power inherent in his acting manifests itself. His enunciation is impeccable—one never misses a word—and his interpretation is always clearly thought out and lucidly expressed."[105] The "sense of reserve power" that added to the interest of Robeson's voice and acting suggested an alternative to the primitivist fantasy that Van Vechten sometimes indulged vis-à-vis black performance as radically desublimated and capped by expressive expenditure without reserve. The black artist's expert interpretation of "primitive expression" on stage called for careful artistic control and discipline.

Robeson was, for his part, very sensitive to the criticism that the tragic roles of the jungle-bound Brutus Jones in *Emperor Jones* and the noble Pullman porter Jim Harris in *All God's Chillun Got Wings* presented demeaning racial images. He defended O'Neill's plays at the time and wrote that the "reactions to these two plays among Negroes but point out one of the most serious drawbacks to the development of a true Negro dramatic literature. We are too self-conscious, too afraid of showing all phases of our life,—especially those phases which are of greatest dramatic value. The great mass of our group discourage any member who has the courage to fight these petty prejudices."[106] Robeson's performances, as described by Van Vechten, approximated what some critics saw as the achievement of the Fisk Jubilee Singers in the 1870s. Colin Brown, we recall, believed that the college singers reached a high artistic level in creating a seamless and invisibly formalized imitation of natural expression. Van Vechten's criticisms of Hayes's approach to the spirituals did not center on the appearance of refinement per se but on a strategy of refinement he found unconvincing and imperfectly suited to the material at hand. Although Hayes deserved a partial exception as "an unusually gifted artist," Van Vechten still preferred Robeson's "deeply sympathetic and authentic renderings of the Negro Spirituals."[107] In writing that he did "not think that white singers can sing Spirituals" and that "white singers had better leave them alone," Van Vechten wanted to render obsolete the insulting legacy of blackface minstrelsy.[108] Robeson's all-spirituals recitals suggested to Van Vechten that African American folk and popular music offered distinctive alternatives to European concert music. The hybridization of the two traditions from the particular perspective that Hayes represented was not the only path to aesthetic vindication or modernist surrogation for the black folk inheritance. Thus, Van Vechten welcomed George Gershwin's jazz-based symphonic composition *Rhapsody in Blue* with far more fanfare than he could muster for the art song spirituals of Dett and Burleigh.[109]

Van Vechten regularly played the role of a modernist flaneur in an urban quest for exotic forms of stimulation. His gleeful report on a Bessie Smith concert in Newark, New Jersey—with "not a mulatto or high yellow visible among these people"—typified his ethnographic posture: "And now, inspired partly by the lines, partly by the stumbling strain of the accompaniment, partly by the power and magnetic personality of this elemental conjure woman and her plangent African voice, quivering with pain and passion, which sounded as if it had been developed at the sources of the Nile, the crowd burst into hysterical shrieks of sorrow and lamentation. Amens rent the air. Little nervous giggles, like the shivering of venetian glass, shocked the nerves."[110] He confessed to Mencken in 1925 that "writing men . . . seek a sort of Nirvana in music, a . . . nervous excitement or the exalting of the nerves." Van Vechten explained that the music of Beethoven and Wagner no longer excited him intensely, despite his enduring appreciation of their greatness. His taste for new sensations placed an especially high premium on nervous stimulation, and the witnessing of exotic, but contagious, forms of "hysterical" music-making took precedence at that time. "Well," he concluded, "a long letter—and about music, which, as is well known, is my discarded mistress. Jazz, the blues, Negro spirituals, all stimulate me enormously for the moment. Doubtless, I shall discard them too in time."[111]

Readers of Van Vechten's fiction encountered a monstrously proportioned cycle of sensual obsolescence in the behavior of Lasca Sartoris, the brutal and insatiable black femme fatale of *Nigger Heaven*. As a talent scout for his friend Alfred Knopf, Van Vechten helped insure Knopf's publication of Langston Hughes's first collection of poetry, *Weary Blues*, James Weldon Johnson's *Book of American Negro Spirituals*, and further books by both of those authors and others. Van Vechten joked in his correspondence that he was turning black despite his unchanging appearance as a pale, middle-aged, white-haired Midwesterner of German descent. As he wrote to one friend in 1925, "If I were a chameleon my colour would now be at least seal-brown. I see *no one* but Negroes . . . and presently I shall begin work on my Negro novel [*Nigger Heaven*]."[112] Van Vechten's efforts, of course, did not make him a racial or class chameleon, for he always retained his financial comforts, social networks, and racial privileges. While the value of Van Vechten's assistance to the black writers and artists he befriended should not be underestimated, his writings, activities, and influence also inspired strong criticisms of white primitivism and counterproductive patronage. Du Bois was hardly the only black intellectual to insist that *Nigger Heaven* took the white author's famous advocacy of the "natural Negro" to an unacceptable extreme.

The subtitle of Van Vechten's essay "Moanin' Wid A Sword In Ma Han" spelled out one of his goals, "A Discussion of the Negro's Reluctance to Develop and Exploit His Racial Gifts." Educated African American artists and audiences were too bashful about their indigenous expressive materials, Van Vechten insisted. He argued that "the low-life of Negroes offers a wealth of exotic and novel material while the life of the cultured Negro does not differ in essentials from the life of the cultured white man." Van Vechten therefore assigned himself the role of a knowing patron who would help younger African American artists discover the true "beauty of a black voice." "Perhaps even in the case of Roland Hayes," Van Vechten concluded, "it may be discovered that more people attend his concerts to hear him sing Spirituals than to hear him sing Schubert *lieder*."[113] With his literary creation of Mary Love, the refined and demure librarian of *Nigger Heaven*, Van Vechten escalated an already sensitive issue from a discussion of middle-class black bashfulness to a portrayal of full-blown neurotic anxiety in the "cultured Negro" protagonist's painful alienation from "natural" black exuberance. Mary, a New Negro intellectual in search of a passionate and fulfilling love affair, adores the spirituals and Roland Hayes. She curates a display of classical African sculpture to educate others about the great lost civilizations of Africa, but she cannot cut loose her excessively sublimated passions to dance the Charleston with all due gaiety and abandon.

Although Van Vechten helped some black writers find white publishers and introduced them to the estimable segments of the Manhattan social elite he counted among his friends, Sterling Brown, among others, strongly disapproved of Van Vechten's patronage.[114] Brown, like his friend and fellow folklorist Arthur Huff Fauset (whose essay on "American Negro Folk Literature" appeared in *The New Negro*), regarded Van Vechten as a decadent aesthete who slaked his thirst for new sensations through an abominably primitivized image of blackness. Fauset later wrote of Van Vechten as a paternalistic and "deceiving ogre." "Old and young hopefuls fell over each other," according to Fauset, "catering to his [Van Vechten's] whims—he was their liege lord, not only a brilliant literary light, but enormously rich, and that endowed him with power to promote the interests of aspiring young Blacks willing to pay him homage."[115] Brown also admitted to a "tremendous distaste for Carl Van Vechten." He particularly "disliked . . . black writers' reliance on Van Vechten and their acceptance of his leadership. I felt that he set up an exotic primitive. His heart was not really with us in that he was a voyeur." Instead of being a solid patron of progressive interracialism, Van Vechten was a "very false friend," in Brown's diagnosis of the situation.[116] Brown's 1932 volume of poetry, *Southern Road*, depicted a folk world far removed from the "theory of Harlem" brought to life in *Nigger Heaven*. Zora Neale Hurston, by contrast, did not go on record criticizing Van Vechten's patronage and friendship. She instead referred to Van Vechten as the first "Negrotarian." The white writer was especially pleased to learn from his friend Fannie Hurst (Hurston's one-time employer) that Hurston had been quoted as announcing, "If Carl was a people instead of a person, I could then say, these are my people."[117]

Sterling Brown undertook a long-term effort to articulate a left populist alternative to Locke's elitist New Negro evolutionism and Van Vechten's modernist primitivism. Intra-racial class and cultural stratification worried Brown deeply and made him especially eager to stress cultural continuities between the popular musics of blues and jazz and the older secular and sacred folk forms. Finding that the "sorrow songs" represented only one of the many vital idioms indigenous to black folks, Brown insisted that the blues were no less rich and representative.[118] He carved his own path in aiding younger African American intellectuals and artists to shed lingering discomforts about the rich expressive traditions of black folk. Brown's privileged background made him a somewhat unexpected and surprising defender of the "old Negro" (as he defined himself). "For a 'New Negro' generation too conscious of character and class as color (and vice versa)," Henry Louis Gates has noted, "Brown had all the signs of the good life: he was a mulatto with 'good hair' whose father was a well-known author, professor at Howard, pastor of the Lincoln Temple Congregational Church, and member of the D. C. Board of Education who had numbered among his closest friends both Frederick Douglass and Paul Laurence Dunbar." Gates suggests that it may have been "just this remarkably secure black aristocratic heritage that motivated Brown to turn to the folk."[119] Brown, who taught at Howard University from 1929 to 1969, is remembered as one of the most influential figures in the African American literary world.[120] Alain Locke, Brown's colleague at Howard for decades, once judged Brown's poetry in *Southern Road* superior even to that of the premier "jazz poet," Langston Hughes. Locke judged Brown "a bolder and more detached observer, [who] has gone deeper still, and has found certain basic, more sober and more persistent qualities of Negro thought and feeling." Brown had thereby "reached a sort of common denominator between the old and the New Negro." "Underneath the particularities of one generation," Locke explained, "are hidden universalities which only deeply penetrating genius can fathom and bring to the surface."[121]

As we have seen, Toomer read black urbanization as having a devastating impact on the folk culture that gave birth to the spirituals; he allowed for no vital lines of continuity between the folk culture and a new urban African American popular culture. Brown's youthful essay on Hayes, by contrast, represented the spirituals not as tokens of a "song of an end" but as lasting vehicles of social memory. For Locke, the pursuit of "common denominators" and "hidden universalities" meant looking further into the past beyond the folk spirituals and blues to the African civilizations from which the black folk of America had been first torn. The more urgent demands of folkloric research among black folk in America—especially as rural folkways waned in the face of urban migration and cultural modernization—remained Brown's first priority. He later commented that "jumping over" the folk tradition of "the old Negro preacher in the South" in order "to get back to Africa is not as sound as first finding our own tradition here and getting that true tradition and then finding out how African it is."[122] The appeal of African research helps to illustrate some important divergences between Locke and Brown.

The Lesson of African Classicism

Sterling Brown's essay on Roland Hayes concludes by evoking sacred ancestral memories: "Yea, we wept, when we remembered Zion." African life before the epochal catastrophe of European bondage and transatlantic removal summoned a different image to Walter Damrosch when he presented Hayes with the Spingarn Medal in 1924. The maestro of the New York Philharmonic did not discuss the loss of civilization but rather its novelty to "the colored race":

> The so called civilization of the colored race dates back a few hundred years since they first left darkest Africa. Their participation in what we might call the culture of the white race dates back hardly more than fifty years, and yet, during that short period of time, they have amply demonstrated not only their potentiality for civilization, but their actual achievement—what they have accomplished in this short time. Throughout the previous history of their race, throughout the period of their slavery in our country, they have always cultivated music, the one cultural outlet of their emotions which they as a race have always possessed to a supreme degree, to accompany not only their religious rites with the intense feeling of the old spirituals, but in their moments of recreation.[123]

"I did not have very much to say in reply," Hayes remembered about the moment. "My heart and my throat were too full, and my mind overflowed with images of the 'dark hours' through which my great-grandfather, my grandfather, and my mother had passed in order to produce the music which I was destined to sing."[124] Hayes's 1942 autobiography refers to his African ancestry with pride (he had recently named a daughter "Africa") and notes a great-grandfather who had been of Ivory Coast royalty.

Many of Hayes's black contemporaries would also have questioned Damrosch's claim that the "so called civilization of the colored race dates back a few hundred years since they first left darkest Africa." The most popular spokesman in the United States for the riches of a diasporic African civilization was Marcus Garvey, the Jamaican immigrant and founder of the United Negro Improvement Association, then the largest mass movement among African Americans. Du Bois, Locke, and many other leading African American intellectuals refused to support Garvey's economic program and his separatist agenda, but they agreed with some of the broad themes of his anti-colonial message of racial pride and pan-Africanism. Locke contended in 1924 that "the perspective of time" might show the Garvey's movement "chief service and mission" not to have been the "financial mal-administration" and "over-ambitious ventures" of the Black Star shipping venture but rather its thrilling capacity to stir "the race mind to the depths with the idea of large-scale cooperation between the variously separated branches of the Negro peoples." The pan-African ideal that united enemies like Garvey and Du Bois, according to Locke, was "without doubt the great constructive idea in the race life during the last decade and must become the center of constructive endeavor for this and the next generation."[125] Others, like socialist A. Philip Randolph, were less conciliatory. In a fiery open letter to Garvey from 1922, Randolph clarified his hopes that "the aroused and awakened, militant, intelligent Negro masses will see to it that you and all that you stand for will be driven from the American soil."[126]

The valorization of African art offered a less divisive approach toward the pan-African ideal for the liberal integrationist journals *Opportunity* and the *Crisis*. The French art critic and collector Paul Guillaume wrote about Africans in *Opportunity* that "these men were the first creators, the first warriors, the first poets; they invented art as they invented fire."[127] Du Bois found Guillaume's formulations appealing and quoted them at length in the June 1924 and May 1925 issues of the *Crisis* and in his contribution to Maurice Maeterlinck's 1926 anthology, *What Is Civilization?*[128] Guillaume was an adviser to the American art collector and philanthropist Albert C. Barnes. Barnes composed an essay for *The New Negro* on "Negro Art and America" that revealed his informal education under Guillaume's tutelage. "Through the means of Paul Guillaume," Barnes exclaimed in *Opportunity*, "that black primitive is still revealing his soul to us in his own marvelous sculptures and the souls of the great creators of our own age in the painting, sculpture, music, and poetry which connoisseurs everywhere arc sure will live as distinctive contributions of our epoch to great art."[129] Barnes referred to Guillaume's Paris residence, with its brimming collection of African masks and fetishes, as "the Temple." Nevertheless, Barnes's interest in black expressivity preceded the influence of Guillaume and other white Europeans. As the literary scholar George Hutchinson points out, "Barnes did not come to black art as a result of European-inspired exotic primitivism; he came to European modernism by way of the aesthetic inspiration of black gospel singing, which melded with philosophical pragmatism."[130] Barnes gained access to the African American intelligentsia while writing "Contribution to the Study of Negro Art in America" in 1923. Locke introduced him to other New Negro spokesmen including James Weldon Johnson, Walter White, and Charles S. Johnson. As a consequence, *Opportunity* devoted several issues to African art, featuring essays by Barnes, Guillaume, Thomas Munro, and Laurence Buermeyer (all associated with the Barnes Foundation), and images of works owned by the Barnes Foundation.[131]

Guillaume held that the "black race" in Africa had enjoyed a Golden Age before the sustained destruction wrought by the European slave trade and colonialism. The rediscovery of Africa's Golden Age consequently demanded new respect for great black achievements made independent of white influence. Guillaume introduced the grandeur of classical African art with an extraordinary flourish in the 1924 Barnes Foundation issue of *Opportunity*:

> At a time when the black race seems to give to the world only the spectacle of its agony, and the men of that race seem doomed by the world to a contempt which nothing can appease, at the time when they seem to have renounced all hope of moral rehabilitation, and where their memory has broken so completely with the past that it seems they would never be bold enough to pretend to intellectual heredity—at this moment is torn the heavy veil of prejudices amassed by the centuries; at this moment appears resplendently, luminous and delightful, a past without equal, perhaps, in civilization known even to this day.[132]

On Guillaume's reading, the black race of the distant past could be recognized as a grand participant in the history of cultural achievement, but at the price of being estranged from contemporary Africans. The collective memory of today's black Africans had "broken so completely with the past," Guillaume contended, "that it seems they would never be bold enough to pretend to intellectual heredity." Therefore, the brilliant African artistic legacy was more accessible to forward-thinking Europeans, according to Guillaume, than to Africans still suffering under European domination, for Africans "seem to have renounced all hope of moral rehabilitation." White modernists' fascination with classical African sculpture deserved credit for tearing away some part of "the heavy veil of prejudices amassed by the centuries." The black contribution to progressive contemporary art was historically premodern, Guillaume concluded. Thus he declared that "African art, the most modern of the arts, by this spirit is also the most ancient."[133] Black artists would have to learn their native "intellectual heredity" through the mediation of white modernists, Guillaume's theory implied. There was an inescapable odor of colonial paternalism to Guillaume's portrayal of intercultural exchange and his modernist recoding of African art.

Guillaume's narrative of a Golden Age in the distant African past was, in effect, an elegy for African art. His sad tale of cultural decline elaborated a modernist swan song in which the violence of European contact initiated the entropic degeneration of black originality and artistic freedom. The swan song account of cultural modernization was, of course, hardly original to Guillaume. The anthropologist James Clifford notes that in the "death of culture" narrative common to modernist ethnography, "the real or genuine life of tribal works always precedes their collection." Therefore, the collection of tribal artifacts is often interpreted as "an act of salvage." The prototypical ethnographic swan song "repeats an all-too-familiar story of death and redemption. In the pervasive allegory the non-Western world is always vanishing and modernizing—as in Walter Benjamin's allegory of modernity, the tribal world is conceived as a ruin. . . . Turning up in the flea markets and museums of late nineteenth-century Europe, these objects are destined to be aesthetically redeemed, given new value in the object system of a generous modernism."[134] Guillaume positioned his own collecting and criticism as a generous and redemptive modernist practice. Throughout the twentieth century, Western art collectors and museums consistently sought out African tribal art as premodern artifacts untainted by contact with European civilization. These same collectors, as Christopher Steiner has detailed, eschewed more hybridic and cosmopolitan African art.[135] "If the notion of the African 'fetish' had any meaning in the twenties," Clifford comments, "it described not a mode of African belief but rather the way in which exotic artifacts were consumed by European aficionados."[136] By contrast, Locke argued that "unless we approach Africa in the spirit of the finest reciprocity, our efforts will be ineffectual or harmful." Exoticism was to be replaced by a non-fetishizing commitment to cultural reciprocity and dialogue. The process had a particular importance for African Americans and other diasporic blacks educated in the West. He insisted that "the meeting of mind between the African and the Afro-American is dependent upon a broadening of vision and a dropping of prejudices from both sides." "The meeting of the two," Locke predicted, "will mean the inauguration of a new era for both."[137]

Locke wrote of African art in 1924: "Its chief need is to be allowed to speak for itself, to be studied and interpreted rather than to be praised or exploited." "It is high time that it was understood," he exhorted, "and not taken as a matter of oddness and curiosity, or of quaint primitiveness and fantastic charm."[138] To such ends, Locke called for a truly "comparative aesthetics" in response to the recent European vogue for African art. The comparative work he desired would not only study differences between African and European art forms, but also between African and African American forms. The set of associations Locke eventually drew between the African art legacy and African American expressive life helped crystallize his agenda for New Negro art. His essay on "The Legacy of the Ancestral Arts" in *The New Negro* foregrounded points of contrast rather than continuity between a variety of expressive idioms:

> The characteristic African art expressions are rigid, controlled, disciplined, abstract, heavily conventionalized; those of the Aframerican,—free, exuberant, emotional, sentimental, and human. Only by the misinterpretation of the African spirit, can one claim any emotional kinship between them—for the spirit of African expression, by and large, is disciplined, sophisticated, laconic and fatalistic. What we have thought primitive in the American Negro—his naiveté, his sentimentalism, his exuberance and his improvising spontaneity are then neither characteristically African nor to be explained as an ancestral heritage. They are the result of his peculiar experience in America and the emotional upheaval of its trials and ordeals. True, these are now very characteristic traits, and they have their artistic, and perhaps even moral compensations; but they represent essentially the working of environmental forces rather than the outcropping of a race psychology; they are really the acquired and not the original race temperament.[139]

Locke included a decrease of artistic discipline and a compensatory heightening of exuberance and "improvising spontaneity" among slavery's consequences in the United States. Classical restraint characterized African art, while improvisational expressivity dominated the "Aframerican." Briefly put, a living legacy of black classicism deserved greater attention than it presently enjoyed. Locke's broader implication, aptly crystallized by George Hutchinson, was that the "Negro renaissance, informed by African classicism, would be the central project of a modernist American renaissance."[140]

The capturing of black classicism as an "intellectual heredity" of the "original race temperament" lent to Locke's classicist tendencies a non-European imprimatur. The formal restraint he cherished in classical African sculpture needed to be reconciled with the immediacy and emotionalism of African American expression. He concluded that "what the Negro artist of to-day has most to gain from the arts of the forefathers, is perhaps not cultural inspiration or technical innovations, but the lesson of a classic background, the lesson of discipline, of style, of technical control pushed to the limits of technical mastery."[141] He could easily have detailed the exemplarity of Roland Hayes in the next sentence. Locke, in contrast to Guillaume, argued that the racial inheritance was best understood not as a lost grandeur but as a rich tradition especially accessible in a non-imitative manner to black artists. "The Legacy of the Ancestral Arts" thus wove together the retrospective swan song of discontinuity and the prospective art song (with its promise of evolutionary continuity and cosmopolitan reciprocity).

Paul Guillaume contended that European artistic traditions had become an ossified burden, and Albert Barnes largely agreed. "Many centuries of civilization," Barnes added about the white man, "have attenuated his original gifts and made his mind dominate his spirit."[142] Barnes evaded the themes of discontinuity and black cultural decline when he noted that in the United States the black race remained spiritually superior to a deracinated and overcivilized white host society. The "abject, downtrodden slave," Barnes wrote, had created "America's only great music—the spirituals." "These wild chants," he continued about the spirituals, "are the natural, naive, untutored, spontaneous utterance of the suffering, yearning, prayerful human soul." Barnes's manifest theme was the desirability of an interracial "working alliance." He concluded "Negro Art and America" by outlining his sense of what African Americans would bring to a progressive coalition: "what the Negro singers and sages have said is only what the ordinary Negro feels and thinks, in his own measure, every day of his life. ... nearly all of his activities are shot through and through with music and poetry." "If . . . he is the simple, ingenuous, forgiving, good-natured, wise and obliging person that he has been in the past," Barnes wrote of the contemporary African American, "he may consent to form a working alliance with us for the development of a richer American civilization to which he will contribute his full share."[143] If Barnes moved toward romantic primitivism in his idealization of exuberant and "untutored" black expressivity in music, Locke answered with the racial authenticity of classical sobriety in black art. Nevertheless, the two agreed when Locke echoed the theme of European artistic exhaustion as a cause for the turn to Africa for inspiration. The "discovery of African art happened to come at a time where there was a marked sterility in certain forms of expression in European plastic art, due to generations of the inbreeding of idiom and style."[144]

Locke found "a vital connection between this new artistic respect for African idiom and the natural ambition of Negro artists for a racial idiom in their art expression."[145] The narrative of European artistic exhaustion, the prestige of white modernist primitivism, and Locke's assertion about the racial authenticity of "rigid" and "abstract" expression would inspire New Negro artists to create daring new styles and overcome a "timid conventionalism" rooted in racial disparagement.[146] Mindful of the popular tendency to use the term "primitive" haphazardly, Locke offered a formal definition. "Technically speaking an art is primitive in any phase before it has mastered its idiom." By contrast, an art becomes "classic when it has arrived at maturity and before it has begun to decline. Similarly art is exotic with relation only to its relative incommensurability, in influencing them at all vitally it ceases to be exotic."[147] Locke swam against the dominant tide in his efforts to de-exoticize African and African American art and music and to rechannel the "Negro vogue" toward the more sustained efforts necessary for a "comparative aesthetics." He needed to decouple the romantic image of black primitivism as a racial trait, whether negative or positive, from classical African artistic styles.

"As Harlem became a fashionable fad," Locke later wrote about the mid-1920s, "a certain amount of irresponsible individual and eccentric exhibitionism inevitably followed, and some of the . . . younger talents were warped and diverted from the sounder courses of serious work and development."[148] Locke's New York patron Charlotte Osgood Mason contributed to this exhibitionist atmosphere by indulging in antimodernist exoticism as a therapy against neurasthenic exhaustion. She was also the patron of Zora Neale Hurston, Langston Hughes, and other leading African American talents during the 1920s. Hughes wrote that Mason "felt that there was mystery and mysticism and spontaneous harmony in their souls [Negroes], but many of them had let the white world pollute and contaminate that mystery and harmony, and make something of it cheap and ugly, commercial and, as she said, 'white.' She felt that we had a deep well of the spirit within us and that we should keep it pure and simple."[149] Mason preferred black spirituality, unrepressed spontaneity, and rhythmic exuberance over the lessons of discipline and abstraction. Locke learned to keep his classicism to himself in order to keep the money flowing. He was probably not shocked when Mason relayed her disappointment after a 1928 Roland Hayes concert. "Alain, I pulled myself together and heard Roland Hayes' concert while he was here," Mason confided. "It made me very sad because he sang awfully well, like a white man and not at all with his old reverent spirit." "This is a thing that always makes me sad," she continued, "that an artist loses his faming spirit. . . . It does seem so sad that when he had climbed thro so much he could not keep his balance and be a light to his people."[150] From Mason's perspective, Hayes had lost touch with his racial gift—"his old reverent spirit"—and was singing imitatively, like a white man. Such statements surely tried Locke's patience, though he refused to sever his ties to the wealthy white "Godmother." Jon Michael Spencer suggests that Locke, Hurston, and Hughes "engaged in 'chicken-thieving' deception for varying lengths of time." "Each of them gave Charlotte Mason the Negro (or African) primitivism she insisted should be expressed through their arts and letters in order to continue to benefit financially from her patronage," Spencer argues, "but to Hurston and Hughes the masking eventually became too miserable."[151]

The black and white intellectuals discussed in this chapter situated the contested legacy of the "sorrow songs" within debates about global processes of modernization, local processes of cultural diffusion and transformation, and the particular burdens and opportunities of the African American artist. As we have seen, the swan-song logic of Western spiritual exhaustion and deracination popular among modernist aesthetes in the postwar period gave new life to exoticizing and aestheticizing images of blackness as racial difference. Related romantic narratives of a lost Golden Age in Africa or of the survival of the "natural Negro" in the United States and elsewhere preferred antimodernist fantasies of black naturalness, equilibrium, and spontaneity. These fantasies often spoke to desires for aesthetic antidotes to the inhumane rhythm and rationalism of machine civilization. Meanwhile, the ongoing colonial domination of Africa and race and class stratification in America helped maintain the "overcivilized" comforts and hyperstimulation that prominent bourgeois modernists found so burdensome. Many of the figures discussed in this chapter rarely imagined direct political strategies or class-based agitation for social justice and economic equality as appropriate responses to either modernist disenchantment or racial and class hierarchy. The relative success of their culturalist strategies for racial advancement remains very hard to judge.

As we have seen, Jean Toomer wielded a swan-song logic of modernist disenchantment and racial reinscription to mesmerizing effect in the poetry and fiction of *Cane*. More controversial among his fellow modernists was Toomer's lived ambition toward a new "birth song." He sought to write himself out of America's racial logic and to escape his reputation as a bright and rising star of African American literature. By contrast, distinctive encounters with Roland Hayes's spirituals and with African art characterized Locke's Renaissance project: in the face of assimilatory and racist pressures, Locke sought to preserve the vitality and relative distinctiveness of certain African American expressive styles while guiding those styles to mature and classic idioms. The 1920s, of course, are more often recalled as the Jazz Age than as the period when concert spirituals were in vogue. Indeed, Renaissance intellectuals regularly addressed jazz music and its broader implications as a cipher of black social memory and intercultural transformation in popular culture. Did the new popular music belong to an apolitical Jazz Age aesthetic of hedonistic release and expressive individualism, or could it serve a collectivist New Negro aesthetic of self-conscious refinement and racial vindication? Chapter 3 focuses on what jazz music and traditional concert music said to Alain Locke about the intellectual and social prospects of cosmopolitanism and the mechanisms of racial ideology in interwar America.

THREE

"The Twilight of Aestheticism":

Locke on Cosmopolitanism

and Musical Evolution

Folk elements do not necessarily make folk music. Only when pure and in the form originally used by the people for themselves, do they yield us true folk music. This is why real folk music is rare; but it is the most precious musical ore we have.
—Alain Locke[1]

All art constantly aspires towards the condition of music. For while in all other works of art it is possible to distinguish the matter from the form, and the understanding can always make this distinction, yet it is the constant effort of art to obliterate it.
—Walter Pater[2]

Alain Locke aspired to guide the evolution of African American expression from folk idioms to formal art. It was with this goal in mind that the 1936 monograph *The Negro and His Music* reiterated his sentiments from *The New Negro* (1925) about W. E. B. Du Bois's "great services" in illuminating the innermost meanings of the "sorrow songs." Locke celebrated how *The Souls of Black Folk* (1903) had taught readers to understand that the "naive and simple" spirituals "were really very profound." "Underneath broken words, childish imagery, [and] peasant simplicity," Locke continued, "was an epic intensity and a tragic depth of religious emotion for which the only equal seems to have been the spiritual experience of the Jews, and for which the only analogue is the Psalms." The spirituals stood, in short, "as one of the great classic expressions of all time of religious emotion and Christian moods and attitudes."[3]

The collection and transcription of folk spirituals—a project emblematic of New Negro cultural work—reached a high point with the publication of *The Book of American Negro Spirituals* (1925). James Weldon Johnson (field secretary of the NAACP), his brother J. Rosamond Johnson, and the pianist Lawrence Brown assembled the anthology. Du Bois welcomed the anthology and commented on how "it is one thing for a race to produce artistic material; it is quite another for it to produce the ability to interpret and criticize this material. This is particularly true when the artistic gift is a matter of primitive development in the rich childhood of a people." Du Bois added about the new transcriptions that it was "as though something unknown and wild and yet sensed in the song of the black folk had been caught and caged forever."[4]

Du Bois's representation of the spirituals in terms of "the rich childhood of a people" underscored his paternalistic attitude toward the black folk and his romanticizing fascination with the spirituals as redemptive fragments of a fading stage of folk life. More generally, his formulations bring to mind what social theorist Slavoj Žižek has called the "ambiguous and contradictory nature of the modern *nation*." Žižek dissects a peculiar contradiction in many strains of modern nationalism where these ideologies depend on the enabling force of a "pre-modern leftover" in the idealization of an organic national folk "as an inherent impetus of its progress." "On the one hand," Žižek theorizes, " 'nation' of course designates modern community delivered of the traditional 'organic' ties, a community in which the pre-modern links tying down the individual to a particular estate, family, religious group, and so on, are broken. . . . On the other hand, 'nation' can never be reduced to a network of purely symbolic ties: there is always a kind of 'surplus of the Real' that sticks to it—to define itself, 'national identity' must appeal to the contingent materiality of the 'common roots,' of 'blood and soil,' and so on." One such premodern residue or sublimely expressive "surplus of the Real" was the "unknown and wild" quality that Du Bois "sensed in the song of the black folk." For some readers, Du Bois's references to an "unknown and wild" quality might evoke the Lacanian language of a "surplus of the Real" as a presymbolic Thing and an unrepresentable object-cause of desire. The "unknown and wild" quality characteristic of the folk spiritual, for Du Bois's imagina-

tion at least, thus took on the anamorphic shape of a sublime and dangerous source of jouissance that seemed to resist all efforts at neutralization
through dialectical negation and sublation. That mysterious quality had
been at least partially "caught and caged" (and therefore preserved) in
transcribed form by white enthusiasts in the first decades after slavery and
later by black composers and arrangers in the early twentieth century, including the Johnson brothers, John W. and Frederick Work, Harry Burleigh, and others.[5] It was not always clear from these composers' published
statements whether American nationalism, a more specific black nationalism, or some combination of the two was the extramusical referent for new
arrangements of the spirituals. Žižek contends that " 'nation' designates at
one and the same time the instance by means of reference to which traditional 'organic' links are dissolved *and* the 'remainder of the pre-modern
in modernity.' "[6] His analyses focus on nationalisms in Europe, but the
insight can be applied to debates about the aesthetic contours of the black
nation in the Negro Renaissance. From the Du Boisian perspective, the
revised spirituals worked to recover and preserve a black national spirit at
a stage of "primitive development" while elevating the aesthetic representation of that spirit through the "talented tenth" prism of elite cosmopolitanism. Cosmopolitan African Americans, as Du Bois read the situation,
next needed "to produce the ability to interpret and criticize this material."
The popularity of newer and less easily "caught and caged" vernacular
forms, including gospel, ragtime, blues, and jazz, presented musical and
ideological challenges to Du Bois's black nationalism and related Renaissance assurances about racial uplift and cultural progress.

The simultaneously recuperative and prospective thrust of *The New Negro* displayed Locke's approach to the relationship between old folkways
and new urban frontiers. Cut loose from the baggage of the "old Negro"
("long more of a myth than a man," Locke explained about the racist image
underwriting segregationist stereotypes of the "Old South"), Locke
sensed that the New Negro's "cultural racialism" sprang largely from a
transformed relationship to aesthetic antecedents.[7] "Cultural racialism"
was a term Locke used to differentiate his views from paradigms of scientific racialism and racial essentialism, as well as Du Bois's more overtly
mystical sense of black racial difference. Along with a racial inheritance
worthy of celebration, Locke defined the New Negro in terms of urban
migration, educational opportunities, and increased interracial cooperation—especially, but not exclusively, in the arts. He voiced optimism in
1925 about the relative expansion of opportunity for new black migrants

and chose not to linger over the mixed effects of increased class stratification. In sharp contrast to the economic radicalism of black socialists in the 1920s, for example, Locke then interpreted new social divisions as inevitable signs of urban modernization. Many contributors to *The New Negro* followed the preferences of Locke and Charles Johnson in highlighting cultural elements of the African American and African past well-suited to paving the way for liberal New Negro leadership into a more democratic future. Although the anthology contained a diverse list of contributors, strong dissents over the political and economic repercussions of New Negro liberalism and cultural evolutionism did not appear in it. It would not take long, however, for contributors like Hughes, Hurston, and Du Bois to pen critiques of New Negro liberalism and its aesthetic tendencies.

As both a philosopher and a public intellectual, Locke claimed to abhor dogmatism and polemics. He was eager to synthesize new findings and critical insights and thereby refine his positions. Consequently, Locke's critical and philosophical positions were often open-ended, and he treated his adoption of new directions as timely shifts in emphasis. He pointed out the strategic, and at times contradictory, character of his intellectual commitments in a 1935 anthology edited by the pragmatist philosophers Sidney Hook and Horace Kallen. Locke recognized that a "key of paradox" dominated his social, aesthetic, and philosophical thought. His cultivation of paradox extended from interpretations of cosmopolitanism, cultural pluralism, and cultural racialism to connoisseurial prognoses for the future of the spirituals, jazz, and African American concert music. Locke's revealing self-portrait included these comments:

> Philadelphia, with her birthright of provincialism flavored by urbanity and her petty bourgeois psyche with the Tory slant, at the start set the key of paradox; circumstance compounded it by decreeing me as a Negro a dubious and doubting sort of American and by reason of the racial inheritance making me more of a pagan than a Puritan, more of a humanist than a pragmatist. . . . Verily paradox has followed me the rest of my days: at Harvard, clinging to the genteel tradition of Palmer, Royce and Munsterberg, yet attracted by the disillusion of Santayana and the radical protest of James. . . . At Oxford, once more intrigued by the twilight of aestheticism, but dimly aware of the new realism of the Austrian philosophy of value; socially Anglophile, but because of race loyalty, strenuously anti-imperialist; universalist in religion, internationalist and pacificist [*sic*] in world-view, but

5. Alain Locke, 1941. Photo by Carl Van Vechten. Courtesy of Carl Van Vechten Trust and Yale Collection of American Literature, Beinecke Rare Book and Manuscript Library.

forced by a sense of simple justice to approve of the militant counter-nationalisms of Zionism, Young Turkey, Young Egypt, Young India, and with reservations even Garveyism and current-day "Nippon over Asia." Finally, a cultural cosmopolitan, but perforce an advocate of cultural racialism as a defensive counter-move for the American Negro, and accordingly more of a philosophical mid-wife to a generation of younger Negro poets, writers, artists than a professional philosopher. Small wonder then, with this psychograph, that I project my personal history into its inevitable rationalization as cultural pluralism and value relativism, with a not too orthodox reaction to the American way of life.[8]

This dizzying passage catalogs some of the sources behind Locke's self-image as "a philosophical mid-wife to a generation of younger Negro poets, writers, [and] artists." He took pride in both elucidating and attempting to reconcile the paradoxes and tensions of his assorted attachments.[9] Along with his commitments to "cultural racialism" in art and folk nationalism in music, strong undercurrents of universalism and aestheticism informed Locke's theoretical and critical writing on music, literature, drama, and visual art.[10] In particular, the "twilight of aestheticism" cast a rarely analyzed glow over his writings on the relation between folk and formal expression; it also motivated his ritualized denials of the influence of "art for art's sake" perspectives over what he proudly called the Negro Renaissance. The residue of aestheticism figured in Locke's tendencies toward formalism and his enthusiasm for the recruitment of folk materials into the service of purportedly universalist ideals of formal sublimation and pure artistry.

The strategy by which Locke confronted the paradoxical appeals of cosmopolitan formalism and undiluted folk expressivity distinguished his criticism from Du Bois's less detailed but more consistently content-driven and political approach to African American art. The artistic legacy of the spirituals and the emergence of jazz music presented themselves to Locke as cosmopolitan dilemmas. He regarded the formalization of the spirituals as inevitable and desirable, but he contended that the "increasing popularity" of the spirituals had "brought a dangerous tendency to sophistication and over-elaboration." Locke distinguished himself from Du Bois by chiding the elder intellectual for missing the friendly point behind Olin Downes's criticisms of the Fisk Choir in 1933. "Even Negro composers,"

Locke concurred, "have been too much influenced by formal European idioms and mannerisms in setting them," thereby diluting the songs' full power.[11]

Although Locke wrote often on the spirituals in the 1920s and later, he did not confront jazz music at length until the 1930s, in such texts as *The Negro and His Music* (1936) and "Toward a Critique of Negro Music" (1934). His early efforts to challenge an ethnocentric European cosmopolitanism and theorize a pluralistic and nonethnocentric alternative grounded his writings on musical development. Along with a lingering attraction to an older cosmopolitanism and its implicitly unilinear developmental narrative, Locke's new cosmopolitanism emphasized cultural reciprocity, racial hybridity, and a position close to what recent theorists have referred to as strategic essentialism. This chapter reads Locke's social philosophy and aesthetic criticism together so that they might illuminate one another. His cosmopolitan ideals about the sublimation and hybridization of "precious musical ore" can and should be read in conjunction with his critique of the more static ethnic essentialism in Horace Kallen's pluralist critique of the "melting pot."

Locke was more than impressed by the achievements of European high culture, but he was also outraged by the brutality of white racism and ethnocentrism. The "key of paradox" revealed itself as early as his 1908 lecture "Cosmopolitanism." The lecture called for a rethinking of the Eurocentric logic of cosmopolitanism. Throughout his efforts to articulate a new pluralistic cosmopolitanism for music, a regulative ideal of formal composition remained effectively unshakable for him. Thus, he looked forward to the establishment of classic scored-through symphonic idioms based in the spirituals and jazz even as he issued regular warnings about misguided adaptations and "cheap alloys" of black folk music's "precious musical ore." Locke positioned himself in an intellectual space between Du Bois, who alienated many with his idiosyncratic fusion of racial propagandism and aesthetic idealism, and those among a younger generation who eschewed Du Bois's directives and instead put greater emphasis on the populist legacies of the blues and the ecstatic, improvised music of the sanctified church. Hughes, Hurston, Brown, and like-minded New Negro revisionists defined their innovations through and against Du Bois's perspective and what they saw as Locke's inescapably Eurocentric cosmopolitanism. The protean cast of Locke's thought rendered him a ubiquitous but oddly evasive spokesperson for and critic of African American music and art.

Cosmopolitanism and the "Key of Paradox"

One of Alain Locke's early public confrontations with the notion of cosmopolitanism was a paper he read to the Cosmopolitan Club at Oxford University in June 1908. He had graduated the year before magna cum laude from Harvard and was the first African American awarded a Rhodes Scholarship. He attended regular meetings of the Oxford Cosmopolitan Club, an international student group. Locke's biographer, Jeffrey Stewart, refers to the club as one "comprised primarily of outsiders—colonial students from India, Egypt, and South Africa, and students from Norway, Russia, and Scotland—who seemed brought together as much by their marginality at Oxford as by their devotion to the ideal of cosmopolitanism." At Oxford, Locke took on the persona of the "Oxford aesthete, man of letters, and dandy about town," according to Stewart, even as he "recast himself in terms of the international movement against imperialism and colonialism" and "began to find his own Afro-American identity."[12] Locke's handwritten "Cosmopolitanism" lecture, complete with no less than three references to the authority of Harvard's George Santayana, displays a new sense of cosmopolitanism's attractions and perils. Locke understood the concept's roots in the profoundly racist geographical thinking of Enlightenment philosophers like Immanuel Kant. Nevertheless, he hoped to weld the allure of cosmopolitanism to the struggle against institutionalized racism in the United States and elsewhere. "Cosmopolitanism," Ross Posnock notes, "became the crucial mediating term enabling Locke's move from expatriate aesthete to race man."[13]

A call for a revised and truly pluralistic cosmopolitanism arrives through Locke's distinction between two cosmopolitanisms. The lecture first defines cosmopolitanism as "a comparatively modern creed or belief in a community of ideas as resulting from the complex and inter associated life of Occidental and particular European civilizations."[14] Locke associates this original modern European cosmopolitanism with the eighteenth-century French Encyclopedists and such Romantic figures as Rousseau, Madame de Staël, the Schlegels, and Goethe. Among the cosmopolitan assumptions Locke associates with such thinkers are these. First, every "man owns the ideas he can think." Second, "from the normal experience all necessary ideas can be evolved spontaneously and without traditional obligation to culture institutions or civilization." Third, through "sympathetic imagination, in sympathy rather than in critical judgment . . . we attain to the normal and true mental attitude."

Locke credits de Staël, who helped import Kantianism into France, with the term "cosmopolitan culture" and with fostering cosmopolitanism against the odds "at a time when there was in both Germany and France a reassertion of the national genius."[15] "A new psychological standard was thus introduced," Locke conjectures, one that "has maintained itself in contrast to but not in contradiction with the feeling for nationality and desire for specialization in learning which sprang up about the same time." No necessary contradiction separated patriotic nationalism from international cosmopolitanism (a point familiar from our discussion of Du Bois's early essays). Sympathy and personal feeling could play a broadly humanizing role in extending personal interest beyond the known and local. "In fact through the doctrine of romantic sympathy," Locke continues, "the mind is more or less a subtle extension of the body—something that is sent out wherever the body cannot go to take possession."[16] Well aware of the point's bearing for his international audience, Locke registered the hint of colonialism in the figure of far-flung possession.

"Education and its result culture are the extension of this sympathetic knowledge—first instinctively to that body of tradition which is your national heritage," Locke argues, "then by courtesy and contrast effect to the international tradition which the Humanists called the Humanities without perceiving that its first need was to be humanized—that is to say incorporated into a systematic body of tradition by each individual for himself."[17] The lecture sounds a warning about certain damaging styles of cross-cultural sympathy that lack reciprocal understanding and exchange.[18] Thus Locke criticizes the cosmopolitan who "judges of the value of any extrinsic stray fact by its place in his system rather than in [the] system to which it belongs." For an example, Locke points to "the man . . . who adopts the mannerisms of Japanese painting without its general principle—or prizes a Japanese colour print without knowing that it is the subordinate medium in Japanese art as to oil colour."[19] The example from visual culture foreshadows Locke's demand (in his mid-1920s essays for *Opportunity* and the 1936 monograph *Negro Art: Past and Present*) for comparativist and nonexoticizing approaches to black art. How beneficial to intercultural understanding could artistic appropriation be if it were interested only in collecting raw materials for formal experimentation or countercultural transgression at home in the metropolis? The cosmopolitan's fetishizing pursuit of exotica or raw source materials among colonized peoples and nondominant populations hardly amounted to reciprocal exchange. Indeed, the ideal of intercultural reciprocity gave Locke a standard for measuring the approach toward a truly pluralistic cosmopolitanism. He often suggested during and after the 1920s "Negro vogue" that a racially inflected doctrine of romantic sympathy both motivated and limited the success of the Negro Renaissance, especially in the field of music. The persistence of counterreciprocal exoticism and a primitivizing notion of racial essentialism, in other words, too often restricted the progress of Locke's Renaissance vision of cosmopolitanism as interracial hybridity and intercultural reciprocity.

Locke anticipated the corrective possibilities of a newer cosmopolitanism in his 1908 lecture. The new "rational cosmopolitan is not an inclusive culture of a universal education," he explained to the Oxford audience. Instead, a truly improved cosmopolitan understanding—"heightened through contrast effect of one tradition by another"—might lead to a deeper appreciation of various traditions. At one point in the argument Locke equated his revised cosmopolitanism with a rigorously pluralistic emphasis on difference.

> Each tradition if it is organic must be exclusive—to illustrate Japanese art and western art must be the consistent development of two different art principles . . . —and the true cultured attitude toward them is not the eclectic blending of the one with the other, but a distinct sense of the parallel evolution of the two. So . . . no sympathetic imagination can find a single standard of comparison outside the two—and the sense for parallel/but not equal values is the true criteria of cosmopolitan taste.[20]

Members of Locke's audience may have wondered how his ideal of "parallel evolution" could assert parallelism about cultural evolution without an implicit expectation of predictive teleological foresight (i.e., "a single standard of comparison outside the two"). A teleological model of cultural evolution needs an evolutionary norm against which to measure the comparative progress and developmental maturity of cultural forms. The very concept of "parallel evolution," in other words, incorporates a normative thrust by assuming compatibility through parallelism. Locke emphasized parallelism as similarity in a 1928 summary of the Negro Renaissance and its cosmopolitanism. He concluded in the summary that the "Negro temperament" "stands today in the position of the German temperament in Herder's day."[21] A century and a half after Herder, the long-suppressed "Negro temperament" was reemerging and standing on its own two feet.

Moreover, thanks to a trailblazing black elite in the United States, it was traveling down the path to self-consciousness as a national culture. The 1928 essay ("Beauty Instead of Ashes") implicitly reconstituted Du Bois's fusion of a "disembodied idea of statehood" with a "race ideal."

"There is in America," Locke continued in the "Cosmopolitanism" lecture, "a considerable number of a transplanted race, who are well on the way toward assimilating what is called American civilization." Despite the trend of cultural modernization through assimilation, "the ideal heritage of that transplanted race will reassert itself not as political ambition or economic greediness, but as a distinctive and vital national idea embodied in a race literature, a race art—a race religion and a sense of corporate history and destiny." "There will be a divided nationalism," Locke outlined, and "an ideal difference within a geographical unity, and you will be surprised to hear me say a cosmopolitanism within a nation."[22] In some respects, Locke's black nationalism resembled Du Bois's philosophical musings in the 1890s and early 1900s as well as views circulated in the American Negro Academy. The aesthetic emphasis on "a race literature" over "political ambition" appeared at least this early in Locke's career; Booker T. Washington, it is worth noting, wielded his power to help Locke secure a position at Howard University in 1912. Despite their differences in the first decade of the century, Locke and Du Bois both felt the pull of the aestheticist dream of elite cultural production and contemplative appreciation as independent of and superior to the exigencies and crude materialism of the marketplace. Both men kept faith with that dream insofar as they found the commercial world absolutely counterproductive to the fullest development of African American artistry and collective self-consciousness. Moreover, Locke's continual denunciation of the culturally enfeebling market logic of commercial music helped push him to the political left in the 1930s.

The developmental narrative that Locke explicated about African American music, especially in the 1920s and 1930s, was attuned to pluralism about "parallel evolution," but it nevertheless bore the distinctive signs of its origins in white European cosmopolitanism. Locke maintained the preeminence of symphonic and scored concerto forms in music, although elite musical culture in the United States continued to reflect the dominance of European influence. Even nonassimilationist evolution implied to Locke (and Du Bois, for that matter) that the formal development of African American music would parallel the direction of recent European concert idioms.

The predicament, according to Locke, was less an irreconcilable contradiction than a temporary paradox. His writings straddled contrasting ideals of a universalizing cosmopolitanism and a pluralizing racialism, and they habitually implied the possibility of reconciling these oppositions. As Rutledge Dennis astutely characterizes the predicament: "Locke seemed to have been working to achieve a balance between the Scylla of potential alienation from a too hasty movement toward cosmopolitanism and the Charybdis of deadening cultural narrowness through the constraints of parochialism." "The idea of cosmopolitan nationalism is semantically contradictory," Dennis suggests, "but the process is dialectical."[23] For such a dialectic to unfold cleanly, the opposed terms of Locke's dialectic would have to be transformed; they would be cleansed of whatever he saw as their ideological detritus and unnecessary surplus (by contrast, the black nationalist's racially characteristic "premodern leftover" would remain) and elevated in the pursuit of reconciliation. Locke critiqued the ethnocentrism and geographical racism of European cosmopolitanism as he struggled to escape its gravitational pull (what Dennis calls "the too hasty movement toward cosmopolitanism") and articulate a more pluralistic cosmopolitanism. But, as we shall see, Locke also contended against the "constraints of parochialism" and the essentializing, antihybridic threats of what some scholars refer to as "pure pluralism." He ultimately hoped to reorder the cultural values of universality and particularity so that neither would be slighted; both could stimulate the progress of cultural reciprocity and enlightened loyalty toward the "functional constants" that united the world's diverse cultures.

The intellectual landscape of bourgeois aesthetics was a particularly inviting destination for Locke's synthetic imagination. Pandemic to nineteenth-century European discourses of Romanticism and its modernist successors was a notion of the aesthetic as a privileged site for the reconciliation of the otherwise alienated realms of the sensuous and the rational. For some intellectuals (including Du Bois), the aesthetic also figured as a site for anticipating the utopian reconciliation of hostile or alienated social sectors, whether in the life of humanity writ large or in that quintessentially modern unit, the nation. The intellectual inheritance of Romantic idealism about art's distance from and superiority to the marketplace and the everyday world, in association with a redemptive hope for a progressive transformation of the everyday world, retained a talismanic allure for many modernists across the political spectrum.[24] Some American modernists took advantage of the discursive opportunity to fuse an elite aesthetic agenda to a passionate advocacy of radical political critique and action. In Alain Locke's case, explicitly political matters almost always took a backseat to more detached philosophical and critical analyses of intercultural understanding and the implicitly political strategies of cultural racialism and cosmopolitan interracialism.

Influence in the acquisition of artistic patronage hardly succeeded in making Locke a universally beloved figure in intellectual and artistic circles. Indeed, his methods of obtaining and sustaining patronage from white philanthropists, the grandiose flavor of his judgments, and even his dandyism and pseudoaristocratic manner inspired distaste and ridicule among prominent contemporaries. In a 1923 speech on "The Ethics of Culture," Locke exhorted freshmen at Howard University to pursue a rarefied life of self-culture. The lecture alluded to an aphorism attributed to Oscar Wilde, that most famously controversial of late Victorian aesthetes, and sketched a model of self-invention in keeping with the spirit of aestheticism. Locke pointedly critiqued Matthew Arnold's notion of culture as excessively external and institutional and echoed Wilde, Wilde's mentor Walter Pater, and other anti-Arnoldian aesthetes in the articulation of an antinomian alternative that focused on the aesthetic sensibility. True culture, Locke argued, proceeds only "from personality to personality" and "is the capacity for understanding the best and most representative forms of human expression, and of expressing oneself, if not in similar creativeness, at least in appreciative reactions and in a progressively responsive refinement of tastes and interests."[25] The comment echoes Pater's explanation that aesthetic criticism depended above all on the rare sensibilities of those with "a certain kind of temperament, the power of being deeply moved by the presence of beautiful objects. He will remember always that beauty exists in many forms. To him, all periods, types, schools of taste, are in themselves equal."[26] "The stamp of culture," Locke concluded in "The Ethics of Culture," "is, therefore, no conventional pattern and has no stock pattern: it is the mould and die of a refined and completely developed personality. . . . The defense of culture is a modern chivalry, though of some hazard and proportional glory."[27] Such pseudo-aristocratic views later came to haunt Locke and his posthumous reputation amid the generational sea changes of African American intellectual and academic life.

In his panoramic study of the Harlem Renaissance, *When Harlem Was in Vogue*, David Levering Lewis quotes George Schuyler's colorful snapshot of Locke as "the high priest of the snobbocracy." Lewis crystallizes negative reactions to Locke by referring to him as "Eurocentric to the tip of his cane" and a "fanatic on culture, and by 'culture' he [Locke] meant all that was not common, vulgar, or racially distasteful."[28] Zora Neale Hurston (the recipient of mixed literary reviews from Locke) referred to Locke as a "malicious spiteful little snot" and warned in a letter, "God help you if you get on without letting him 'represent' you."[29] On the other hand, Locke's positions on political issues were typically well to the left of Schuyler and Hurston and altogether too radical for some. He was dismissed from Howard in the busy year of 1925, for example, for supporting a single pay scale for black and white faculty and for agreeing with student demands to end compulsory chapel and ROTC attendance. Howard's white president at the time, J. Stanley Durkee, did not appreciate Locke's outspokenness and radicalism. Du Bois secretly wrote to a Howard trustee on behalf of Locke's reinstatement. The elder intellectual admitted that Locke was "not a particularly close friend" but insisted that Locke was "by long odds the best trained man among the younger Negroes." "Nothing will discourage young men more from taking training which is not merely commercial and money-making," Du Bois affirmed, "than the fact that a man like Locke is not permitted to hold a position at Howard."[30] Locke returned to Howard two years later through the supportive action of Mordecai Johnson, the university's first African American president.[31]

Locke remained a "fanatic on culture" in the 1930s, but he managed to reconcile his aestheticist commitments with friendly support for Soviet and American Communist Party policies toward minority art and social realism. In a 1949 talk to students at Howard, Locke moved to recant his earlier elitism and expressed regret for earlier considering culture to be "cake as contrasted with bread." True culture is democratic rather than aristocratic, he noted in a Whitmanesque gesture, for it is "baked into our daily bread." Locke accounted for his attempts to force a note of aesthetic aristocracy into his publicity for the Negro Renaissance by exclaiming, "What price Harvard and Oxford and their traditional snobbisms!"[32] Nevertheless, Locke revealed his sustained commitment when he published a poignant encomium in 1951 to George Santayana, perhaps his most enduring role model from Harvard. Locke defended the Spanish-born philosopher against derisive characterizations of him as an "ivory-tower esthete" who draped himself in "the detachment of pampered withdrawal" and the ethereal language of "Socratic serenity and ironic delight." Caricatures of Santayana hit close to home because Locke was also defending himself and some of his most dearly held commitments to the life of the mind.[33]

One should consider Locke's advocacy of formal evolution in African

American music in terms of his own language about the need for a newer and more pluralistic cosmopolitanism. An analysis of his approach to jazz and African American formal concert music reveals the paradoxical afterglow of the "twilight of aestheticism." He wanted to interpret jazz music in the "system to which it belongs" (to borrow the language of his early "Cosmopolitanism" lecture). But to which "system" did that most mercurial of idioms truly belong? Moreover, how was it to be linked to the inheritance of the spirituals and to their iconic importance for the Renaissance as energizing sites of black social memory? Locke's understanding of cultural pluralism and its roots in philosophical pragmatism, to which we now turn, provided a context for his developmental interpretation of African American musical history.

Cultural Pluralism and "The Symphony of Civilization"

In an essay on the emergence of an important new trend around the time of World War I in New York City, the historian David Hollinger argued that a cosmopolitan ideal enabled American intellectuals of varied ethnic backgrounds to fabricate a community characterized by secular and liberal discourse. Most importantly, the new cosmopolitanism provided a transethnic nationalist ideal that repudiated the implicit or explicit "Nordicism" or "Anglo-Saxonism" of previous American nationalist ideologies. At the core of the new ideal was the desire

> to transcend the limitations of any and all particularisms in order to achieve a more complete human experience and a more complete understanding of that experience. The ideal is decidedly counter to the eradication of cultural differences, but counter also to their preservation in parochial form. Rather, particular cultures and subcultures are viewed as repositories for insights and experiences that can be drawn upon in the interests of a more comprehensive outlook on the world. Insofar as a particular ethnic heritage or philosophical tradition is an inhibition to experience, it is to be disarmed; insofar as that heritage or tradition is an avenue toward the expansion of experience and understanding, access to it is to be preserved.[34]

Intellectuals signaled their participation in the transethnic cosmopolitanism of what Randolph Bourne dubbed "trans-national America" by taking aim at targets of intolerant, narrow, or constricting senses of "provincialism." While the various provincialisms offered potential "repositories for insights and experiences," they could only be partial contributors to a more comprehensive cosmopolitan perspective. Alain Locke does not appear in Hollinger's brief sketch, but a cosmopolitan critique of provincialism ran through all of Locke's writings, surfacing most explicitly in "Values and Imperatives" (1935), "Negro Needs as Adult Education Opportunities" (1938), and "Pluralism and Intellectual Democracy" (1942).

Cosmopolitan judgments about "narrow" provincialisms varied, of course, depending on where the intellectual in question stood regarding a variety of transethnic aspirations in the cultural realm. Was the preferred ideal one of preestablished harmony, prospective unity, hybridization, profound mutual transformation, reciprocal exchange, or a protective preservation of discrete local cultural identities? In general, the liberal cosmopolitan ideal expected differences in ethnic and national descent and welcomed these differences. Intellectual unity arrived at through individual consent (rather than ethnic descent) animated a quintessentially contractarian ideal of a tolerant, diverse, and mutually enriching national community. The related perspective of cultural pluralism, especially in its more purist formulations, shared cosmopolitanism's idealistic Americanism but emphasized the primacy of preserving, and indeed reinforcing, ethnic differences. On this view, identity formation was to be approached not so much in terms of individual consent and hybridizing transformation but rather through a retrospective lens focused on group descent and distinctive origins.

Cultural pluralism's foremost proponent, the Harvard-trained philosopher Horace Kallen (who originated and popularized the term), publicized the idea as definitively antiassimilationist. Himself a German Jewish immigrant, Kallen was unnerved by widespread anti-Semitism and hostile to the rigorous "Americanization" (according to the dominant Anglo-American norm) expected of, and often embraced by, each new wave of immigrants. He saw such homogenizing acculturation as disruptive to a more desirable heightening of ethnic heterogeneity, especially in urban centers. In his most famous gesture, he assailed the assimilationist ideal of an American "melting pot" as antidemocratic. Kallen argued in his two-part essay for the *Nation*, "Democracy versus the Melting Pot" (1915), that the nationalism of the "melting pot" evoked a ritual purgation by fire of ethnic (i.e., non-"Nordic") impurities and differences for the sake of reproducing a culturally undemocratic and deracinated ethnic norm.[35] Kallen proposed instead a musical metaphor for pluralistic Americanism as "a multiplicity in a unity." He wrote:

Thus "American civilization" may come to mean the perfection of the cooperative harmonies of "European civilization," the waste, the squalor and the distress of Europe being eliminated—a multiplicity in a unity, an orchestration of mankind. As in an orchestra, every type of instrument has its specific timbre and tonality, founded in its substance and form; as every type has its appropriate theme and melody in the whole symphony, so in society each ethnic group is the natural instrument, its spirit and culture are its theme and melody, and the harmony and dissonances and discords of them all make the symphony of civilization, with this difference: a musical symphony is written before it is played; in the symphony of civilization the playing is the writing, so that there is nothing so fixed and inevitable about its progressions as in music, so that within the limits set by nature they may vary at will, and the range and variety of the harmonies may become wider and richer and more beautiful.[36]

In Philip Gleason's historical analysis of Kallen's pluralist vision and its lasting influence, we learn how "the melting pot came to be looked upon as almost exclusively a purger of 'foreign dross' and 'impurities.'" Gleason details how, after Kallen's critique, "the melting pot 'theory' tended to lose all association with the idea that immigrants could make valuable contributions to a yet unfinished American culture." The cosmopolitan transnationalist's priority of a mutually transforming and hybridizing integration—a cultural stew, as it were, simmering at a temperature less destructive to the valued flavorings of enlightened provincial differences—was pushed off stage in Kallen's polemical battle against the "melting pot." Recounting the impact of Kallen's pro-immigration but antiassimilationist assault on the "melting pot," Gleason adds that "those who were repelled by the narrowness of the more extreme Americanizers tended also to reject the melting pot, which stood, in their minds, for enforced conformity to a repugnant version of Americanism." Kallen's influence was crucial to a fundamental ideological shift: the "melting pot acquired in World War I a bad reputation with liberals which it has not yet fully lived down."[37] The wholesale rejection of the "melting pot" metaphor by some cultural pluralists also marked a contrast to Locke's investment in cross-cultural reciprocity and mutual transformation through nonassimilationist hybridization.

Taken to an extreme metaphoric connotation, the "melting pot" image connotes the white heat of metallurgical refinement, with the burning off of impurities and the forging of an altogether different stable substance. Kallen's "symphony of civilization" image attempted to reconcile prospective cosmopolitan unity to the pluralistic preservation of distinctiveness. Thus his image evaded the dissonances and incongruities of pluralism and ethnic essentialism in empirical practice through an idealistic image of elemental harmony. Peace and harmony would emerge from a nationalist ethos of tolerance toward unassimilated—and, Kallen insisted, ultimately unassimilable—differences. Kallen's harmonious heterogeneity trumped, at least to his satisfaction, a less predictable and mutually transformative integration. Nevertheless, his 1915 essay reintroduced ethnocentric unity through an argumentative backdoor by assuming the sounds and identities of a future "American civilization" to be of European descent.[38] His explicit nationalist ideal remained a harmonized and presumably English-speaking revision of Europe in the United States, a revision purified of Europe's social distress (which for Kallen meant both poverty and the proletarian class struggle), but not its ethnic heterogeneity. To ensure the polyphonic harmony of a "symphony of civilization," Kallen described ethnic differences as permanent, static, and transhistorical. As he put it, "each ethnic group is the natural instrument, its spirit and culture are its theme and melody." Group differences in ethnic descent took on a decidedly mystical and essentialist hue elsewhere in "Democracy versus the Melting Pot." "Behind him in time," Kallen philosophized about the universal human condition, "and tremendously in him in quality are his ancestors; around him in space are his relatives and kin, looking back with him to a remoter common ancestry. In all these he lives and moves and has his being."[39] In contrast to the strategic essentialism that Locke would propound a decade later for the New Negro, a secularized filiopiety and ancestralism undergirded Kallen's pluralist image for a new nationalist ideology.

Apart from the racial exclusivity of "the perfection of the cooperative harmonies of 'European civilization,'" Kallen's nationalist alternative to the "melting pot" offered few hints about shared leadership, substantive goals, or future directions. Traditionally, orchestras depend on composers and conductors to facilitate a noncompetitive traffic flow between discrete sections of strings, woodwinds, brass, and percussion. Through written scores and rehearsed interpretations, leaders direct orchestras with a specific and unifying vision of a given symphony, not with a laissez-faire tolerance of individualistic and conflicting interpretations. Kallen noted how his "symphony of civilization" parted from the realm of music altogether;

the analogy broke down because in "the symphony of civilization. . . . there is nothing so fixed and inevitable about its progressions as in music." Kallen's ideal of a pluralistic American symphony where "the playing is the writing" suits a small improvising jazz band far better than a large traditional orchestra. Indeed, his metaphors of happy social improvisation foreshadow later American nationalist interpretations of jazz music, not least in the New Deal era, as a uniquely democratic, pluralistic, and tolerant cultural form. Jazz came to be seen by many as a nonelitist, improvisational musical form that represented the liberality of the modern American spirit at its heterogeneous best. Kallen's aesthetic metaphor of social reconciliation evoked the appeal of a predominantly African American musical form, although, ironically enough, it illustrated a whitewashed American national ideal.

Kallen's spontaneously orchestrated pluralism admitted no explicit direction on matters of form and purpose, and it shared little meaningful unity beyond peaceful noninterference. Hollinger comments that Kallen "tended to favor the retention of parochial loyalties almost for their own sake; he was not so much for cross-fertilization as for the harmonious cooperation and mutual enrichment of clearly defined, contrasting, durable ethnic units."[40] Kallen defended his cultural pluralism by insisting that "differences are primary." Americanizing assimilation was taking place, he acknowledged, but only on a superficial level of external rather than internal or spiritual change. "The immigrant group is still a national group," Kallen held, "modified, sometimes improved, by environmental influences, but otherwise a salutary spiritual unit, which is seeking to find its way out on its own social level."[41]

The historian John Higham notes the irony that cultural pluralism and Kallen's distinction between external assimilation and internal assimilation actually "relied on the assimilative process which it seemed to repudiate."[42] The very distinction between internal (or, to use Kallen's term, "spiritual") and external ("environmental") assimilation assumed the possibility of successful assimilation. Following successful external assimilation, the revelation of ethnic difference could be transferred onto subtler ideological markers of membership in a "spiritual unit." Jews and other groups of European immigrants suffered enormously, of course, from the ethnic prejudices and institutionalized discrimination of "old-stock" Americans. Kallen presented an ideological alternative to the narrow nationalism of "old-stock" whites and the Americanizing demand of assimilation by moving ethnic diversity to the center of liberal Americanism.

Theoretically, at least some ethnic groups would be suited to an idealized "perfection of the cooperative harmonies of 'European civilization'" and could imagine assuming the benefits of external assimilation on Kallen's ideal of a postprejudicial America. Unfortunately, his ideal of "the perfection of the cooperative harmonies of 'European civilization'" could not fit the circumstances of all American residents. African Americans numbered among those non-European ethnic groups for whom even external assimilation into Kallen's ideal of a happily diverse and democratic America seemed to be foreclosed. Ironically enough, an encounter with an African American student at Harvard, namely Alain Locke, first inspired Kallen's adoption of the cultural pluralist credo.

Kallen later recalled first using the term "cultural pluralism" "around 1906 or 1907 when Alain Locke was in a section of a class at Harvard where I served as assistant to Mr. George Santayana." As Kallen remembered it, his notion of cultural pluralism specifically evolved out of interactions with Locke. The two knew each other at Harvard and remained friendly at Oxford when both were Rhodes scholars. Expressing sympathy for Locke, who was "suddenly shut out of things,—unhappy, and lonely" when the white American Rhodes scholars shunned him at Oxford, Kallen wrote to his Harvard mentor, Barrett Wendell, for advice. Representing his personal view, Kallen stated: "As you know, I have neither respect nor liking for his race—but individually they have to be taken, each on his own merits and value." Wendell's response to the young scholar was unambiguous about Locke's status as a racial inferior. "My own sentiments concerning negroes are such that I have always declined to meet the best of them— Booker Washington, a man whom I thoroughly respect,—at table." Kallen had tea with Locke and dutifully reported the results back to Wendell: "So he is to come to tea again tho' it is personally repugnant to me to eat with him. Shylock's disclaimer expresses my feeling exactly; but then, Locke is a Harvard man and as such he has a definite claim on me."[43] After bringing this disturbing incident to light, the literary scholar Werner Sollors offered a lucid interpretation:

> The birth of cultural pluralism was beset by ironies: a non-religious Jewish student was converted by a Boston brahmin professor [Wendell] who suffered from spells of repugnance brought about by race contacts during dinners; the student denounces assimilation and endears himself to his professor by claiming the same feelings of repugnance toward a black fellow student whom, with the help of his profes-

sor, he yet wants to protect against racism. . . . It seems strange, indeed, that Kallen singled out the early contact with Locke as the stimulus for pluralism when his own letters at the time of the incident make Kallen such an unlikely ancestor for contemporary pluralists. Upper-case "Cultural Pluralism" emerged in a world which also contained lower-case "negroes."[44]

One can wonder if Kallen played up the motif of chummy Ivy League racism to appease Wendell, the conservative Anglo-Saxonist who encouraged Kallen's embrace of Zionism. In any case, Locke formulated an alternative notion of the African American's cosmopolitanism and "divided nationalism" while at Oxford. Locke's theory looked beyond the implicit racial exclusivity of the pluralist ideal that Kallen would make famous in 1915. Kallen later looked back on his adoption of cultural pluralism as a technique for representing the philosophical basis of friendship between people "who are different from each other but who, as different, hold themselves equal to each other." "By 'equal,'" Kallen detailed, "we commonly mean 'similar' or 'identical.'" His cultural pluralism, by contrast, intended "by 'equal' also parity of the unequal and equality of the unlike, not only of the like or the same." "It postulates that individuality is indefeasible," he added, "that differences are primary, and that consequently human beings have an indefeasible right to their differences and should not be penalized for their differences, however they may be constituted."[45]

Kallen interpreted his emphasis on the indestructibility of ethnic differences as an extension of William James's rejection of all forms of monism and his call for a pluralistic ontology. The contribution that Kallen made to a memorial service for Locke took as its theme Locke's slow conversion from universalism to cultural and metaphysical pluralism. Locke was for too long committed to a disappointingly monistic view of the universe, Kallen upheld in his strangely argumentative eulogy. "He would have preferred reality to be basically a One and not a Many," Kallen reminisced, "and human relations to be expressive of this Oneness." Locke's "preference interposed an active reservation to the actuality of the plural," Kallen continued, and "long kept him from completely committing himself."[46] Locke's reservations about the ultimate values of pluralism gradually subsided, according to Kallen. Indeed, Locke's publications often displayed hesitations about pluralism as an ultimate or final value. Perhaps Kallen should have added that Locke's monism was also pluralistic, if in a different way from Kallen's more explicitly essentialist account of ethnic difference. Rutledge Dennis suggests that "it is possible for Locke to have accepted the substance of the pragmatists' ideas [about a pluralistic ontology] and the logical structure of the Hegelians'."[47] Simultaneously embracing both the One and the Many, such dialectical universalism would signify a dynamic process of differentiation, negation, reciprocity, and mutually transformative integration. Ross Posnock argues that Locke and Kallen took away different lessons from James's Oxford lectures on pluralism (published posthumously in 1910 as *A Pluralistic Universe*). Kallen held tight to a "minor point" in James's "depiction of the pluralistic world as a 'federal republic,' which Kallen interpreted to mean separate ethnic nationalities coexisting harmoniously in an 'orchestration of mankind.'" In the course of an original interpretation of pragmatic antiessentialism in African American thought, Posnock surmises that Locke "grasped Jamesian pluralism" more firmly than Kallen "as an indictment of philosophical thought that is grounded in the logic of difference/identity."[48] Locke's hesitations about the essentializing thrust of Kallen's pluralism, in other words, may have been more dynamic and Jamesian in spirit than Kallen's eulogy supposed.

Kallen's purism about ethnic difference and cultural pluralism should be distinguished from Locke's instrumentalist defense of cultural racialism as minority counterassertion in *The New Negro*. "The racialism of the Negro," Locke strategized, "is no limitation or reservation with respect to American life; it is only a constructive effort to build the obstructions in the stream of his progress into an efficient dam of social energy and power."[49] The functional image of "an efficient dam" implied that the elaboration of African American cultural difference would *not* exclude a mutually transforming integration; integration would be fulfilled only when white racism and its pervasive institutional and ideological effects had been decisively eviscerated. Locke rephrased the strategic quality of his racialism ten years later in his self-estimation as "a cultural cosmopolitan, but perforce an advocate of cultural racialism as a defensive counter-move for the American Negro." His juxtaposition of cultural racialism and cosmopolitanism sounded "the key of paradox" because cultural racialism hinted at essentialist notions of ethnic purity and restrictive pluralism instead of Locke's preferred values of intercultural hybridity and reciprocal exchange. Minority counterassertion through purist or essentialist varieties of cultural racialism, he habitually warned, threatened to harden into the kind of chauvinistic and hypostasizing obstructions that blocked the development of intercultural reciprocity and hybridic exchange.[50] Rigid racialism and notions of unassimilability made for a counterproductive and inefficient "dam of social energy and power." Purist and antihybridic notions of racialism lacked historical sensitivity, Locke insisted, and leaned toward the fixed identities of undynamic stasis. Pluralism and racialism seemed to present Locke with strategic terms open to progressive negation in a synthesis that did not sacrifice the values of cultural difference.

Locke's work evidenced the tension in the role of an African American public intellectual addressing both an academic audience and a broader reading public. His essays in the National Urban League's *Opportunity*, for example, articulated the bases of his cultural racialism and aesthetic connoisseurship in the course of discriminating critiques of the "literature of the Negro." His philosophical essays, by contrast, argued the necessity of a skeptical and self-critical relativism as a tool for weeding out narrow and misguided provincialisms. He presented scholarly essays on relativism, including "Pluralism and Intellectual Democracy" and "The Need for a New Organon in Education," in academic forums such as the New York symposiums of the Conference on Science, Philosophy and Religion, which first gathered at the Jewish Theological Seminary. Locke summed up his career when he asked a scholarly audience in 1950 whether "we can have the advantage of cultural differences without their obvious historical disadvantages?" The fact of "obvious historical disadvantages," including the ongoing injustices of ethnic discrimination, legalized racial segregation, and de facto racial discrimination, drove Locke toward a nonrelativistic cosmopolitan hope to transcend the limitations of all provincialisms, beginning with the toxic provincialism of hegemonic white racism. "If I thought it irreconcilable with the future development of internationalism and the approach toward universalism to . . . help revive the lapsing racial tradition," he confessed, "I would count myself a dangerous reactionary, and be ashamed."[51]

The "key of paradox" also energized Locke's estimation of value relativism and his occasional willingness to underscore the arbitrariness and incommensurability of evaluative standards. He evoked value relativism hesitantly and with qualifications as part of a strategic path toward a new understanding of universal ideas and practices. Value relativism in the interwar American intellectual milieu presented one face of a larger philosophical campaign against epistemological foundationalism. Often associated with the pluralistic logic and antiracism of Boasian cultural anthropology, value relativism functioned as a cross-cultural tool to lay bare the local or provincial features of ostensibly universal and objective value commitments. Locke welcomed these developments and aligned himself with the progressive Boasian school. As we have seen, the related philosophy of cultural pluralism offered as a normative ideal an ideally harmonious interrelation between different cultures and a shared commitment to tolerant coexistence. Kallen later restated the "symphony of civilization" metaphor during the cold war: "it designates that orchestration of the cultures of mankind which alone can be worked and fought for with least injustice, and with least suppression or frustration of any culture."[52] The orchestration of any prospective tolerance, according to Locke, called for value relativism to expose the absolutist biases of harsh and unjust provincialisms. His essays, including "Values and Imperatives," "Pluralism and Intellectual Democracy," and "Pluralism and Ideological Peace," thus esteemed value relativism and a correlate pluralism as intellectual strategies that would aid the discovery of deeper universalities beneath apparent cultural differences.

Locke contrasted his pluralistic cosmopolitanism against the absolutist features of narrow provincialisms that a proper relativism would undercut. In "Values and Imperatives" (1935) and later essays, he urged the necessity of value and cultural relativism while noting his distaste for any "value anarchist" mode of relativism. "In de-throning our absolutes, we must take care not to exile our imperatives, for after all, we live by them."[53] Stressing the inevitable epistemic inertia of cultural traditions and provincialisms, he argued in "Pluralism and Intellectual Democracy" that "we could not, even if it were desirable, uproot our own traditions and loyalties." Locke recognized the practical inescapability of provincial understanding, but he would not accept provincial defenses of segregation and institutionalized racism or moderate pleas for patience in the black freedom struggle. The United States had "no justification for identifying *en bloc* with an ideal like democracy, as though they were a perfect set of architectural specifications for the concept itself." Moreover, Locke urged, "the only way of freeing our minds from such hypostasizing, from its provincial limitations and dogmatic bias, is by way of a relativism which reveals our values in proper objective perspective with other sets of values."[54] "Pluralism and Intellectual Democracy" centered on the point that value relativism effectively clarified evaluative commitments by showing their justificatory bases to be largely local and contingent upon custom rather than objectively or ahistorically grounded. Attachments arrived at through everyday socialization would do well to undergo a relativizing self-examination. Relativist thought would not only combat the absolutist faiths of U.S. foes in World War II, but it would stand against oppressive absolutism at home as well.[55] Locke critiqued the provincial loyalties of racial supremacist thought and phrased his enthusiasm for black folklore research in terms of a strategic cultural racialism and a nonchauvinistic interest in all classic folk materials.

For Locke, relativism, like racialism and pluralism, offered not a final position but a tool for measuring the character and depth of cultural differences. His use of relativism, in other words, was largely strategic and directed toward nonrelativistic ends. After quoting a passage from Kallen about James's embrace of pluralism and diversity, Locke softly hinted in "Pluralism and Intellectual Democracy" about how his position diverged from that of his friend Kallen.

> I do not quote for complete agreement, because I think we have come to the point where we can and must go beyond this somewhat anarchic pluralism and relativism to a more systematic relativism. This becomes possible as we are able to discover through objective comparison of basic human values certain basic equivalences among them, which we may warrantably call "functional constants" to take scientifically the place of our outmoded categoricals and our banned arbitrary "universals."[56]

A careful and "systematic relativism" would lead to a deepening and widening of desirable cosmopolitan values rather than to their erosion. "After an apparent downfall and temporary banishment," Locke promised, "many of our most prized 'universals' would reappear, clothed with a newly acquired vitality and a pragmatic validity of general concurrence."[57] Relativism, from Locke's perspective, counteracted mistaken metaphysical impulses to objectivity and the false universalization of provincial values; it also invited greater tolerance and heightened knowledge of other cultures' value frameworks.

With any number of malicious provincial targets in view, Locke held back from training his relativizing antiprovincial perspective onto his own aesthetic commitments and his perception that "the cosmopolitan should share the loyalties of the group, but upon a different plane and with a higher perspective."[58] Having asserted this point of friction between Locke's philosophical theory and critical practice, we should turn from his broad theoretical statements to the vocabularies of racialism, universalism, and aestheticism operative in his writings on African American musical development.

Locke's cosmopolitan ideal fused a forward-looking "common consciousness" among African Americans to a deepened respect for convergences and nonantagonistic differences between national and ethnic traditions.[59] He encouraged African American composers to forge concert works that spoke to a black folk nationalist aesthetic, American musical nationalism, and a more general cosmopolitan ethos.[60] Enthusiasm for the Negro Renaissance did not make Locke especially generous with judgments of aesthetic success. Triumphs of pure artistry, he insisted, never came frequently. Many of Locke's critical essays also catalogued the gauntlet of social hurdles and audience problems faced by African American artists in their pursuit of cosmopolitan success.

Locke was forthright in *The Negro and His Music* (1936) about what might be called premature cosmopolitanism among nineteenth-century black formal composers. According to his early "Cosmopolitanism" lecture, an enriched African American cosmopolitanism required a "divided nationalism," as true cosmopolitanism began with a proud self-consciousness about provincial starting points (what Josiah Royce, whom Locke admired, labeled "wholesome provincialism"). For American composers of African descent, identifying and accessing the quintessential provincial bonds was no simple matter; extraordinary intracultural heterogeneity and regional differences separated African Americans from each other, the African continent, and the vast diaspora produced by modern European slavery and colonialism. Institutionalized racism enforced the outsider status of the black minority in the United States with violence and a flood of damaging stereotypes in elite and popular culture that only seemed to rise with each passing year of black freedom. Locke saw premature cosmopolitanism as an understandable response to an impossible predicament where racist stereotypes powerfully distorted black folk traditions. Black folk nationalism in music could hardly flourish in a corrupt postbellum world of comic Jubilee and ragtime songs, pseudospirituals, minstrelsy, and "coon songs." That African American ragtime and minstrel performers (like Ernest Hogan, author of the 1896 hit "All Coons Look Alike to Me") were central to popular music sensations in the United States gave small comfort to Locke.

The chapter on "Early Negro Musicians" in *The Negro and His Music* lists a number of black "formal musicians who early pointed the way to higher attainment in music," including Chevalier St. Georges, George Bridgetower, Edmund Dede, Joseph White, Elizabeth Taylor Greenfield, the Hyers Sisters, Thomas Bethune, and Frank Johnson. For Locke, the pervasiveness of premature cosmopolitanism in the nineteenth century had limited the effectiveness of American concert music in general. In moving so quickly to assimilate recent European models of formal music, American composers bypassed their particular folk inheritances. "They were as sophisticated as the folk music we have been discussing was primitive," Locke wrote of early African American composers, "and there was a complete gulf between them. They were cut off, like the earlier Negro poets and writers, from the folk tradition. Their story is one, therefore, of isolated promise and achievement."[61] The bridging of the "complete gulf" between folk idioms and formal music was a nationalistic priority for African American concert music in the period between the world wars. Locke's depiction of the previous distance between the worlds of black folk music and formal music recalls the metaphoric chasm that swallowed Du Bois's tragic protagonist—another sensitive black aesthete cursed with "isolated promise and achievement"—in the story "Of the Coming of John." Du Bois attended to the "sorrow songs" as a bridge from the slave past to a fully emancipated future, and he enlisted the songs in his effort to reconcile African American class and cultural disparities (disparities highlighted and exacerbated by his "talented tenth" rhetoric). Locke pursued a related dialectical response to the "complete gulf" that had hitherto "cut off" African American cosmopolitanism from the folk inheritance.

The "isolated promise" of African American concert music before the Renaissance was "typical of the individual achievements of the first and second generation of Negro musicians on the art-level," Locke contended, "at a time when even the folk music had not yet broken through to recognition."[62] He believed that African American concert music experienced its watershed moment in the 1870s with the Fisk troupe's revelations to audiences, critics, and composers of the folk spirituals' universality and appeal as listeners' music. Du Bois acknowledged in his 1903 salute to the Fisk Jubilee Singers that the "sorrow songs" were hardly the most authentically African of African American musics. Instead, the songs' blending of African-derived rhythms, melodies, and timbral characteristics with Anglo-Protestant hymnody and lyrical content crystallized the musical and ethnic reality of African American distinctiveness.[63] Locke agreed that the Fisk Jubilee Singers "put Negro music and musicianship on the path of world recognition" as a result of their tours of Northern and European cities in the 1870s.[64] He considered "the path of world recognition" an indispensable detail in the Fisk story.

Identity, as the philosopher Charles Taylor has noted, "is partly shaped by recognition or its absence, often by the *mis*recognition of others, and so a person or group of people can suffer real damage, real distortion, if the people or society around them mirror back to them a confining or demeaning or contemptible picture of themselves. Nonrecognition or misrecognition can inflict harm, can be a form of oppression, imprisoning someone in a false, distorted, and reduced mode of being."[65] For Du Bois and Locke, the Fisk Jubilee Singers contributed to antiracist activism by deliberately refusing to mirror the demeaning images of blackness perpetuated in minstrelsy. Not all critics and historians have shared this interpretation of undistorted recognition and a relatively reciprocated gaze in the singers' cultural work. The historian Robert Cantwell, for example, counters that the Fisk Jubilee Singers of the 1870s inaugurated "a kind of genteel minstrel show" that substituted the solemn distortions of "highbrow" racial sentimentalism for the ridicule of "lowbrow" blackface minstrelsy. The tradition of the Jubilee Singers contributed to "the further confinement of black people," Cantwell suggests, "in some ways more invidiously than in minstrelsy itself, into the stereotype of Christian patience, humility, and other-worldliness that Victorian sentimentality had projected."[66] One finds no shortage of corroborating evidence for this interpretation in the publicity surrounding the original Fisk Singers, as in Theodore Seward's praise for the "simple, ecstatic utterances" from the singers' "child-like, receptive minds."[67] Critiques of the "invidious" representational strategies of the Fisk tradition are considered elsewhere in our analysis; they offer valuable fugal responses to less skeptical visions of concert music's role in the articulation of black social memory and cosmopolitan aspiration.

While a condition of isolation from folk materials had limited the achievements of earlier black composers, Locke looked forward to the promise of black composition "in the universal mode." Here again we encounter the "key of paradox." Locke did not want black folk nationalism and cultural racialism to contradict contributions to music "in the universal mode." By "the universal mode," he meant formal music "without trace of folk idiom and influence." Locke ranked music "in the universal mode" in relation to folk, commercial, and formal music as a "fourth separate strand of art music representing the Negro's participation in the general mainstream of cosmopolitan or classical music." Did the pursuit of a "universal mode"—a mode that transcended all provincial attachments—contradict the ideal of a pluralistic "new cosmopolitanism" based on "parallel evolution?" Not for Locke. He folded his anticipation of black cosmopolitanism into a single developmental narrative that moved from the "great dialect music of the Spirituals" to the "petty dialect of popular music, ragtime and jazz and finally 'classical jazz' and the transition to the universal speech of formal art music."[68] His commitments to a sense of teleological evolution that could be universalized and to a pluralistic "sense for parallel/but not equal values" have already been outlined. The appeal of "universal speech" in music marks a point of tension between the two models of cosmopolitanism sketched in Locke's early "Cosmopolitan" lecture.

The musical meaning of "universal speech" is thinly explicated in *The Negro and His Music*. Locke's use of the term perhaps alludes to the conventional musicological notion of "musical logic," a mainstay of European aesthetics since the nineteenth-century heyday of German Romanticism and the theorization of nonprogrammatic instrumental music as pure or absolute music. The musicologist Carl Daulhaus explains: "that music presents itself as sounding discourse, as development of musical thoughts, is the compositional justification of its esthetic claim that it exists to be heard for its own sake; a claim that was nothing less than self-evident in the late eighteenth century."[69] Dahlhaus notes that Johann Herder originated the term "musical logic" in 1769. Herder argued that harmonic development and logical understanding in music were secondary to the evocative and devotional power of melodies and what he called "the bond of their sequence in their pleasantness for the ear, in their effect on the soul."[70] In other words, the leading German folk nationalist's focus on melody and sentiment prevented him from celebrating the new harmonic and structural emphases and nonfunctional formalism of what critics would call absolute music.

The primacy of musical logic in musical aesthetics gained a positive valence later in the eighteenth century through the writings of Johann Nikolaus Forkel, Ludwig Tieck, and Friedrich Schlegel. We can also surmise that Locke wrote of "universal speech" to imply vocal and instrumental music's capacity to satisfy universally appealing preferences across cultures. Borrowing the language of his 1942 essay "Pluralism and Intellectual Democracy," one might imagine that by "universal speech" in music Locke contemplated a musical language of nonrelativistic "'functional constants' to take scientifically the place of our outmoded categoricals and our banned arbitrary 'universals.'" The music's universality would commence, as it were, not from foundational claims about aesthetic value (to be counted among "our banned arbitrary 'universals'") or national superiority, but from "a pragmatic validity of general concurrence." Locke assumed "universal speech" in music to be qualitatively different from the "great dialect music of the Spirituals" and the "petty dialect of popular music." He never paused, however, to explain or defend the mechanisms by which these rigid generic determinations had been reached.

"Universal speech" would present no "trace of folk idiom and influence," Locke proposed; it involved no musical analogs to provincial or vernacular dialects. A reader skeptical of the Lockean strategy for overcoming conceptual contradictions through synthesis might ask how such "universal speech" would be distinguishable from established musical languages in European and Euro-American art music? Or did Locke believe that European classical music had already attained its teleological consummation—only to wait for the rest of the world to catch up? At certain points in his criticism, basic assumptions of Locke's new cosmopolitanism were indistinguishable from the old Eurocentric cosmopolitanism he had set out to correct and transcend. His statements oscillated between the pluralistic implication of "parallel evolution" as an end in itself and the different appeal of "universal speech." On the one hand, the pluralistic thrust of "parallel evolution" and the call for black folk nationalism in music appeared as strategies for prodding African American artists to forge ahead toward a distant universal goal. Strictly parallel lines, by contrast, stretch out into infinity without ever touching.

Locke's formulation about a kind of "universal speech" stripped clean of "folk idiom and influence" warrants close scrutiny because it bears on a prominent criticism of much African American literature associated with the Harlem Renaissance, and the Negro Renaissance more broadly. For an example of the long-standing critique, one might consider Henry Louis Gates's argument about the tendency toward a self-destructive universalism in New Negro poetics:

> With very few exceptions—notably Sterling Brown and Langston Hughes . . .—poetic expression, and hence poetic image, became a stylized, literate experience for the printed page and the outside reader. And because of this, black poetry—that is, the oral component of black poetry, which even the formalized abuse of black language in its parodies failed to smother completely—was sacrificed on the altar

of the universal to the spirit of Western art. . . . [the] political considerations of the black poet made the value of dialect especially dubious to the "New Negro," for dialect was an oral remnant of slavery, and it was that degradation to the dignity of a proud people that these artists, both consciously and unconsciously, intended to abolish. Abolish dialect they did, and with the bathwater went the baby.[71]

Analogous critiques about the sacrifice of black specificities in formal music could be raised against Locke's appeals to music "in the universal mode." Locke attempted to insulate his position from such criticisms by consistently flagging the pitfalls and idiomatic dilutions of prematurely cosmopolitan black concert music. A cosmopolitan urge toward the universal did not limit his idealization of certain forms of black folk expression (especially the spirituals) in a manner consonant with the romantic nationalism he shared with Du Bois, James Weldon Johnson, and others. In particular, Locke took great pains to underscore his sensitivity to subtle folk characteristics in performances of the spirituals and to what he called the "dangerous tendency to sophistication and over-elaboration" in formal presentations. In "The Negro Spirituals" (1925), for example, he worried about premature cosmopolitanism in the genre of concert spirituals, and he displayed his own concern that a precious "baby" was being sacrificed along with the "bathwater" of the original sacred folk context of musical performance. Nevertheless, the glittering prospect of intercultural reciprocity in a new cosmopolitanism dimmed whenever Locke gave primacy to the "general mainstream of cosmopolitan or classical music" over the work of folk interpretation among New Negro performers. He wrote, for example:

the spirituals, in these glorious times of Roland Hayes, Paul Robeson, Marian Anderson, and Dorothy Maynor, and others have brought our interpretive artists a welcome opportunity, after mastery of the great universal language, to pay their racial homage to the native source of their artistic skill and spiritual strength, and to express their artistic indebtedness to the singing generations behind them and to the peasant geniuses who were, in James Weldon Johnson's apt phrase, "the black and unknown bards" of long ago.[72]

Locke did not promote the renunciation or sacrifice of the "great dialect" music of the spirituals "on the altar of the universal to the spirit of Western art." Instead, he proposed a delicately calibrated transformation and formalization of folk materials. To what extent the postures of renunciation and formalization ultimately differed remains a point of conflict among critics and musicians to this very day. Zora Neale Hurston lambasted New Negro formalizers and insisted that there had "never been a presentation of genuine Negro spirituals to any audience anywhere." The formalized concert spirituals misrepresented not only the "genuine Negro spirituals" but the songs' deceased and living creators. "The real Negro singer," unlike the Europeanized singer beholden to a formal score, "cares nothing about pitch. The first notes just burst out and the rest of the church joins in—fired by the same inner urge."[73] Hurston's perspective will be explored more carefully in chapter 4. Locke understood Hurston's emphasis on idiomatic authenticity in folk expression (he quoted her sympathetically in *The Negro and His Music*), but he retained his enthusiasm for the sublimation or distillation of folk elements in scored-through concert music.

Locke's appreciation for Hurston's attention to ethnographic detail in folk expression distinguished his perspective from Du Bois, who assumed that a sufficient degree of folk authenticity could be summoned through performers' expressive sincerity far outside the original folk performance idiom. To Hurston and other skeptics about New Negro formalization, the newly scrubbed and upscaled representations of black folk materials were fundamentally inauthentic and, in almost every case, inferior to the best nonelite uses of the source materials. Locke was more than sensitive to this line of criticism; in fact, he sometimes doled it out himself. Skeptics like Hurston interpreted New Negro formalization as the self-aggrandizing effort of an anxious black bourgeoisie eager to silence, if not abolish, the unruliness of black vernacular expression. Moreover, the debate demonstrated how the distance between unwritten and formally transcribed spirituals, and their respective performance sites, signified a profound social cleft. An older "complete gulf" between folk and formal forms, as Locke would have it, was being bridged. At the same time, however, newer divisions were revealing themselves on the contested musical terrain of a supposed "common consciousness." Despite the overheated pronouncements of some publicists for the Renaissance, racial vindication through the success of individual artists could go only so far toward solving larger social problems and cementing intra-racial solidarity. "To suppose," David Levering Lewis has argued, "that a few superior people, who would not have filled a Liberty Hall quorum or Ernestine Rose's 135th Street library, were to lead ten million Afro-Americans into an era of opportunity and justice seemed irresponsibly delusional."[74] True this may be, but the "delusional" project of avant-garde national leadership was hardly the invention of such New Negro intellectuals as Charles Johnson and Locke. Moreover, not all of the artists associated with the Renaissance subscribed to the messianic supposition that Lewis denounces.

Locke's argument in *The Negro and His Music* oscillated between folk-derived "Negro music" and dialect-free "universal music," and between the alternate appeals of racialism and cosmopolitanism. Did this symptomatic tension ultimately point to an irreducible paradox or to a synthetic and dialectical vision of musical "double-consciousness"? We can understand Locke's approach by looking to his language about folk authenticity, artificiality, and idiomatic dilution in music. At a turning point in his book's argument, we learn that folk elements are completely submerged in the final stage of musical development. Locke explains the complete interpenetration of folk substance and scored-through forms.

> Only when pure and in the form originally used by the people for themselves, do they [folk elements] yield us true folk music. This is why real folk music is rare; but it is the most precious musical ore we have. When folk elements are stereotyped and artificially imitated, we have popular music with a folk flavor. . . . When developed and blended with the technique of formal music, they are no longer content with the simple forms of the folk ballad or sentimental ballad, and yield classical music of folk origin. . . . When so thoroughly blended as to be recognized only upon technical musical analysis, folk music has become completely universalized and has made its final contribution, as the German chorale in a Bach instrumental *Chorale* or a Polish folk dance in a *Polonaise*.[75]

The passage captures the universality of the folk-to-formal developmental process as a matter of "parallel evolution." The complete and seamless fusion of substance and form—the process constitutive of successful formal music, Locke seems to have believed—leaves the folk elements undetectable except upon "technical musical analysis."

The depiction of folk music as a "most precious musical ore" offers a metallurgical metaphor for the process of aesthetic refinement and recalls the critical vocabulary of Walter Pater (1839–94). Pater was not, it should be clarified, a notable advocate of folk expression or folk nationalism in concert music. The Paterian vocabulary that we mean to recall here lies in other moments of his aesthetic criticism. In the second half of his life, Pater was a high priest of aestheticism at Oxford University where he taught and from where he wielded a profound influence. Locke admitted that he was "intrigued by the twilight of aestheticism" at Oxford and earlier inspired at Harvard by the aesthetic philosophy of Santayana.[76] Because explicit references to Pater are rare in Locke's published writings, this statement from 1928 deserves particular attention:

> Now that the time has come for some sort of critical appraisal, what of our much-heralded Negro Renaissance? Pathetically pale, thinks Mr. Mencken, like a candle in the sunlight. . . . I wonder what Mr. Pater would say. He might be even more sceptical, though, with the scepticism of suspended judgment, I should think; but one mistake he would never make—that of confusing the spirit with the vehicle, of confounding the artistic quality which Negro life is contributing with the Negro artist. Negro artists are just the by-products of the Negro Renaissance; its main accomplishment will be to infuse a new essence into the general stream of culture. . . . If then it is really a renaissance—and I firmly believe it is, we are still in the hill-town stage, and the mellowness of maturity has not yet come upon us.[77]

Locke's characterization of Pater as one who would not confuse "the spirit with the vehicle" refers to the analysis of the Italian Renaissance made in Pater's classic work, *The Renaissance: Studies in Art and Poetry* (1873). Pater argued there that "the Renaissance of the fifteenth century was, in many things, great rather by what it designed or aspired to do, than by what it actually achieved." According to Pater, "the movement of the fifteenth century was two-fold": the Renaissance looked forward and backward simultaneously as it struggled to break the grip of "those limits which the religious system of the middle age imposed on the heart and imagination." The Renaissance "comprehended a return to antiquity" (i.e., the heritage of classical Greece) even as it anticipated "what is called the 'modern spirit,' with its realism, [and] its appeal to experience."[78] Locke theorized a parallel "two-fold" movement—recuperative and at the same time anticipatory—for Negro Renaissance music, art, and literature. Locke's passage on "our much-heralded Negro Renaissance" transplanted a Paterian theme in arguing that the incompleteness of "our little Renaissance" did not render it a failure; instead, the Negro Renaissance was a "vehicle" for setting in motion a "spirit" larger than its individual achievements. Its "main accomplishment," Locke proudly concluded, "will be to infuse a new essence into the general stream of culture."

The literary critic Perry Meisel has demonstrated that "metallurgy is the most persuasive historical source and model Pater has for the chemical fusion of medium and sensibility." A metallurgical model of artistic refinement pervades Pater's writings, from the early essay "Diaphanete" (1864) to later works like *Marius the Epicurean* (1885), *Appreciations* (1889), and *Plato and Platonism* (1893). Meisel notes that Pater also wished "to naturalize his account of culture by speaking of it through [a] second or covering language of organicism and natural growth." As a result, Pater's contrasting metallurgical and organicist accounts create an impression of paradoxicality. "How," Meisel asks, "can a single model for culture accommodate the requirements of sublimation on the one hand and those of organic presence on the other?"[79] A similar rhetorical operation takes place in *The Negro and His Music* and elsewhere in Locke's writings. In particular, Locke's account of the sublimation of folk roots in the cosmopolitan work of "the great masters" passes from metallurgical images of "precious musical ore" and the process of "refining out" to a contrasting organicist language of "folk elements" as "taproots" and "sub-soil." In the organicist or botanical mode, Locke writes:

But though the great masters often use this highest kind of universal musical speech in which the layman does not recognize the folk elements, they themselves know it and often admit that the finest taproots of their art run down deep into the sub-soil of folk music. Even after the themes, harmonies and color have been refined out, basic rhythms betray the original folk sources. Thus the forms of Italian opera come from provincial folk songs; the great classical music of Germany from German folk songs and dances; Spain and Russia likewise. . . . So when the folk songs of the Negro or the Georgia plantations or the Carolina rice-fields or the Mississippi bayous turn up as spirituals and blues in European concert-halls, as they do, or as ingredients in the symphonies of European composers like Dvorak, Delius, Milhaud or in the equally elaborate formal work of Negro composers like Dawson, Dett, and Still, they are following a path common to all musical development.[80]

After one registers Locke's metallurgical and botanical passages, his perspective on the character of "universal musical speech" becomes less obvious. "Even after the themes, harmonies and color have been refined out" in the later stages of musical evolution, "basic rhythms betray the original folk sources." Locke's statement contrasts with his comments elsewhere about folk aspects being "refined out" in formal music to the point of imperceptibility, except upon "technical musical analysis." In other words, Locke defers the presentation of perfectly consummated aesthetic development; he oscillates between the metallurgical image of refinement as a fundamental transformation of a "most precious musical ore" and the organicist image of gradual cultivation and continuity with distinctive "taproots" and "sub-soil."

The ambiguity of Locke's statements about aesthetic consummation neatly captures his courting of paradox and "suspended judgment" in the "twilight of aestheticism" and his twinned commitments to black folk nationalism in music and the "universal speech" of cosmopolitan music. One can look elsewhere in his writings for the intertwining of metallurgical and botanical images and find similarly paradoxical formulations. A passage from an article that Locke wrote for the *Nation* in 1928 evokes the tension between universal cosmopolitan forms and culturally distinctive idioms in literature. "Beauty Instead of Ashes" (published the same year as the explicitly Paterian "Our Little Renaissance") offered a generous progress report on Negro Renaissance writing.

> Already our writers have renewed the race temperament (to the extent there is such a thing) by finding a new pride in it, by stripping it of caricaturish stereotypes, and by partially compensating its acquired inferiority complexes. It stands today, one would say, in the position of the German temperament in Herder's day. There is only one way for it to get any further—to find genius of the first order to give it final definiteness of outline and animate it with creative universality. A few very precious spiritual gifts await this releasing touch, gifts of which we are barely aware—a technique of mass emotion in the arts, a mysticism that is not ascetic and of the cloister, a realism that is not sordid but shot through with homely, appropriate poetry. One wonders if in these sublimated and precious things anyone but the critic with a half-century's focus will recognize the folk temperament that is familiar today for its irresistibly sensuous, spontaneously emotional, affably democratic and naive spirit. Scarcely. But that is the full promise of Negro art as inner vision sees it.[81]

The passage holds out the promise of reconciliation between Locke's developmentally-minded pluralism and his universalizing cosmopolitanism. The application of "genius of the first order" would guarantee "sublimated and precious things" and lead to "beauty instead of ashes."

The contrast between beauty and ashes implies a shared condition through the metaphoric link of heat. Undergoing the application of heat leads either to destruction (ashes) or to a new and superior product (beauty).

Locke's metallurgical metaphor refers to a transformation of primary substances or source matter through heat, with a goal of "sublimated and precious things." Analogous imagery circulates throughout his critical reviews, as when he wrote "with all the improvement of fact and attitude, the true Negro is yet to be discovered and the purest values of the Negro spirit yet to be refined out from the alloys of our present cultural currency."[82] Elsewhere he claimed "the substance of modern life brings a heavy sediment not easy to filter out in the poetic process. Only a few can distill a clear flowing product." The filtering out of "heavy sediment" in the liquid distillation of a "clear flowing product" of mature art amounts to the same figurative dynamic as the refinement of pure alloys. In that same review of Countee Cullen's *Color*, a book of poetry, Locke contended: "Here as indubitably as in Petrarch or Cellini or Stella, there is the renaissance note. What body of culture would not gladly let it in!"[83]

Although the selective survey undertaken in Pater's *Renaissance* did not take up musical matters, music inspired his best-known formulation about the ideal sublimation of matter into form. He wrote in the course of a discussion of Renaissance painting in "The School of Giorgione" about how *"all art constantly aspires towards the condition of music."* "For while in all other works of art it is possible to distinguish the matter from the form," Pater continued, "and the understanding can always make this distinction, yet it is the constant effort of art to obliterate it."[84] Pater's sense of music as the role model for all the arts did not emerge from a special estimation of music in the era of the Italian Renaissance. He alluded instead to the absolute music ideal of contemporary concert music theorized in German Romantic thought and exemplified in the purely instrumental work of Beethoven. Pater clarified his allegiances elsewhere in *The Renaissance* to "that essential music, which presents no words, no matter of sentiment or thought, separable from the special form in which it is conveyed to us." "Music of greater compass perhaps than words can possibly yield" extended a possibility to transcend functionality and referentiality and obliterate the distinction between matter and form. Pater urged, in short, the extension of a certain Romantic paradigm of music to all aesthetic criticism. "That the mere matter of a poem, for instance—its subject, its given incidents or situation; that the mere matter of a picture—the actual circumstance of an event, the actual topography of a landscape—should be nothing without the form, the spirit, of the handling; that this form, this mode of handling, should become an end in itself, should penetrate every part of the matter: this is what all art constantly strives after, and achieves in different degrees." Metallurgical refinement offered Pater an analogy for the active obliteration of the distinction between matter and form and the penetration of "the form, the spirit," and "the handling" into "every part of the matter." Thus he wrote of Leonardo da Vinci waiting for "the moment of invention" and "alchemy" when "the idea is stricken into colour and imagery" and a "cloudy mysticism is refined to a subdued and graceful mystery." Pater added into his powerful brew of Platonism and German idealism the decidedly secular and protomodernist note of the French *l'art pour l'art* school of Gautier and Flaubert. Thus, he sometimes portrayed the artistic process as a scientific matter of extreme discipline in pursuit of perfectly unified and complete works. "Few artists," he stated in *The Renaissance*, "work quite clearly, casting off all *débris*, and leaving us only what the heat of their imagination has wholly fused and transformed."[85] Pater detailed in "Style" (1888) how "all art does but consist in the removal of the surplusage."[86] One finds traces of these Paterian themes throughout Locke's critical writings.

A completed process of aesthetic sublimation as purifying refinement, or *ascesis*, was a chief indicator of success according to the criticism of both Pater and Locke. Both imagined an aesthetic cauldron or melting pot where the impure elements of merely spontaneous expressivity are boiled off in the process of formalization through which great works of art must be forged and refined.[87] The aestheticist themes of matter sublimated into form and sensibility transmuted into medium help us to understand Locke's efforts to inspire the "maturation" of African American music in a movement from provincial idioms to universal forms and from "petty dialect" music to "great dialect" music and finally to "universal speech" in art. According to Locke, the aesthetic ideals of formal sublimation and "great art" were still best encountered outside African American formal music. His examples were not all European. As we have seen, he argued in 1924 that a new pride in the "race temperament" would commence from a more thorough appreciation of classical African sculpture's formal maturity.

Locke's essay on "The Legacy of the Ancestral Arts" in *The New Negro* presented classical African sculpture as the highest achievement of black art to date and an inspiring model for artists in all media. He approvingly quoted the comments of British critic Roger Fry about the surprising formal success of an exhibition of African sculpture from the collection of Paul Guillaume. It should be noted that the philosophical roots of Fry's canonizing essays on French "post-impressionist" painting and his commentaries on such matters as the "purely aesthetic organization of form" and the "disinterested intensity of contemplation" (collected in the 1920 book *Vision and Design*) are in part traceable to Pater and Victorian aestheticism. *Vision and Design* includes "Negro Sculpture," Fry's commentary on Guillaume's collection. In the essay, Fry emphasizes formal achievement and the African genius for "plastic" expression and finds himself a bit stunned by his own conclusions. He confesses that he had "to admit that some of these things are great sculpture—greater, I think, than anything we produced even in the Middle Ages." The best of the sculptures realized the achievement of "complete plastic freedom; that is to say, these African artists really conceive form in three dimensions. . . . Without ever attaining anything like representational accuracy they have complete freedom."[88] According to Fry, the African sculptors' failure to achieve mimetic or "representational accuracy" (the crowning achievement of the greatest Greek sculptors) meant that even the greatest African art betrayed backward cultures trapped in an evolutionary stage of barbarism.

Fry was anti-imperialist in political sentiment, and his appreciation of African art displayed a relatively high degree of sympathy for African civilization. Moreover, his cosmopolitan connoisseurship stretched far beyond the exclusively European interests of earlier aesthetes like Pater. The racist assumptions of the colonial mind remained unmistakably strong, however, in Fry's evolutionary judgments about the pre-mimetic barbarism of the "Negro mind."[89] J. B. Bullen has commented that "the very remoteness" of the African cultures represented in Guillaume's collection "was a positive advantage for Fry's method." A blissfully decontextualized encounter with alien art guaranteed a free reign for Fry's critical imagination. Thus, he interrogated the African artworks only "through the formal relations—the way in which mass and volume was created in each piece— and though Fry does not mention the modernist connection in his essay, there is no doubt that the resemblance between the plastic sense of Negro art and the solid geometry of Cubism brought the sculpture alive for him."[90]

Locke adopted Fry's complimentary point about "complete plastic freedom" from the restraints of mimetic representation, but he sought to counter Fry's poorly informed cross-cultural understanding. In response to Fry's influential but flawed analysis, Locke called for a truly "comparative aesthetics" and tried to add details about the African artists and their cultural contexts in commentaries that nevertheless highlighted formal characteristics. His analyses displayed a particular affection for the most austere and nonmimetic works as signs of superior refinement and self-discipline.[91] Locke's attraction to Fry's critical method revealed itself in this passage from *Negro Art: Past and Present*:

> The common denominator between African art and modernist art is the cult of form for form's sake. That is to say form as a satisfaction in itself without reference to realistic representation or immediately intelligible symbolism. This is the same as to say that most primitive art and most modernist art are highly abstract or stylized. Of course the motives are different, but the results are startlingly the same. . . . But the contemporary artist cannot count on his audience grasping his symbolism, which is one way of saying that our artists are out of tune with their audience. In primitive tribes, the group is able to follow the artist for the double reason that they are able, like children, to reduce all their forms to their simplest components, and that they have closer contact with the mechanics of carving or decoration and therefore a feeling for the purely technical effects of these media,—in short they are themselves more artistic. . . . As yet, a great deal of this modernistic art is not appreciated by the majority of us western moderns. And yet Africans would prefer the type of art which is admired by our ultra-modern sophisticates to that which attracts the gaze and warms the heart of our "man in the street."[92]

The notion of "form as a satisfaction in itself without reference to realistic representation" evokes an intellectual lineage stretching from German Romanticism and the idealization of absolute music, to the late Romanticism of Pater's aestheticism, to Fry's approximation of modernist formalism in art criticism. With the specific aims of our present discussion in mind, one might read Locke's comment on "the cult of form for form's sake" in the context of Pater's idealization of music and art that obliterated—or at least came the closest to obliterating—the distinction between matter and form.

Pater and Locke intertwined the implicit formalism of the metallurgical rhetoric about refinement and sublimation with organicist rhetoric about expressivity and semantic meaningfulness. Moreover, both of them maintained that it was the expressive and instructive power of great art to illuminate beauty's ultimate inseparability from truth. "In the highest as in the lowliest literature, then, the one indispensable beauty is, after all, truth," Pater wrote in "Style." The maligned prophet of Victorian aestheticism made a distinction for literature between "great art" and "good art" that ultimately rested "not on its forms, but on the matter." The "greatness of literary art," Pater concluded, depended on subject matter of the highest quality in "its compass, its variety, its alliance to great ends, or the depth of the note of revolt, or the largeness of hope in it."[93] Pater's critique of Wilde's controversial novel *The Picture of Dorian Gray* was, after all, ultimately moral in substance.

Locke had no quarrel whatsoever with these Paterian sentiments on the obliquely humanizing value and social function of "great art." Locke likewise wrote of the moral potential for "sublimated folk-poetry on the Negro theme" and a literature revelatory of "a black beauty that is truth,—a Negro truth that is purely art."[94] A consistent tenet of his annual reviews of the "literature of the Negro" from 1929 to 1953 was that "tractarian" authors of overwrought antiracist literature and poetry forgot that "excess is never good art" and thereby missed the opportunity for an effective fusion of truth and beauty in "poetic realism."[95] Even as a radicalized Marxian critic in the 1930s, Locke maintained a stated commitment to "the golden mean of sober interpretation."[96] "Poets, like birds, sing at dawn and dusk," he wrote in 1935, "they are hushed by the heat of propaganda and the din of work and battle, and become vocal only before and after as the heralds or the carolling serenaders."[97] "Notwithstanding his famous disagreement with Du Bois's "all art is propaganda" argument, Locke's convictions about the coexistence of truth and beauty promised an ultimately moral and social justification for great art. Moreover, metallurgical images of sublimation in Locke's aesthetic criticism also spoke to his broader American nationalist agenda for progressive cultural fusion, not through simple assimilation to a Nordic ideal (or, *pace* Kallen, through a cultural purist's repudiation of assimilation), but through ethnic hybridization and reciprocal transformation. The aestheticized utopian ideal behind Locke's cosmopolitan melting pot of aesthetic and social transformation was not something standard and monolithic, but rather a proliferation of new and beautiful combinations. The passage above from "Beauty Instead of Ashes" explicitly referred to Herder and the development of German cultural nationalism as a model for the New Negro artist's nationalism, but it also prophesied the imperceptibility of folk roots in the sublimated cosmopolitanism of the future. The metallurgical and formalist strains of

Locke's criticism might be interpreted together with the nationalist organicism he espoused for the Negro Renaissance and American art overall.

As his 1935 "psychograph" announced, the "twilight of aestheticism" was only one of the many sources behind Locke's self-identification as the "mid-wife to a generation of younger Negro poets, writers, and artists." To counterbalance a recent scholarly emphasis on Locke's pragmatism, the preceding pages have stressed affinities between the critical formulations of Locke and Paterian aestheticism. What remains to be discussed here is the fact that Locke's references to the "art for art's sake" label typically affixed to aestheticism were nearly always accompanied with caveats, if not denunciations. He was acutely sensitive to aestheticism's public reputation and its associations with decadent antinomianism, amoral literature and art, political quietism, and, not least, homosexuality and gay-identified sexuality. Pater and Wilde, the leading voices of British aestheticism, were gay. Moreover, the list of homosexual or gay-identified men associated with the Harlem Renaissance includes, but is not limited to, Carl Van Vechten, Alain Locke, Claude McKay, Countee Cullen, Wallace Thurman, and Richard Bruce Nugent. "Gay social networks played a key role in fostering the Renaissance," the historian George Chauncey has concluded.[98] Locke, who preached Paterian restraint to his more flamboyant and Wildean gay colleagues, responded to the simmering controversy in the article "Art or Propaganda?" (1928), published in the same year as "Our Little Renaissance" and "Beauty Instead of Ashes." "Art or Propaganda?" critiqued "propagandism" (Du Bois's explicit stance as of "Criteria of Negro Art"), but it also clarified in self-defense that "our espousal of art thus becomes no mere idle acceptance of 'art for art's sake.'" Locke's Renaissance ideal was not a "cultivation of the last decadences of the over-civilized, but rather a deep realization of the fundamental purpose of art and of its function as a tap root of vigorous, flourishing living." The article's argument struggles to evade any association with the unhealthy "decadences of the over-civilized." Thus Locke defined art's "fundamental purpose" botanically "as a tap root of vigorous, flourishing living" that contradicted idle solipsism and exoticism. "Not all of our younger writer writers are deep enough in the sub-soil of their native materials," Locke warned; "too many are pot-plants seeking a forced growth according to the exotic tastes of a pampered and decadent public."[99] The "forced growth" of exoticism for the sake of a "decadent public," in other words, contradicted the health of art and its fundamentally social function. Passages like these (and others elsewhere that focus on the functional values of "beauty in use") suggest Locke's sympathies for the socially minded (but also formalistically inclined) pragmatist aesthetics of John Dewey.[100]

In *Negro Art: Past and Present*, Locke criticized unnamed black artists who were "still beating the thin air of art for art's sake long after the art of our time has passed to a creed of social analysis and criticism. Negro art, more logically, falls in with an art of social interpretation and criticism."[101] The Negro Renaissance, he reiterated self-defensively in 1939, had been "committed to no one cult of aesthetics (and least of all to the creed of 'art for art's sake,' since it tried to focus the Negro creative writer upon the task of 'folk interpretation')."[102] The statement posed the formalist and antisocial thrust of "art for art's sake" against a purportedly more accessible and democratic aesthetic of "folk interpretation." More characteristic and non-dogmatic were the occasions when Locke allowed aesthetic ideals to mingle intimately without contradicting one another. Such was the case in his appreciation in 1945 of a set of African American artists (including Elizabeth Catlett, Ernest Crichlow, and Jacob Lawrence) who displayed "an ability to blend the somewhat conflicting approaches of a social message with the abstractly aesthetic into a balanced, mutually reenforcing synthesis."[103]

Beyond the panorama of African American art worlds, Locke also trained his imagination on another horizon, a cosmopolitan utopia where the world's provincialisms and nationalisms could be preserved, cultivated, and sublimated into a new pluralistic universalism. As he exclaimed in 1936, "Deep river; deeper sea!—even a landlubber knows that!" Locke's self-assigned responsibility was to insure that the nationalistic exploration of such "precious musical ore" as the folk spiritual "Deep River" emboldened a journey outward to an even deeper sea of unrealized and uncharted cosmopolitanism. "Before too very long, the tang, taste, color and rhythm of our art will have changed irreparably from the purely racial to the universal," Locke predicted in that benchmark year of hope for the radicalized "art of social analysis." Upon reaching the universal waters of cosmopolitan art, "those who have cried for the sea will doubtless cry for the loss of their river."[104]

"The Negro Never Had a Jazz Age"

"The greatest accomplishment to date," Locke wrote in *The Negro and His Music*, "excepting the joy of the music itself, lies in the fact that there is now no deep divide between our folk music and the main stream of world music."[105] Locke interpreted mass-produced popular music, by contrast, as the dubious zone of economically motivated ephemera—the "great gulf" that estranged the best folk music from its cosmopolitan fulfillment as formal music. He thus targeted exoticizing interpretations of jazz and the disabling perceptions of desublimated expressivity in the improvisational music's supposedly delirious spontaneity and intoxicating syncopated rhythms. By the 1930s Locke was certain that the previous decade's "Negro vogue" had largely reinforced double standards and racial stereotypes. "Its devotees, especially at the height of the craze," he recalled in *The Negro and His Music*, "rationalized this [the seizure of "Negro emotional elements"] in a complete creed and cult of primitivism. But it was not original and genuine primitivism; only a sophisticated substitute."[106] By contrast, Locke consistently sought to canonize folk and formal art practices in ways that ran counter to decadent primitivism. His hesitations about jazz music and various popular music vogues in the 1920s and 1930s stemmed from more than an exceptionally high regard for the polished maturity of scored-through concert music in the larger forms and the raw and undiluted purity of authentic folk forms. Market pressures also constricted African American musical aspirations to a few popular genres; the full artistic development of jazz faced severe nonmusical hurdles on the difficult path to cosmopolitanism and true intercultural reciprocity.

Locke took pride in how black creativity had driven the jazz revolution of the 1920s and influenced new directions in modern art music. Jazz music, he wrote, "has educated the general musical ear to subtler rhythms, unfinished and closer harmonies, and unusual cadences and tone qualities. It has also introduced new systems of harmony, new instrumental techniques, novel instrumental combinations, and when fully developed, may lead to a radically new type of orchestra and orchestration. Thus jazz has been a sort of shock troop advance, which the regular line advance of modernistic music has intrenched and consolidated."[107] The depiction of American jazz musicians as a "shock troop advance" reiterated the popular music's inspirational power over compositional practices in "modernistic music." Locke's martial imagery suggested that jazz and scored-through concert music were not only moving in the same direction but fighting the same war; jazz musicians provided raw technical innovations and idiomatic flavors, while formally trained composers stayed behind the battle lines to measure new advances according to a more comprehensive strategy. According to Locke's metaphor, the relatively detached analyses made possible by distance from the "shock troop advance" of popular musicians allowed concert composers to logically adjust their longer-term battle plans. Locke's image of the activity of formal composers fit the Apollonian task of poets who remain silent during the "work of battle" and "become vocal only before and after as the heralds or the carolling serenaders." Indeed, the reflective thrust of "carolling serenaders" perfectly suited Locke's folk nationalist agenda for African American composers.

The actual relationship between jazz and the "regular line advance of modernistic music" presented too varied a situation for any unilinear image of jazz musicians marking out new expressive territory in functional popular music prior to the subsequent phase of formalizing composition and interpretation. The musical realities of developmental incongruity and discrepancy put pressure on Locke's formalist assumptions and his pluralistic but unilinear narrative of "parallel evolution." While West African sculpture had long ago attained formal maturity and classical achievement, Locke argued, "Negro music" remained in a less mature stage of development. His timetables for classical achievement in "Negro art" and "Negro music" were strikingly off-kilter; while "Negro art" had soared highest in the distant past (and since collapsed, according to Locke, into disarray under European colonial domination), "Negro music" still awaited its consummatory achievements. The developmental lag on the path toward formal maturity in "Negro music" required a balanced apprenticeship toward the traditions of European art music and the inspiring lessons of African sculpture along with a studious avoidance of imitativeness, premature cosmopolitanism, and exoticism.

The fetishization of "blackness," one of the most common "decadences of the over-civilized," relied on fantasies of desublimation and deep cultural difference regarding the presumably native primitivism of people of African descent. Such fantasies created a false and "sophisticated substitute" for the realities of ethnic pluralism, and they hardly inspired expectations of intercultural reciprocity. Locke estimated in "Toward a Critique of Negro Music" that fully four-fifths of existing commentary on African American music was analytically useless because poorly informed, hopelessly romanticizing, or both. Serious criticism was a developmental necessity, he insisted, for those ready to hold African American music to the highest cosmopolitan standards. "For from the enthusiasts about Negro music," Locke complained, "comes little else than extravagant superlatives and endless variations on certain half-true commonplaces about our inborn racial musicality, our supposed gift of spontaneous harmony, the uniqueness of our musical idioms and the infectious power and glory of our transmuted suffering."[108]

As a critic with classicist and formalist inclinations, Locke repudiated the extravagant praise of formless expressivity and spontaneity from "enthusiasts about Negro music." Such uncritical praise was counterproductive, if not pernicious on racial grounds, he believed; also, from his perspective, it was aesthetically unsound in any case. His distrust of the vulgar Romanticism of any overemphasis on unmediated emotional expressivity in music dovetailed with the views of Pater, Fry, and Santayana. Santayana, for example, held that the "beauty of form . . . is what specifically appeals to an aesthetic nature; it is equally removed from the crudity of formless stimulation and from the emotional looseness of reverie and discursive thought."[109] Locke might have agreed on the importance of the appreciation of form as a contemplative process involving imaginative synthesis. Rather than "emotional looseness" and a desublimating urge toward primitive sensuousness, true aesthetic contemplation offered sublimation and an imaginative transcendence of the sensuous realm. Santayana, for whom the "illusion of disembodiment" was "very exhilarating," employed an idealistic notion of aesthetic pleasure to underwrite his own vision of cosmopolitanism. "The mind passes from China to Peru without any conscious change in the local tensions of the body."[110]

In keeping with the "key of paradox," one can occasionally find Locke refiguring his interracial notion of "established reciprocity" into alignment with primitivist rhetoric about the "untarnished instincts" of the "Negro temperament." He sometimes agreed that prominent African American cultural work was expressing an appealing emotional reaction—a "recoil from the machine"—against industrialized life and its alienating effects. Although the "sophisticated substitute" or surrogate of a false primitivism worried Locke, he participated in the transvaluation of stereotypical notions about black expressivity and "untarnished instincts" from negative to positive.

The modern recoil from the machine has deepened the appreciation of hitherto despised qualities in the Negro temperament, its hedonism, its nonchalance, its spontaneity; the reaction against oversophistication has opened our eyes to the values of the primitive and the importance of the man of emotions and untarnished instincts; and finally the revolt against conventionality, against Puritanism, has found a strong ally in the half-submerged paganism of the Negro. With this established reciprocity, there is every reason for the Negro artist to be more of a modernist than, on the average, he yet is, but with each younger artistic generation the alignment with modernism becomes closer.[111]

The values of formalization and sublimation usually took a prominent place in Locke's writings on art, but here he applauded the "values of the primitive" as a matter of "established reciprocity" between black and white artists and a sign of their shared modernism. If understood in the larger context of Locke's developmental vision, his statement about "untarnished instincts" does not necessarily conflict with comments made elsewhere about "sublimated and precious things" in the African American art of the near future. The sublimated achievement of superior aesthetic creation, Locke always believed, depended on superior alloys and base materials. "Real folk music" yielded "the most precious musical ore we have" and avoided (through its authentic primitivism) the damaging artificiality of decadent "oversophistication." In other words, the proper cultivation of a "half-submerged paganism" contributed to the achievement of a mature classicism.

Locke regularly inveighed against the ways in which the monolithic power of popular music threatened the transfiguring sublimation of authentic folk alloys expressive of the folk's natural "paganism." Despite his optimism about "established reciprocity," he came to distinguish between a Jazz Age inclined toward informality and false primitivism and a simultaneous Negro Renaissance inclined toward a formalizing memorialization of the "Negro temperament" and the maligned folk inheritance. "The Negro . . . never had a jazz age," according to Locke, because the Jazz Age best suited a predominantly white revolt against residual Victorianism; the Jazz Age revolt used jazz music and related dance idioms as weapons against established codes of bourgeois psychic repression. "The Negro," Locke countered, "strictly speaking, never had a jazz age" because "he was born that way, as far as the original jazz response went." The music's pure folk roots defined the "original jazz response" for Locke. "But as a modern and particularly as an American also," he continued, the Negro "became subject to the infections, spiritual and moral, of the jazz age." The "original jazz response" was "primitively erotic," while the Jazz Age response was "decadently neurotic."[112] "Primitively erotic" folk impulses and idioms suggested to Locke the promise of efficient and successful sublimation;

"decadently neurotic" sources, by contrast, were too compromised and impure. In a nameless attack on Carl Van Vechten as a decadent influence, Locke argued in 1938 that "one wing" of the 1920s Renaissance "was caught up and diverted in the neurotic jazz age with its freakish aesthetics and its irresponsible individualism."[113] (Locke clarified the situation to a white colleague that year; "I am I believe persona non grata with him [Van Vechten], and not ashamed of that.")[114] The other "more positively toned movement of cultural racialism and solidarity" assigned to itself "a realistic rediscovery of the folk." Both trajectories took place "over the common denominator of racialism," and Locke added that "the depression and the second disillusionment of the elite" marked a movement away from racialism toward "the reformist and socialistic reaction of the present day."[115]

The "realistic rediscovery of the folk" took on a less folkloric emphasis and a more markedly left-wing focus in Locke's commentaries from the 1930s. He wrote that the radicalized response of "the latest generation" of African American writers and artists to the Depression meant that "realistic, socialistic, and proletarian" values were "again changing the whole cast and direction of Negro expression in literature and art."[116] Locke interpreted the shifting emphasis as entirely continuous with his own long-standing priorities, and he warned, as always, against the counterproductive pitfalls of dogmatism and merely propagandistic art. While visiting Leningrad in 1936, he took to the radio airwaves to praise the new "Theater of People's Art" and related Soviet programs aimed at cultivating the national arts of Soviet minorities. Locke's address outlined how state support for the arts of minority populations in the Soviet Union resonated with his hopes for stronger folk art advocacy in the United States.

> As a Negro interested in the rich but as yet only half-emancipated folk art of my own people, I am deeply touched and inspired by this. For us, such a program and policy could mean cultural salvation. It would mean instead of a folk art commercialized and prostituted to the frivolous entertainments of others, a healthy artistic expression for the fuller life of the people themselves and the serious enrichment of our national American culture. And so, the cultural lesson in which Russia is so successfully pioneering, is a lesson of supreme importance, not only to suppressed and disparaged minority cultures, but to the whole world of art.[117]

The Soviet program of subsidizing minority nationalism in the arts told Locke that the stultifying dominance of the capitalist marketplace could be overcome. He bitterly contrasted "a folk art commercialized and prostituted to the frivolous entertainments of others" in the United States. The development of a "half-emancipated folk art" had the chance to proceed on the Soviet model, as Locke understood it, at a natural pace toward maturation and a fulfilled emancipation. Leninist-style pluralism and its "lesson of supreme importance" vindicated Locke's early dream of a "divided nationalism." He quoted from the radio address in a letter to Charlotte Osgood Mason, and reported mentioning "to Langston [Hughes] the duty I thought we had to make connections with the Russians." "They are the only nation," Locke insisted, "treating racial and national minorities honestly and decently through and through. . . . If they ever get hold of Africa, some of our hopes can be realized."[118]

Locke returned to the link between what he called "the cultural racialism of the art philosophy of the 1920's and the class proletarian creed of today's younger generation" in notes for a 1937 speech delivered to the radical National Negro Congress. He defended his own and the Negro Renaissance's reputation among black leftists critical of New Negro elitism and petit bourgeois nationalism. His own work and the creative writings of Langston Hughes and Sterling Brown bridged the two generations and demonstrated the fundamental consistency of "folk interpretation" in the 1920s and 1930s, Locke argued, despite apparent divergences of tone and emphasis. As a second line of self-defense, Locke pointed to the "cultural minorities art program being consistently and brilliantly developed in the Soviet Federation for the various racial and folk traditions of the vast land." The Soviet program only reinforced "the consistency between the sounder aspects of cultural racialism and proletarian art, and between cultural regionalism and socialistic culture."[119] From Locke's perspective, the combined forces of capitalism, segregation, and institutionalized racism rendered impossible the true emancipation of African American folk art and the actualization of democratic pluralism in the United States.

The pluralistic promise of Leninist-style nationalities' policies gave way to monocultural Stalinist nationalism in the late 1930s. Although circumspect on the matter, Locke did not repudiate the Soviet Union after Stalin made his nonaggression pledge to Hitler in September 1939. He retained into the 1940s at least a measure of sympathy for the Soviet experiment and the Communist Party in the United States and its flagship periodical, *New Masses*. One finds an admiring comment from Locke about Soviet pluralism in his 1942 anthology for the Progressive Education Association on internationalism, imperialism, and cultural conflict, and an absence of polarizing rhetoric on the Soviet threat in his commentaries from later in the 1940s. "The Soviet policy and program," Locke wrote in *When Peoples Meet*, "represents an almost complete divorce of cultural from political nationalism" and "offers the possibility of stable cosmopolitan societies based upon cultural pluralism, and dependent for their functioning upon legally guaranteed minority equality."[120]

As a longtime resident of "voteless Washington," Locke was, to at least one close observer, "not very political minded." Radicalized by the events and opportunities of the 1930s, he became "a fervent New Dealer and saw in this political philosophy a fulfillment of the democratic ethos, particularly for the disadvantaged minority to which he belonged."[121] In any case, Locke was evasive in print about his political sentiments. The point is made especially obvious when one compares Locke's Marxian commentaries to the voluminous editorials of W. E. B. Du Bois, who was unambiguously socialist and pro-Soviet in the 1930s. The differences between them came to a head when Locke served as the editor of Du Bois's invited contribution to the Bronze Booklet Series in the 1930s. Locke returned Du Bois's manuscript, "Social Reconstruction and the Negro," and labeled it unpublishable on account of its dangerous radicalism. Du Bois's manuscript included his socialist "Basic American Negro Creed" (printed in his 1940 autobiography, *Dusk of Dawn*) and an agenda for voluntary racial separatism that was surely anathema to Locke. "A co-operative Negro industrial system" should be established, Du Bois argued, "in the midst of and in conjunction with the surrounding national industrial organization."[122] Locke wrote Du Bois that "it would be unwise to print the Basic American Negro creed" as it opened Du Bois's book and Locke's entire Associates in Negro Folk Education book series to "criticism on grounds of direct propaganda."[123] The short books that did appear in the Bronze Booklet Series included, among other titles, Locke's *The Negro and His Music* and *Negro Art: Past and Present* and two studies in literary criticism by Sterling Brown.

Locke's political inclinations and his aestheticism merged in his analysis of jazz music in the 1930s. His idealization of early jazz conveyed an interpretation of folk music as essentially noncommercial and anathema to the capitalist marketplace. The "original jazz response" had since undergone a distorting commercialization such that its modernization had not followed Locke's normative folk-to-formal trajectory. Early jazz, Locke wrote, had been of a piece with a distinctive and fading African American folk culture:

Today's jazz is a cosmopolitan affair, an amalgam of modern tempo and mood. But original jazz is more than syncopation and close eccentric harmony. With it goes, like Gipsy music, a distinctive racial intensity of mood and a peculiar style of technical performance, that can be imitated, it is true, but of which the original pattern was Negro. Moreover, it is inborn in the typical or folky type of Negro. . . . So jazz is basically Negro, then, although fortunately, also human enough to be universal in appeal and expressiveness.[124]

Locke's sense of the "almost complete disappearance of the pure soil peasant" and the concomitant decline of the original spirituals had implications for jazz as a music rooted in the milieu of the "typical or folky type of Negro."[125] Indeed, one finds him echoing the elegiac modernism of Toomer's "Song of the Son" in some passages of *The Negro and His Music*. "Though late, there is still some precious time left for the study of the original folk sources of this music before it vanishes in its original forms. Some primitive communities, some older links have miraculously survived, but researchers must hasten."[126] (Toomer wrote: "Though late, O soil, it is not too late yet/to catch thy plaintive soul, leaving, soon gone.") The folk idioms of jazz had also fallen victim to commercial distortion and idiomatic dilution; Locke contrasted the healthy "peasant paganism" of early jazz against the "freakish" primitivism of a "neurotic jazz age."

The development of jazz into an informally "cosmopolitan affair" intimated to Locke a story about its diluted potency as folk music. The superior alternative to the predicament of "a folk art commercialized and prostituted" was successful refinement and hybridic fusion according to the highest artistic ideals. "The golden age of jazz artistically occurred long before the flood of popularity and profit" since the late 1920s, Locke insisted, because true "jazz is more at home in its humble folk haunts even than in Harlem." "Often wholly illiterate," the music's pioneers had been "humble troubadours [who] knew nothing about written music or composition, but with minds like cameras they would listen to the rude improvisations of the dock laborers and the railroad gangs and reproduce them, reflecting perfectly the sentiments of these humble folk." "But as jazz has spread out from its Mississippi headwaters and become the international ocean it now is," Locke lamented, "it has become more and more diluted, more cosmopolitan and less racial. It was the early jazz that was the most typically racial—and musically the most powerful."[127] Similar accounts of jazz's musical decay (dependent on a conception of the dilution of its folk authenticity) rose to prominence as founding narratives in the jazz criticism of the 1930s and 1940s. By contrast, Locke captured his optimal cosmopolitan narrative for successful aesthetic sublimation without dilution in the earlier-noted essay "Deep River, Deeper Sea." The threat of dilution was so great in the case of jazz and related popular music because the authentic idioms were innately fragile and vulnerable to pollution in commercial exploitation. "Surface jazz," Locke warned, was "the cheap alloy of Tin Pan Alley."[128]

An ambiguous but ultimately hopeful analysis of "symphonic jazz" countered Locke's gloomy prognostications in *The Negro and His Music* about dilution and blocked development. A reversal of musical dilution was possible through a properly guided agenda of hybridic fusion, even as Locke found himself troubled by questions of leadership and interracial reciprocity in the development of black-identified idioms. "Toward a Critique of Negro Music" foreshadowed the conclusions that appeared a few years later in *The Negro and His Music*. Locke suggested that "the whole field is full of paradoxes, for after all the most original and pioneering creative use of Negro musical idioms still goes to the credit of white composers from Dvorak down to Aaron Copland, Alden Carpenter, George Gershwin, Paul Whiteman, and Sesana."[129] The description of a field "full of paradoxes" encompassed the realities of white bandleaders and ensembles dominating the commercial marketplace for jazz-related music and white critics commandeering the music's interpretation in periodicals and books. "Thus, it has been white musicians and critics," Locke concluded, "who for the most part have capitalized jazz, both commercially and artistically."[130]

Few had capitalized jazz so thoroughly as the white bandleader Paul Whiteman, widely regarded in the 1920s as the "King of Jazz." In contrast to the majority of jazz critics writing in the 1930s, Locke welcomed Whiteman's aspiration to shape a canon of symphonic jazz suited to the concert hall (though Locke credited an African American, Will Marion Cook, as the real father of symphonic jazz). Whiteman's 1924 premiere of Gershwin's *Rhapsody in Blue* struck Locke as the turning point for the hybridization of jazz into concert music. "Paul Whiteman, guided by Gershwin and Ferde Grofé, was exploiting and popularizing jazz tone color, harmony and rhythm in the larger forms. This was no inconsiderable service: Whiteman has converted the American public to the seriousness of jazz and clinched Dvorak's prophecy that future American music would draw its substance from Negro sources."[131] Whiteman's artistic success vis-à-vis

"Dvorak's prophecy" raised a problem for Locke's black folk nationalist agenda. Among other critics, Carl Van Vechten enthusiastically celebrated the success of Gershwin's *Rhapsody in Blue*.[132] Locke shared Van Vechten's nationalistic sentiments but added in *The Negro and His Music* that "our music should not be at the mercy of a popular fad, which may die down at any time, or be exploited, or even developed most seriously by other than Negro musicians."[133]

Agitated by the pitfalls of "cultural chauvinism" and insiderism, Locke moved back and forth betweel ideals of American cultural nationalism, a distinctly African American nationalism, and a cosmopolitan ideal of international music in the "universal mode." If white musicians and critics were forging paths for the transformation of jazz into art music, what could be foreseen about the future of black folk nationalism in music? The top white musicians, Locke concluded in *The Negro and His Music*, equipped themselves with "a guiding thread of theory" and were therefore "able to go farther by logic in the development of the more serious aspects of jazz than the Negro musicians have, moving too much under the mere guidance of instinct. Besides too great familiarity has bred, if not contempt, at least a certain short-sighted perspective on the best possibilities of jazz."[134] Comments like these led Sterling Brown to later describe *The Negro and His Music* as "not a good" book and one "full of errors." As Brown put it, "Locke did not know jazz, and he did not know the blues, but intellectually he knew their importance. . . . For Locke, if Stravinsky liked it, it had to be good. And that's bad." Brown added that Locke undoubtedly knew "the importance of jazz on the world scene, but he could not hear jazz and he did not see jazz in its own terms."[135] One can conclude that Locke learned about jazz and grasped its importance in terms that made sense to him, terms based on prior European musical developments. Brown set for himself an alternative challenge: to see "jazz in its own terms" at a point in the music's history when these terms remained entirely up in the air.

Brown praised the art of Jelly Roll Morton, Bessie Smith, and other early blues and jazz musicians for their "pioneering creative use of Negro musical idioms" without holding their music hostage to the mediating structures of Locke's comprehensive developmental vision. Roland Hayes, who did not share Brown's misgivings, reassured Locke that *The Negro and His Music* was "a significant treatise" and "the best organized and the most comprehensive setting-forth of matter on the subject . . . that I have yet read."[136] Carl Van Vechten wrote Locke that he would have liked more attention paid to the great popular singer Ethel Waters. "After hearing her recently," Van Vechten explained, "I wrote her that the only reason she couldn't sing Isolde or the leider of Schubert is because she doesn't want to. She in her line is as great as Marian Anderson."[137] As we have seen, Locke preferred to imagine a single developmental line that would wind its way from the deep river of pure folk music through the rocky shoals of commercialized popular music and out to the deeper sea of mature cosmopolitan music.

To preserve and elevate folk idioms without diluting them, to cultivate cosmopolitan forms and artistry without descending into imitativeness or academicism, and to find an escape from both propagandism and the decadent and racist commercialization of the black folk inheritance: these were the musical and critical goals for African American music that Locke outlined in the "twilight of aestheticism." Defined by the "guiding thread of theory," fully scored concert music presented itself to him as a model of mature cosmopolitan art. Locke did not, however, entirely rule out alternative modes of formal self-consciousness in musical idioms rooted in the "petty dialect" of blues and jazz, nor did he elaborate these alternative modes. Others, including Sterling Brown, Langston Hughes, and Zora Neale Hurston, would undertake the articulation of these alternative paths. Nevertheless, Locke's commentaries on jazz always incorporated defenses of the music and its developmental prospects. He lamented how Maud Cuney Hare wrote her otherwise "indispensable" *Negro Musicians and Their Music* (1936) "with a pronounced bias against jazz and popular music in general, and with what the writer believes a false conception of an antithesis between folk forms and art forms in music."[138] If an antithesis existed at present, it would be overcome in a nondiluting fusion of jazz idioms and classical forms, Locke urged in *The Negro and His Music*. He rejoiced that leading African American jazz composers and arrangers like Duke Ellington were finding the materials for developing "the more serious aspects of jazz" in unexpected paths less dependent on European traditions of formal musical structure. In particular, the avenues of solo and group improvisation, based not on the "mere guidance of instinct" but rather on an ever-expanding idiomatic vocabulary offered alternatives to Locke's philosophical mapping of cosmopolitan development.

FOUR

"Beneath the Seeming Informality":

Hughes, Hurston, and the Politics

of Form

Song is both a complaint and a consolation dialectically tied to that ordeal, where in back of "orphan" one hears echoes of "orphic," a music that turns on abandonment, absence, loss. Think of the black spiritual "Motherless Child." Music is wounded kinship's last resort.
—Nathaniel Mackey[1]

So, having looked at the subject from many sides, studied beliefs by word of mouth and then as they fit into great rigid forms, I find I know a great deal about form, but little or nothing about the mysteries I sought as a child. As the ancient tent-maker said, I have come out of the same door wherein I went.
—Zora Neale Hurston[2]

"The path of progress passes through a series of vital centers whose succession is the most significant line of human advance," Alain Locke wrote in 1929. He hoped to guide New Negro cultural development onto the rails of cosmopolitan success. "A province conscious of its provinciality has its face turned in the right direction," he continued, "and if it follows through with effort can swerve the line of progress to its very heart."[3] The cosmopolitan "line of progress" for music, as Locke saw it, followed a direction from folk to formal idioms. Any critical foresight into the truest path toward that end, he believed, demanded the discrimination of African American progress in music from mere imitations of European and Euro-American concert models and the ephemera of popular music.

As a self-styled modernist dissatisfied with the preoccupations of an older generation of artists and critics, Locke campaigned against the reduction of African American literature to the explicit demands of genteel taste, middle-class uplift, and antiracist propaganda. Nevertheless, he always presumed that progress in black art would pay generous social dividends; the cosmopolitan success of African American artists would clarify a true "line of progress" for all of society. Less forward-looking tastes among black artists and audiences, by contrast, stood as predictable signs of an assimilationist stage of development. "The average Negro writer," Locke argued in 1936, "has thus been characteristically conservative and conformist on general social, political and economic issues, something of a traditionalist with regard to art, style and philosophy, with a little salient of racial radicalism jutting out front—the spear-point of his position. Many forces account for this, chief among them the tendency the world over for the elite of any oppressed minority to aspire to the conventionally established values and court their protection and prestige." The "conservative and conformist" temperament had to be overcome, Locke contended, through the successful vindication of black modernist art. In passing through a conformist stage on the road to cosmopolitan self-understanding, the conservative African American elite "has been no exception" among elites of oppressed minorities, Locke explained, "but on that very score [it] is not entitled to exceptional blame or ridicule."[4]

Carl Van Vechten's best-selling novel, *Nigger Heaven* (1926), and Langston Hughes's first collection of poetry, *The Weary Blues* (1926), both generated controversy during the Harlem Renaissance as affronts to genteel traditionalists. Van Vechten, always a controversial icon of white patronage during the Renaissance, championed Hughes's writing and helped to ensure that Alfred Knopf published the young black writer. For his part, Hughes defended his friend against those outraged by primitivist depictions of black decadence in *Nigger Heaven*. Countee Cullen, a conservative on matters of poetic form, gave *The Weary Blues* a negative review in *Opportunity* (February 1926) and made clear how far Hughes had gone in disappointing black traditionalists. The controversy swirling around Hughes's new poetry only heightened with a second book of poems published the following year, *Fine Clothes to the Jew*.

6. Langston Hughes, 1936. Photo by Carl Van Vechten. Courtesy of Carl Van Vechten Trust.

Hughes's new poetry raised the ire of critics who felt betrayed by his transformation over the preceding five years. The changes in his aesthetic were so "sweeping and all-encompassing," the literary critic Richard Barksdale remarked much later, "that the young poet whose 'The Negro Speaks of Rivers' had charmed the black literary elite in 1921 found himself, five years later, almost a literary persona non grata."[5] Hughes's first published poem, "The Negro Speaks of Rivers," had indeed delighted black traditionalists, including Du Bois. Accepted for publication by Jessie Fauset, literary editor of the *Crisis* and an important novelist in her own right, the poem earned its nineteen-year-old author instant recognition as a major talent. "The Negro Speaks of Rivers" eulogized the dawn of civilization and ancient Africa in a Whitmanesque cadence at once sweeping and compact. The lyrical poem perfectly summoned the noble spirit of the anonymous "black and ancient bards" that James Weldon Johnson and others credited with forging the classic folk spirituals. Hughes's poem evoked Du Bois's understanding of the long black memory captured in the "sorrow songs," while the stately uplift of the poem's final line—"my soul has grown deep like rivers"—referenced the spiritual "Deep River." (Du Bois did not include "Deep River" in *The Souls of Black Folk*, but it had since been treated to a highly acclaimed formal arrangement by Harry Burleigh.) Hughes's next major poem, "The Weary Blues," may have won first prize in the 1925 *Opportunity* literary contest, but it registered a distinct tonal and conceptual shift. Under the editorial leadership of Charles Johnson, The National Urban League's periodical departed from the urgent political tone of Du Bois's *Crisis* and instead pursued a more indirect and culturally focused strategy for racial progress. A major aesthetic goal held by Johnson, Alain Locke, and other leading lights at *Opportunity* was to encourage literary experiments that fused modernist and folk forms.[6]

Locke greeted the publication of *The Weary Blues* as a positive breakthrough and wrote that "techniques of folk songs and dance are instinctively there, giving to the individual talent the bardic power and touch." Because Hughes's individual talent served so effectively as a poetic medium for the folk tradition's "bardic power," Locke applauded Hughes's new explorations of vernacular materials.

> Especially if Hughes should turn more and more to the colloquial experiences of the common folk whom he so intimately knows and so deeply loves, we may say that the Negro masses have found a voice, and promise to add to their natural domain of music and the dance the

conquest of the province of poetry. Remember—I am not speaking of Negro poets, but of Negro poetry. Poetry of a vitally characteristic racial flow and feeling then is the next step in our cultural development. Is it to be a jazz product? The title poem and first section of *The Weary Blues* seem superficially to suggest it.[7]

Locke was grateful that the "Negro masses" had found a poetic voice unburdened by the minstrel overtones of dialect literature, but he preferred not to hear too much in the volume's "superficial" suggestion about the centrality of jazz and the blues. Indeed, he seemed to hesitate when given the chance to encourage the "vitally characteristic racial flow and feeling" of poetry inspired by jazz and the blues. Never one to unconditionally trust the developmental possibilities of those new musical forms, Locke hoped instead that Hughes might fashion "new beauty" from "the rhythm of the secular ballad but the imagery and diction of the spiritual."[8] Locke praised Hughes's fine ear for vernacular idioms but quietly registered Hughes's shift from the solemn grandeur of "The Negro Speaks of Rivers" to the grittier (but, compared to the more outré blues songs, not particularly explicit) realism of the blues poems.[9] In any case, Hughes pursued the blues lyric form further in *Fine Clothes to the Jew*, and Locke again wrote a glowing review, this time lauding the profound and "tragic vision" of the blues poems.[10]

Hughes's influential blues poetry and other writings argued that neither Du Bois's "talented tenth" nor Locke's "cultured few" were directing the creative efflorescence of African America. Even though Locke wrote of the urban "Negro masses" as the unsung heroes adding "to their natural domain of music and the dance the conquest of the province of poetry," it was Hughes who defended the contemporary blues and its nonelite social world without apologies. The popularity of "classic blues" singers like Mamie Smith, Bessie Smith, and Alberta Hunter demonstrated that the elite New Negro focus on the older spirituals as ciphers of folk culture was out of tune with newer vernacular forms emerging from the urbanizing "Negro masses." Hughes's literary work and criticism often reflected on cultural dissonances exacerbated by the intraracial class divide. Indeed, his work amounted to a case study in New Negro revisionism by highlighting nonelite elements in urban African American music that Du Bois and Locke attempted to subdue or evade in their developmental mappings of the true "line of progress" for black art with a "vitally characteristic racial flow and feeling." Hughes's blues poetry, for example, sought to alter the relationship between elite African American literature and popular music. His focus on the urban blues exposed a blind spot of the folk-to-formal paradigm enshrined in the formal concert spirituals identified with classical composers and musicians like Roland Hayes, Harry Burleigh, Nathaniel Dett and Marian Anderson.

As we have seen, the rural folk romanticism that Du Bois and Locke shared often led them to interpret black folk culture less as a living reality than as residue from a fast-receding past. Besides feats of conceptual prestidigitation, elite New Negro nationalists struggled to ventriloquize an archaic "black folk" and thereby assume prophetic command over the heterogeneous voices of contemporary African Americans. The strategy was hardly unique; indeed, comparisons and intersecting analyses with insurgent nationalist currents throughout the world deserve far more attention than they have received. Romantic nationalist intellectuals of every nation frequently have moved to underwrite their authority as spokespeople by wielding appealing, and usually pastoral, images—"pre-modern leftovers," in Slavoj Žižek's terms—of an archaic national folk culture. In nationalist discourses that eschew the kind of democratic pluralism so prominent in New Negro thought, the impulse to aestheticize the past and to imagine "a vitally characteristic racial flow and feeling" can fuel a brutal cultural narcissism and a violent hostility to foreign contamination in the name of national purity. Hughes's revisionist critique in the 1920s assented to the fundamental "common sense" of African American cultural nationalism, even as he pulled back a curtain of class mystifications, a kind of intraracial veil, in black middle-class ideologies of uplift and elite leadership. As Hughes read the situation, these class mystifications were unnecessary and counterproductive; they ultimately limited the untapped democratic potential of black cultural nationalism and (as he came to emphasize in the 1930s) the international workers' movement.

In the 1920s and 1930s, Zora Neale Hurston also protested against elite New Negro strategies of cultural representation. Her classic studies of African American folk culture and religion in the Deep South mounted highly original defenses of traditional folk practices against elite New Negro demands for formal development and urban-focused hybridization. Hurston challenged Du Bois's famous vision of black anxiety and self-overcoming in "double-consciousness." She also targeted Locke's beloved concert spirituals and ridiculed them for "squeezing all of the rich black juice out of the songs and presenting a sort of musical octoroon to the public." As Hurston would have it, too much of the New Negro cultural

7. Zora Neale Hurston, 1938. Photo by Carl Van Vechten. Courtesy of Carl Van Vechten Trust.

nationalist project for black cosmopolitan development was "some more 'passing for white.' "[11] Her charge of idiomatic impurity against the concert spirituals contributed to the era's intellectual debate over music, memory, and racial authenticity; at least in Hurston's comments on the spirituals, the fundamental meaning of racial authenticity itself seemed to rise or fall on specific aesthetic points about performance and style. While Hughes emphasized the extent to which the "low-down folks" of the black urban milieu had developed or adapted vernacular forms appropriate to their changing social conditions, Hurston assaulted the urban black elite's patronizing, if not always explicitly condemnatory, image of rural folk culture. In particular, she rose in defense of the unappreciated aesthetic complexity of the black folk church. "Beneath the seeming informality of religious worship," Hurston wrote, "there is a set formality. . . . The individual may hang as many new ornaments upon the traditional forms as he likes, but the audience would be disagreeably surprised if the form were abandoned."[12]

Although polarizing political differences and a lifelong rift developed between Hurston and Hughes after their frustrating 1930 collaboration on the stage play *Mule-Bone*, a broadly defined dissent against what Hughes called the destructive "race toward whiteness" and what Hurston called the "flight from blackness" united their intellectual and artistic projects. Both of them looked "beneath the seeming informality" of black vernacular idioms and demanded a rethinking of basic assumptions behind the folk-to-formal narrative of New Negro cosmopolitan development. Their distinctive but nevertheless related efforts ultimately reshaped the terrain of aesthetic debate in African American intellectual life.

The "Racial Mountain" and Blues Form

Langston Hughes wrote "The Negro Artist and the Racial Mountain" as a riposte to "The Negro-Art Hokum," George Schuyler's skeptical critique of New Negro cultural racialism. The *Nation* published both Schuyler's and Hughes's essays in 1926. In his, Hughes defended the unifying idea of "Negro art," but he attacked the black middle-class for an assimilatory "race toward whiteness." The "racial mountain" that black artists struggled to climb over was a product of both white racism and middle-class assimilationism, Hughes argued. One face of "the mountain standing in the way of any true Negro art in America" was an internalized white ethnocentrism and a "desire to pour individuality into the mold of American standardization, and to be as little Negro and as much American as possible."[13] The racializing process of "whiteness" marked the mold of standardization; through fits and starts, the process bestowed on the majority of the ethnically diverse American population the national privileges of racial unity. Although Hughes's condemnation of "the mold of American standardization" echoed Horace Kallen's pluralist critique of the "melting pot," Kallen's antiassimilationist alternative of an American "symphony of civilization" was itself white and implicitly restricted to those of European descent. Where Kallen focused on the "Anglo-Saxon" norm of assimilation, Hughes specified "Nordicism" as the ideal type of American whiteness. Moreover, Hughes lent the ideal type of whiteness an unmistakably privileged, bourgeois shading.[14] His critique of the "race toward whiteness" among blacks, then, included a sharp political edge by linking cultural assimilationism to the intraracial enforcement of class and status stratification. Kallen, by contrast, stressed not class divisions (in fact, he positively deemphasized the impact of class on cultural differences) but the primordial ties of descent-based belonging within an ethnic group. For his part, Schuyler lampooned the quest for a unified and distinctively "Negro" racial culture; he claimed instead that "the Aframerican is merely a lampblacked Anglo-Saxon."[15]

Against the homogenizing aspirations of African American cultural nationalism, Schuyler argued that the spirituals, jazz, and the blues were "contributions of a caste in a certain section of the country." As such, these class and region-specific idioms were incapable of representing or giving voice to a unified "Aframerican" culture. The national orientation of the "Aframerican" should be American, Schuyler wrote, because primitivism and pernicious racialism always accompanied notions of racial difference. There is, as George Hutchinson notes, a "great contradiction" in Schuyler's essay. "The Negro-Art Hokum" wraps a skeptical antiracialist argument in a positive presentation of a substitute hokum, namely, "Americanism" as an authentic national mentality. For Schuyler's essay, an asserted "Americanism" not only takes precedence over any imagined differences in racialized mentalities but actively negates the possibility of any relatively distinctive African American culture or "Negro art." Schuyler's antiracialist assault on "Negro art" as a hokum (and, with "Negro art," the "cultural racialism" Locke posited in defense of the Renaissance) suffered through its dependence on counterassertions about a culturally non-differentiated

"Americanism." "If racism is a powerful factor in American society (as Schuyler acknowledges)," Hutchinson asks, "and if racialist thinking is an ingrained aspect of the American character, then does not the very 'Americanism' of whites and blacks in the United States . . . effect cultural differentiation along 'racial' lines?"[16]

Far more sympathetic to the ideal of a "true Negro art in America," Hughes rejected Schuyler's view and mobilized contemporary, nonelite black music to represent a dominant sensibility among the national black community. In other words, the restrained singing and subdued rituals of the "Nordicized" and "upper-class Negro church" needed to be understood as an exception to the culturally distinctive music and rituals of the true black majority. The church music comparison, painted by Hughes in broad polemical brush strokes, showed that the "race toward whiteness" entailed the repression of long-standing black traditions and the innovations of gospel music. Exuberant styles of evangelical worship and sacred singing were being sacrificed by the "upper-class Negro church" in a conversion to what Hughes perceived as an aesthetically unappealing and nonparticipatory liturgy. "The Negro Artist and the Racial Mountain" did not, however, address how the concert spirituals enacted a kind of halfway covenant for New Negro cosmopolitans aspiring to create a new, more pluralistic formal culture through an elevation—rather than an outright evasion—of the folk inheritance.

Hughes's celebration of jazz and the blues, rather than a full-blown defense of the black church or the spirituals (whether in folk or concert form), guaranteed that "The Negro Artist and the Racial Mountain" would be remembered less as a bitter polemic than as an ebullient, secular manifesto. The wide success of the blues and hot jazz music and dance, Hughes maintained, crystallized a generational revolt against obsolete bourgeois norms of morally appropriate behavior. As Du Bois's condemnation of Van Vechten so powerfully demonstrated, an irony of historic proportions marked the mid-1920s cultural moment. A highly influential Jazz Age subculture of urban whites was pursuing a fantastical quest for liberatory desublimation in the taboo territories of black nightlife. Meanwhile, middle-class New Negroes were assailing stereotypes of black hypersexuality and labeling them as malicious weapons of a racist culture and a complicitous entertainment industry. Many middle-class African Americans worried that practitioners of jazz, blues, and related music and dance styles were overshadowing the controversial antiracist agendas of uplift and institution-building and the professional achievements of those who Hughes referred to as the "Nordicized Negro intelligentsia."[17] In an oft-quoted passage from "The Negro Artist and the Racial Mountain," Hughes stepped into the fray.

> Jazz to me is one of the inherent expressions of Negro life in America: the eternal tom-tom beating in the Negro soul—the tom-tom of revolt against weariness in a white world, a world of subway trains, and work, work, work; the tom-tom of joy and laughter and pain swallowed in a smile. Yet the Philadelphia clubwoman is ashamed to say that her race created it and she does not like me to write about it. The old subconscious "white is best" runs through her mind.[18]

Hughes welcomed the exuberance of much black popular music as an honest expression of "the tom-tom of revolt against weariness in a white world." Jazz combined a delicious frisson of counterbourgeois transgression with the "tom-tom" appeal of racial authenticity. Hughes did not pause to address how white audiences were likely to translate the "tom-tom" appeal into a transgressive but deeply racist primitivism; as we have seen, traditional romantic racist stereotypes of unrepressed and unrefined blackness were being repackaged in the 1920s as glittering icons of unrestrained, liberated modernity. Instead, Hughes directed the force of his remarks at other black intellectuals. "Let the blare of Negro jazz bands and the bellowing voice of Bessie Smith singing Blues penetrate the closed ears of the colored near-intellectuals," he prodded, "until they listen and perhaps understand."[19] For Hughes, the hostility of the "Philadelphia clubwoman" toward jazz and the blues demonstrated above all how intra-racial shame and insecurity motivated the "race toward whiteness." The challenge was clear. In order to move ahead on the most valid path toward a "true Negro art in America" rooted in folk idioms, the black artist had to walk without undue haste through the social territories of jazz and the blues at their most "low-down." When Langston Hughes defended Carl Van Vechten's *Nigger Heaven*, the white writer wrote back in comradely terms, "The situation is *easy* to explain: You and I are the only coloured people who really love *niggers*."[20]

Published less than a year after Locke's *New Negro* anthology, "The Negro Artist and the Racial Mountain" eschewed diplomacy toward African American traditionalists and prophets of uplift as it ridiculed the provincialism of a "smug Negro middle class." Locke, always a proponent of aestheticized ideals of social reconciliation, had collated *The New Negro* to build bridges between overt race propagandism, black nationalism, a strain of aesthetic idealism he identified with Santayana and Pater, modernist experimentalism, and the dialect interests of black and white modernists. The intra-racial problem, as Hughes saw it, was born of class divisions and transcended generational and tactical differences between traditionalists and modernists. To clarify the point, he aimed an accusatory finger in a later essay at "the younger colored people, sons and daughters of the pompous gentlemen and . . . ladies, some of them students at Northern colleges or at Howard." The ideals predominant among elite black youth, he contended, "seemed most Nordic and un-Negro."

Hughes based his views on firsthand knowledge. He had attended Lincoln University near Philadelphia and was bitter about the elite professionals and supposed race leaders who "appeared to be moving away from the masses of the race rather than holding an identity with them." Confessing his distaste for black "society" in Locke's Washington, D.C., Hughes praised the contrasting graciousness of the city's black working class: "Seventh Street was always teemingly alive with dark working people who hadn't yet acquired 'culture' and the manners of stage ambassadors, and pinks and blacks and yellows were still friends without apologies." "Now I can live in Harlem," he wrote with relief, "where people are not quite so ostentatiously proud of themselves, and where one's family background is not of such great concern."[21] Hughes's own pedigree, like Sterling Brown's, was distinguished. His free maternal grandparents had worked heroically with the Underground Railroad. The husband of his maternal grandmother was one of five blacks killed with the radical abolitionist John Brown during the historic armed raid on Harpers Ferry, Virginia; President Theodore Roosevelt later honored the martyred abolitionist's widow.[22] Hughes was raised in Lawrence, Kansas, mostly by his grandmother. According to his first autobiography, *The Big Sea* (1940), a deep well of racial self-hatred poisoned the spirit of his father, a successful lawyer. The young Langston rejected his father's elitism and authoritarianism. Through his long and prolific career as a writer and celebrity, Hughes lavished attention on the rich humor, lack of pretension, and democratic spirit he found among working-class African Americans.

If the "colored near-intellectuals" targeted in "The Negro Artist and the Racial Mountain" were not able to understand jazz, the blues, and poetry influenced by the new popular music, at least some black intellectuals could. Jessie Fauset reviewed *The Weary Blues* for the *Crisis* and cast her vote in favor of Hughes's new poems. She wrote of one poem as "indeed a universal subject served Negro-style and though I am no great lover of any dialect I hope he heartily will give us many more such combinations." In addition to subject matter and dialect, Hughes's apparent lack of concern with form caught Fauset's attention. "Never is he preoccupied with form," she noted. "But this fault, if it is one, has its corresponding virtue, for it gives his verse, which almost always is imbued with the essence of poetry, the perfection of spontaneity."[23] Fauset's comment on the "perfection of spontaneity" reinforced Van Vechten's sense of Hughes's work. Van Vechten called attention to the "highly deceptive air of spontaneous improvisation" in Hughes's new poems in the preface to *The Weary Blues*. The observation resembled Van Vechten's praise for the "complete control" and "sense of reserve power" he heard in Paul Robeson's "evangelical, true Negro rendering" of the spirituals. The impression of graceful spontaneity—a hard-won impression achieved only through the deceptive appearance of naturalness and spontaneity—played an important role in the appeal of Hughes's blues poetry.

Hughes's second volume of poems, *Fine Clothes to the Jew*, further pursued the poetic possibilities of the blues lyric. His prefatory "Note on Blues" in that volume addressed the structural frame in which the apparent spontaneity took place.

> The first eight and the last nine poems in this book are written after the manner of the Negro folk-songs known as *Blues*. The *Blues*, unlike the *Spirituals*, have a strict poetic pattern: one long line repeated and a third line to rhyme with the first two. Sometimes the second line in repetition is slightly changed and sometimes, but very seldom, it is omitted. The mood of the *Blues* is almost always despondency, but when they are sung people laugh.[24]

The comment on "strict poetic pattern" in the blues lyric illuminates Fauset's comment on "the perfection of spontaneity" and Van Vechten's point about the "highly deceptive air of spontaneous improvisation." Moreover, the comment implicitly challenged Locke's analysis of African American expressive practices. Locke's essay on the "Legacy of the Ancestral Arts" in *The New Negro* regarded spontaneity and exuberance in African American expressive practices as overwhelming; he interpreted these characteristics as understandable reactions to—and fleeting releases from—the trauma of enslavement and its legacy of brutalization. The limitations of unrehearsed spontaneity and unbounded affect drove Locke's campaign for unmistakable discipline and restraint in New Negro art indebted to folk sources and the formality of classical African sculpture. By contrast, Hughes's preface to *Fine Clothes to the Jew* asserted that, even as "Negro folk-songs," the blues had strict formal rules, which provided an indigenously African American model of discipline and restraint.

Hughes wrote regularly on the contrast between the blues and the spirituals. For him, the spirituals seemed to possess a less constricting formal frame than the blues—or at least the twelve-bar "classic blues" form that he tended to focus on. Lacking the "strict poetic pattern" of the blues, the spirituals (especially the up-tempo "jubilees") better suited the characterization of unrestrained, affective extravagance than the more spartan and formalized idiom of the twelve-bar blues preferred by Hughes and the "classic blues" singers of the 1920s. The Protestant hymns sung by the "upper-class Negro church" or the fully scored concert spirituals drew clear formal frames around musical performance, thereby cutting short the opportunities for the loose improvisation, unbounded spiritual expressivity, and ecstatic "possession" identified with the sanctified black church. Like a plain setting for a fine gem, the generically strict frame of the "classic blues"—the twelve-bar form constructed of the tonic, subdominant, and dominant chords of any given key and the characteristic AAB lyric structure—cast the originality of a solo vocal performance into the highest possible resolution. Hughes appropriated terms of praise long accorded the folk spirituals when he wrote, "[blues] songs approach all great art in their simplicity and directness. They say what they want to say with no twists and turns, no decorations, no pretty words. Their terseness is their beauty."[25] As Hughes read the mid-1920s situation, the "bellowing voice of Bessie Smith" deserved no less artistic respect than the formal works of elite New Negro composers.

In addition to the consideration of form, the secular blues struck Hughes as more thematically appropriate to understanding African American urban life than the sacred spirituals. He contended that an otherworldly escapism dominated the spirituals, while a more appropriately secular realism typified the blues. Hughes's hyperbolic thematic contrast between the blues and the spirituals underplayed Du Bois's secular emphasis on the complex and masked double meanings of the "sorrow songs'" lyrics, even as it set aside the theoretical edifice and dialectical machinery of Du Bois's idealistic aesthetic. Hughes's focus on subject matter also evaded the musical commonalities shared by the two genres. His review of W. C. Handy's anthology, *Blues*, depicted the spirituals through the ideas of "escape from this world, faith, hope, and a certain 'joy in the

Lord."[26] Although he argued for the equal importance of the spirituals and the blues, Hughes did not tax himself in trying to hide his preference.

> The Spirituals are group songs, but the Blues are songs you sing alone. The Spirituals are religious songs, born in camp meetings and remote plantation districts. But the Blues are *city* songs rising from the crowded streets of big towns, or beating against the lonely walls of hall bed-rooms when you can't sleep at night. The Spirituals are escape songs, looking toward heaven, tomorrow, and God. But the Blues are today songs, here and now, broke and broken-hearted, when you're troubled in mind and don't know what to do, and nobody cares. . . . The real Negro Blues are as fine as any folk music we have, and I'm hoping that the day will come when famous concert singers like Marian Anderson and Paul Robeson will include a group of Blues on their programs as well as the Spirituals which they now sing so effectively.[27]

The blues, a newer idiom than the spirituals, focused on solo vocal performances with instrumental accompaniment (whether piano, guitar, or an ensemble) rather than communal singing. Despite their urban character and the dominance of highly individualized performers, Hughes still insisted on applying the label of "folk music"—rather than the more desultory commercial label of "popular music"—to the blues.

In accepting the "real Negro Blues" as a commercial urban music and a folk music, Hughes disturbed a delicate web of aesthetic and sociological assumptions prevalent in Renaissance aesthetic thought. He especially upset Locke's hope that New Negro poetry would follow the "imagery and diction of the spiritual." In the course of a discussion of the "blues aesthetic" and Hughes's poetry, Sherley Anne Williams emphasized how the classic blues form provides a mediating frame and a marker of distance from the kind of immediate and unrefined expressivity purportedly found in sanctified singing.

> This necessary analytic distance is achieved through the use of verbal and musical irony seldom found in the singing of the spirituals or the gospels. . . . The self-mockery and irony of the blues pull one away from a total surrender to the emotions generated by the concreteness of the experiences and situations described in the song. Even where the verbal content of the song is straightforward and taken at face value the singer has musical techniques that create ironic effects.[28]

One of Williams's points is that the "aesthetic distance" created in the blues through "verbal and musical irony" achieves an impact distinguishable from the sincerity and "total surrender to the emotions" expected from sacred folk singing. It might be added that many of the greatest blues and jazz vocal performances shift in unexpected and dramatic ways between the poles of irony and utter emotional involvement. Williams stresses how the repertoire of blues techniques furnishes strategies of mediation that cultivate ironic distance between the singer's self-possessed performance and the song's content, often about lost or frustrated love and other personal disappointments. The highly skilled blues or jazz singer can stretch and make elastic the cognitive distance between a song's lyrical subject matter and the content of the performer's idiosyncratic performance. Such elastic stylization—the skill of turning a song inside-out to create something entirely unexpected—calls attention to the performer's musical mastery through personalized and often improvised signals of artifice. About blues singers, Williams writes, "at their best they disengage meaning from feeling." "Put another way," she continues, "the singer objectifies, almost symbolizes, the emotional content of the song through the use of melisma, stuttering, and variations in stress and, in so doing, places the situation in stark relief as an object for discussion."[29]

Hughes's approach to the spirituals/blues binary colored many later elaborations of the blues aesthetic, including the influential formulations of Ralph Ellison and Albert Murray about improvisation in the blues and jazz as, at its best, a heroic modernist triumph of folk-rooted formal mastery over existential chaos.[30] Williams focuses on "analytic distance" and the ironic disengagement of "meaning from feeling" in blues performances. Her point about the blues frame as a device for emotional distancing might be compared to Hughes's formula about laughter and despair: the "mood of the *Blues* is almost always despondency," he explained, "but when they are sung people laugh." One may ask whether the performer, like the audience, is laughing at the stylized portrayal of despondency or if the performer's laughter originates in the blues mood of despondency. In other words, what happens to what Williams calls the "emotional content of the blues" during the interval when the song-text is not, or not yet, stretched out on the blues frame and made elastic for the sake of emotional analysis and formal stylization? The distance between lyrical meaning and stylized performance (subject matter and content) does not necessarily add up to the detachment of cool self-analysis. Thus Hughes pointed to the "hopeless weariness" of the blues mood. It was a weariness that "mixed with an absurdly incongruous laughter" to make blues songs "the most interesting folk songs" that Hughes had heard. "Blues are sad songs sung to the most despondent rhythm in the world, yet people always laugh at them."[31] Perhaps the "absurdly incongruous laughter" attending the blues performance could leave the original misery untouched and thereby cast a shadow over the existential promise of aesthetic self-mastery. Hughes commented on the inconsolability of the blues mood in a letter to Van Vechten. The blues, Hughes wrote:

> always impressed me as being very sad, sadder even than the spirituals because their sadness is not softened with tears but hardened with laughter, the absurd, incongruous laughter of a sadness without even a god to appeal to. . . . the worthless lovers with hands full of gimme, mouths full of much oblige, the eternal unsatisfied longings. There seems to be a monotonous melancholy, an animal sadness running through all Negro jazz that is almost terrible at times.[32]

The staged confrontation with "animal sadness" at the intersection of meaning and feeling—deliberative stylization and "monotonous melancholy"—promises neither a present nor a prospective final triumph over the existential blues mood. Temporary triumphs over the pull of some unknown "animal sadness" promise a different, but not insubstantial, kind of relief. In contending that the sadness of the blues was "not softened by tears but hardened with laughter," Hughes suggested that the "animal sadness" motivating the blues was interminable and immune to any perfected sublimation of grief or melancholy. At such moments, Hughes's interpretation of the blues grants no redeeming glimpse at a transfigured future. The contrast with Du Bois's dialectical and ultimately utopian interpretation of the "sorrow songs" as a catalyst to social transformation is striking.

"I think we would all agree," Locke stated, "that the spirituals symbolize, as nothing else can do, our racial past. They are as well the taproot of our folk music."[33] Hughes located the spirituals rurally, as "born in camp meetings and remote plantation districts," and he represented the blues as "*city* songs rising from the crowded streets of big towns, or beating against the lonely walls of hall bed-rooms when you can't sleep at night." Hughes's depiction of the blues as urban was not absolutely accurate, since the blues had begun as a rural form and new rural variants regularly emerged. The exaggeration revealed more about his polemical intent than about the music. While Locke praised the spirituals as the preeminent symbol of the racial past, Hughes defended the blues as worthy symbols of the racial

8. Bessie Smith, 1936. Photo by Carl Van Vechten. Courtesy of Carl Van Vechten Trust.

present. The popularity of the "classic blues" in the 1920s struck Hughes as deeply symptomatic of black modernization and its cultural impact; blues divas like Bessie Smith, Clara Smith, and Mamie Smith, were selling records by the millions and offering inspiring new role models of success and independence for African American women. Although Hughes characterized the spirituals as "group songs" and the blues as "songs you sing alone," the genres' shared origin in collectively sung folk forms retained its imprint on the "classic blues" song form. Even when only one voice delivers the lyric, the generic structure of the blues lyric mimics, and often incites, a call-and-response exchange with the audience as a collective. Socialization and group communication imply themselves in the idiom's very form.

Locke contended in *The Negro and His Music* that the "dominant blues mood is a lament, beginning in a sentimental expression of grief or hard luck, sometimes ending on an intensification of the same mood and sometimes turned to ironical self-ridicule or fatalistic resignation. Self-pity tends to dominate."[34] Readers were to contrast the blues' recapitulation of unpleasant details for the sake of self-pity with the serene nobility of Locke's preferred subset of folk and concert spirituals and the "tragic vision" of Hughes's best poetry. In a stimulating discussion of Hughes's blues poetry, the literary critic Jahan Ramazani redescribed the spirituals/blues binary in similar, but more specifically Freudian, terms. The spirituals, he wrote, "tend to be poems of normative mourning, whereas the blues are typically melancholic, non-redemptive and anti-consolatory like many modern elegies."[35]

The Freudian binary of mourning and melancholia offers a useful theoretical perspective from which to compare Hughes and Locke's readings of the spirituals/blues contrast. As the central aesthetician of the Negro Renaissance, Locke implicitly called for the dialectical purification of the folk spirituals' expressive essence and the cancellation of their merely contingent idiomatic elements. If one were to follow the dialectical implications of self-overcoming in the Freudian model of "normative mourning," Locke's ideal of the New Negro spirituals would be to serve as secularized sites of collective mourning. Locke and others clearly approached the concert spirituals as retrospective monuments to the fading folk culture of the racial past. The pressing question was whether or not these newly styled compositions and performances were appropriate memorials. Did these surrogates give full aesthetic and moral justice to the past? Hughes's interpretation of the melancholic grief of the blues disrupted the uplifting dialectic of New Negro affirmation with an alternative paradigm for celebrating the blues as racially representative. As "today songs," the blues inspired no idealism "looking toward heaven, tomorrow, and God." Hughes's readings of formal mastery in the blues and the idiom's "absurd, incongruous laughter" highlighted an antidialectical trail for the reformulation of a black nationalist aesthetics. The emerging paradigm of a blues aesthetic would counter and eventually supersede the spirituals-based New Negro developmental narrative.

Sublimation and Whiteness

A critique of the "race toward whiteness" and a defense of jazz and the blues drove Hughes's manifesto "The Negro Artist and the Racial Mountain." Hughes pursued both themes again in a short story, "The Blues I'm Playing," published nearly a decade later. The story critiques "whiteness" through a satire of characteristically "white" and elite ideals of "art for art's sake" and sexual sublimation. It appeared in Hughes's first collection of short stories, *The Ways of White Folks* (1934), a title that alludes to Du Bois's *The Souls of Black Folk* and to Du Bois's rumination on "The Souls of White Folk" in *Darkwater* (1920). Hughes's stories offer portraits of white racial privileges in America and their bitter consequences for African Americans. Although only "The Blues I'm Playing" will be discussed here, the collection of stories approaches whiteness less as a transhistorical racial identity (a relevant comparison might be Du Bois's 1896 manifesto, "On the Conservation of Races") than as a historically specific set of class-coded beliefs and practices. Du Bois, it should be noted, also took a historical approach to whiteness and its connection to imperialism in *Darkwater.*

The historian David Roediger has argued that whiteness "describes not a culture . . . but precisely the absence of culture." As an abstract and ethnically nonspecific blank screen, the essence of whiteness emerges as "the empty and therefore terrifying attempt to build an identity based on what one isn't and on whom one can hold back."[36] *The Ways of White Folks* follows Hughes's comments on "Nordicism" from "The Negro Artist and the Racial Mountain" to portray whiteness as something more, although perhaps not much more, than an "absence of culture." Criticizing the rare book in which whites rather than blacks suffer the pitfalls of stereotyped characterizations, Sherwood Anderson complained about how "the Negro people in these stories of his are so alive, warm, and real" while "the whites are all caricatures." Anderson, the author of *Dark Laughter* (1925) and no stranger to racial romanticism, protested that Hughes granted "life, love, laughter, [and] old wisdom all to the Negroes and silly pretense, [and] fakiness, pretty much all to the whites."[37] The one-dimensional quality of the book's white characters serves Hughes's polemical purpose; as caricatures, they bring to life certain broad-based ideological mystifications flowing from race and class hierarchies. Through a series of deceptively simple stories, *The Ways of White Folks* exposes racial mystifications clouding the social vision of many putatively nonracist white Americans. E. C. Holmes noted in his enthusiastic review for *Opportunity* that Hughes, enlightened by a new "class approach," did "not mean all white folks" in his indictment. Instead, Hughes only targeted "those white people who in their control, circumscribe and influence the lives of the Negro masses." "Taken together," Holmes concluded about the short stories, "they show an indictment against the decadences of capitalistic society."[38] Hughes wrote the stories during and after a year-long visit in 1932 to the Soviet Union, and they reflected the spirit captured in his book of poetry *Good Morning, Revolution* (written in 1933 but published in 1938).[39]

"The Blues I'm Playing" charts a relationship between two women in New York City, Oceola Jones, a young black pianist, and Dora Ellsworth, an older white philanthropist. (To capture the story's tone, I will follow the narrator's practice of referring to the pianist by her first name and to the patron as "Mrs. Ellsworth.") The childless and widowed Mrs. Ellsworth develops a strong interest in Oceola and intends to craft a new career path for the pianist, one exclusively aimed toward European concert music. Though thankful for the financial support, Oceola resists the much older woman's intrusiveness from the beginning. She studies classical music in Paris for several years at Mrs. Ellsworth's expense, but she refuses to divorce herself from her native African American musical and social worlds. Tensions between patron and artist escalate, and the affirmative power of the blues emboldens Oceola to part ways with Mrs. Ellsworth. Oceola, doubly cursed by her patron's dogmatic traditionalism in musical matters and unconscious erotic fixation on the pianist's blackness, will carve her own unpredictable career path without the white benefactor's interference.

The story opens with Oceola Jones, a Wilberforce College graduate and the child of professional musicians from Mobile, Alabama, at work in Harlem. She plays European classical pieces for church services (perhaps requested by the kind of elite black congregations excoriated in "The Negro Artist and the Racial Mountain"), rehearses a church choir, and gives private lessons. In addition to her active professional schedule, she enjoys playing blues and jazz styles at Harlem rent parties. Shortly after being introduced to each other by a music critic, Oceola and Mrs. Ellsworth intuit an imperfect pairing but forge ahead in a patron-pupil relationship. "Mrs. Ellsworth had the feeling that the girl mistrusted her generosity, and Oceola did—for she had never met anybody interested in pure art before. Just to be given things *for art's sake* seemed suspicious to Oceola."[40] Oceola's skepticism proves well-founded when Mrs. Ellsworth demands sacrifices in exchange for financial support. Her philanthropic generosity "for art's sake" is always a carefully monitored investment, never an outright gift. Obsessed with the idea that "pure art" demands undistracted creativity, Mrs. Ellsworth discourages Oceola from seeing her Harlem roommate and lover Pete Williams. Williams plans to attend medical school in Nashville and hopes to marry Oceola.

Mrs. Ellsworth imagines her patronage to be motivated solely by an abstract ideal of "pure art"; in reality, she takes more pleasure in sharing "her richness with beauty" than she is willing to admit to anyone, including herself. Thus, the narrator reports that Mrs. Ellsworth "was sometimes confused as to where beauty lay—in the youngsters or in what they made, in the creators or the creation." She provides a stipend with the expectation that Oceola will study and practice nothing but the European classical repertoire and "no longer have to take in pupils or drill choirs or play at house parties." The stipend is also given "so Oceola would have faith in art, too."[41] Certain that the Harlem environment is inappropriate for Oceola's artistic development, Mrs. Ellsworth wants to relocate Oceola to Greenwich Village. Oceola accepts the offer and moves downtown alone, but she is not easily converted to Mrs. Ellsworth's near-religious devotion to classical music. "She no longer had pupils or rehearsed the choir, but she still loved to play for Harlem house parties—for nothing—now that she no longer needed the money, out of sheer love of jazz. This rather disturbed Mrs. Ellsworth, who still believed in art of the old school, portraits that really and truly looked like people, poems about nature, music that had soul in it, not syncopation." Mrs. Ellsworth steps up her efforts to limit Oceola's contact with Harlem social life and the world of syncopated music. For the sake of "pure art," the older woman organizes trips for the two women highlighted by special moments meant to facilitate Oceola's aesthetic and spiritual conversion. On one occasion, the patron takes the pianist on a trip to the mountains "where Oceola could look from the high places at the stars, and fill her soul with the vastness of the eternal, and forget about jazz."[42] By maximizing the physical distance between Oceola and Harlem, however temporarily, Mrs. Ellsworth hopes to fill the pianist's "soul with the vastness of the eternal." But even when Oceola spends two years in Paris studying classical piano at the patron's expense, she regularly plays the blues at parties and cabarets that evoke what she remembers as Harlem's insuperable joie de vivre.

Acting in a characteristically self-deceiving "way of white folks," Mrs. Ellsworth misrecognizes designs that she has on the attractive young pianist. These designs stray far from the pure disinterestedness of aesthetic contemplation. The patron's official and conscious position is that Oceola must "learn to sublimate her soul" and separate herself from the man, the home, and the popular music she loves; Pete Williams, Harlem, and the blues are all impeding Oceola's success in sublimation and art-making.[43] Oceola's erotic life, according to Mrs. Ellsworth, must shift away from intimacy with her longtime sexual partner and other "low" pleasures and be sublimated or rechanneled into the pursuit of "pure art."

Sketching his psychoanalytic thesis about sublimation, Sigmund Freud contended that "the origins of artistic activity" sprang from a process of sublimation in which "excessively strong excitations arising from particular sources of sexuality . . . find an outlet and use in other fields."[44] Freud's influential notion was that a kind of hydraulic libidinal circuit could detach and then shift a charge of excitation from the "lower," more animalistic, sources of libidinal attachment to the "higher," more refined, activities constitutive of advanced "civilization." The circuit of sublimation flowing between base, animalistic, and antisocial desire and refined, idealized, and pro-social activity powered the motor of artistic activity. The notion of desublimation maintains the model of a libidinal circuit but reverses the flow's direction. As we have seen, Du Bois and Locke frequently criticized exoticizing transvaluations of the "natural Negro" and adjacent primitivist detours from the civilizing promise of a cosmopolitan and antiracist "kingdom of culture." "When we have learned to channel down our emotional power, to run it through a cylinder," James Weldon Johnson argued similarly in a 1923 commencement address at Hampton Institute, "it will be transformed into great music, poetry, literature, and drama." Johnson complained that the Negro's "greatest God-given endowment . . . our emotionalism . . . is being recklessly dissipated in loud laughter, boisterous dancing, and a general good time."[45] Hughes did not accept his elders' idealistic campaign for racial uplift through sublimation and his antibourgeois polemics only grew sharper in the radicalized context of the 1930s.

The shifting emphases of Hughes's work, however, "constituted no giant ideological step for the poet," as Richard Barksdale has effectively shown.[46] E. C. Holmes concluded that Hughes's "ability to generalize" in *The Ways of White Folks* was "characteristic of his anti-bourgeois outlook. This characteristic enables him to apply his scalpel to Negroes and whites alike."[47]

"The Blues I'm Playing" takes up the question of whether the libidinal circuit of sublimation could ever so regulate itself as to work at full efficiency, assimilating all surplus excitation and undirected desire without waste or residue. When Mrs. Ellsworth reflects on what makes Oceola particularly appealing as a beneficiary of her largesse, she fixates on the pianist's "rich velvet skin, and such a hard young body!" A comic treatment of Ellsworth's erotic investment and self-deception appears when the women share a bed. On one occasion, the patron reads "aloud Tennyson or Browning before turning out the light, aware all the time of the electric strength of that brown-black body beside her, and of the deep drowsy voice asking what the poems were about." What the patron imagines as the arousing idealism of romantic poetry mediates and displaces her racialized and altogether corporeal fascination with Oceola's body. On the one hand, Mrs. Ellsworth proscribes sexual behavior for "art's sake." On the other hand, she experiences proximity to the "electric strength of that brown-black body" as inexplicably thrilling. "Mrs. Ellsworth couldn't recall ever having known a single Negro before in her whole life," the narrator explains, "so she found Oceola fascinating. And just as black as she herself was white." Simply fascinated by Oceola's "brown-black body," Mrs. Ellsworth feels compelled to reshape the pianist's musical vision to conform to the most extreme demands of whiteness in terms of an ideological agenda of sublimation and disembodied, etherealized "pure art." The white woman's aesthetic Manicheanism and displaced erotic fixation on the pianist's body reveal her racialized self-deception. A tangle of confusions "as to where beauty lay" and an implicit critique of the model of sublimation as a fully efficient circuit contradict the white patron's stern commitment to "pure art." Unconvinced by Mrs. Ellsworth's passion for sublimation, Oceola wonders to herself, "Why did white folks think you could live on nothing but art?"[48] Oceola's faux naive question clarifies the satire of bourgeois notions of sublimation in "The Blues I'm Playing."

The musical battleground of Oceola's resistance to Mrs. Ellsworth speaks directly to the Renaissance debate over musical evolution, cultural authenticity, and the concert spirituals. Indeed, Oceola's reasoning nearly replicates Hughes's position, as stated in "The Negro Artist and the Racial

Mountain" and other texts. The narrator's explanation in "The Blues I'm Playing" for Oceola's lack of interest in Mrs. Ellsworth's aesthetic of sublimation is of particular interest.

> Music, to Oceola, demanded movement and expression, dancing and living to go with it. She liked to teach, when she had the choir, the singing of those rhythmical Negro spirituals that possessed the power to pull colored folks out of their seats in the amen corner and make them prance and shout in the aisles for Jesus. She never liked those fashionable colored churches where shouting and movement were discouraged and looked down upon, and where New England hymns instead of spirituals were sung. Oceola's background was too well-grounded in Mobile . . . and the Sanctified churches where religion was a joy, to stare mystically over the top of a grand piano like white folks and imagine that Beethoven had nothing to do with life, or that Schubert's love songs were only sublimations.[49]

Mrs. Ellsworth's exclusive program of classical study fails to weaken Oceola's attachment to sacred and secular black folk music. Classical training only reinforces the appeal of the folk spirituals, blues, and jazz. For Oceola, it is a liberating appeal that calls for something distinct from etherealizing sublimation in music. "In her playing of Negro folk music, Oceola never doctored it up, or filled it full of classical runs, or fancy falsities. In the blues she made the bass notes throb like tom-toms, the trebles cry like little flutes, so deep in the earth and so high in the sky that they understood everything." Although Oceola finds pleasure in listening to and playing European classical music, she never reaches Ellsworth's ideal state, a state of consciousness the patron finds not only desirable but compulsory. Formal European music does not make Oceola's soul float "on clouds of bliss," nor is she ever overcome with the disembodied impression of a soul elevated and adrift in the "vastness of the eternal."[50] Instead, the pianist maintains her earlier belief that the most joyous music demanded not silent immobilization for the sake of solitary contemplation, but "movement and expression, dancing and living to go with it."

Oceola's ecstatic performances of Negro folk music follow the music "high in the sky" but also, and perhaps more importantly, "deep in the earth." It is in overlooking the second imperative that Mrs. Ellsworth's idealistic aesthetic fails; it cannot recognize the imaginative value of the blues' emphasis on corporeality or the dance-based rhythms that rapturously transport Oceola's body and soul to a place "deep in the earth." At their final meeting, Oceola responds to Mrs. Ellsworth's protests by taking to the piano; "her fingers began to wander slowly up and down the keyboard, flowing into the soft and lazy syncopation of a Negro blues, a blues that deepened and grew into rollicking jazz, then into an earth-throbbing rhythm."[51] The "earth-throbbing rhythm" of Oceola's blues challenges Mrs. Ellsworth's understanding of how spirit and eros relate to one another. Oceola's earthbound blues and "rollicking jazz" summon the patron's thwarted desire to dominate and redirect the "electric strength of that brown-black body" and send unexpected shock waves through Mrs. Ellsworth's frail frame. As was the case with "The Negro Artist and the Racial Mountain," Hughes's story short-circuited bourgeois ideals of whiteness and civilization on the cultural battleground over the less respectable and more joyously corporeal idioms of "Negro folk music."

In preferring the "rhythmical Negro spirituals" and avoiding the importation of "fancy falsities," Oceola echoes Hughes's critique of the "race toward whiteness." Superfluous hybridizations or "fancy falsities" would only diminish the integrity of folk idioms. Although formally trained, the pianist preserves differences between "rhythmical Negro spirituals" and "New England hymns." She does not blend the idioms together, but instead deliberately shifts between the blues, spirituals in the form of "a syncopated variation from the Sanctified Church," and the classical European repertoire.[52] Her musical life, in a sense, is that of a pluralist fluent in the alternative idioms of disparate cultures. Her approach tends toward cultural purism insofar as she eschews the hybridizing path of reframing folk idioms to match expectations for self-consciously cosmopolitan formal music. Oceola's pluralism and relative purism do not, however, prevent her from appropriating and mastering classical European repertoire and training. Locke's publicity on behalf of concert spirituals and New Negro musical hybrids must have struck Hughes as too aggressive, anxious, and overdetermined by bourgeois notions of racial uplift. Hughes's collaborations with James P. Johnson (Hughes wrote the libretto for the "folk opera" *De Organizer*), William Grant Still (Hughes wrote the libretto for Still's opera *Troubled Island*), and his later collaborations with such modern jazz masters as Randy Weston, Max Roach, and Charles Mingus made clear, however, that he was not afraid of adventurous hybrids of music and poetry.

Rather than making an urgent priority out of the seamlessly blended folk-formal hybrid, Hughes more often shifted between alternative registers. A prominent example of how this code-switching can take place occurs in his poem "The Weary Blues."[53] The narrator recalls a blues performance he witnessed the night before. The poem demonstrates how Hughes sometimes deliberately straddled "the discursive gap between literary and 'folk' culture." "The Weary Blues" marks that "discursive gap" in its explicit shifts from the narrator's standard English voice to the black vernacular of the blues singer. In Jahan Ramazani's view, the poem serves more generally as "an intricate meditation on the simultaneous distance and proximity between Hughes's blues poetry and blues song."[54] On the one hand, the nonelite blues singer inspires the narrator to his own "drowsy syncopated tune." On the other hand, Hughes's poem contains within it a blues lyric identified with the singing representative of black oral tradition—the six lines that begin "I got the Weary Blues / And I can't be satisfied"—while the narrator's surrounding material does not have the form of a song lyric. Thus, the embedded blues lyric carries its own unmistakable rhythm and diction and is not seamlessly fused with the substance and form of the narrator's response.

"The Weary Blues" captures a symptomatic kind of doubleness in Hughes's artistic stance as a New Negro. He argued for the developmental integrity of black folk cultural idioms (as with Oceola's antihybridizing protest against "fancy falsities") even as he crafted literature that could only encourage further elite appropriations of folk idioms. Hughes made the case for the integrity of the blues lyric form in the blues poems that appeared in *Fine Clothes to the Jew*. In that volume, the blues lyrics stand alone and no longer appear embedded within a double-voiced context. While Hughes's implicit argument may have been that blues artists and other creators of "Negro folk-songs," past or present, did not depend on elite New Negro appropriation and hybridization for artistic validation, the volume nevertheless provides exactly that kind of validation. "No longer the intrusive amanuensis of 'The Weary Blues,'" Ramazani contends, "the poet discards the frame and vanishes behind various blues personae."[55] The "simultaneous distance and proximity" made explicit in the double-voiced framing of "The Weary Blues" appeared to evaporate in Hughes's later blues poems. Hughes continued to straddle the divide between black folk and formal culture as he crafted an alternative vision for black modernist art. As an unapologetic defender of the blues and jazz, he wanted "Negro folk-songs" to evolve at the pace set by their actual practitioners and consumers, not simply at the pace demanded by bourgeois cosmopolitans eager to speed up development. Moreover, Hughes did not restrict himself to an ideal of folk authenticity as premodern and rural, and hence endangered by the breakneck speed of black urbanization. Older, rural styles commanded no privilege of superior authenticity in his thinking.

For Hughes, the decisive modernity of the blues—the music he read as *"city* songs rising from the crowded streets of big towns"—in no way threatened its authenticity as folk music. When Hughes spoke against economic and cultural modernization and the changing black urban milieu, his motivation was not backward-looking. He eschewed rural nostalgia and instead embraced a populist urban radicalism aligned with the expansive 1930s left-wing coalition that Michael Denning has labeled the "cultural front."[56] Throughout his career, Hughes protested the injustices of urban working-class living conditions and what he considered to be the condescending alienation of the black middle class. As we have noted, many of the stories in *The Ways of White Folks* refracted his radicalized views on white racial and class privilege and the particular burdens of African Americans. Locke may have shared E. C. Holmes's Marxist conclusions about *The Ways of White Folks*, but he softened the point for readers of the *Survey Graphic*: "in most of the stories there is the double motif of the inconsistency of racial discriminations and the injustice of class lines, with frequent hints of the recent radical insistence that the two are below the surface closely related."[57] This "double motif" works together with veiled autobiographical references in "The Blues I'm Playing."

Hughes described Charlotte Osgood Mason as an elderly white woman both fascinated by the racial exoticism of blacks and eager to have them "stay true" to the natural exuberance and spirituality of their race. By 1930, the "Godmother's" condescending patronage had overwhelmed the benefits of the relationship, and Hughes cut himself loose. In "The Blues I'm Playing," Oceola's racial otherness, as "the blackest—and most interesting" beneficiary, inspires her white patron's investment. Mrs. Ellsworth, unlike Mrs. Mason, hoped to break her beneficiary's spirited commitment to "Negro folk music" in the name of European classical music and a bourgeois ideal of artistic sublimation. Mrs. Ellsworth remains a traditionalist who believes "in art of the old school, portraits that really and truly looked like people, poems about nature, music that had soul in it, not syncopation."[58] Hughes reversed the polarity of the patron's explicit aesthetic commitments in "The Blues I'm Playing," but he saw the maintenance of racial and class hierarchy as one of patronage's hidden costs in both cases. He pursued the association of racial and class hierarchy further elsewhere, as in his 1937 plea for interracial proletarian unity at the Second International

Writers Congress. Arguing that "we represent the end of race," Hughes concluded "the Fascists know that when there is no more race, there will be no more capitalism, and no more war, and no more money for the munitions makers, because the workers of the world will have triumphed."[59]

Unlike Hughes or his fictional creation Oceola Jones, Zora Neale Hurston had her own reasons for maintaining friendly relations with Mason. Hurston may have been Hughes's model for the Jones character.[60] "Born so widely apart in every way," Hurston wrote of her bond with Mason, "the key to certain phases of my life had been placed in her hand. I had been sent to her to get it. I owe her and owe her and owe her! Not only for material help, but for spiritual guidance."[61] One should presume a dose of ironic overstatement in Hurston's paean to Mason. The elderly patron reveled in Hurston's folk humor and unforgettable storytelling performances. The "spiritual guidance" that Mason gave was for Hurston to remain faithful to her roots in rural Southern life and to resist any devitalization of the rural black folk inheritance. Hurston turned away from the radical political priorities that inspired Hughes and others in the 1930s to keep their appointment with a transformed American landscape by swerving the "line of progress" through a path of Marxian protest and analysis. Hurston influenced future generations less by her political commitments than by hewing to a profoundly intimate rendezvous with the recent black Southern past. Focusing on the black world of the rural South that she knew best, her work offered a different path for memorializing the black folk inheritance.

"What We Really Mean By Originality"

As we have seen, the following was a prototypical Negro Renaissance question: to what extent did "fancy falsities" negate the presence of folk authenticity in concert spirituals? Locke referred to the 1933 Fisk Choir review by Olin Downes that left Du Bois incensed and argued that Downes "advises us rightly to sing in the Negro idiom and to lift it to the level of formal art." Setting aside Du Bois's sweeping condemnation of Downes's perspective, Locke responded, "it is easy to turn such good advice aside on the false interpretation of advising Negroes to stick to their own limited province. It is a deeper problem than this; that of developing a great style out of the powerful musical dialect we have."[62] All parties agreed that "elevating" black folk idioms through a mere imitation of European classical forms did a disservice to the folk music. The spirituals debate focused instead on distinguishing criteria of imitativeness, idiomatic corruption, and unoriginality in the stages of cosmopolitan development toward a new "great style."

In "Toward a Critique of Negro Music" (1934), Locke enumerated some things that had "blocked the fusion of classical forms with the Negro musical idiom when they have not resulted in an actual watering-down of these idioms by the classical tradition." Rather than a static or essentializing pluralism focused on racial homogeneity or unalterable cultural differences, dynamic hybridization informed his vision of musical cosmopolitanism. As chapter 3 detailed, the call for a seamless hybridization or "fusion of classical forms with the Negro musical idiom" was symptomatic of Locke's developmental perspective. He also asserted that "except in choral singing,—the one vein of Negro music inherently orchestral, there is yet a deep divide between our folk music and the main stream of formal music."[63] Locke viewed this "deep divide" not so much as the distance between a valley and a peak, but rather as a contrast between two impressive, but utterly dissimilar, mountains of value. The spirituals' "inherently orchestral" choral quality, he believed, could help bridge the gap between the folk forms and the "main stream of formal music." After the successes of Roland Hayes, Paul Robeson, Marian Anderson, and other soloists, the spirituals' ultimate formal presentation required a triumphant return to the choral idiom, according to Locke.

If European classical forms overwhelmed the previously unstandardized "Negro musical idioms," the resulting hybrid would unilaterally dilute the folk idioms; uneven hybridic development contradicted Locke's demand for cultural reciprocity. He outlined his disappointment with the state of musical affairs in the mid-1930s when he asked readers to "remember that much has also fallen upon our own stony ground of shallow appreciation or been choked by the hostile thorns of a false and blighting academic tradition." "No musical idiom that has arisen from the people," he continued, "can flourish entirely cut off from the ground soil of its origin. Even in the sun of popular favor it is baked to an early death unless it has deep under it roots of vital nourishment."[64] Locke mobilized metaphors of fragility in describing folk music as raw "ground soil" and a "most precious musical ore" for high art and in warning that "the sun of popular favor" might bake the folk idioms "to an early death."

The valley of commercial music, a "deep divide" between the peaks of folk and concert music, constituted a threatening transitional space for Locke. African American musicians were masters "so far as the execution or performance" of folk-rooted black music was concerned, but he doubted "whether the Negro has yet become an undisputed master in the creative composition of music based on his native racial idiom and tradition."[65] The ultimate artistic challenge, Locke assumed, rested not in interpretation but in formal composition. "The Negro's admitted excellence in song," he wrote, "has not been an unmixed musical blessing." The hypertrophic "emphasis on the interpretative rather than the creative aspect of musical art" reversed the valence of a putatively flattering racial stereotype into a desultory sign of lack. "The public still expects the Negro to sing and dance principally. In fact prejudice has seriously handicapped the Negro musically, even through admitting his special musical aptitude."[66] Performance, interpretation, and improvisation figured for Locke as secondary aspects of creativity and originality, aspects dependent on prior material.

Zora Neale Hurston fully embraced the notion of a black gift for musical interpretation and performance and argued that musical performance, interpretation, and improvisation were primary aspects of creativity. Her powerful 1934 essay, "Characteristics of Negro Expression," inverted the desultory idea of interpretation as secondary or inferior. Interpretation and imitation, she insisted, were neither secondary to, nor even distinct from, originality in its truest sense.

> What we really mean by originality is the modification of ideas. . . . So if we look at it squarely, the Negro is a very original being. While he lives and moves in the midst of a white civilization, everything that he touches is re-interpreted for his own use. . . . Everyone is familiar with the Negro's modification of the whites' musical instruments, so that his interpretation has been adopted by the white himself and then re-interpreted. In so many words, Paul Whiteman is giving an imitation of a Negro orchestra making use of white-invented musical instruments in a Negro way. Thus has arisen a new art in the civilised world, and thus has our so-called civilisation come. The exchange and re-exchange of ideas between groups.[67]

Interpretation and the "modification of ideas" deserved no less claim to originality than the exaggerated ideal of autotelic and primordial creativity. Hurston's attentiveness to "characteristically Negro" techniques of revisionary interpretation in her ethnographic and fictional writings blazed an important alternate path for approaching African American expressivity. Henry Louis Gates's landmark work of literary criticism, *The Signifying Monkey* (1987), offered a particularly influential postmodern appropriation and revision of Hurston's theory of originality. In the book, Gates explicitly follows Hurston's lead in claiming that "Imitation is the Afro-American's central art form." "For Hurston," Gates explains, "the distinction between originality and imitation is a false distinction, and for the black writer to suffer under the burden of avoiding repetition, revision, or reinterpretation is to succumb to a political argument that reflects a racist subtext."[68] *The Signifying Monkey* contains intertextual readings of African American literary landmarks (including Hurston's *Their Eyes Were Watching God*, Ralph Ellison's *Invisible Man*, Ishmael Reed's *Mumbo Jumbo*, and Alice Walker's *The Color Purple*). Gates's virtuosic interpretations detail how these literary texts revise and comment on preceding texts in the African American tradition: the individual talent finds his or her own voice through a critical, often ironic, engagement with the tradition. In turn, formal literary practices that can be generalized recapitulate and revise vernacular practices of competitive commentary (e.g., "the dozens") and parodic signifying, or what Gates labels "signifyin(g)." Thus, Gates's canonizing theory of the African American novel is not a mere transplanting of European formalist criticism, most particularly the techniques of deconstruction much in fashion during the 1980s. His theory is instead a hybrid partly based on native African American oral practices. The vernacularist theory propounded in *The Signifying Monkey* reaches toward a Lockean cosmopolitan goal through a postmodernist exegesis of Hurston's approach to black orality. This chapter will return later to Hurston's posthumous career, but first we should examine her arguments in the context of Renaissance debates.

Hurston addresses revisionary imitation and the "modification of ideas" in "Characteristics of Negro Expression" as emblems of the "will to adorn." The adornment practices in home decoration, oral traditions, dancing, and music outlined by Hurston constitute a vernacular aesthetic among African Americans in the rural South. Unlike Locke's decidedly classical ideals of restraint, austerity, and harmonic resolution, the additive impulse toward pastiche in the "will to adorn" suggests to Hurston that "there can never be enough of beauty, let alone too much." Accordingly, music situated within Hurston's black vernacular aesthetic interweaves parts and voices without submerging their disparate elements into a seamlessly unified product.

Hurston contributed "Characteristics of Negro Expression" and "Spirituals and Neo-Spirituals" to Nancy Cunard's landmark 1934 anthology, *Negro*. In both essays, Hurston pitted African-rooted techniques of improvised variation, rhythmic asymmetry, harmonic angularity, and tonal impurity in the black folk spirituals against the scored-through composition, rhythmic regularity, harmonic symmetry, and idealized tonal purity of European-style concert music. Referring to the scored compositions of Harry Burleigh and Nathaniel Dett and performance styles of the Fisk Jubilee Singers and other black college groups, Hurston refused any attribution of black cultural authenticity to the arranged spirituals; hence the "neo-" label. "There never has been a presentation of genuine Negro spirituals to any audience anywhere," she declared unequivocally. "What is being sung by the concert artists and glee clubs," she continued, "are the works of Negro composers or adaptors *based* on the spirituals." New Negro proponents of the concert spiritual saw transcription and formalization as a way to both salvage and elevate the fragments of a fading folk culture in the tumultuous wake of modernization. Hurston begged to differ. "Contrary to popular belief," she asserted, the folk spirituals' "creation is not confined to the slavery period. Like the folk tales, the spirituals are being made and forgotten every day."[69] She therefore regarded formalized adaptations as musically inferior and deleterious to the proper memorialization of the folk inheritance. The concert spiritual was a "conservatory concept," she wrote elsewhere, in which the real spirituals "are twisted in concert from their barbaric rhythms into Gregorian chants and apocryphal appendages to Bach and Brahms."[70]

If the true folk spirituals were not obsolete, then the projects of transcription and concert formalization represented far more than a salvaging response to inevitable modernization. Hurston rejected the mainstream New Negro surrogation of the folk spirituals as a harmful appropriation performed for the sake of middle-class uplift and a misguided narrative of cosmopolitan evolution. She singled out Du Bois's politically charged interpretation of the mood and message of the spirituals as especially misinformed. The "idea that the whole body of spirituals are 'sorrow songs' is ridiculous," Hurston countered. The real spirituals "cover a wide range of subjects from a peeve at gossipers to Death and Judgment."[71] By labeling the "sorrow songs" as but another subgenre of spirituals, Hurston wanted to shift the spirituals' symbolic and emotional valence away from the solemn Du Boisian project of memorializing the inhumanities suffered during slavery. Hurston's critique of Du Bois's "sorrow songs" paradigm also reflected how her ethnographic and creative interests merged with her anti-collectivist campaign against what she called the "school of sobbing Negrohood." Du Bois undoubtedly struck Hurston as the prime mover in that "school." From her perspective, he and other critics of racial and economic injustice were responsible for a monolithic and dehumanized image of the African American as a tragic victim of racism. "I have seen that the world is to the strong regardless of a little pigmentation more or less," Hurston responded in 1928.[72] She considered much of the spectrum of African American political critique, moral uplift, and economic empowerment strategies polluted by either urban middle-class biases or political radicalism. Her response was to eschew the various campaigns for critique and improvement and instead to defend the resiliency, self-sufficiency, and undiminished humanity of African American folk culture in the Deep South. Personal memories of growing up in the all-black town of Eatonville in rural Florida energized her revisionist agenda for rescuing black folk culture from its "false friends."

There is a revealing tension between Hurston's sense of originality as revisionary imitation and the more demanding standard of folk authenticity in her critique of the "neo-spirituals." To contrast genuine folk spirituals against inauthentic "neo-spirituals" merely "*based* on the spirituals" presumed a special qualitative gap between the two idioms. The contrast put her apparently fluid definition of originality as "the modification of ideas" under pressure; more precise calibrations of originality and authentic "modification" were called for. If imitations or variously modified copies, properly understood in their originality, constituted the very fabric of black cultural distinctiveness, how could a critic go about condemning anything as lacking in originality (including the concert spirituals)? In short, Hurston's outline of a vernacular aesthetic of originality as the revisionary "modification of ideas" might be distinguished from the more protectionist folk purism that she expressed elsewhere. Gates's postmodernist interpretation, for example, appropriated key themes of Hurston's vernacular aesthetic but reshaped them to fit a relatively porous and nonprotectionist approach toward folk purity and cultural authenticity.

"Spirituals and Neo-Spirituals" begins its denial of authenticity to the "neo-spirituals" by contrasting an idea of unmediated and raw expressivity with an idea of aesthetic meaning as necessarily mediated through artifice and self-conscious formalization. To this end, Hurston points to the informality, exuberance, and spontaneity of authentic black folk singing as qualities antithetical to the "neo-spirituals." "*Negro songs to be heard truly must be sung by a group, and a group bent on expression of feelings and not on sound effects.*" The expressive dimension of the folk church service begins to take on the appearance of anarchic spontaneity. "The real Negro singer cares nothing about pitch," Hurston clarifies. "The first notes just burst out and the rest of the church join in—fired by the same inner urge. Every man trying to express himself through song. Every man for himself. Hence the harmony and disharmony, the shifting keys and broken time that make up the spiritual." An apparent communal indifference to pitch and an "every man for himself" mood help in generating an idiomatically distinctive effect of "jagged harmony." The specific conditions of spontaneous production within the church service give "jagged harmony" its status as an authenticating characteristic of real spirituals. "The jagged harmony is what makes it [the folk spiritual], and it ceases to be what it was when this is absent. Neither can any group be trained to reproduce it. Its truth dies under training like flowers under hot water."[73] Hurston strategically overstates the contrast between "the expression of feeling" and the presentation of "sound effects," with the former's suggestion of a complete absence of formalization in the real folk spirituals. She extends the hyperbole and claims that "the truth" of the folk spirituals "dies under training like flowers under water." In this case, the floral metaphor poses an unreproducibly organic religious event against an inauthentic artifact cut off from the sanctified context by the mediation of training and deliberation. The contrast with Locke's language of organic development is striking.

Hurston did not shrink from the stereotype about black musical informality implicit in the dichotomy that set black expressivity and "feelings" against artifice and "training." Neither did she fully reinforce the stereotype; instead, as with the originality/imitation binary, she sought to deconstruct it. Her contention was that the "neo-spirituals" emphasized a distinct regime of musical "training" that was both less desirable and, for musicians in the vernacular tradition, less culturally and thus racially authentic. The essay's opening contrast between inauthentic "training" in the "neo-spirituals" and anarchic informality in the performance of authentic spirituals silently passed over the role of aesthetic form in the sanctified church. The essay's second half, however, clarified the distance between an imagined artlessness in unmediated informal expressivity and the specific formal aesthetic practices of the black folk church. "Training," the cultivation of "sound effects," and formal rules emerge in the later part of Hurston's short essay not as definitive indices of European-style formalization but, rather, in their appropriate context as essential characteristics of "Negro expression."

The formal dimension resurfaces when Hurston points to the participatory call-and-response dynamic of the sermonic form. She notes the loosely scripted moments when the congregation sits in silence, responds with quick interjections, and finally "bears up" the preacher at the sermon's climax. Hurston extends the observation in order to pursue a more general claim about the black church.

> Beneath the seeming informality of religious worship there is a set formality. Sermons, prayers, moans and testimonies have their definite forms. The individual may hang as many new ornaments upon the traditional forms as he likes, but the audience would be disagreeably surprised if the form were abandoned. Any new and original elaboration is welcomed, however, and this brings out the fact that all religious expression among Negroes is regarded as art, and ability is recognised as definitely as in any other art. The beautiful prayer receives the accolade as well as the beautiful song. It is merely a form of expression which people generally are not accustomed to think of as art.[74]

The formulation about originality in the folk church as a matter of hanging "new ornaments upon the traditional forms" appears near the conclusion of "Spirituals and Neo-Spirituals." In pointing the reader's attention "beneath the seeming informality," the argument matches the perspective of "Characteristics of Negro Expression" regarding revisionary interpretation and the "will to adorn." Moreover, the argument directs the reader back to the emphasis on drama that opens "Characteristics of Negro Expression." Hurston's enduring interest was not with the theological or supernatural content or consequences of spiritual "possession." A professed religious skeptic, she most often focused not on what she called the "inner thing" but rather on the "definite forms" and "high drama" of the black folk church.[75] One should compare this emphasis on the dramatic appeal of vernacular forms, including the spiritual, with Du Bois's focus on the "internal" content of the "sorrow songs" as crystallizations of folk memory and a collective desire for liberation.

The conclusion of "Spirituals and Neo-Spirituals" ingeniously reverses the argument with which it began. Hurston critiqued the formalization and "sound effects" of the inauthentic "neo-spirituals," but she ultimately sketched an alternative model of formal self-consciousness and the production of "sound effects" in authentic "Negro expression." Far from the anarchic spectacle of "every man for himself," a host of "definite forms" shape the church service into a highly stylized aesthetic event. The preacher both plans and improvises the prayers and sermon for emotional, doctrinal, and aesthetic values. Thus, in the matter of preaching, "ability is recognized as definitely as in any other art." Hughes made a similar rhetorical shift from the impression of informal performance and unbounded sincerity to the framing conditions of formalized idioms with regard to the blues in "The Negro Artist and the Racial Mountain," "The Weary Blues," and *Fine Clothes to the Jew*. Vernacular strategies of artifice and formalization provided an alternative to Locke's emphasis on "the fusion of [European] classical forms with the Negro musical idiom." For Hurston, folk storytellers, dancers, preachers, singers, and musicians were all self-conscious artists working within and constantly modifying a shared repertoire of aesthetic practices. "The truth is," she asserted, "that the religious service is a conscious art expression. The artist is consciously creating—carefully choosing every syllable and every breath."[76] Some of Hurston's pious consultants would have recoiled from her interpretative principles; she ironically shifted the most interior and religious ideals of spontaneity in spiritual "possession" into hyperaesthetic and self-conscious markers of formal structures. All claims to religious and supernatural truth-value in a sermon or prayer dissolved in her anthropological evaluations of sacred rituals as dramatic performances.

It is consistent with the idea of imitation as signifying modification that Hurston chose to amend and revise the folk stories she collected in order "to emphasize the esthetic significance of the folklore performance" rather than reproduce them through an attempted replica or social-scientific account.[77] Hurston's biographer, Robert Hemenway, notes that her "ambivalence about folklore study grew from her dual identity between 1925 and 1927 as academic researcher and creative artist. Before going to the field in 1927, she had relatively little difficulty in maintaining both identities." Actual field experience, however, clarified that "the type of reportorial precision required of the scientific folklorist bored Hurston; she was used to assimilating the aura of a place and letting that stimulus provoke her imagination."[78] In *Mules and Men* (1935), a monograph on black folklore in the rural South, Hurston described her return to Eatonville, Florida, after years in New York City. "It was only when I was off in college, away from my native surroundings," she wrote in the volume's introduction, "that I could see myself like somebody else and stand off and look at my garment. Then I had to have the spy-glass of Anthropology to look through at that."[79] As a college-educated ethnographer, she was at home with, but also distanced from, her consultants, while her native connection to Eatonville gave her a degree of access and trust unavailable to visiting white folklorists and ethnographers.

Always horrified at the prospect of flattening living folk traditions for the sake of artless and clinical scholarship, Hurston instead wanted to flesh out the traditions' inventiveness and cull their dramatic resonances. The training she received under Franz Boas while a student at Barnard College "provided more than an explanation for Eatonville's existence." Hemenway adds that the Boas training "also revealed how folklore could be preserved without transformation into conscious art." As Hurston saw it, no wrenching transformation was necessary; African American folk expression was not raw and uncooked, but had already achieved its own distinctive kind of aesthetic refinement. She saw highly articulate dramatic performances where many earlier observers saw only a "natural Negro" limited to raw emotionalism. According to Hemenway, Hurston assented to "the existence of particular cultural differences while simultaneously positing a basic sameness in the human condition." In shifting gears from the ethnographic "Eatonville Anthology" (1928) to the complex structure and lyrical narrative of *Their Eyes Were Watching God* (1937), among her other novels, she wanted to "maintain the integrity of black culture without sacrificing it to the mythical American melting pot."[80]

Hurston comments in "Characteristics of Negro Expression" that "decorating a decoration, as in the case of the doily on the gaudy wall pocket, did not seem out of place to the hostess." She also offers a pluralistic gloss to her comments on the "grotesque" pursuit of asymmetry and angularity. "We each have our standards of art, and thus are we all interested parties and so unfit to pass judgment upon the art concepts of others."[81] More often, however, Hurston's prevailing condemnation of cultural assimilationism among urban and urbanizing African Americans—the process she decries in *Dust Tracks on a Road* as the "flight from blackness"—drops any suggestion of pluralistic equanimity or value neutrality. Cultural modernization, spurred by unmistakable realities of rural-to-urban migration and new patterns of interracial contacts, threatened to eclipse black folk traditions with an assimilative integration into the Euro-American mainstream. From the vantage point of the urban New Negro cosmopolitanism publicized in the *Crisis* and *Opportunity*, the "neo-spirituals" laudably evidenced a petit bourgeois, African American intention to reinforce the continuity of a changing black culture through a proud memorialization of the slaves' perseverance and creativity. Hurston condemned such

New Negro memorialization as tantamount to burying black folk culture as it if was already dead. In announcing a very exacting folk standard of cultural authenticity, Hurston erected a firewall against what she interpreted as insidious assimilationism and destructive hybridization. On this important point, Hurston's conclusions markedly departed from those of Boas. Where Boas welcomed porous boundaries between cultures, Hurston underscored the threat of assimilation. Her sense of cultural authenticity in genuine folk expression, in other words, foreshortened the legitimating scope of the hybridic "exchange and re-exchange of ideas between groups."

Hurston's formulation about "the exchange and re-exchange of ideas" in "Characteristics of Negro Expression" appeared in the course of an ambiguous comment on the white bandleader Paul Whiteman. Hailed in the press of the 1920s as the "King of Jazz," Whiteman was the chief proponent of the hybridic "symphonic jazz" idiom. Hurston turned Whiteman's self-image on its head; while Whiteman aspired to bourgeois respectability as an original artist who was elevating jazz into a formal concert music, Hurston wrote that he was "giving an imitation of a Negro orchestra making use of white-invented musical instruments in a Negro way." Playing on the ambiguities of the term "imitation," the comment seemed to deny the value or originality of the innovations that Whiteman symbolized (Duke Ellington, by contrast, later named Whiteman an influence on—and a popular rival for—his own "symphonic jazz" projects). The standard logic of the elite appropriation of subcultural expressive forms followed a unilinear "upward" direction; it was not, in short, a logic of reciprocal exchange. Hurston's notion of "the exchange and re-exchange of ideas" also seemed to flow in only one direction. But in her case that flow was in the unexpected "downward" direction of African American revisionary hybridization and the subcultural black appropriation of elite white forms. The point about imitation reinforced Hurston's pluralism and her skepticism toward arguments about hybridization that appeared to her as equivalent to Eurocentric assimilationism.

Hurston's strategies for defending the particular authenticity of rural black culture in the South met with searing criticisms from other members of the overwhelmingly male African American intellectual establishment. Many of the most prominent black intellectuals (including Hughes, Locke, Brown, Robeson, and Du Bois) took up political agendas, especially in the 1930s, far to the left of Hurston. Hurston rejected the activist pleas for economic and racial justice associated with the loose-fitting left-populist "cultural front," and she did not hold her tongue when she resisted the turn leftward among black modernists. She famously condemned Richard Wright's first book, *Uncle Tom's Children*, a cycle of short stories set in contemporary, small-town Mississippi. "Mr. Wright's author's solution, is the solution of the PARTY—state responsibility for everything and individual responsibility for nothing, not even feeding one's self. And march!"[82] Wright returned the critical volley in his stinging review of *Their Eyes Were Watching God*. Even Sterling Brown, the poet, critic, and educator who shared many of Hurston's passions as a conservator of black Southern folklore and music, criticized *Their Eyes Were Watching God* on social grounds in the pages of *Opportunity*. He argued that Hurston's Southern fiction smoothed over the realities of black anger and resentment and the poisonous atmosphere of violence that arose from institutionalized racial discrimination and peonage.[83]

Hurston's profoundly enigmatic autobiography, *Dust Tracks on a Road* (1942), suggested the extent of her self-identification as a politically nonaligned individualist determined to honor the folk legacy without recourse to political progressivism or propaganda. The book sang a unique swan song to a rural folk world she knew to be slowly fading; beneath that public swan song was Hurston's personal song of mourning and reparation for a mother whose passing had deeply traumatized her.[84] Hurston faithfully maintained her ambivalent rendezvous with the past for a variety of public and private reasons. Scholars and other readers continue to debate whether Hurston's strategy for memorializing and recuperating the voices of Southern black culture veered too close to a politically mute or nostalgic approach to the folk inheritance, or whether it effectively evaded the short-sighted blandishments of propaganda. Among her many defenders, Françoise Lionnet writes of Hurston's heroism in struggling "to be the voice of that occluded past, to fill the void of collective memory."[85] In a partial reconfiguration of Wright's critique, Hazel Carby has warned of the pitfalls of an uncritical celebration of Hurston's vision. Carby argues that Hurston's lyrical depiction of the rural folk world, despite its visionary feminism, romanticized a particular slice of black life and idealized it as an all but exclusive locus of African American cultural authenticity. To whatever extent this was the case, Hurston's artful repository of social memory and folk resources could harden into an antidevelopmental and purely retrospective archive. Thus Carby warned that the Hurston revival since the 1970s, though built on a progressive feminist edifice, could degenerate into the memorialization of a static and politically disengaged

cultural inheritance; such degeneration could silence the politically challenging, though nonfeminist, writings of Richard Wright and other black
modernists. To the question of whether or not Hurston's image of black
folk culture constructs a seductive ahistorical refuge from the challenges
of modernity, Carby answers in the affirmative. In one of her most forceful
criticisms of Hurston's politics of folk authenticity, Carby contends:

> Hurston's criticisms were not reserved for the elitist manner in which
> she thought the authentic culture of the people was reproduced. The
> people she wanted to represent she defined as a rural folk, and she mea-
> sured them and their cultural forms against an urban, mass culture.
> She recognized that the people whose culture she rewrote were not
> the majority of the population, and that the cultural forms she was
> most interested in reproducing were not being maintained. . . . When
> Hurston complained about "race records" and the commercialization
> of the blues, she failed to apply her own analysis of processes of cul-
> tural transformation. On the one hand, she could argue that forms of
> folk culture were constantly reworked and remade when she stated
> that "the folk tales" like "the spirituals are being made and forgotten
> every day." But, on the other hand, Hurston did not take seriously the
> possibility that African-American culture was being transformed as
> African-American peoples migrated from rural to urban areas.[86]

Hurston's model of "the exchange and re-exchange of ideas" presented
an image of black vernacular openness toward innovative hybridic creativity. An examination of her position in the debate over the spirituals shows
that such an exchange was to take place within a restricted, but never fully
articulated, continuum of the black folk tradition. The hybridizing cosmopolitanism of the Lockean New Negro, for example, betrayed Hurston's sense of the folk continuum and produced an inauthentic "musical
octoroon." The concert spiritual degraded rather than elevated the folk inheritance, she insisted, by squeezing "all of the rich black juice out of the
songs." Hurston's increasingly lonely campaign included a populist critique of elite New Negro assimilation but tended to silently pass over how
urban migration and proletarianization were also transforming the nonelite realms of African American culture. Unlike Hughes, Hurston did
not rush to embrace the "classic blues" of African American female entertainers of the 1920s. The ambivalence behind her ethnographic work revealed itself in an unpublished 1938 text for a work to be titled *The Florida
Negro*: "Folklore in Florida is still in the making. Folk tunes, tales, and

characters are still emerging from the lush glades of primitive imagination before they can be finally drained by education and mechanical inventions."[87] On the one hand, the hybridizing motors of "characteristically Negro" imitation, drama, and adornment fueled by the folk's "primitive imagination" were still running. On the other hand, salvage ethnography was necessary because the "folk tunes, tales, and characters" were dying at an even faster rate than they could be organically produced. For Hurston, the modernization of African American culture mostly implied a disenchanting eclipse of black distinctiveness. She regrettably concluded that such symbols of modernization as "education and mechanical inventions" spelled assimilative deracination rather than new hybridizing opportunities for authentic "Negro expression." The facts of her own education and artistic practice in these very years, however, suggested an alternative conclusion.

One of Hurston's responses to the "neo-spirituals" and other "ersatz Negro music," in which "the shadow became the man," was to produce what she considered a "real Negro concert." In 1932, after mounting several New York concerts featuring folk singers and Bahamian folk dancers, she felt "satisfied in knowing that I established a trend and pointed Negro expression back towards the saner ground of our own unbelievable originality."[88] Ten years later, she was certain that there had been "a sharp trend towards genuine Negro material."[89] In her own artistic practice, Hurston hoped to push the appropriation of the black folk inheritance away from the assimilationist "flight from blackness" and "back towards the saner ground of our own unbelievable originality." Her fiction, largely obsolete and out of print until the 1970s, not only looked backward but also helped push African American writing and criticism forward toward new horizons of both vernacular appropriation and cosmopolitan memorialization.

"The Rhythm of Segments"

"There is this fundamental difference between Negro dancing in Africa and America," Alain Locke wrote in The Negro and His Music. "The African dance is largely ceremonial and is associated with a fixed ritual. It is really primitive ballet. . . . Contrary to general belief, African dances are formally stylized and the tradition held for generations; they only appear to be improvised."[90] Readers familiar with Locke's "The Legacy of the Ancestral Arts" may have expected him to argue that African American dance was one more expressive realm where development would be hastened not by returning to "fixed ritual" but by taking lessons from African discipline and creativity. Instead, Locke took a complimentary approach to African American dancing in *The Negro and His Music*. He suggested that with the Negro

> dancing has always been a spontaneous and normal mode of expression rather than an artificial and formalized one. No matter how set the general pattern is, the Negro always improvizes as he dances, whether in solo or group dancing. Moreover, it is the typical Negro reaction to embroider whatever basic rhythm is set,—changing, doubling, skipping beats in a fashion bewildering to those less expert in rhythmic patterns and designs. . . . These subtle ways of varying the simplest of rhythmic patterns is the secret of their unusual and basic musical ability. Modern jazz and dance artists have proved that this art can be learned after close study and familiarity with Negro performers and dancers; however, experts usually detect a more mechanical regularity to even the best Anglo-Saxon imitations. Many think the Negro expression of rhythm inimitable in its naturalness, lack of self-consciousness, its freedom and technical assurance.[91]

Locke's imagery hews closely to Hurston's fecund insight in "Spirituals and Neo-Spirituals" about hanging "many new ornaments upon the traditional forms" without abandoning the basic forms. Sophisticated improvisational styles, in Locke's words, "embroider whatever basic rhythm is set." The parallel imagery was no mere coincidence. Locke was incorporating, but also restricting, Hurston's insights.

How, according to Locke, would the movement of jazz from a folk music through the stages of popular and formal music bear on the improvisational impulse? In the typical African American jazz band, he wrote, the "music comes alive from the activity of the group, like folk-music originally does, instead of being a mere piece of musical execution." The improvising jazz musician, according to Locke, summoned the informal conditions of folk music and the early folk purity of jazz. "Improvising," he continued, "is an essential trait of the genuine jazz musician: with the assurance that 'there is plenty more where it came from,' he pours his music out with a fervor and freshness that is unique and irresistible." The "essential trait" of improvisation in dance and music may have displayed the "typical Negro reaction," but Locke looked to advances in compositional formalization as indices of the consummatory stages of music as a fine art;

fully scored formalization might transcend an "essential trait" like improvisation, but it could still retain its authenticating links to the vernacular tradition. Earlier, the authenticity question had agitated Locke's argument in "The Negro Spirituals" for formalizing the spirituals in a manner that did not sacrifice their most valuable indigenous characteristics. The "titanic originality of the jazz orchestras," he concluded in *The Negro and His Music*, "has only to be harnessed and seriously guided to carry jazz to new conquests."[92]

Guardedly optimistic by the late 1930s about the long-term prospects of jazz, Locke rejected the developmental skepticism of Winthrop Sargeant's widely noted *Jazz: Hot and Hybrid* (1938). Locke wrote that he did "not share Mr. Sargeant's skepticism over the potential contributions of jazz and Negro folk music to music in the larger forms." Intermittently quoting Sargeant, Locke insisted that "jazz does not need to remain . . . even 'at its most complex' still 'a very simple matter of incessantly repeated formulas,' or even, as it is later 'most successful in the looser forms of ballet and opera, where music plays a subsidiary atmospheric role.'" As with the spirituals, jazz was only beginning to find its place in the folk-to-formal developmental narrative of much concert music. "Negro folk music, properly maturing, has the capacity to produce new musical forms as well as new musical idioms; that is indeed the task of the trained musician who has the sense and devotion to study seriously the folk music at its purest and deepest sources."[93] For Locke, the future of jazz was hopeful but precarious. A highly commercialized music at the peak of its popularity in the late 1930s, its artistic future depended on a studious devotion to its receding folk roots and a high-minded distance from the fickle demands of the popular music marketplace. The greatest contributions of jazz would have to wait for the future, Locke predicted, and the music's "capacity to produce new musical forms as well as new musical idioms."

Hurston's perspective on music was neither future-oriented nor oriented toward the "potential contributions of jazz and Negro folk music to music in the larger forms." The comprehensive formalization of improvised "rhythmic patterns and designs" was anathema to her for numerous reasons. "Characteristics of Negro Expression" includes a telling comment on the role of asymmetrical rhythm and the relation of parts to wholes in black vernacular music. "The presence of rhythm and lack of symmetry are paradoxical, but there they are. . . . it is the rhythm of segments. Each unit [in a performance] has a rhythm of its own, but when the whole is assembled it is lacking in symmetry. But easily workable to a Negro who is accustomed to the break in going from one part to another, so that he adjusts himself to the new tempo."[94] Both asymmetrical and orderly, the "rhythm of segments" imparts a formal coherence to dense rhythmic embroidery that Locke reported as "bewildering." Hurston posed her formulation about black vernacular music against the symmetrical rhythms and linear organization associated with Western classical music. The expectation of an asymmetrical "rhythm of segments," periodically punctuated by abrupt breaks, counters the dominant European ideal of unbroken thematic development in classical composition.

The cosmopolitan "path of progress" and the "line of human advance" toward a progressive future joined together Locke's social and aesthetic ideals. Hurston's dissenting emphasis on the "rhythm of segments" crystallized her challenge to far more than Locke's long-form ideals for black formal music. Although he did not refer to Hurston as a source, James Snead drew out some philosophical implications latent in the "rhythm of segments" in his 1984 essay, "Repetition as a Figure of Black Culture." "As European music uses rhythm mainly as an aid in the construction of a sense of progression to a harmonic cadence," Snead wrote, "the repetition has been suppressed in favor of the fulfillment of the goal of harmonic resolution." Snead's argument seizes on the prominence of the "cut" or "break" in black music in order to elaborate two contrasting visions of repetition. The regularity of a "cut" or "break" forestalls any semblance of unbroken thematic development. As such, it suggests an African-derived alternative to teleological notions of unbroken progress encoded in Hegelian dialectics and much Western classical music.

> In black culture, repetition means that the thing *circulates* . . . there in an equilibrium. In European culture, repetition must be seen to be not just circulation and flow but accumulation and growth. In black culture, the thing (the ritual, the dance, the beat) is "there for you to pick it up when you come back to get it." If there is a goal (*Zweck*) in such a culture, it is always deferred; it continually "cuts" back to the start, in the musical meaning of "cut" as an abrupt, seemingly unmotivated break (an accidental *da capo*) with a series already in progress and a willed return to a prior series. . . . In European culture, the "goal" is always clear: that which always is being worked towards. The goal is thus that which is reached only when culture "plays out" its history. Such a culture is never "immediate" but "mediated" and separated from the present tense by its own future-orientation.[95]

Snead's hypotheses about differences between "black culture" and "European culture" (with regard to music's place as a social text) help us to further elaborate Hurston's disagreements with Locke and Du Bois. Snead's Derridean animus against the vision of growth and progress in Hegelian dialectics is especially pertinent. Du Bois's sense of art's role in black liberation has been a reference point throughout our analysis. "Criteria of Negro Art" (1926) boldy outlined the future-oriented cast of Du Bois's criticism and his insistence on wedding black aesthetic work to a long campaign of progressive propaganda and activism directed toward a distant utopian fulfillment. Hurston, by contrast, argued that "literature and other arts are supposed to hold up the mirror to nature."[96] Du Bois's idealistic orientation toward matters of art and nature more closely approximates Snead's picture of "European culture," wherein "the 'goal' is always clear" as something "which is only reached when culture 'plays out' its history." The "sorrow songs" kept vital collective memories in circulation, according to Du Bois, and simultaneously memorialized a demand for liberation. The repetition and remembering of the "sorrow songs" thereby served the political goals of progressive transformation. Paul Gilroy has recently theorized a revised Du Boisian interpretation of music's place of prominence in the black Atlantic imaginary. *The Souls of Black Folk* strikes Gilroy as an especially resounding text because it speaks to "the project of liberating music from its status as a mere commodity and by the associated desire to use it to demonstrate the reconciliation of art and life, that is, by exploring its pursuit of artistic and even aesthetic experience not just as a form of compensation, paid as the price of an internal exile from modernity, but as the favoured vehicle for communal self-development." For Gilroy, the formal features of the "cut" or "break" in the popular music of the black Atlantic world (including such recent idioms as funk and hip-hop) do not conflict with a future-oriented "politics of transfiguration." He argues that popular music can offer the relatively immediate compensatory pleasure of circulation within an infectiously repetitive dance groove (what he dubs a "politics of fulfilment") as well as utopian anticipation of a better world in the future. The musically encoded "politics of transfiguration," Gilroy writes, "strives in pursuit of the sublime, struggling to repeat the unrepeatable, to present the unpresentable."[97] On this model, the musicalized "politics of transfiguration" takes place in a dramatic and performative dimension independent of a composition's manifest musical logic. Gilroy's theoretical conception of a "pursuit of the sublime" in black music fuses the power of musical remembrance to a utopian critique of the present; his model thus recalls and reconfigures Du Bois's dialectical suggestions about the "unvoiced longings" operative in the peculiar "double-consciousness" of the "sorrow-songs."

The New Negro, according to Du Bois and Locke, needed to mediate forward-looking social goals through a recuperation of black folk culture and the aesthetic triumphs of ancient African civilizations. Hurston's non-dialectical observations on the "will to adorn" and the "rhythm of seg-ments" found their most explicit postmodernist appropriation in Henry Louis Gates's rhetorical analyses of irony and "signifyin(g)" as revisionary doubling in *The Signifying Monkey*. The ethnomusicologist Ingrid Mon-son has expertly detailed how musical "signifying" operates in the practice of mainstream jazz improvisation. A musical variant of "signifying" is prevalent in the interpretation of "standards" (i.e., classic Broadway show tunes and popular songs by George Gershwin, Irving Berlin, Johnny Mercer, Cole Porter, and others, and the traditional repertoire of jazz com-positions by Ellington, Monk, Mingus, Coltrane, and others).[98] Monson follows Gates's lead and locates a characteristic style of black-coded "double-consciousness" in jazz improvisations that ironically comment or "signify" on prior interpretations and pieces from the standard jazz and show tune repertoire. An ethnographically detailed adaptation of Bakh-tin's rhetorical model of dialogics thus replaces the dialectical narrative of Du Boisian "double-consciousness." By revisiting the Renaissance debate over the spirituals, we are reminded of the important differences between the aesthetic views of Hurston, Du Bois, and others. "Gates's conceptual-ization of Du Bois's ideal of 'double-consciousness' as a 'repeated trope of dualism' . . . through the epiphaneous repetition of parodic doubling," Shamoon Zamir contends, "reenacts, in postmodern or Derridean guise, the drama of the divided self and of the transcendence of division through liberatory verbal gesture."[99] Zamir notes Gates's antidialectical revision-ism in order to warn readers against anachronistic interpretations of Du Bois's philosophical and political imagination.

Dialogical analyses of "parodic doubling" and ironic "signifying" need to be distinguished from more dialectical interpretations of "double-consciousness" in music. It can at least be agreed that the performance of a standard allows jazz musicians to manipulate an immensely pliable frame. Jazz improvisers proceed to hang their spontaneous compositions (as well as novel scored elaborations) on the standard's durable and flexible frame. Originality—or the spontaneous "modification of ideas"—emerges in the moment of performance out of the musicians' improvisational prowess.

Soloists lead with the call to a musical dialogue, hanging "new ornaments upon the traditional forms," while the accompanists actively respond with improvised challenges and unpredictable "commentaries" in a shared musical rhetoric. According to Monson, "at least part of the pride many African-American jazz musicians take in their versions of standards derives from their ability to 'upstage' the European-American versions of these tunes—something acknowledged by both black and white audiences. In asserting a musical 'superiority' even when measured against the (white) hegemonic standard, musicians make ironic the presumption of racial inferiority."[100] "Free jazz" playing (spontaneous improvisation with no basis in a prior score, tune, or schematic melody and chord "chart") bears a less obvious relationship to a dialogic model of African American "signifying," but the well-trained listener can still explicate the music's dialogic qualities despite the lack of an established score or frame. The musicologist Samuel Floyd has further demonstrated that the rhetorical analysis of musical compositions and performances in terms of African American traditions of "musical Signifyin(g)" can be applied to formal music in the African American tradition as well, including large-scale compositions that bear little obvious relation to vernacular sources. He approaches "the rhetorical use of preexisting material as a means of demonstrating respect for or poking fun at a musical style, process or practice through parody, pastiche, implication, indirection, humor, tone play or word play" as a point of commonality among all forms of African American music.

Floyd's elaboration of a dialogical model of "musical Signifyin(g)" gives a formal grounding to his valuable conclusion that "all black-music making is driven by and permeated with the memory of things from the cultural past and that recognition of the viability of such memory should play a role in the perception and criticism of works and performances of black music."[101] All of the Harlem Renaissance figures discussed in this chapter and preceding ones would have agreed with Floyd's statement about the memorializing function of African American music. Nevertheless, as the Hurston-Du Bois rift demonstrates, each of them had a distinctive approach to which "things from the cultural past" were to be remembered, how those things would be best memorialized, and the larger social implications of the various memorializing strategies. Contrasting visions of possible and desirable futures fueled divergent strategies for memorializing the musical past.

The presence of a singer or lyrics only renders more explicit the interpretive conventions of what Floyd calls "musical Signifyin(g)." In the case of instrumental performances of standards, the familiar lyrics are implied and thus available for musical commentary. A deliberately maintained tension between the song text and the improvising event—the subject matter and the content—is very often cultivated in jazz and blues music. Indeed, "repetition with a difference" (to borrow a term from Gates) in the form of ironic signifying pervades the improvised adornment strategies of African American popular music. The novelist Leon Forrest presented a trenchant reading of how one of the greatest jazz singers revealed "the true relationship between refinement and baseness" through a process legible in terms of "musical Signifyin(g)." Billie Holiday shaped her brilliant renditions of popular songs through a characteristic "modification of ideas" at once profoundly original and profoundly traditional. Forrest's essay does not address Hurston, Hughes, or the other critics and theorists discussed here, but his trenchant comments on "refinement" and "baseness" in Holiday's vocal art offer a venue for synthesizing several interlocking concerns and preparing readers for a concluding chapter on the Swing Era.

> Lady Day took the essentially Ofay Tin Pan Alley lyrics and made them raw, real, and on occasion regal, with her "sulphur-and-molasses voice". . . . She attempted—in the main—to strip these lyrics of their slurpy sentimentality and then polish them down until a deeper grain reflected up in the wood and revealed something of the true relationship between refinement and baseness, culled from her life, and her knowledge of human relations. Where there was a wrinkle of a water-mark, then let it be, Baby.[102]

The juxtaposition of the "'sulphur-and-molasses'" grain of Holiday's voice and the many blithely sentimental popular tunes she reconstructed—one thinks, for example, of "Sailboat in the Moonlight," "Pennies from Heaven," or "Them There Eyes"—offers a final twist to this chapter's exploration of vernacular strategies. Alain Locke's ideal of aesthetic sublimation as a seamless "fusion of classical forms with the Negro musical idiom" was ill-suited to appreciate Holiday's stylistic contribution to the vocabularies of jazz. "Where there was a wrinkle of a water-mark," Forrest affirms about Holiday's interpretive style, "then let it be, Baby." The form, subject matter, and content of a Holiday interpretation, in other words, did not blend to the point of undifferentiated unity; instead, she kept contrasting elements of "refinement" and "baseness" in a state of tension and irresolution. What Forrest calls "the true relationship between refinement and baseness" refuses the unearned promise of final resolution. He further

9. Billie Holiday, 1949. Photo by Carl Van Vechten. Courtesy of Carl Van Vechten Trust.

notes that Holiday's voice, like that of the gospel-rooted Ray Charles, epitomized "the grain or timbre in the African-American singing voice." Holiday's "singing voice," Forrest explains, "was a blend of the husky and the pure, one overlapping the other."[103] The grain of Billie Holiday's voice and its overlapping timbres represented a characteristically African American alternative to the European ideal of the beautiful singing voice. Holiday's grainy and distinctly nonoperatic voice never suggested a soul's breath set free, however briefly, from the accidental qualities of its material vessel.[104] Forrest tells us that although Holiday knew "spiritual hunger" well, her art remained deeply secular. "One hears in Billie's music very little if any of the cathartic cry that is so essential to the fervor of the religious Gospel utterance and shouting ecstasy," Forrest observes.

Holiday pioneered a different kind of vocal artistry in polishing a song until "a deeper grain reflected up in the wood." The wrinkles and knots of her performances and her vocal equipment revealed not artistic failure but her understanding of "the mysteries of love and life, race and loneliness."[105] "Song," Nathaniel Mackey suggests, "is both a complaint and a consolation dialectically tied to that ordeal." Hughes's reflections on the "eternal unsatisfied longings" in the blues can lead toward Forrest's points about Holiday and her representatively African American vocal grain. Hurston's reflections on the "great rigid forms" in the folk spirituals can lead toward Snead's points about the values of repetition and "the cut" in black culture. "Music," Mackey concludes, "is wounded kinship's last resort." One might imagine a point that stretches and separates into two line segments. Both segments push outward, create a curve, and nearly meet again. "If there is a goal (*Zweck*) in [black] culture," Snead reminds us, "it is always deferred." If a culture never "plays out" or consummates its history, Hughes and Hurston offered suggestive visions of something else—how a culture finds, recovers, or invents itself, in the course of playing and singing.

ϜΙϞϜ

Saving Jazz from Its Friends:

The Predicament of Jazz Criticism

in the Swing Era

The principle of nobility . . . achieves a kind of
consummation in the idea of the folk, for here
it strips itself of the outward conditions of
birth or fortune, discovering what is surpass-
ingly fine among the lowly and least favored,
thereby validating itself at the deepest levels.
—Robert Cantwell[1]

Although even the best colored bands rarely
acquire the gloss and cohesion that now
belong to Goodman's, they do have an
enthusiasm that is born of the fact that every
single man in the band would rather make
music than anything else in the world.
—John Hammond[2]

Zora Neale Hurston intended "Spirituals and Neo-Spirituals" to help save
the folk spiritual from those she considered to be its false friends. Her essay
cast a spotlight on the cultural divide separating the spiritual's function
in the sanctified church of rural black folk from the more Europeanized
hymns, spirituals, and liturgy of the middle-class urban black church. It
first appeared in Nancy Cunard's omnibus *Negro* anthology of 1934, nes-
tled among a wildly mixed set of texts. Essays, poems, and manifestoes by
white American and European surrealists and radicals jostled for attention

alongside essays by Hurston, Du Bois, Locke, and other African Americans. Although "Spirituals and Neo-Spirituals" offered no political commentary, its antibourgeois polemic must have appealed to Cunard's aristocratic radicalism and her ideas about the expressive authenticity of black proletarian and folk cultural life. Had Hurston been more explicit about her own antileftist perspective, the British heiress might have excluded her from the anthology.

Cunard's *Negro* anthology proved that Hurston's views on folk expression, black authenticity, and the perils of assimilation were eminently portable beyond the Harlem Renaissance context. As further proof of the essay's portability, the obscure British magazine *Jazz Music* (the self-described bulletin of the Jazz Sociological Society) reprinted "Spirituals and Neo-Spirituals" in 1943. The connoisseurial magazine was representative of the little magazines devoted to jazz recordings and related forms of popular and folk music; the genre also included, among others, the *Record Changer, Jazz Record, Hot Record Society Rag, Tempo, La Revue Internationale de la Musique de Jazz*, and *Jazz Forum*. Issues of *Jazz Music* featured record and book reviews, detailed surveys of musicians' careers, and discographies that indexed a musician's recorded output by title, date, personnel, and catalog number. The magazine rarely included interviews with major musicians or firsthand accounts by them. By contrast, the widely circulated *Down Beat*, a major new periodical of the American popular music business, filled its pages with interviews, advertisements, economic data, "cheesecake" photos of young female singers (or "birds"), and promotional articles. Anticommercial biases and connoisseurial perspectives nevertheless dominated *Down Beat* record reviews and historical articles.

Disquisitions on the roots and development of jazz music dominated the pages of *Jazz Music* and similar small fan magazines. When did the "real jazz" emerge, many of the writers asked, and what defined it? To what extent was it true that only African American musicians had played real or authentic jazz in the past? Could the orchestrated, commercial styles of the big bands possibly stay true to the guiding spirit and genre rules of authentic jazz? Was it appropriate to tie together ragtime compositions, rural and urban blues, early New Orleans style jazz, the sweet symphonic jazz of the 1920s and 1930s, and big band styles in a single overarching narrative? If a unilinear narrative of development was unworkable, what could replace it? What did the present predicament of jazz suggest about the music's future, considering the ascendancy of big band music and the decline of the collectively improvised New Orleans style? Were new musical innovations and folk-formal hybrids to be welcomed or lamented? In short, debates about basic matters of genre definition and the alternative valences of folk, popular, commercial, and formal music framed the early discourse of jazz criticism.

White jazz critics in the 1930s and 1940s, for the most part, did not put themselves into a dialogue with relevant African American debates on racial identity, the folk inheritance, musical evolution, and the social consequences of art. Hurston's "Spirituals and Neo-Spirituals" appeared on the pages of *Jazz Music* without editorial commentary. It can be surmised that the essay appealed to *Jazz Music* readers who, like the majority of its purist contributors, approached the early history of jazz as the unfolding of a folk music. Such readers could appreciate Hurston's disdain for the concert spirituals and other "neo-spiritual" hybrids, and they could extend her conclusions to other fusions of black folk idioms and European formal idioms. The velocity and international variety of jazz's stylistic changes from its genesis up to 1943, however, clouded any generic analogy between the purer strains of "real jazz" and Hurston's "real spirituals." The mercurial character of stylistic change in jazz only emboldened connoisseurs to redouble their searches for the least diluted and most authentic idioms.

Jazz music, unlike the folk music that Hurston celebrated, found commercial applications very early; consequently, it underwent stylistic transformations with incredible speed. The new idiom emerged around the turn of the century in New Orleans, the port city that jazz historian Ted Gioia describes as "the most seething ethnic melting pot that the nineteenth-century world could produce."[3] The new popular music loosened its anchoring to the religious context of funeral parades from which it may have originated and adapted to nightclubs, cabarets, medicine shows, dance halls, riverboats, and the vaudeville stage. Jazz quickly spread across the musical landscapes of rural and urban America and found enthusiastic international audiences of musicians, dancers, and listeners.

The geographic reach, commercial success, and dizzying transformations of early jazz were integrally linked to the success of new recording and broadcasting technologies. New sonic worlds emerged as listeners further familiarized themselves with the imaginative practice of traveling to distant places and times with a turn of a dial or a flick of a switch. Recorded jazz was available as early as 1916 to facilitate the music's dispersion and influence. The music was disseminated widely over the radio by the 1920s, even as that new technology threatened to destroy the phonographic recording market. Records survived the radio threat, but the bottom fell out of the music business in the aftermath of the 1929 stock market crash. As of 1934, when Hurston wrote "Spirituals and Neo-Spirituals," black folk spirituals had not undergone the kind of worldwide dissemination that blues and jazz recordings had.

The music business rebounded in the 1930s through the popular vogue known as "swing." Big bands specializing in swing ruled popular music in a period (roughly 1935 to 1948) since remembered as the Swing Era. The connoisseurs who wrote for specialty magazines like *Jazz Music* usually derided the swing vogue as the commercial triumph of inferior or artistically compromised musicians.[4] The rhetoric of folk authenticity provided these connoisseurs with a dramatic but notoriously imprecise weapon for rendering their disappointments with the music's commercialization and its consequent dilutions and hybridizations. The rhetoric made its strongest appeals at moments of perceived crisis when threats of obsolescence or mutilating transformation endangered the purity of a cherished genre.

For some purist fans, the music was in a state of permanent crisis. Narratives of cultural decline and eroded authenticity constantly invited the lamentation of an absent golden age and a turn away from a still young music's unknown future.[5] The elegiac commemoration of forgotten musical moments energized innumerable articles in *Jazz Music* and similar magazines. Idealizations of the earliest, unrecorded New Orleans jazz fueled especially powerful longings to recapture the music's folk genesis, longings nicely captured in Jelly Roll Morton's classic song "I Thought I Heard Buddy Bolden Say." By the 1940s, a core of white aficionados engineered an influential "New Orleans revival" by sponsoring documentary recordings and concert and club engagements for elderly musicians (most of whom were African American) thankful to be rescued from obscurity.[6] True-believing jazz revivalists held that the best hopes for the future of the music lay in salvaging its lost folk roots and eschewing the chimerical progress of big band innovation and modernistic or formal hybrids. In particular, portable recording devices offered an exceptional technique for memorializing, if not fully reigniting, the styles and careers of nearly forgotten jazz masters. Others were more pessimistic about such eleventh-hour salvage missions. "Of course, there is very little hope for new recordings," the pianist Art Hodes wrote sourly in the *Jazz Record*, "and even then we'd get little if any of the old style jazz on wax."[7] A niche market demand for such novelties, along with the ethnographic aura of folk exotica, helped fuel the salvage and resuscitation of obsolete musical styles. The critic Roger Pryor Dodge accurately marked the growing centrality of recorded music as the dividing line between the first two phases of jazz criticism. "The early critics occupied themselves with the *extension of jazz* but entertained little consideration for jazz itself. On the other hand the recent critics have concentrated upon the living recording as an end in itself. Without doubt the disc is a priceless innovation towards the preservation of jazz. . . . if the musicians themselves are becoming conscious of written music with constant recourse to their own records, such awareness, *built* on the past, will be more lastingly significant than taking off from scratch every day."[8]

Jake Trussell's article "Why Fusion?" followed Hurston's "Spirituals and Neo-Spirituals" in the September 1943 issue of *Jazz Music*. A shared skepticism about folk-formal hybrids linked the two essays. Hurston's essay did not critique Duke Ellington, though Trussell (or, more likely, the editors of *Jazz Music*) might have imagined his own essay as a logical extension of Hurston's. In particular, Ellington's recent *Black, Brown and Beige* raised Trussell's ire. The composer and bandleader premiered the nearly hour-long formal composition at Carnegie Hall on January 23, 1943.[9] According to Trussell, Ellington and those who encouraged his long-form composition were "off-the-beam gentlemen who have been doing their damndest to de-naturalize Jazz as a folk art." "Denaturalization," or the disauthentification of folk idioms, was inimical to the informal spontaneity and unself-consciousness that Trussell preferred. To reinforce his attack, Trussell referred to John Hammond's critique of Ellington's efforts in extended forms (published in the *Jazz Record*) as an especially "wonderful review."[10] The title of Hammond's article forebodingly asked "Is the Duke Deserting Jazz?" Answering in the affirmative, Hammond remarked on Ellington's dissatisfaction with the reputation of jazz as a "minor art" and the musician's efforts "to achieve something of greater significance." Ellington had indeed stated as early as 1931 that "what is still known as 'jazz' is going to play a considerable part in the serious music of the future." The popular bandleader insisted that the music had a serious role to play in "elevating the race," and his publicity statements echoed quintessential New Negro concerns with musical innovation as a forum for uplift, memorialization, and racial vindication.[11] Hammond's review of *Black, Brown and Beige* made clear the powerful critic's sense "that by becoming more complex, Ellington has robbed jazz of most of its basic virtue and lost contact with his audience." Hammond and Trussell agreed that in their view Ellington's pursuit of formal complexity through compositional refinement entailed a "denaturalizing" sacrifice of the music's "basic virtue." "Despite all that I have said," Hammond concluded, "Duke is still the greatest creative force in jazz."[12] Hammond hoped that Ellington would resist straying further from the idioms of short-form jazz composition and arrangement—arenas in which he remained without rival.

As a Swing Era tastemaker, Hammond had a great deal of influence. A 1959 *Esquire* profile rated him as nothing less than "the most important nonperformer in the history of jazz."[13] Another commentator singled him out as the person "in the period between 1930 and 1955, [who] did more to improve the position of blacks in the United States than any other white man."[14] Neither the musical nor the social claims should be taken at face value, but they suggest the necessity of exploring the intersections of Hammond's career in music and his social activism. This chapter addresses such concerns through Hammond's early ideas about jazz's development, especially as revealed in the historic "From Spirituals to Swing" concert he produced in December 1938. On some matters, Hammond challenged the tiny minority of backward-looking connoisseurs who were more vociferously purist than himself. He insisted, for example, that contemporary hot jazz and big band styles were not hopelessly detrimental to the artistic ideals of the finest jazz; they could succeed, Hammond argued, and on an artistic level they could be elevated higher than any preceding jazz genres.

For a contrasting jazz critic's approach to folk authenticity and formal development, we can turn to Roger Pryor Dodge. Dodge shared Hammond's judgment about the dangers of sacrificing jazz's "basic virtue," but he dissented from other themes in Hammond's buoyant Swing Era advocacy. Rather than celebrate the democratic and pluralistic possibilities of the Swing Era, Dodge preferred to canonize lesser-known jazz traditionalists, particularly ones identified with the New Orleans style of collective melodic improvisation. These musicians, Dodge held, preserved the complexity and aesthetic rigor of the music's classic early styles despite the temptations of commercialization and mediocre arrangements. "Jazz needs protection not so much against its enemies as against its friends," Dodge concluded. And he assigned himself the responsibility of protecting the music's richest folk-rooted genres from false friends—errant Swing Era populists and misguided formalizers alike.[15]

More than any other musician of the era, Duke Ellington was often caught in the cross fire of jazz criticism. Both Hammond and Dodge, for example, admired him profoundly but dissented from his genre-crossing ventures into long-form composition. The bandleader and composer disagreed with many of his critics; he saw no contradiction between the folk roots of jazz and his own cosmopolitan ambitions. Ellington also took exception to the "jitterbug" euphoria of the swing vogue at high tide in 1939, explaining that his orchestra was "not interested primarily in the playing of jazz or swing music, but in producing musically a genuine contribution from our race." "We try to complete a cycle," Ellington wrote of his band.[16] The conception of "Negro music" that Ellington articulated at certain times during the Swing Era fused the vocabularies of jazz with the formal concert aspirations of the New Negro artist and the Renaissance project of memorializing the black folk inheritance. These aspirations often cut against the grain of Swing Era jazz criticism. Indeed, the turns of this conflict over genre purity, folk authenticity, and cosmopolitan experimentation continue to resonate in ongoing debates about the evolution, idiomatic identity, and future of jazz.

John Hammond's Swing Era

As a young man, John Hammond dreamed of hosting a concert of "talented Negro artists from all over the country who had been denied entry to the white world of popular music." He succeeded in staging a concert featuring a hand-picked selection of obscure and well-known musicians late in December 1938. The concert's "musically sophisticated audience" encountered "Negro music from its raw beginnings to the latest jazz." The evening, according to Hammond, combined "both primitive and sophisticated performers, as well as all of the music of the blacks in which jazz is rooted."[17] When "at the last minute [stage director] Charles Friedman, the concert's scheduled announcer, failed to appear as master of ceremonies," Hammond nervously took the stage to introduce the performers. Problems with the sound system left Hammond inaudible at first, and he later remembered "Carl Van Vechten yelling 'louder' from his front row perch." The soundman misinterpreted Hammond's cue for increased volume and "instead put on the record of wild African chanting." The three-and-a-half-hour concert was a "continuous ball" for the sold-out house, Hammond proudly recalled.[18] "Hammond's performance," according to one commentator, "was hardly less engrossing than any of the official ones. An ear-to-ear grin, a slap of the hand on the thigh, a bobbing from right to left showed the pleasure that lesser (more inhibited) folk merely expressed by a pounding of palms."[19] The concert secured his reputation as a music producer, tastemaker, and social activist.

John Henry Hammond Jr. was born in 1910 into a prominent New York family. His mother was a granddaughter of the railroad magnate Cornelius Vanderbilt, and his father was a prominent New York lawyer. One of four children, Hammond grew up in opulence in a fabled six-story residence on East 91st Street on Manhattan's Upper East Side complete with a private ballroom, sixteen bathrooms, and more than a dozen servants. The young Hammond witnessed his first live jazz with a performance by the Georgians, a white American jazz band, while on family vacation in London. The opportunity to see an African American stage show, "From Dixie to Broadway," excited him even more. Hammond later reminisced that because the London Pavilion "had matinees I was able to sneak away from my family and see Florence Mills and hear a rather sensational pit band which had in it on baritone and soprano saxophone Sidney Bechet."[20] Mills reached popular stardom after her appearance in *Shuffle Along* (1921), the enormously successful and influential all-black show with music and lyrics by Eubie Blake and Noble Sissle (other cast members included Paul Robeson and Josephine Baker). "After a record 504 performances on Broadway, *Shuffle Along* went on the road to play for two more years."[21] One of the leading African American popular entertainers of her day, Mills appeared in numerous musical revues, sang in William Grant Still's 1926 chamber suite *Levee Land*, and died at the age of thirty-two in 1927. Bechet, one of the most commanding virtuosos of New Orleans jazz, would later appear in Hammond's "From Spirituals to Swing" concert of 1938.

The teenage Hammond found himself gripped by an insatiable passion for African American blues and jazz recordings. He avidly sought out the music, hunting all around New York City in the early 1920s for the latest in "race records." "You had to go up to Harlem or the various Black ghettos in other boroughs . . . before you could even listen to such a record," he recounted with relish. The twelve-year-old Hammond "had no fears," so he "started going around to these stores."[22] His zeal for black popular music did not slacken when he was sent to the Hotchkiss School in Connecticut. While at Hotchkiss, Hammond "subscribed to every periodical, trade and critical, in which phonographs were mentioned, and built his collection of records to imposing proportions." Classmates may have preferred the more popular, but less improvisational, jazz of Paul Whiteman, but Hammond was "already a partisan of the most authentic jazz."[23] Weekend commutes to Manhattan under the reassuring pretense of violin lessons allowed the prep school student to stay current with the latest recordings. Entering Yale College in 1929, Hammond swiftly became a central authority in the school's undergraduate clique of jazz and blues recording collectors, a breeding ground for Swing Era jazz critics. The historian David Ware Stowe notes that "during the early post-Crash years, when the music and recording industries were crippled by the Depression, the Ivy League sustained its demand for hot music."[24] Hammond undoubtedly made a disproportionate contribution to the Ivy League demand for new jazz records.

Bedridden with jaundice, Hammond left New Haven after a year and a half, thus ending his formal education. His health crisis passed, and Hammond was eager to pursue a life backstage in the music world. He took an apartment in Greenwich Village for himself and his record collection and began reporting on American jazz for the British magazines *Parlophone* and *Melody Maker*. Musicians, distributors, and publishers were struggling to survive during the massive economic downturn. The domestic market and radio exposure for jazz "had dwindled sharply." Record companies shifted their attention to "peddling theme-songs from the then-emerging talkies," according to Irving Kolodin. It was the "inevitable lag in trans-Atlantic influences" that saved the "esoteric art of improvised jazz," Kolodin wrote, because the specialty idiom of improvised small group music known as "hot jazz" was only then "beginning to attract attention in England and France."[25] Hammond began producing hot jazz recordings by top American talent for the European market.

Hammond's connoisseurial approach held new recordings and nightclub performances to the highest possible standards, and he measured all popular music according to a hot jazz ideal. He decried all "corny" novelty recordings along with "sweet" music styles as tainted by artless commercialism. Typical was Hammond's comment from 1936 about a bad week for popular music in New York City. "But for the most part it is the same dreary bunch of music manufacturers: Guy Lombardo at the Roosevelt, Cab Callaway [*sic*] at the Cotton Club, Enoch Light at the McAlpin, Lopez, Clyde McCoy, Jerry Freeman, Russ Morgan, and all the other dispensers of a commodity rather than an art."[26] Sweet jazz, according to Hammond, was by definition a commercialized and diluted echo of the real thing, hot jazz. The cognitive dissonance between Hammond's anti-commercialism (an article of faith among his fellow jazz critics) and the lowest-common-denominator sensibility of "all the other dispensers of a commodity rather than an art" guaranteed plenty of antagonism and righteous indignation. On the other hand, musicians lucky enough to be favored by Hammond enjoyed fawning adulation, free publicity, and voluminous unsolicited advice. Some critics also came to follow Hammond's model by taking on an ever-expanding role in the work of promotion and production.

Hammond insisted that the very landscape of American popular music, in terms of public taste and music production, needed to be reshaped. For one thing, greater prominence needed to be given to hot jazz recordings and performances by expert African American and white musicians. Most American popular music, Hammond argued, was mindlessly sentimental, rhythmically bland, and musically unappealing. He wanted to push aside the excesses of sweet jazz to make room for intense hot jazz styles characterized by energetic solos, improvisational freedom, and what he saw as a more distinctly African American approach to syncopation and rhythmic propulsion.

Hammond idealized and produced studio recordings that successfully re-created (or at least mimicked) the informal spirit and spontaneous creativity of the late-night "jam session." The quality of jazz never rose, he maintained, when the musicians approached composition and performance in the formal, studied manner better suited to classical music. The liberated spirit of authentic jazz triumphed, Hammond implied, when performances and recordings hewed close to an African American blues aesthetic and the functional imperatives of swinging dance music. Hammond did not hide his feeling that white musicians were at a distinct cultural disadvantage when it came to meeting the demands of hot jazz, though he was quick to assist worthy white musicians.[27] Nevertheless, he eagerly promoted the interracial unionization of the music business and the wholesale exposure and reform of that industry's exploitative and racist labor practices. Overall, Hammond presented himself as a crusading reformer of the popular music business, a reformer unhindered by shortsighted financial imperatives. His Swing Era career richly illustrates the class and cultural ambiguities of what Robert Cantwell has dubbed "the principle of nobility."

In September 1933, Hammond urged the white clarinetist Benny Goodman, little-known in hot jazz circles, to move away from the popular sweet jazz style and undertake some hot jazz recordings for the English market. Hearing this contrarian advice from a scion of the WASP elite must have struck the virtuoso jazz stylist as a challenge. Goodman confessed in his 1939 autobiography that he "was not overly enthusiastic about the proposition at first" because he "had not done work of that sort for some months, and the money involved was not much."[28]

Goodman, the Chicago-born son of poor Eastern European Jewish immigrants, was more of a realist than Hammond; his main goal was professional stability as a full-time musician during the lean years of the Depression. Hammond, always quick to suggest musical personnel and repertoire, proceeded to recruit suitable musicians for the recordings, including trombonist Jack Teagarden and drummer Gene Krupa. The records were a musical and financial success and Goodman soon made additional "sides" with some of the most sophisticated African American specialists of new jazz styles, including tenor saxophonist Coleman Hawkins and pianist Teddy Wilson. Through Hammond's efforts, Goodman also played on the last recording date of Bessie Smith, the great blues diva whose faltering career had not bounced back during the Depression. Goodman had long admired leading black jazz clarinetists like Johnny Dodds, Jimmie Noone, and Buster Bailey, but he acknowledged that "the idea of working with" black musicians "had never come my way before." Integrated recordings were still "a pretty unusual thing," Goodman explained.

Feeling confident that things were looking up for his new career in hot jazz, Goodman turned down an offer to join Paul Whiteman's ever-popular touring band. Instead, Goodman formed a twelve-piece band of hot jazz specialists in the spring of 1934, a time when "there were practically no hot bands using white musicians." The band included no black musicians, but Goodman soon came to rely on arrangements by black bandleaders including Benny Carter and, thanks to Hammond's friendly intercession, Fletcher Henderson. Hammond was not alone in the opinion that Henderson had led the most advanced and virtuosic big band of the 1920s. Fabled for their exciting live performances, the African American band successfully fused the improvising freedom of hot jazz with the organized power and elegance of brass and saxophone section playing. Henderson's New York-based ensemble never saw the kind of financial success enjoyed by Paul Whiteman (or later by Goodman). Nevertheless, it was held in the highest regard by musicians and jazz connoisseurs for its groundbreaking arrangements and the cultivation of an unparalleled roster of improvising soloists, including (at various times) the trumpeters Louis Armstrong and Roy Eldridge and the tenor saxophonists Coleman Hawkins, Lester Young, and Chu Berry. Goodman recognized that he "still didn't have the right band to play that kind of music," but the Henderson arrangements convinced him "more than ever which way the band should head."[29]

With Hammond's assistance, Goodman recruited and rehearsed a band capable of meeting the expectations of Henderson's arrangements. The Goodman big band enjoyed a weekly engagement for six months on the national radio show "Let's Dance" before breaking through as a popular phenomenon during a touring engagement at the Palomar Ballroom in Los Angeles. The Swing Era began on August 21, 1935, according to jazz critic Gary Giddins, "because on that night middle-class white kids said yes in thunder and hard currency."[30] A national fad for swing music and a new social type—the dancing, teenage "jitterbug"—ensued. Goodman took advantage of the situation and won the race to capture a new popular vogue for hot jazz styles translated into the idioms of medium, big, and bigger band sizes. The musicologist Scott DeVeaux notes:

> Benny Goodman's youthful listeners may not have been aware, or have cared, that the core of his repertory was provided by prominent black arrangers, including Fletcher Henderson (and his brother, Horace), Edgar Sampson, and Jimmy Mundy. But through these arrangements—and more important, the performance practices the arrangers took for granted—white musicians brought the rhythmic sensibility that had for several years been the stock-in-trade of the black dance orchestras to a vast new audience, one at the center of all subsequent dance crazes in the twentieth century: the white adolescent market.[31]

In 1935, Goodman also began performing regularly in a trio setting with Teddy Wilson and Gene Krupa. Racially mixed small group performances—music meant for listening rather than dancing—became a regular feature of Goodman's popular big band shows.

The "coronation of Goodman as 'King of Swing,'" David Ware Stowe points out, "brought a corresponding increase in prestige for Hammond in the music industry."[32] Indeed, Hammond welcomed his share of credit for Goodman's success and the bandleader's steps toward desegregating American popular music. Goodman capped his popular reputation as the "King of Swing" with a hugely successful evening of jazz at Carnegie Hall in January 1938. The concert led Hammond to offer a confession in his review for *Tempo*, house periodical of the United Hot Clubs of America (the fan network over which he presided). "There were many of us who had looked with suspicion on anything so pretentious as a concert hall presentation of swing, but we were thoroughly disarmed by the simple, well arranged program, the fairly successful jam session, the supremely modest behavior of Benny—and to a lesser degree—his band."[33] Goodman's first

Carnegie Hall concert featured his big band as well as a racially mixed jam session. The later portion of the show included the pianist Count Basie and some of his sidemen (bassist Walter Page and tenor saxophonist Lester Young) and members of the Ellington band (including alto saxophonist Johnny Hodges, trumpeter Cootie Williams, and baritone saxophonist Harry Carney, but not Ellington). The evening followed jazz concert protocol and included a "Twenty Years of Jazz" segment that sampled various styles (including music by black composers Will Marion Cook and Ford Dabney) and suggested a general line of evolution behind contemporary hot jazz and swing music.[34]

Most earlier concerts of jazz-related music in elite settings, Hammond worried, had fallen prey to excessive self-consciousness and idiomatic dilution. The Goodman concert succeeded, Hammond was happy to report, because of Goodman's mastery of authentic hot jazz approaches to small band and big band styles and his avoidance of inappropriate symphonic jazz hybrids. (The clarinetist performed and recorded classical music by Mozart, Bartók, and others as a side project to his vocation as a popular musician, but he eschewed symphonic jazz ambitions.) From Goodman's perspective, his first Carnegie Hall concert fit a personal ambition to craft a respectable career, for himself and for jazz music, that overcame the music's lower-class and morally questionable roots. As Gerald Early comments, the clarinetist's historic 1938 concert crystallized how Goodman "made people listen to dance music and thus, even more than the boppers who came later, effected the transformation of hot jazz music to an art music and reoriented the public to accepting jazz as high art without the trapping of classical European art music."[35]

Goodman and Hammond knew well that performances of popular music in elite settings identified with the rituals of classical music carried connotations of a populist challenge, a carnivalesque transgression, or an upward-climbing effort at cultural vindication. Goodman's Carnegie Hall concert joined a tradition of concerts that had its roots in James Reese Europe's massive African American orchestra, the Clef Club, and its 1912 Carnegie Hall concert of ragtime and other popular music.[36] The prominent blues arranger and composer W. C. Handy offered his own orchestral concert at Carnegie Hall in 1928 and started "the vogue for the 'historical survey' concert" by including a variety of African American styles from the folk music of slavery to the symphonic music of the present.[37] For hot jazz partisans, the most important (because most ill-conceived) precedent to Goodman's concert occurred on February 12, 1924, when Paul

Whiteman led his all-white orchestra in a historic performance at New York's Aeolian Hall. Whiteman's "Experiment in Modern Music" opened with improvised small group jazz and then proceeded toward fully scored symphonic jazz. The didactic concert presented an evolutionary narrative from jazz music's raucous plebeian origins in New Orleans to the restrained bourgeois prospect of symphonic jazz. The "Experiment in Modern Music" featured an intentionally parodic version of "Livery Stable Blues" (a song made famous by the Original Dixieland Jazz Band in 1917) and the premiere of a popular songwriter's first concert work, George Gershwin's *Rhapsody in Blue*.

When the Aeolian Hall audience "laughed and seemed pleased with *Livery Stable Blues*, the crude jazz of the past," Whiteman confessed, "I had for a moment, the panicky feeling that they hadn't realized the attempt at burlesque—that they were ignorantly applauding the thing on its merits."[38] The bandleader intended *Rhapsody in Blue* as solid proof of the obsolescence and inferiority of "Livery Stable Blues." Gershwin's composition for piano and orchestra was an instant success and soon became Whiteman's signature finale.

Critics at the time were not unanimous about Whiteman's symphonic jazz. Olin Downes, for example, found the "Livery Stable Blues" performance especially appealing and wrote that the song "was introduced apologetically as an example of the depraved past from which modern jazz has arisen." "The apology is herewith indignantly rejected," Downes wrote, "for this is a gorgeous piece of impudence, much better in its unbuttoned jocosity and Rabelaisian laughter than other and more polite compositions that came later."[39] The performance of New Orleans-style jazz generated "Rabelaisian laughter" by suggesting a parodic lower-class riposte to the somber rituals of bourgeois respectability otherwise pursued by Whiteman. Whiteman, hoping to elevate his own and jazz music's cultural capital, presented symphonic jazz as a vindication of American musical nationalism. Carl Van Vechten shared some of Downes's hesitations but applauded Gershwin's first foray into formal music as nothing less than the fulfillment of prophecy.[40]

In the 1930s and later, hot jazz partisans decried Whiteman's symphonic jazz as an unworkable paradox. Robert Goffin, the Belgian author of *Aux Frontiers du Jazz* (1931), interpreted Whiteman's musical conception as a failed "compromise between real jazz and the prejudices of the bourgeois public."[41] Whiteman's genre-bending compromise was the musical target against which Hammond and most other jazz critics hurled their sharpest critical barbs; Whiteman was their *bête blanc*. Even in 1970, Hammond looked back on "that brief but horrible period when Paul Whiteman foisted something called symphonic jazz on the public." The critic engaged in a measure of wishful thinking when he concluded that Whiteman's music "did not have too much effect on the history of jazz."[42]

Marshall Stearns, a co-officer with Hammond in the United Hot Clubs of America, articulated the critical orthodoxy as of 1936: "Whiteman was adapting colored music to the white tradition and the result was simpler, spiritless, and without swing." Stearns interpreted Whiteman as a structural antipode of authentic hot jazz in the course of a twenty-installment historical survey of jazz for *Down Beat*. Whiteman's music "was publicized and popular," Stearns noted, "presenting an introduction to the real thing for those with vitality enough to follow it up to its distant but genuine source." As for the "genuine source" of jazz in the 1920s, Stearns stressed that "racial prejudices kept it in the background. It was almost entirely confined to the colored race and a few pioneer white musicians who recognized and absorbed the real thing. Very few recordings were made by these bands compared to the mountains of wax melted to perpetuate the sweet innocuous ballads of such white bands as that of . . . Paul Whiteman, and others."[43]

Whiteman's project of fusing characteristics of jazz with the scored-through techniques of European formal music struck almost all jazz critics as fundamentally misguided. They argued that his symphonic jazz hybrid failed to meet the highest critical standards of both hot jazz and European classical music. The critics' vilification of Whiteman also evidenced their habit of describing authentic jazz as a folk music—and often a specifically African American folk music—utterly divorced from long-form ambitions, ambitions that Whiteman shared with many African American composers and musical enthusiasts. Gerald Early approaches Whiteman's reputation as an opportunity to defuse a simplistic and unnecessarily polarizing binary in jazz criticism that pits black folk authenticity against elite white expropriation:

> Whiteman was no more racist than other whites of his era and there is, indeed, evidence to indicate that he may have been less so. He wanted to hire black musicians to play in his band in the mid-twenties but was talked out of it by other band members and commercial sponsors. . . . What Whiteman's 1924 concert was trying to establish was the idea that from its beginnings to its most fully realized form as sym-

phonic concert music, jazz was and is an undeniable *American* music; and inasmuch as Whiteman wanted to convince himself and his audience that it was an American music, he was bound to convince both himself and others that it was, officially, a white music. Otherwise, history taught him that the only way he could perform black music would be in blackface or as a kind of minstrel. Whiteman, whatever his faults, did not want jazz to become another minstrel music and it is, in part, through his popularizing efforts that the music did not become that. . . . Whiteman mediated a major shift in American culture. And while his concert could attempt to deny a mongrelized American cultural past, it could not ultimately deny a kind of racial syncretism that suggested that the sharing of art between black and white, from commercial co-option to friendly collaboration, would not be used exclusively as a method to further denigrate and oppress blacks within the culture.[44]

The racist tradition of blackface minstrelsy negotiated the "mongrelized American cultural past" and present through white and black performers' blackface mask, a mask that marked and perpetuated racial fascination and repulsion.[45] Whiteman broke with minstrelsy and substituted the performance rituals of respectable bourgeois entertainment, though his symphonic jazz still involved a distorting mask of "whiteface" entertainment; white performers could eschew the literal "blacking up" of blackface while still mimicking or depending on African American performance styles. Early contends that "inasmuch as Whiteman wanted to convince himself and his audience that it was an American music, he was bound to convince both himself and others that it was, officially, a white music." Whiteman's critics saw in the bandleader's presentation a middlebrow misconstrual of jazz's authentic properties and prospects, a grotesque repression of the music's African American and plebeian roots, or both.[46] Early concurs on the inescapable presence of racial expropriation, but he emphasizes that Whiteman did not simply replicate or mimic African American styles. Even Whiteman's "whiteface" gesture involved creative hybridization, thus contributing to musical development according to a long-standing, if ultimately inequitable, cultural dynamic of "racial syncretism."

Early's approach to the contested terms of "mongrelization" and "racial syncretism" revisits Whiteman's reputation as a bumbling middlebrow bandleader and appropriately named icon of the white cultural theft of African American idioms. Although Early's argument does not engage with specific hot jazz partisans, it sheds considerable light on early jazz criticism. Whiteman's contributions to the syncretic history of American music failed the purity test administered by hot jazz advocates. They habitually denounced his long-lasting success and ridiculed his "King of Jazz" title as the ill-gotten gains of musical dilution, commercial co-optation, and racial expropriation. On the one hand, as Early notes, Whiteman's "Experiment in Modern Music" presented a "jazz history of the world or a history of the jazz world" that "excised the presence of blacks as creators of this music." Without question, the distorting absence of "references to blacks in the entire concert" systematically obscured jazz's deep roots in African American culture.[47] Swing Era critics like Hammond and Stearns went to great lengths to correct such distortions. On the other hand, jazz critics wrote themselves into a rhetorical corner by constantly reiterating polarizing denunciations of Whiteman and his formal ambitions.

Early answers their rhetoric by shifting focus to issues repressed in the ritualized denunciation of Whiteman: the musician's rejection of blackface minstrelsy and his consequential formal hybrid. Moreover, both Whiteman and Goodman helped to break down "the prejudices of the bourgeois public," Early stresses, and thereby they helped elevate the cultural capital of jazz as an indigenous American art form. Whiteman and the composers and arrangers he relied on were not alone, after all, in fusing vernacular source materials with large-scale and orchestral instrumentation and scored-through compositions. New Negro composers and concert artists were pursuing a simultaneous campaign of syncretism, idiomatic formalization and bourgeois vindication. Not surprisingly, Alain Locke did not attack the patent impurities of Whiteman's popular music with the ferocity that Hammond brought to the matter. Locke publicized the African American roots of jazz, but his musical goals were, after all, close to Whiteman's.

Hammond treated Goodman's racially mixed and more informal and improvisational Carnegie Hall concert of 1938 as a corrective to Whiteman's continuing influence. Much stronger medicine was necessary, according to Hammond, to counteract Whiteman's relative silence about the black folk roots of jazz and the improvisational and rhythmic imperatives of what Hammond regarded as the most promising forms of jazz. The first "From Spirituals to Swing" concert thus turned Whiteman's developmental narrative qua symphonic jazz ideal on its head. Hammond's concert expanded on Goodman's precedent and aimed to legitimate hot jazz, boogie-woogie, and blues and gospel styles without diluting or commercializing these vernacular forms or suppressing them to meet traditional concert hall expectations.

The respected jazz critic Frederic Ramsey Jr. wrote in 1946 of "From Spirituals to Swing" as "the first successful attempt" to "bridge the gap between 'unbuttoned jocosity' and the unbending pomp of more formal affairs."[48] The concert program asked the audience to make an indulgence: "Most of the people on the program are making their first appearance before a predominantly white audience; many of them have never visited the North before. They will do their very best if the audience will cooperate with them by creating an atmosphere of informality and interest. The most memorable hot music comes when the performer can feel his audience. May we ask that you forget you are in Carnegie Hall?"[49] Hammond first approached the NAACP about sponsoring the concert (Walter White had recruited Hammond for the group's board of directors in 1935) but was turned down. The International Ladies Garment Workers Union also passed on the opportunity. Finally, *New Masses* agreed to sponsor a December 1938 concert. "The people at the *New Masses* just hated jazz," Hammond commented later, "but, since it was the days of the United Front . . . they thought this would be good for their cultural image to have somebody write about jazz, particularly black jazz."[50]

Hammond was active in the broad-based movement for democratic unionism and racial integration in the thirties and forties that Michael Denning has provocatively interpreted as the "cultural front." Hammond had contributed articles to the *Nation* and *New Masses* about the Scottsboro Boys and other progressive concerns. He had written sympathetically on the labor unrest of 1932 in Harlan County, Kentucky, as part of a contingent of New York writers (including Waldo Frank, John Dos Passos, Edmund Wilson, and Malcolm Cowley). Hammond's unionist and integrationist politics and his vision of authentic jazz as a commercially uncompromised popular music—in essence, an urban folk music representing the American spirit at its best—fit comfortably with the agenda of *New Masses*, especially during its coalition-minded Popular Front period.

Hammond did not approach the planning of "From Spirituals to Swing" as a simple evening of entertainment. The evening would be ripe with social and political implications. A related event at Carnegie Hall, "An Evening of Negro Music," took place a month earlier in honor of W. C. Handy's sixty-fifth birthday. The Handy celebration featured such African American musical stars as Fats Waller, Cab Calloway, Maxine Sullivan,

Lionel Hampton, and Teddy Wilson, along with several formal music groups. The Harlem Musicians' Committee to Aid Spanish Democracy sponsored the "Evening of Negro Music" to benefit the Spanish Children's Milk Fund. A week before the Handy event, the New York State Committee of the Communist Party presented a "dramatic spectacle" with a "cast of hundreds of actors, dancers, musicians, [and] chorus" titled "Truth to Your Eyes" at Madison Square Garden in celebration of the twenty-first anniversary of the Soviet Union.[51] When editors at *New Masses* agreed to sponsor the talent search, publicity, and production of "From Spirituals to Swing," Hammond sought assurances that the concert would not be turned into an explicitly political spectacle. At the time, Communist Party strategists were divided between emphasizing the radicalization of a racially segregated but internally united black "nation within a nation" (possibly as a precursor to interracial class unity) and advocating a desegregated and interracial labor-based radical politics. *New Masses* editors latched on to Hammond's crusade for "the music nobody knows" to reinforce Popular Front themes about the national representativeness of folk and regional expression then filling the magazine's pages.[52] The editors prepared readers for an evening of unexpected revelations.

> And what we now have promises to be an evening of great discovery, a presentation that may well be to modern music what the Armory show of cubist painting in 1913 was to modern art. The idea is to give musical New York an evening of American Negro music, not the warmed over, heavily arranged, symphonic stuff with which most people associate Negro musical forms, but the true, untainted, entirely original works that the American Negro has created. We mean spirituals sung in their primitive majesty. . . . This is something that grew up unnoticed in America, the music that only a few enthusiasts really know but which has never been heard by a public, never gathered into an expository concert, rarely played above the Mason and Dixon line.[53]

The promise of "true, untainted, entirely original works" that had "never been heard by a public" elevated an "expository concert" into a virtual bonanza of black folk authenticity. The advertisement's emphasis on the folk music's "primitive majesty" betrayed an inappropriate analogy between the Armory Show's introduction of European modernist art to American audiences and Hammond's production. Many of the European and American artists featured in the scandalous Armory Show of 1913 were self-conscious members of a forward-looking artistic elite; if their cosmopolitan art was deemed primitive (as was the case with Marcel Duchamp's painting *Nude Descending a Staircase*), their modernist primitivism reflected deliberate calculation. The "primitive majesty" of the "untainted" performances in Hammond's concert, by contrast, highlighted no such avant-garde self-consciousness.

Hammond's concert of folk music would offer tough-minded folk realism and a desperate jubilation rooted in the everyday life of doubly oppressed black workers in the South. For those sympathetic to the aesthetic priorities of *New Masses*, Hammond's concert might even contribute to a diminution of the Armory Show's decadent bourgeois legacies of formalism, apolitical "bohemianism," and modernist subjectivism. Along similar corrective lines, *New Masses* sponsored its first art exhibition in 1938. Titled "We Like America," the exhibition brought together Popular Front patriotism, regionalist art, and radical politics. It is not surprising that discussions of classical music in *New Masses* carried fewer direct political implications than commentaries about folk music, as the folk music commentaries usually focused on the music's authentic proletarian basis and its implicitly radical and oppositional flavor. In preconcert publicity for "From Spirituals to Swing," Hammond referred positively to Lawrence Gellert's writings (collected in his 1934 book, *Negro Songs of Protest*) on the frequently overlooked motif of labor protest in African American folk music. On the one hand, Hammond noted the importance of securing "some untrained group who can rouse the Carnegie Hall audience and demonstrate that the Southern Negro worker goes farther than the defeatism of most blues."[54] On the other hand, his aesthetic sensibility led him a year later to criticize "Strange Fruit," the antilynching ballad popularized by Billie Holiday, as "artistically the worst thing that ever happened to her." "The more conscious she was of her style," Hammond grumbled, "the more mannered she became."[55]

New Masses promoted "From Spirituals to Swing" through weeks of preconcert publicity. The editors quoted one reader's letter insuring that the upcoming event was "something not to be missed." "With John Hammond producing, one can be sure that there will be no fakery, no concessions to popularity," the writer promised.[56] An editorial on pianist Meade Lux Lewis hinted at the magazine's web of concerns:

> One of the most stimulating Negro musical forms which will be heard at NEW MASSES' December 23 concert at Carnegie Hall is the style of

piano playing called "Boogie-woogie." . . . The Boogie-woogie piano style came out of the poverty of the American Negro who could not afford an orchestra on his festive occasions. One player of a battered piano had to furnish the drive of a jazz orchestra. . . . "Lux" Lewis' life story is typical of the neglect of these native geniuses. . . . In the early twenties he recorded one of his own compositions . . . for a cheap-record company. Through the years this single recording came to be a classic of jazz to a handful of American and European enthusiasts. But no one knew what had become of Lewis. Five years ago, John Hammond . . . started to look for Lewis. Hammond asked musicians everywhere, without success. Finally, last year, he discovered the Boogie-woogie master washing cars in a Chicago South Side garage. Hammond brought him to New York where he arranged to record four sides for English Parlophone, because no American phonograph company would take a chance on such records selling. These records . . . became sensations in Europe. . . . Lewis dropped into obscurity because there was no appreciation in America for his talents. Lewis' return to New York . . . will bring him before an audience whose interest may finally break the jinx for this talented musician.[57]

Was the reader to locate the crux of the Meade Lux Lewis story in outrage regarding the musician's personal poverty and obscurity, the general "poverty of the American Negro," the bad taste and racism of American recording companies, or Lewis's original piano concept? All of these things were to interact and heighten feelings of personal sympathy, political outrage, and musical appreciation. "Most of the people you will hear," Hammond's program notes baldly stated, "are absurdly poor," and "the greatest of these artists die of privation and neglect."[58] An evening spent following the historic trajectory from black folk spirituals to contemporary swing idioms was to help correct a tragic history of high artistry and personal deprivation. At least for those musicians highlighted by Hammond, a history of unrelenting injustice would be partly ameliorated by a joyous "Spirituals to Swing" narrative of musical progress.

After the recording of West African drum music blared unexpectedly through the hall's speakers, the concert's live portion began, not with spirituals, but with three boogie-woogie pianists: Pete Johnson, Albert Ammons, and Meade Lux Lewis. Hammond praised the pianists to a writer for the *New Yorker*: " 'They're terrific,' he said. They can't read music, which Hammond thinks is a good thing, on the theory that if they ever studied technique and harmony, they might lose their natural feeling for their art. 'You can't intellectualize boogie-woogie,' Mr. Hammond said."[59] The blues singer Big Joe Turner, accompanied by Pete Johnson, followed the trio of pianists. Next came the gospel singer Sister Rosetta Tharpe, joined by a piano-led rhythm section. Tharpe, the quintessential crossover artist of the period, made a name for herself "by presenting for the first time to a night-club audience the exciting hymns (which have much in common with the blues) that the sect commonly known as Holy Rollers uses in its devotional practices."[60] Ruby Smith then sang blues with the celebrated virtuoso pianist James P. Johnson. Smith was the niece of Hammond's favorite blues singer, the recently deceased Bessie Smith. Hammond had eulogized Bessie Smith as "the greatest folk-singer ever to spring from American soil" and "the greatest artist American jazz ever produced."[61]

Switching over to sacred music, an obscure vocal quartet, Mitchell's Christian Singers, then took the stage. Hammond had recently "discovered" the group in the small town of Kinston, North Carolina, as a result of his incomparably energetic talent scouting. His companion on the trip, Goddard Lieberson (a future vice-president at Columbia Records who wrote for *New Masses* under the pseudonym "John Sebastian"), gave *New Masses* readers a description of the singers worth quoting for its implications about folk authenticity.

> From the moment they started (with no one giving a mechanical pitch), the room was filled with some of the most glorious music conceivable. Unaffected voices joined in creating harmonies and counterpoint which defy description no less than they defy comparison. Each singer's voice is so sure, so flexible, so filled with emotion, so alternately ecstatic and somber, so perfect for the music sung, so liquid, so fresh, and unique. . . . The voices when joined raise the significance of a single word to poignant heights. . . . Negro spirituals, through arranging, misinterpretations, jim-crow alterations, have come to be considered a more or less fixed type. In reality, the character of spirituals is made up of innumerable facets of temperamental and intellectual timbres. It is safe to say that Mitchell's Christian Singers will give you an entirely new feeling of what a spiritual may be.[62]

The singing group had several recordings to their name but were not widely known. Hammond reacted to the group's initial recordings as "just about the finest and most natural group singing ever recorded, as well as the first authentic spirituals I've heard on records." The records captured an informal vernacular style at its untainted best. "No arrangements, no accompaniment, complete freedom." Hammond exclaimed, "everybody who has been bored or disgusted by the castrated versions of spirituals we hear on the concert stage should get hold of this record."[63] H. Howard Taubman, in his review for the *New York Times*, agreed that Mitchell's Christian Singers "represented in their concentration, true musical feeling, integrity and unaffectedness Negro music in its pristine aspects."[64] The singers' "unaffected" musicality and relative obscurity matched Hammond's ideal for "From Spirituals to Swing" in representing folk spirituals and gospel music as part of the history of "the music nobody knows."

Turning from the spirituals to the blues, Sonny Terry took the stage to play solo harmonica. In what may have been the evening's only lapse from Hammond's ideal of stylistic authenticity, an ensemble of well-known jazz musicians followed Terry's performance with a reportedly awkward performance in the early New Orleans style of jazz. Soprano saxophonist Sidney Bechet led an impromptu band including several musicians uncomfortable with the New Orleans idiom (including members of the Basie band). A Kansas City swing sextet, and finally the blues singer Big Bill Broonzy, backed by a small band, concluded the concert's first half.

Count Basie and his band dominated the second half of the show, along with an all-star jam session. The band matched Hammond's contemporary jazz ideal and was given the last word. Hammond first witnessed one of the band's club performances in Kansas City several years earlier. He immediately heralded the Basie band's music to *Down Beat* readers in 1936 as "miraculous" and definitive of the best jazz. Celebrating the unpolished looseness of an ensemble that was "more rocking than any I have known," the road-touring talent scout declared that "whatever rough edges there still are can either be removed or made more jagged, preferably the latter."[65] Indeed, the removal or smoothing away of the band's "rough edges" would threaten its appeal to Hammond, and he worried about the transition from Kansas City's Reno Club—"the ideal stage for unselfconscious and direct music"—to the nightclubs of New York. "Basie's band is at its best," Hammond declared, "when it is playing a single good tune for about twenty minutes, with the rhythm section exerting a drive unlike that of any other, and a couple of good soloists playing against brass figures which could only originate in Kansas City. Once it becomes mannered and pretentious the group will have lost its only reason for existence."[66] Luckily for all involved, Hammond found the band's first performances in New York more than satisfactory and offered his highest possible compliment:

"Basie is the only one who could compare with the original Fletcher Henderson orchestra . . . a driving rhythm section more exciting than any in American orchestral history."[67]

"Throughout the Count's life," Alan Pomerance has noted, "John fussed and worried about the makeup, sound, and exposure of the band like a mother hen."[68] Others have commented less generously on Hammond's paternalistic manner, not least in ensuring that the Basie band remained "at its best." Billie Holiday's tenure with the ensemble in 1938, for example, was apparently cut short because of Hammond's intercession. Drummer Jo Jones maintained that Holiday "was fired" by Hammond, "but nobody's got guts enough to tell the people because he's the great white father." Hammond always denied responsibility for the firing, while Basie characteristically demurred from commenting on the matter in his autobiography. According to Jones, Hammond "fired her because he wanted her to sing the blues."[69] Holiday biographer Donald Clarke concludes, "As far as we can ever reach a conclusion, it certainly looks as though Hammond meddled between Basie and Billie and helped to wreck what must have been one of the era's greatest partnerships."[70]

"From Spirituals to Swing" was sold out, and its producer claimed that "reviews hailed it as unlike anything in New York before."[71] "A good time was had by all," the *New York Times* reviewer commented, "except, perhaps, by the manager of the hall, who might have been wondering whether the walls would come tumbling down." The concert demonstrated "the Negro's contribution to our music" and showcased that contribution "in its sincere, unspoiled forms."[72] A reviewer for the *New York Herald Tribune* also noted the show's novelty in presenting "its hearers an informative and varied account of types of American Negro music which seldom reach this or other sophisticated auditoriums."[73] The evening's historic sweep underscored the sacred and secular folk music pedigrees of hot jazz and big band music.

Some audience members might have wondered what place, if any, white musicians were to assume in Hammond's musical narrative. Hammond answered the question in the 1939 "From Spirituals to Swing" concert by including Benny Goodman. Sponsored by the Theatre Arts Committee (TAC), a Popular Front entertainment alliance, the second concert's otherwise exclusively African American presentation featured Sterling Brown as master of ceremonies and concluded with a racially mixed jam session. African American musicians and styles dominated the stage, despite Goodman's commercial power and prestige. Rarely at a loss for words on such matters, Hammond had a racial explanation for the inferiority of Goodman's white big band—and, by extension, all white bands. "Benny's band has attained such a high degree of superficial polish," the critic once remarked, "that one occasionally wonders why it does not have the same feeling of relaxation and suppressed power that Fletcher Henderson's old group used to possess." The answer was "fairly simple," according to Hammond.

> Although even the best colored bands rarely acquire the gloss and cohesion that now belong to Goodman's, they do have an enthusiasm that is born of the fact that every single man in the band would rather make music than anything else in the world. With white bands—and I know it is dangerous to generalize—there is always that minority to whom music is only a means of making a living and not the expression of a personality. In an improvising band the presence of only one "commercial" guy can subtly and irrevocably ruin the spirit of a whole band. Perhaps this is why one sometimes has the feeling that Benny, Gene Krupa, Jess Stacy, and three or four of the rest of the guys are carrying—even pushing—the rest of the orchestra.[74]

Some musicians and critics complained that Hammond, Marshall Stearns, and like-minded partisans of "the real thing" were prejudiced against white jazz practitioners. The leading European jazz critic, France's Hugues Panassié, likewise trafficked in racial stereotypes about African Americans' "natural feeling for their own music." "When you want to know the likes of a colored man," Panassié wrote to American readers in 1946, "don't make him talk! Just watch his reactions while he is listening to the music."[75] Rather than critiquing racial ideologies about Negro musicality and its "naturalness" the revisionism of white liberals eager to credit African Americans with the creation and sustenance of jazz too often devolved into essentialist stereotypes.[76] Jake Trussell (earlier quoted as a fan of Hammond's critique of Ellington) offered the observation that "the majority of the Big name jazz critics had become so engrossed over the fight against Jim Crow that they had let an extreme breed an extreme." The result, Trussell concluded unhappily, was "inverted Jim Crow."[77] Nevertheless, white critics retained the right to chastise African American jazz musicians who failed to meet stereotypical expectations of racially characteristic performances. The disciplinary privileges of Jim Crow, in other words, were not rescinded.

The success of the "From Spirituals to Swing" concerts led *New Masses* to advertise boogie-woogie recordings (from the new Blue Note label's recordings of artists from Hammond's concert) as subscription incentives in 1939. Hammond's 1938 concert helped inspire the founding of Blue Note records as a specialty label dedicated to authentic and noncommercial jazz-related music. The concert also inspired a boogie-woogie vogue and the programming of folk and swing music styles at Café Society. The popular New York nightclub with a nonsegregated patron policy opened its doors in December 1938. Hammond held to his ideals even as his involvement deepened in the business side of popular music, whether as talent scout, informal manager, or producer for industry giant Columbia Records. Irving Kolodin's friendly profile of him for *Harper's* in 1939 addressed the seeming paradox of Hammond's idiosyncratic personal taste and vast public influence. Kolodin referred to the swing vogue itself as a repercussion of Hammond's noble crusade.

> To his credit is the almost single-handed creation of a vogue for the type of music known as "swing," which has made a large-scale industry of the playing of dance music in a forthright, vigorous style. It has been a factor of striking importance in the revival of the phonograph business, creating for the first time dance music whose interest outlives the momentary interest of a pleasant tune or an unexpected rhythm. . . . No less than four prominent dance bands—those of Benny Goodman, "Count" Basie, Teddy Wilson, and Harry James— whose aggregate income is well over half a million dollars annually, base their position largely on his interest; and the number of vocalists, piano players, saxophonists, and drummers who owe their jobs to Hammond, for whom he has "made a call," or "told Benny," or whom he has got into the union, or otherwise discovered, promoted, patronized, and in the fullness of time disavowed, is virtually limitless. . . . Their status as individuals and their earning power as performers have both been tremendously enhanced by the spread of "swing," which is, basically, no more than a reversion to the kind of "hot jazz" that was played by the Dixieland Jazz Band of 1916 and derived from the Negroes of New Orleans.[78]

Historians often count the Original Dixieland Jazz Band or ODJB as the first New Orleans jazz band to play in New York City. The all-white ensemble was also the first New Orleans jazz band to record and enjoy national success. Twenty years later, white bands dominated the jazz-related music industry during the swing vogue, notwithstanding the publicity efforts of Hammond and others on behalf of leading African American bands and soloists. Nick LaRocca, spokesman of the ODJB, exchanged sharp words with swing critics (notably, Marshall Stearns) over the extent to which the ODJB's music was "derived from the Negroes of New Orleans" (as Irving Kolodin asserted). LaRocca fancifully insisted on his band's total independence from black influence. The Jim Crow policy of racial segregation, in LaRocca's mind, had been successful in New Orleans.

Most white listeners did not vote with their wallets in favor of the African American replotting of jazz history propagated by Hammond and other critics. Despite important symbolic successes against racism in the Swing Era, African American bands never shared equally in the popular vogue's financial rewards. The crowded field of white bands enjoyed too many commercial and social advantages, while black big bands suffered institutionalized barriers to media exposure, commercial support, and access to various hotel ballrooms, dance halls, nightclubs, and concert stages. As David Ware Stowe explains, "of the five major sources of big-band receipts—record sales, one-night engagements, theater shows, hotel location jobs, and commercially sponsored programs—black bands were essentially restricted to the first three." After detailing the economics of the big band business, Stowe concludes: "Despite the ideology of pluralism and racial equality promulgated by the swing critics . . . racial prejudice pervaded the swing industry."[79] The swing critics' contribution to the crusade for racial progress was not, however, without its success stories.

Hammond's Swing Era activism stemmed in part from his determination to engineer a shift in American popular taste and social attitudes. He organized many of the finest jazz recordings of the 1930s and had a hand in picking songs, arrangers, and band personnel for the musicians with whom he worked. The imperiousness of the young, upper-class taste-maker occasionally put him at odds with those whose records he was producing—or not producing, as in the pointed case of Duke Ellington—but his power in the industry was so great that few musicians openly criticized him. Unrivaled social capital, industry connections, and financial independence (on his twenty-first birthday he began receiving an annual trust income of $10,000) allowed Hammond to voice blistering critiques of industry practices even as he condemned antiblack racism in labor unions. In one typical 1937 exposé, he attacked an article that had praised James C. Petrillo, the powerful leader of the American Federation of Musicians (AFM). Hammond complained that the whitewashing article included "nothing about the sweatshop conditions in Chicago's innumerable taverns, the appallingly inadequate relief for unemployed musicians, the jim-crowing of Negro musicians into a puppet and helpless subsidiary local, the complete lack of democratic procedure (elections have not been held there in years) and the threats against members so bold as to question Petrillo's motives and wisdom."[80] The advocacy of top-quality jazz, racial integration, and progressive union politics melded into a single project for Hammond. One might argue that the "From Spirituals to Swing" concert simply repeated, through a reversal of racial valences, Whiteman's earlier mistake in "attempting to deny a mongrelized American cultural past." Although partly true in the case of the 1938 concert, we should also bear in mind the integrationist agenda Hammond advanced when he was not publicizing the underrepresented African American titans of jazz.

Hammond's adherence to a folkish hot jazz paradigm set the stage for his relative disillusionment with the development of modern jazz in the 1940s and later. Whole fields of "modern jazz" (usually meaning post–World War II jazz influenced by bebop) seemed to move outside or even against Hammond's taste for accessible, blues-based, and danceable music—though he was always too intense a listener to dance. He contended that bebop and other new elements of postwar jazz modernism "defied the jazz verities without improving on them." According to Hammond, too much modern jazz "offered a new self-consciousness, an excessive emphasis on harmonic and rhythmic revolt, [and] a concentration on technique at the expense of musical emotion." "Instead of expanding the form," he complained of jazz avant-gardists, "they contracted it, made it their private language."[81]

Hammond's derision of the "private languages" of jazz avant-gardists suggests the limitations of his folkish populism. He held that jazz and popular musicians had the opportunity, and perhaps the obligation, to provide an inspiring national soundtrack for an egalitarian and pluralistic society. By the early 1940s, however, some of New York's most innovative black jazz musicians had grown tired of the familiar public languages of hot jazz, big band, and swing music and their own minority status in the commercial marketplace of popular music.[82] Hammond did not outrightly reject the new music, but he worried when young rebels strayed from the unpretentious dance music origins of jazz music and focused instead on relatively obscure complexities in rhythm, harmony, and improvisation. Less than fully impressed by the "new self-consciousness" of modern jazz, Hammond maintained his long-standing tastes and looked to emerging popular genres more harmonious with his ideals. His later major "discoveries" would include Bob Dylan, whose early career first blossomed by following the Popular Front model of folk singer Woodie Guthrie, the soul diva Aretha Franklin, and rock star Bruce Springsteen.

Hammond's perennial disdain for Paul Whiteman's symphonic jazz foreshadowed his unhappiness with some of the most challenging jazz of the 1940s. In the particular cases of Duke Ellington's "Reminiscing in Tempo" (1935) and *Black, Brown and Beige* (1943), Hammond's accusation about betraying the "basic virtue" of jazz shifted from an easily ridiculed white band leader to the preeminent black jazz composer. Ellington's project revisited not only Whiteman's ambitions but also those of African American formal musicians. Ellington's extended works, which grew in number during the late 1950s and through the 1960s, reflected a cosmopolitan aspiration to compose in a public language rooted in African American folk and vernacular materials but irreducible to folk music, hot jazz, swing, or traditional concert music.

Hot Jazz as a New Classicism

Roger Pryor Dodge reported in the little magazine *HRS Rag* (the house organ of the New York–based Hot Record Society) that "From Spirituals to Swing" struck him "both in variety and distinction of soloists . . . [as] the best concert I have ever heard." The concert "was a cross between an art lecture and a concert," Dodge noted, "the art lecture consisting of progressive demonstrations of what fine stuff make up the basis of jazz, the concert presenting some rarely heard piano compositions in jazz played by the outstanding virtuosi of our time."[83] The boogie-woogie piano variations of Meade Lux Lewis, Albert Ammons, and Pete Johnson satisfied Dodge's vision of jazz, though he found the gospel and blues acts and the Count Basie orchestra lacking. Dodge wrote of Hammond not long after the 1938 concert as a critic overly compromised by involvement in the swing business. "John Hammond occasionally gives evidence of being a critic," Dodge claimed, "but for the most part he seems to be deeply embroiled in the commercial ambitions of a band—its desire for smoothness, or for more personality in its singers, etc., etc. All of this is purely the business of a publicity agent—not of a hot jazz critic."[84] Dodge presented himself, of course, as a truly independent critic.

The fascination with jazz manifest in Dodge's writing did not flow from the formulas of primitivism condemned by Locke, Du Bois, Brown, and other African American critics, or from the antiracist, populist climate of the "cultural front." Dodge did not herald African American jazz as a cipher of folk simplicity or unrepressed naturalness or plebeian protest. His more classicist approach to jazz countered the modernist and populist perspectives of Carl Van Vechten and John Hammond and, in certain respects, resembled Alain Locke's enthusiasm about the formal achievements of African sculpture. Dodge's criticism implied that the best jazz held out nothing less than a classicist alternative to the romantic subjectivism and antiformalism of much modernist art. Though fragile and susceptible to the pervasive vulgarity and cheap romanticism infecting modern civilization, true jazz exposed—and could possibly help to repair—the decadence of contemporary music.

Dodge's jazz criticism began with "Jazz Contra Whiteman." Though written in 1925 as a response to "An Experiment in Modern Music," it did not see print until 1929. The essay appeared in the London journal *Dancing Times* under the title "Negro Jazz" and fairly crystallized Dodge's theory of jazz. "Jazz Contra Whiteman" (or "Negro Jazz") explicitly counterposed the "real jazz" against "pseudo-jazz." By "pseudo-jazz," Dodge meant Whiteman's symphonic jazz along with jazz-related popular songs, whether by George Gershwin, Irving Berlin, and Cole Porter, among others, or by legions of lesser songwriters. He approached authentic jazz as an organic and evolutionary product that emerged from the same cultural interaction that created the African American spiritual. The spiritual, Dodge theorized, was "the result of straining a formal and highly cultivated music [i.e., the Anglo-American hymn] through the barbaric and musical mind of the Negro." Although the blues constituted "the basis of true jazz," the spirituals preceded the blues with "the savage rhythms that had shaped or been shaped by the ancestral dances of the tribe and these formed in time a definite playing style; and in recognizing this style we recognize jazz."[85]

Credit for the genius of true jazz, Dodge wrote, belonged to the "barbaric and musical mind of the Negro." Nevertheless, jazz attracted Dodge not through its informality or supposed simplicity and accessibility but through its complexity, a complexity he saw as recapitulating key steps in the linear development of mature idioms. He assumed a universal model of cultural development (based on European formal music) and sketched a developmental sequence from African chants and the "ancestral dances of the tribe" to New World spirituals, blues, and jazz. In short, the path to jazz retraced earlier phases in European music. "The development from the hymn and spiritual to the blues and stomp," Dodge contended in "Negro Jazz," "is paralleled in the history of classical music by the development of the fundamental chant as influenced by the rhythms of the dance tunes; a movement which culminated in the rhythmic, but certainly not drum-like, works of Bach."[86]

Dodge's exercise in cultural parallelism might bring to mind Alain Locke's 1908 lecture at Oxford on the "parallel evolution" of discrete cultures. Locke's notion of parallel evolution emphasized the promising evolutionary future of African American artistic culture. Dodge's foreboding sense of cultural decline made for dimmer hopes regarding the developmental future of jazz and African American folk music in general. He dated the golden age of jazz to the 1920s flowering of small-group jazz and warned that the idiom would collapse when its musicians succumbed to fatal influences in the surrounding culture — idiomatic and commercial influences best represented by Paul Whiteman, the self-declared spokesman of symphonic jazz.

Dodge held that the benefits of eighteenth-century classicism for European culture collapsed with Romanticism's hyperbolic expressivity. Romantic music's introspective character made evident the regrettable triumph of bourgeois individualism, a process that only accelerated when prominent musical modernists disavowed either classical structures or music's function as an accompaniment to dance. Therefore, the best jazz, Dodge suggested, shared features with the healthiest moments of European classical music. He wanted discerning listeners to appreciate music's ineradicable dance function as well as the more specific values of counterpoint and melodic development as pursued in the virtuosic art of collective improvisation. Certain jazz idioms presented themselves to Dodge as evidence of a new classicism and an authentic resurgence of healthy folk music.

> Jazz is certainly, as was the contrapuntal music, a music of the people. And like the music of the contrapuntal period, it is distinguished by the same bare melodies, stripped to fundamentals, driving with a continuous flow of musical thought to a natural and inevitable conclusion. There is no pause, no turning to one side, no attempt to lift the music to uncertain heights, as in romantic music of the pre-decadent period. Jazz melodies, like contrapuntal melodies, inspire both melodic and contrapuntal development and do not depend on full-throated orchestration to cover a lack of fundamental virility.[87]

Dodge's sense of the best jazz and its "fundamental virility" centered on a core set of characteristics; an absence of these characteristics indicated the impurities of derivative "pseudo-jazz." The essay "Negro Jazz" thereby fused a stereotype about "the musical and barbaric mind of the Negro" to an antimodernist classicism.

Dodge pushed a double-edged compliment to its limit in praising a classic music born of "barbaric" minds incapable of recognizing their own creation's value. A perusal of early jazz periodicals like *Jazz Music, Jazz Forum*, and the *Record Changer* reveals the frequency of such compliments among connoisseurs wedded to romantic and folkloric interpretations of early jazz. "The creative playing found in *low-down* jazz," Dodge argued, "is establishing a stronger form than any that has arisen for centuries. It is a musical form produced by the primitive innate musical instinct of the Negro and of those lower members of the white race who have not yet lost their feeling for the primitive." The primitive musical instincts definitive of Dodge's "Negro" were also within the reach of whites; these were elements of an early stage in cultural evolution rather than ahistorical features of an essentially different race. In jazz and other musics, Dodge placed highest priority on melodies "stripped to fundamentals" that drove "with a continuous flow of musical thought to a natural and inevitable conclusion." Recorded and live jazz performances that bore "masterpieces of structural beauty" made their claims on Dodge's connoisseurship as alternatives to lesser forms of scored-through formal music.[88] He demanded a premium of melodic development from jazz and a logical path toward an "inevitable conclusion." The growing popularity of repetitive solo "riffing" and ensemble parts (basic elements of big band jazz) that abandoned the "continuous flow of musical thought to a natural and inevitable conclusion" frustrated Dodge profoundly. As he later wrote: "riffs are about the easiest type of music to assimilate and for this very reason become obnoxious when they are 'overloaded.'"[89]

Partisans of the New Orleans style regularly complained that riffs had "taken the place of spontaneous improvisation" in recent big band and small-group jazz styles.[90] Influential critics friendlier to recent styles, including Hammond and Hugues Panassié, made a point of defending the potential for genuine aesthetic excitement in contemporary "riff" playing.[91] Skepticism about the dependence on "riffs" in section writing for big bands grounded Dodge's tepid response to the Basie ensemble's performance at the "From Spirituals to Swing" concert. The repetitiveness of boogie-woogie piano, however, did not incur a similar judgment from

Dodge, perhaps because boogie-woogie's highly percussive and harmonically stable style made for a strong alternative to the pianistic romanticism he abhorred. The material on a series of Blue Note records by Meade Lux Lewis in 1945, for example, suggested to Dodge that Lewis had "the greatest imagination of any keyboard artist." "The music is so highly charged in its own way that, like Bach's fugues, no individual side stands out separate from the group."[92] Unfortunately for Dodge, Whiteman's symphonic jazz and the many big bands (including Basie's) that followed Fletcher Henderson's model of section playing parted ways with some of the New Orleans style precedents that he preferred.

Dodge's disappointment with the greater share of jazz-related music could hardly surprise readers familiar with his classicist ideal. He unleashed a special virulence on musicians who betrayed precious jazz idioms by fusing them together with postclassical European structures. Thus, Whiteman's hybridic symphonic jazz earned Dodge's greatest condemnation: "Whiteman, Gershwin, Berlin, and others are exponents of frivolous art; if there is anything bogus about jazz it is certain to be found in their type of jazz." Dodge's complaints about the "frivolous art" of *Rhapsody in Blue* built on his distaste for the nonjazz genre to which Gershwin appealed. "Gershwin selected that stalest of decadent forms, the rhapsody," Dodge fumed, "an episodic form that allows the furthest possible departure from the logical carrying to completion of a single musical idea, and hence, probably the form more remote from the genuine jazz ideal than any other." The supposed "jazz contribution of Whiteman's famous orchestra which consists in the application of little jazz rhythms or syncopation to popular songs and popular classics" could never impress Dodge.[93] Whiteman treated jazz less as a distinctive idiom than as a loosely defined method of treatment, a technique of "jazzing." Dodge utterly rejected Whiteman's claim (in the 1926 book *Jazz* and elsewhere) that jazz was best understood as a verb rather than as a noun. Authentic jazz involved specific idiomatic practices, Dodge insisted; it was an advanced folk music with a set of formal procedures that demanded improvisational virtuosity from its players. These principles did not render jazz racially exclusive for Dodge. He argued in "Negro Jazz as Folk Material for Our Modern Dance" (1936) that "the blackface comedian was an imitation of the Negro idiosyncrasy, [while] white jazz music and dancing, on the other hand, is our reaction to the Negro reaction to our culture." "Blackface is imitation of racial idiosyncrasy," Dodge suggested, "whereas modern jazz is doing something vital in our own way." "There is a great difference," he concluded, "between expressing a natural impulse within our own medium ... and making an effort to imitate another in either his personal or racial idiosyncrasy."[94]

Dodge ended "Negro Jazz" by looking to the music's future. "Much as jazz is supposed to dominate our modern music," he wrote, "it is really rare in its pure state."[95] Although some modernist composers saw in jazz a resource for refreshing new ideas, their appropriations of folk music only destroyed its finest elements.[96] Jazz music, in Dodge's purist understanding of the genre, was a folk idiom more fragile than flexible. Its idiomatic purity would only decline, he assumed, under continued contact with commercial music and such "pseudo-jazz" idioms as symphonic jazz. Decadent commercial or elite influences would only corrupt the pure folk spirit of true jazz.

The growth of discriminating jazz connoisseurship, thanks to the wonders of phonographic recording, promised some support for the pioneers of the authentic music. The music of the pioneers "will grow," Dodge hoped, and the "confusion between true jazz and its bastard children of the polite orchestras will become less" if a sizable audience could make a preference for the real jazz clear. Ultimately, jazz depended on the maintenance of essential cultural differences; the music would "exist so long as the Negro lives *in* our civilization but not *of* it."[97] Dodge's 1934 essay "Harpsichords and Jazz Trumpets" presented an idiosyncratic defense of jazz to readers of the modernist journal *Hound & Horn*. The essay extended Dodge's earlier musings on jazz music's folk roots and formal characteristics, its recapitulation of "the contrapuntal period" of European music, and the challenges facing its development. He focused on the dance function inherited from folk music and the exuberant power of group and individual improvisation. Beyond these local reflections, Dodge contemplated the relative obsolescence of these characteristics in European art more generally. "Of the old technique of ballet," he lamented, "all we have left is disintegration; and a revolt ... as intellectually manufactured as Schonberg's revolt against harmonic accord." The rigors of improvisation had fallen on hard times in formal music and dance, despite an apparent vogue for expressionistic dance. "What passes for improvisatory art in our exclusive little studios of both dancing and music, where the girls and boys find new freedom in expressing the machine-age or the dynamic release of the soul, or in musical combinations in the manner of the written works of Liszt, Scriabin, Milhaud or Gershwin, is not the art of improvisation that I discuss."[98] In European music's golden age, Dodge countered, leading musicians regularly trained as virtuoso improvisers. The true "art of improvisation" was the result of a dedication to formal principles rather than an undisciplined libertinism dedicated to romantic expressivity and the "dynamic release of the soul." Dodge speculated that J. S. Bach's improvisational defenses of his theory of the well-tempered clavier probably inspired music superior to the written works that he left behind.

Dodge maintained that the musically sophisticated creators of the purest jazz remained ignorant of their own achievement.[99] "The negro," he argued, "is still musically unconscious of what he has done or what he may do." Nevertheless, readers were not to conclude that jazz was "still at the simple folk-tune stage." "Far from it," Dodge exclaimed: "For though the birth of the Spiritual was the birth of a new folk song containing the seed of Jazz, Jazz itself has reached the highest development of any folk music since the early Christian hymns and dances grew into the most developed contrapuntal music known to history."[100]

Jazz music, as of 1934, had reached the far edge of a folk music's development only to hover at a dangerous threshold. The dissonance between the jazzmen's supposed lack of perspective on their achievements and the actual scope of their artistry only highlighted the moment's threshold quality. Folk players with limited exposure to other musics made the greatest jazz, while trained cosmopolitan musicians produced only weak "pseudojazz" or jazz-related music. Throughout the 1930s and 1940s, Dodge continually described jazz music as poised to exit the folk music stage and enter a stage of self-conscious development signaled by formal notation and long-form composition. A comparison with Alain Locke becomes relevant at this point. Locke leaned toward a classicist aesthetic of austerity, restraint, and structural balance, but nineteenth-century European Romanticism and twentieth-century modernism in music hardly left him scandalized. Indeed, Romanticism made possible the paradigm of folk nationalism in music that Locke found so relevant for the cosmopolitan marriage of formal music and African American folk music. Locke further imagined early jazz performers as a folkish "shock-troop advance" for the creators of modern European music. Dodge regarded the purest contemporary jazz as a delicate refuge from a corrupt modernism, while Locke approached jazz music as a vernacular resource for African American concert music, a new tradition that would interact with broader modernist advances and stand beside other national schools of formal music.

The proliferation of jazz arrangements for big bands in the 1920s and 1930s excited Locke about formalization and the music's developmental possibilities. The same developments fell short of Dodge's expectations for the music's evolution. Whiteman's scored-through symphonic jazz had appeared prematurely, Dodge insisted, and therefore failed as a genuine step forward in the music's evolution from a folk to a formal music. The big band arrangements of Fletcher Henderson, Benny Carter, Edgar Sampson, and Duke Ellington did not necessarily point to a proper future either, though Dodge preferred Ellington over Whiteman. Ellington deserved credit, Dodge acknowledged, for understanding that jazz would not advance by merely borrowing European forms and thus reshaping itself for the sake of scored-through arrangements. To whatever extent possible, novel ideas would have to arise from within the idiom and related folk sources. The unusual harmonic density and inventiveness of Ellington's writing that so impressed other critics, however, failed to excite Dodge. He could hardly celebrate apparent influences on jazz from Romantic and post-Romantic music that rejected his strictures on logical melodic development and instead emphasized harmonic experimentation and impressionistic tonal coloring in an effort to "lift the music to uncertain heights."[101] Ellington's distinctive tonal coloring impressed Dodge far less than the soaring improvisational power of the soloists in Ellington's orchestra. Individuals in the Ellington ensemble such as the late Bubber Miley had created entirely new approaches to European instruments. For Dodge, the brilliance of Ellington's 1920s band music rested in its being "very loosely arranged; the whole affair a sort of arranged background for improvisation."[102] Dodge credited Ellington with leading jazz through the late 1920s and early 1930s with a strong focus on improvisation "at a time when big orchestra leaders were letting go the great heritage of jazz improvisation and relying solely on the complete arrangement."[103]

Dodge asserted throughout the 1930s and 1940s that the predominant jazz arranging styles utterly failed to capture the power of the virtuosic instrumental solo. "This being one of the last stages in folk development," he speculated, "the Jazz arrangers are not equal to the task and their output is very tiresome."[104] A "jazz academy" struck Dodge as unavoidable. Invoking a masculinist ideal of folk music similar to Hammond's hot jazz aesthetic, Dodge found the real promise of a "jazz academy" to depend on the "continuance of this virile school of improvisation." The most artistically ambitious jazz arrangers, always at a slight remove from folk music's core, carried a daunting burden: to formalize the brilliant inventiveness of the virtuoso improvisers without diluting the music's power. Dodge worried throughout the Swing Era that jazz arrangers were not proving themselves equal to their developmental mission.[105]

Dodge also took pains to distinguish his views from the counterprogressive tendencies of the New Orleans revivalists. "For jazz to maintain a vital reason for continuing," he argued in an essay calling for advances in the musical notation of jazz, "it must go ahead." Any "improvement of this situation," however, could only be "a matter for the folk themselves."[106] Dodge did not want to set the clock back or eschew the promise of further musical progress. By contrast, the very notion of formal arrangement was anathema to many New Orleans revivalists and their unchanging ideal of collective improvisation. "To build up a theory on the impossibility of arrangement as something outside of jazz" is wrong, Dodge countered. Jazz connoisseurs needed sufficient historical perspective to see that "any music in its earlier stages is as much spot improvisation as is jazz."[107] Nevertheless, Dodge admitted to finding more cause for hope in the New Orleans revival than he did in bebop and the modern jazz of the postwar era.

Duke Ellington's longer compositions of the 1930s and 1940s, such as "Reminiscing in Tempo" and *Black, Brown and Beige*, failed to impress Dodge. Dodge's regrets about Ellington and the progress of bebop somewhat resembled Hammond's disillusionment, but Ellington's development particularly disheartened Dodge. To Dodge, Ellington's supposed shortcomings reflected the incapacity of even the most advanced jazz artists to elevate a classic folk music into a classic formal music, as both internal and external factors thwarted the music's proper development. The music succumbed to the surrounding decadence and failed whenever it stopped offering a refuge from and an active alternative to modern European music. "The present decadence of jazz, with us in spite of great developments in player ability," Dodge concluded in 1955, "owes much to the fact that throughout this last stretch there has been unavoidable and constant contact with the classical music of the 19th century and the modern classical music of the 20th." Modern jazz and the efforts to extend the original folk music into long-form idioms showed "jazz in the process of a losing battle."

Dodge's early faith in jazz as a folk music that would provide the basis for a renewed musical classicism ended in disillusionment. By the mid-1950s he was certain that "jazz will not, as it should, become a part of musical life like the classical music of various periods."[108] In his struggle to "save jazz from its friends," Dodge instituted a barricade of critical demands so high that fewer and fewer exponents of his beloved music could meet his expectations. Within thirty years of Whiteman's "Experiment in Modern Music," Dodge had given up on the music's developmental prospects altogether.

Roger Pryor Dodge's idiosyncratic jazz classicism stressed the vaguely defined values of folk authenticity and idiomatic purity differently than Hammond's far more influential music criticism. Like many partisans of the idealized New Orleans style, Dodge judged jazz performances according to how closely they hewed to a classical model of collective improvisation. The Count Basie orchestra, Hammond's ideal jazz ensemble, never met Dodge's higher criteria. To his exacting ideal of true jazz in its folk stage, Dodge added further demands about the proper shape of jazz in its postfolk stages. His denunciations of Whiteman's symphonic jazz as a weak hybridic dilution of authentic jazz were symptomatic of much broader currents in hot jazz criticism willing to preserve an ideal of folk authenticity even at the cost of hybrids more productive than Whiteman's.

Duke Ellington played a major role in the developmental drama that Dodge regarded as essential. Although he was very close to an ideal shared by Alain Locke and Roger Pryor Dodge of a jazz composer who could organically push the music to further stages demanded by its internal developmental logic, Ellington ended up disappointing Dodge. To other critics, including Hammond, who were less impressed by the possibilities of a renewed classicism in jazz, Ellington's emerging ambitions presented a revised version of an old menace. Would the New Negro role model Duke Ellington, the most widely acclaimed composer in the jazz field, become the new Paul Whiteman?

EPILOGUE

And the traveller girds himself, and sets his
face toward the Morning, and goes his way.
—W. E. B. Du Bois[1]

What is important is the fact that Jazz has
something to say. . . . Still in the throes of
development and formation, it has fought its
way upwards through the effortful struggles
of sincere and irate musicians, has fought to
escape maljudgment at the hands of its own
"causified critics." . . . It has striven in a world
of other values, to get across its own message,
and in so doing, is striving, toward legitimate
acceptance, in proportion to its own merits.
—Duke Ellington[2]

One can appreciate the distinction of Duke Ellington through a contrast
with Benny Goodman and Count Basie, the Swing Era bandleaders most
closely associated with John Hammond. Goodman was eager to play with
top jazz musicians and to lead his popular big band in the work of the very
best arrangers. He publicly parted ways with hot jazz connoisseurs by taking a nonconfrontational stand on jazz music's artistic provenance. In a
1939 article for *Collier's* magazine, Goodman insisted that, above all,
swing meant fun. Those claiming that swing music had a far deeper social
significance were simply missing the point of the music. Using the Swing
Era jargon in which "icky" referred to the more intellectual and analytical

music fan, Goodman wrote: "To me the swing icky is as dismal as the high-brow music icky. Swing isn't as important as the icky thinks it, and certainly not as unimportant as the long-haired classicist thinks it."[3]

Goodman's sarcastic comments matched the oddly impenetrable image he presented in *The Kingdom of Swing* (1939), the autobiographical account of his rise from the immigrant working class to the pinnacle of the American popular music business. The white clarinetist's all-American success story did not so much create the "King of Swing" as "the mirror of swing," in Gary Giddins's apt phrase; in other words, Goodman reflected back upon his national audience "one of the nation's favorite images of itself."[4] Giddins adds that behind the friendly "King of Swing" image, Goodman was a notoriously remote and difficult employer, a workaholic, and a somber perfectionist. To let a "mirror of swing" drop from one's hands—whether it reflects an ideologically unifying image of Goodman, Ellington, Basie, or others—is to expose oneself to more conflicted and unreconciled currents in modern American culture. "The splinter in your eye," Theodor Adorno once wrote, "is the best magnifying glass."[5]

John Hammond played a leading role in crafting the "mirror of swing," not least through his inspiration of Goodman's refabrication and popularization of the 1920s hot jazz legacy in the mid-1930s. As noted, Goodman's band was never Hammond's favorite. "My favorite all-time band," Hammond admitted, "would be a tie—the old Basie band, and Fletcher's band, with maybe an edge to Basie."[6] Henderson's portfolio of big band arrangements made possible Goodman's conquest of the popular music business. About the Basie band, Goodman wrote in 1939 that "there is nothing like the pure swing this outfit has, from the moment it starts playing until it stops . . . [it] is in a class by itself."[7]

Basie, at the time of his band's 1936 "discovery" by Hammond in Kansas City, was embarking on a daringly modest conception of jazz piano, starting to pare down his piano parts to introductions, cues, rhythmic punctuations, and brief flurries of stride-style playing. His generally unobtrusive style led the "All American Rhythm Section" (bassist Walter Page, drummer Jo Jones, and guitarist Freddie Green) in a gravity-defying conception of 4/4 swing, while it supported such star soloists as Buck Clayton, Dickie Wells, Lester Young, Herschel Evans, and Harry Edison. "Basie," Gerald Early has noted, "was so much like the music he played, or at least so much like people thought his music was: the mighty burning of the unassuming."[8]

Duke Ellington represented a distinctive alternative to Goodman's and

Basie's senses of band leadership and Hammond's conception of the Swing Era. Unlike Goodman, Ellington enjoyed a reputation as jazz music's preeminent composer. Unlike Basie, Ellington often wrote pieces that were not so much blues-laced frames for improvisation and "riffing" as idiosyncratic compositions indelibly associated with the specific musical personalities in his band. Ellington's 1939 blast at "causified critics" was not referring to critics who had exaggerated his music's importance, but rather to critics who did not share his own sense of the music's significance. Rather than overestimating Ellington's artistic projects, jazz critics too often failed to view them in their proper context. Moreover, Ellington found the generic labels of "jazz" and "swing" inappropriate for his music. He pointed to the repetition and monotony plaguing the popular music business and explained that his band was "not concerned personally with these conditions, because our aim has always been the development of an authentic Negro music, of which swing is only one element." Widely praised as the creator of a particularly sophisticated product for the popular music market, Ellington intended his music to follow a different track altogether. "We are not interested primarily in the playing of jazz or swing music," he clarified, "but in producing musically a genuine contribution from our race. Our music is always intended to be definitely and purely racial. We try to complete a cycle."[9] Completing a cycle, in Ellington's case, demanded a creative response to the challenge of Whiteman's symphonic jazz and the New Negro aspiration toward black concert music capable of memorializing and elevating the black folk inheritance.

Hammond worked throughout the Swing Era to combine ideas of black-rooted authenticity in popular music together with what he called "the racially mixed stream of contemporary hot jazz."[10] Though he could hardly fault Hammond's antiracism and hot jazz activism, Ellington revisited the prospects of symphonic jazz in order to contribute to the African American concert music tradition. The musicologist Mark Tucker has shown how Ellington's discomfort with the restrictive labels of "jazz" and "swing," like his forthright black cultural nationalism, derived in part from his upbringing in Washington, D.C.

Born in 1899, Ellington was not raised in the segregated black community's most elite strata, but his family and educators nevertheless incited him to set his ambitions as high as possible. "Growing up black in Washington," Tucker notes, "trained Ellington to overcome the destructive effects of racism with patience, an iron will, and the sure conviction that any goal was within his grasp." "Perhaps most significant for a black composer seeking his vocation in the field of popular music," Tucker continues, black Washington gave the young Ellington "a sense of being part of a historical procession."[11] Black Washington showed the young Ellington that black history was something to be commemorated, whether in dramatic pageants like "The Star of Ethiopia" written by W. E. B. Du Bois or in the presentation of African American concert music. Ellington remembered his education at "an all-colored school, [where] Negro history was crammed into the curriculum, so that we would know our people all the way back. They had pride there, the greatest race pride, and at that time there was some sort of movement to desegregate the schools in Washington, D.C. Who do you think were the first to object? Nobody but the proud Negroes of Washington, who felt that the kind of white kids we would be thrown in with were not good enough."[12]

The New Negro vision of cultural production as an uplifting source of racial pride and cosmopolitan progress was not an invention of the mid-1920s Harlem Renaissance. Du Bois's *The Souls of Black Folk* followed Dvořák's suggestion in arguing that the black folk inheritance be honored through the cultivation of music as a site of social memory and formal artistry. Ellington's adult contributions to New Negro cultural nationalism, however, were idiosyncratic. His varied musical output, taken as a whole, challenged prevailing assumptions about boundaries between entertainment and art, between popular and formal music.[13] As a young Washingtonian, Ellington had known African American classical musicians who worked by necessity in the field of popular music. Segregation and racial discrimination had profoundly limited these musicians' career options. Ellington did not pursue an extended study of formal concert music; taking the path of popular music, however, did not cancel his artistic ambitions. He came to public attention in the late 1920s and early 1930s as a jazz composer and bandleader striving for recognition as a serious musical artist. Unlike Paul Whiteman, Ellington led his small jazz orchestra in music drawn from his own pen and the personalities of his highly individualistic players. Ellington's public statements about producing a "genuine contribution from our race" distinguished him from Whiteman, even as they linked him to Whiteman's pursuit of bourgeois respectability through symphonic jazz. "The music of my race is something more than the 'American idiom,'" Ellington announced in a characteristically defiant gesture. "It is the result of our transplantation to American soil, and was our reaction in the plantation days to the tyranny we endured. What we could not say openly we expressed in music, and what we know as 'jazz' is something more than just dance music. It expresses our personality, and, right down in us, our souls react to the elemental but eternal rhythm, and the dance is timeless and unhampered by any lineal form."[14]

As early as 1930, Ellington commented for publication about his own music's potential role in the long-term development of African American music. He wrote admiringly of such Renaissance icons as Paul Robeson and Roland Hayes, adding that "from the welter of negro dance musicians now before the public will come something lasting and noble I am convinced." Ellington was certain that the music popularly known as "jazz" was "going to play a considerable part in the serious music of the future."[15] R. D. Darrell's admiring 1932 essay "Black Beauty" captured Ellington's unusual position among dance bandleaders as an ambitious New Negro composer. Ellington was a "man who knows exactly what he is doing," Darrell pointed out, "while he remains securely rooted in the fertile artistic soil of his race." Darrell went on to note that Ellington "has stated in unmistakable words his own credo, no press agent's blurb of a talented but ungrounded black, but the staunch ideal of a new Negro . . . an artist who has the right to claim, 'I put my best thoughts into my tunes, and not hackneyed harmonies and rhythms which are almost too banal to publish.'"[16]

Ellington initiated a prolific and distinctive stream of band recordings to please and challenge the marketplace as the composer for and leader of a popular band in the late 1920s. Not all of his early output was exceptionally daring, but by 1930 his band had recorded a number of landmark short compositions including "East St. Louis Toodle-oo," "Black and Tan Fantasy," "The Mooch," "Black Beauty," and "Creole Love Call." Discerning listeners quickly found that these early recordings displayed a compositional originality and complexity far beyond the expectations of either popular taste or a more discerning hot jazz connoisseurship. "A lot of Duke's material goes over our heads, because we are not used to having to listen that carefully," Helen Oakley wrote in a 1936 appeal to *Down Beat* readers on behalf of Ellington. "When you say that they don't swing," she continued defensively, "remember that they don't play the tempos or style you are accustomed to. Try paying attention once, and remember that more styles than one can be good . . . and some may be better."[17] Ellington was the bandleader and composer whose creativity most often soared above the competition to expand the very horizons of contemporary music, Oakley insisted. Ellington explained to an interviewer in 1936 that his ensemble made "real Negro music" by "getting the different Negro idioms in cluster forms" and then distributing "those idioms in arrangement and

still retain[ing] their Negroid quality."[18] Among those who supported Ellington's claim for his music as "definitely and purely racial," his music's
racial element often became part of the explanation of his artistic success.
Along these lines, Paul Miller offered some remarks to *Down Beat* readers
on how to understand Ellington's greatness.

> The evolution of swing music has not been without effort, and the
> important landmarks in the process of evolution are curiously though
> definitely all very dark in colour. . . . Despite any recent attacks on El-
> lington, he remains the peer of all jazz musicians, beside whose sheer
> genius the prowess of white pianists pales into embarrassing insig-
> nificance. For Ellington understands jazz as no one else does. While
> the white man has laboriously striven to identify himself and his
> efforts with the essential requirements of swing, this preliminary has
> been unnecessary in the case of the Negro. And while many a white
> musician has been schooling himself in the harsher aspects of what he
> believes to be pure jazz, Ellington has been attacking these same as-
> pects with a soft eraser, toning them down, and in some instances rub-
> bing them out altogether. The result is that in Ellington's music there
> is no suggestion of condecension [*sic*], but rather an elevation to art-
> istry. He substitutes sincere emotion for the white musician's lack of
> feeling and use of mere technical skill. His style is genuine, unaffected,
> graceful, possessing strength. His originality has been unequalled by
> any white man, and his contribution to the evolution of jazz in general
> remains unmatched by anyone. His has been a logical development of
> style, and the culmination of this style in Reminiscing in Tempo is
> perfect testimony to his incontestable genius and vision.[19]

Miller implied that African American musicians arrived at the "essential requirements of swing" through a less trying initiation than that undertaken by nonblack musicians. Although he was defending Ellington's
controversial "Reminiscing in Tempo" against Hammond's criticisms,
Miller reinforced Hammond's racial assumptions about jazz by noting
"the white musician's lack of feeling and use of mere technical skill." Miller's comments on color, "genuine" style, and "unaffected" feeling under-
wrote the idea of African American superiority in jazz and upheld Ellington's special aptitude for more formally ambitious jazz compositions.
Such essentializing statements joined a long tradition of commentaries
about African American musicians' cultural inheritance as a racially specific set of advantages and disadvantages. Ellington's defense of his for-

mally innovative compositions as "definitely and purely racial" added value to the currency of racialized aesthetics in the Swing Era; it also challenged the focus on unself-conscious folk expressivity in much hot jazz connoisseurship. Ellington led the list of possible exceptions from strictures on idiomatic purity among hot jazz critics committed to the struggle between a folk art's purity and primitive naiveté and the formal dilutions of jazz motivated by wayward commercial and cultural aspirations. What Miller called Ellington's "logical development of style" tested the connoisseurial criteria of folk authenticity because Ellington's most ambitious compositions threatened ideals of idiomatic purity that presumed a definitive threshold between entertainment and art, informal and formal music.

Ellington's 1935 recording of "Reminiscing in Tempo" suggested to Hammond a great popular artist gone astray. Jake Trussell's notion of "denaturalization" in Ellington's forays into longer-form music similarly played on the romantic idealization of hot jazz as a humble folk music manufactured without self-conscious artistic effort. Perhaps with Hammond's "recent attack on Ellington" in mind, Paul Miller insisted that Ellington was an artist of "incontestable genius and vision" shaping a path for jazz music's evolutionary development. Ellington had risen to unparalleled mastery of jazz fundamentals and was free to apply a "soft eraser" in refining the harsher qualities of "pure jazz." Hammond, by contrast, esteemed the Basie band above all others precisely because of its "rough edges." Rather than see those edges polished and refined, Hammond hoped that they might be highlighted and made even "more jagged." If the Basie band was to lose its distinctive roughness, Hammond's rhetoric implied, it would lose its fundamental "blackness," the imagined source of its greatness.

Ellington's compositional leadership was refining and directing the "logical development of style" in the mid-1930s, according to Miller, precisely because he was a master of jazz fundamentals and related techniques in blues-based idioms. It was only on the basis of such idiomatic mastery, Miller argued, that a composer could contribute to "the evolution of jazz in general." Perhaps Whiteman and his architects of symphonic jazz had failed to fully reckon with New Orleans idioms and the aesthetics of black vernacular musics before undertaking the famous parody of "Livery Stable Blues" at the 1924 "Experiment in Modern Music" concert. Miller elsewhere defined symphonic jazz as "an attempt to render in academic forms the materials and techniques which are generally associated with jazz."[20]

From this perspective, Whiteman's championing of Gershwin's *Rhapsody in Blue* amounted to a premature cosmopolitan experiment that laid out no original path for the "logical development of style."

From Hammond's perspective, "Reminiscing in Tempo" and *Black, Brown and Beige* signaled a composer's dissatisfaction with jazz not only as a label but as an idiom. Ellington's interest in longer compositions, less dependent on instrumental solos improvised over a cycle of chord progressions, revealed to Hammond the influence of certain misguided critics. The concentration of elite enthusiasm raised by a British tour in 1933, according to Hammond, inspired Ellington to make plans for more ambitious music and betray the charms of jazz as a blues-based dance music. Hammond's influential story about Ellington's seduction by highbrow critics obscured the musical influences that Ellington encountered early on in Washington, D. C., and the composer's "sense of being part of a historical procession."[21] Behind Hammond's narrative of Ellington's highbrow seduction, one finds the hot jazz partisan's elemental repudiation of symphonic jazz. Hammond's long-standing repudiation of the symphonic jazz ideal fed his skepticism about Ellington's ambition to "complete a cycle" and move jazz into the African American concert tradition.

Ellington's ambition proved to be extraordinarily influential because it began from within the jazz idiom. Alain Locke argued that Whiteman's symphonic jazz was not so much an affront to folk purity in jazz or an outrageous case of cultural theft in "whiteface" as it was a serious challenge to African American composers. "Whiteman has converted the American public to the seriousness of jazz," Locke remarked, "and clinched Dvorak's prophecy that future American music would draw its substance from Negro sources."[22] Locke took care to credit less-well-known African American innovators, including James Reese Europe and Will Marion Cook, who had paved the way for Whiteman's symphonic jazz. Nevertheless, Whiteman's ethnicity and his high profile raised the stakes on seizing jazz's folk elements and developing them into self-conscious art. Locke praised Ellington in the mid-1930s as "one of the great exponents of pure jazz . . . [and] the pioneer of super-jazz and one of the persons most likely to create the classical jazz toward which so many are striving." "Ellington projects a symphonic suite and an African opera," Locke added, "both of which will prove a test of his ability to carry jazz to the higher level." Ellington's unique style, Locke contended, "has passed through more phases and developed more maturely than any of his more spectacular competitors."[23]

Hammond's 1938 "From Spirituals to Swing" concert struck Locke as a "high-water mark in the annals of Negro music" for allowing folk musicians to be heard in a concert hall as artists.[24] But even if Hammond's cast had been presented as artists, an implicit theme of the evening was that, as folk artists, the provincial musicians were unaware of the broader cosmopolitan drama into which their art had been positioned. Ellington, on the other hand, struggled to influence the reception of his music and the narrative into which it was to be inserted. He perceived Hammond's advocacy as intrusive, a form of meddling tainted by conflicts of interest and racial paternalism. In 1939, Ellington finally vented his frustrations in *Down Beat* magazine, where he wrote:

> The swing critic who perhaps has stirred the greatest resentment, while at the same time was earning the deepest gratitude of others, has been John Henry Hammond, Jr., son of a prominent New York family and possessed of wealth in his own right. . . . He appears to be an ardent propagandist and champion of the "lost cause." He apparently has consistently identified himself with the interests of the minorities, the Negro peoples, to a lesser degree, the Jew, and to the underdog, in the form of the Communist party. Perhaps due to the "fever of battle," Hammond's judgment may have become slightly warped, and his enthusiasm and prejudices a little bit unwieldy to control.[25]

Ellington did not participate in Hammond's "From Spirituals to Swing" concerts of 1938 or 1939. His own concert ambitions led him to an alternative narrative for the musical inheritance of the spirituals and African American folk culture. Locke played to Ellington's distaste for Hammond when he solicited the bandleader to perform in a *New Masses* concert of African American music scheduled for January 1940. Ellington's orchestra would dominate the concert's second half and would have "a chance at last," Locke confided, "to give a real Negro version without having to have any white producer intruding his ideas or particular whimsies."[26] *New Masses* canceled the concert, but the prospect of circumventing Hammond must have delighted Ellington.

Whiteman, we should note, had been an early fan of Ellington's original seven-piece band, The Washingtonians, who performed regularly at the Club Kentucky near Times Square from 1923 to 1927. Ellington remembered that "Paul Whiteman came often as a genuine enthusiast, listened respectfully, said his words of encouragement, very discreetly slipped the piano player a fifty-dollar bill, and very loudly proclaimed our musical merit."[27] Ellington was proud, for example, to have been asked to contribute an original composition, "Blue Belles of Harlem," for Whiteman's Carnegie Hall concert of Christmas 1938, his eighth "Experiment in Modern American Music." The concert took place two nights after "From Spirituals to Swing" and featured such guest stars as Louis Armstrong and Artie Shaw and new compositions by Ellington, Morton Gould, Fred Van Epps, and the late George Gershwin. As expected, the evening concluded with *Rhapsody in Blue*. Reviews were mixed and less enthusiastic than reviews for Hammond's concert. The New York *Amsterdam News* disapproved of Armstrong's treatment of the spiritual "Nobody Knows [the Troubles I've Seen]" and commented that the jazz clarinetist Artie Shaw "showed just how well ofays can steal the genius of their sepia brothers, make of it an art and reap a fortune."[28] Gama Gilbert wrote in the *New York Times* that Whiteman "brought with him enough live composers and first performances to make a jazz renaissance." Nevertheless, Gilbert (an associate of Hammond's) lambasted not only the concert but Whiteman's entire vision of a jazz renaissance. "It is music that was once jazz, trying to be something better than its own swell self. It is music that has scorned its musical heritage, cut its social roots and fallen for the empty glamour of vaudeville virtuosity. It has clothed innocent tunes in pretentious tonal raiment, and awaited the coming of the second 'Rhapsody in Blue.'"[29] In these pages we have already considered similar critiques of "pretentious tonal raiment" in the Swing Era and the reception of the concert spiritual idiom associated with Harlem Renaissance of the 1920s.

Ellington hoped that the second coming of *Rhapsody in Blue*, the ne plus ultra of symphonic jazz, would commence from his own pen. He and his orchestra finally arrived for their first full evening at Carnegie Hall in 1943. The concert's highlight, *Black, Brown and Beige* "provoked a good deal of controversy," Ellington commented far too mildly in his 1973 autobiography.[30] The long composition's premiere thrilled neither hot jazz purists nor those dedicated to protecting the standards of formal European concert music. Its mixed reception, biographers agree, discouraged Ellington but did not dissuade him from subsequently producing and premiering new long compositions at what became an Ellington tradition of annual Carnegie Hall concerts. To the affront of one group of connoisseurs, Ellington looked beyond the familiar eight-bar and twelve-bar blues and thirty-two-bar popular song structures that dominated jazz music. To the dismay of others, the composer demonstrated insufficient familiarity with long-form structures of European concert music onto which he might have grafted jazz motifs.

Was Ellington's *Black, Brown and Beige* a string of relatively discrete short pieces tied together into a suite, did it aspire to the structure of a classical European symphony, or was it something else? The composer denied that the three-part piece had formal symphonic structural ambitions. It was instead a "tone parallel" to the three-part historical narrative named in the title. Ellington defended his piece's construction by saying that the "things we use are purely Negroid—we want to stay in character." "Quite simply," he concluded, "we are weaving a musical thread which runs parallel to the history of the American Negro."[31] Ellington often infused the short-form music and popular songs that constituted the bulk of his repertoire with a similar seriousness of purpose. "It Don't Mean a Thing (If It Ain't Got That Swing)" went the insouciant title of the 1932 Ellington hit that, for many, crystallized the meaning of jazz. But when Ellington explained to his public just what it meant to actually have "that swing," he often spoke with unexpected seriousness about the historical progression that his music participated in. Swinging, Ellington explained, had a history that long preceded the popular vogue of the Swing Era. His music would help illuminate that history. We are reminded here of Arthur Schomburg's exclamation that "the American Negro must remake his past in order to make his future."

The vogue for big band jazz crested in 1939. Both the explosive commercial appeal of dance music and the slow decline of the big bands led to the stylistic revolution known as "bebop," a revolution centered in Harlem and engineered by young members of a rising African American generation of professional jazz musicians. Hammond's influence as a tastemaker declined somewhat, but the ideological limitations of hot jazz criticism in the Swing Era had been visible for some time.

The variousness of Ellington's musical achievement, which registered the virtuosic challenges of bebop but never parted too abruptly from Ellington's distinctive course, would continue to test the endurance and flexibility of the invisible boundaries between the European-derived culture of formal concert music and the predominantly African American culture of jazz. Ellington's massive output (a steady stream of new music continued until his death in 1974) illuminated the threshold simultaneously constituting and dividing these historical boundaries. We have seen that some of his compositions once resided at the margins of a purist critical discourse about jazz music. In the last decades of the twentieth century, a so-called neoclassical interpretation of Ellington's art arose. The neoclassical paradigm aimed to fix the musical and social meaning of El-

lington's legacy (including his later long-form work) as an inviolable center for the jazz tradition. The brilliant music and provocative ideas of Wynton Marsalis, the most famous and institutionally powerful jazz musician
of his generation, came to represent the neoclassical project. Marsalis's
statements on behalf of a new classicism about the jazz tradition in the
1980s and 1990s publicized his desire to quarantine what he saw as a coherent musical tradition's normative center from wayward influences active
on the art's margins. The neoclassical approach, a musical and ideological
reaction against the legacies of jazz-pop fusion, free jazz, and the fusion of
jazz and European "new music" since the 1960s, might be understood as a
passionate and contentious bid for "saving jazz from its friends." Neoclas-
sicist spokesmen, especially Marsalis and the writers Stanley Crouch and
Albert Murray, often make their inheritance claims upon the Ellington
legacy with a vehemence reminiscent of the claims to inheritance that
W. E. B. Du Bois made on the "sorrow songs" legacy. From the beginning
of the 1980s jazz debate, however, critics of the neoclassical paradigm contended that Ellington's legacy was being distorted and transformed into
an essentially conservative and retrospective defense of a narrowly conceived canon of classic jazz. The basic function of all canonizing processes,
of course, is the elevation and conservation of a preferred genre through
restrictive selection.

The musicologist Gary Tomlinson has looked beyond the particularities of the neoclassicism debate to remind readers of how "by not scruti-
nizing the postulates of earlier canons, jazz historians have engaged in a
wholesale restatement of them."[32] In particular, the appealingly elegant
ideal of a unilinear jazz tradition depends on a notion of unbroken internal
development—as if the music was playing out its own intrinsic possibilities and immanent logic—that is historiographically untenable. Many
aestheticians of European concert music have, of course, been gripped
by such a homogenizing picture of the rational evolution of styles. Those
who seek to vindicate jazz along similar lines replicate rather than critique
the inherited logics of formalism that have long dominated scholarly writing on European music. The ideological postulates and historical specificities that lay behind European formal canons deserve historical scrutiny,
Tomlinson urges, rather than "a wholesale restatement" and replication as
a technique for legitimating parallel studies of a jazz canon.

This book has offered a critical genealogy for interpreting later musical
developments (such as neoclassicism) by exploring Harlem Renaissance
era replications, adaptations, and renunciations of powerful European as-

sumptions about music, nationalism, folklore, and aesthetic formalism. The musicologist Scott De Veaux has demonstrated how the various narratives of a single unified jazz tradition show a "tendency to impose a kind of deadening uniformity of cultural meaning on this music, and [display] jazz history's patent inability to explain current trends in any cogent form."[33] The temptation to a "deadening uniformity" is present whenever the history of jazz is narrated according to a unilinear evolutionary tale that passes from the participatory spaces of the jazz funeral, honky-tonk, and nightclub to the consummatory rituals of the concert auditorium. Too much important music-making takes place at the margins of genres and at the thresholds between musical worlds for such restrictive canonizing narratives to be as historically useful as evolutionists might hope. Canonizing narratives of the jazz tradition, for example, tend to make a strong distinction between jazz music and developments in concert music, especially African American concert music, thereby reinforcing the almost complete cultural invisibility of composers who have contributed to the African American concert music tradition. Early non-Ellington developments in symphonic jazz are similarly evaded, along with the relevant development of the concert spiritual genre. The polemical genre boundaries of Swing Era jazz criticism have long outlasted their usefulness. In the case of the canonizing project of jazz neoclassicists, contemporary popular music is also shunned as a symptom of what Marsalis calls "the whole decline in all of American musical culture."[34] The goal of neoclassicism, as the name suggests, is to rescue and rejuvenate an embattled legacy of classic achievement. Our examples from Harlem Renaissance and Swing Era debates have shown how similar salvage projects of musical recuperation and canonization are always highly concentrated points of ideological conflict.

There exists a methodological double fantasy among some students of the past in which the complete archival contextualization of a historical moment, once achieved (the first fantasy), will magically render forth the complete meaning of that moment (the second fantasy). The scholar might then transform a fully digested archive, according to this fantasy, into a luminous and nondistorting portrait of an age. The study of music and memory in Harlem Renaissance thought pursued in this book does not aim at a comprehensive portrait of a historical moment. Instead, my goal has been to critically reconstruct and juxtapose some of the perspectives of certain historical actors. My hope is that the inevitably partial intellectual portraits sketched here might help us in reframing fundamental questions about the period. The Harlem Renaissance moment demands continual reframing, not least because it is becoming harder and harder to imagine ourselves as truly postmodern or truly independent of its unfinished business. The resonant songs and dreams of the period and perennial desires for a fulfillment of longings captured in spirituals like "Deep River" still energize the imaginations of many. This book has aspired to demonstrate how even the struggles over genre definitions and narratives of idiomatic evolution and canonization in music speak to broader social struggles for institutional legitimacy and authority over the interpretation of the past and present.

Having reached these contemporary questions, our brief historical investigation has come full circle. Remembering and promising to develop a folk inheritance can provide an invaluable sense of continuity in the midst of tumultuous social transformation and cultural modernization. Such retrospective projects can inspire novel progressive ideals or ossify into restrictive and reifying nationalist policies against hybridic adaptations and aesthetic and social freedom. Examples abound for both trajectories. We are left to ask whether the call of Du Bois's beloved "sorrow songs" can still affirm the depth of past struggles and achievements along with a passionate reach into the future toward unfulfilled ideals of social transformation in a postracist world. We might be heartened that such evocative and hopeful ciphers of memory and anticipation can be recollected, sung, and shared around the world.

NOTES

INTRODUCTION

1 This variation on the lyrics of "Deep River" is in Howard Thurman, *Deep River: Reflections on the Religious Insight of Certain of the Negro Spirituals* (Port Washington, N.Y.: Kennikat Press, 1969), 66.

2 Alain Locke, "The New Negro," in *The New Negro*, ed. Alain Locke (New York: Atheneum, 1968), pp. 4, 6. Subsequent citations from the 1925 anthology shall refer to this edition.

3 Ibid., p. 14.

4 Arthur A. Schomburg, "The Negro Digs Up His Past," in *The New Negro*, p. 231.

5 Samuel A. Floyd, Jr., "Music in the Harlem Renaissance: An Overview," in *Black Music in the Harlem Renaissance*, ed. Samuel A. Floyd, Jr. (Westport, Conn.: Greenwood Press, 1990), p. 3. For a probing analysis of memory and modernism in Harlem Renaissance music, see also Samuel A. Floyd Jr., *The Power of Black Music* (New York: Oxford University Press, 1995), esp. pp. 100–135.

6 Alain Locke, "The Negro Spirituals," in *The New Negro*, p. 209.

7 Ibid., p. 208.

8 W. E. B. Du Bois, *The Souls of Black Folk* (New York: Library of America, 1990), p. 9.

9 Jean Toomer, "On Being an American," from "Outline of an Autobiography" [ca. 1931–32], in *The Wayward and the Seeking: A Collection of Writings by Jean Toomer*, ed. Darwin T. Turner (Washington, D.C.: Howard University Press, 1980), p. 123.

10 MacKinley Helm, *Angel Mo' and Her Son, Roland Hayes* (Boston: Little, Brown, 1942), p. 189.

11 Carl Van Vechten, "The Folksongs of the American Negro," *Vanity Fair* (July 1925), p. 92.

12 Quoted in Horace Kallen, "Alain Locke and Cultural Pluralism," *Journal of Philosophy* 54 (February 28, 1957): 121.

13 Ibid., pp. 121–22.

14 Alain Locke, *The Negro and His Music* (Port Washington, N.Y.: Kennikat, 1968), p. 73.

15 Ibid., p. 87.

16 Zora Neale Hurston, "Spirituals and Neo-Spirituals," in *Zora Neale Hurston: Folklore, Memoirs, and Other Writings*, ed. Cheryl A. Wall (New York: Library of America, 1995), p. 870.

17 Duke Ellington, "Duke Says Swing is Stagnant," in *The Duke Ellington Reader*, ed. Mark Tucker (New York: Oxford University Press, 1994), p. 135.

ONE   *"Unvoiced Longings": Du Bois and the "Sorrow Songs"*

1 W. E. B. Du Bois, *The Souls of Black Folk* (New York: Library of America, 1990), p. 148.

2 Herbert Marcuse, *The Aesthetic Dimension: Toward a Critique of Marxist Aesthetics* (Boston: Beacon Press, 1978), p. 73.

3 Olin Downes, quoted by W. E. B. Du Bois, "Our Music," *Crisis*, July 1933, in *W. E. B. Du Bois: Writings*, ed. Nathan Huggins (New York: Library of America, 1986), p. 1239.

4 Jon Michael Spencer, *The New Negroes and Their Music* (Knoxville: University of Tennessee Press, 1997), p. 68.

5 For an analysis of nineteenth-century American abolitionists, folkloric ideologies, and romantic racialism, see Ronald Radano, "Denoting Difference: The Writing of the Slave Spirituals," *Critical Inquiry* 22 (Spring 1996): 506–44. On Du Bois in particular, see Ronald Radano, "Soul Texts and the Blackness of Folk," *Modernism/Modernity* 2, no. 1 (1995): 71–95.

6 J. B. T. Marsh, *The Story of the Jubilee Singers: With Their Songs* (Boston: Houghton, Osgood, 1880), p. 66.

7 Eileen Southern, *The Music of Black Americans: A History*, 2d ed. (New York: W. W. Norton, 1983), p. 226.

8 Neil Harris, *Humbug: The Art of P. T. Barnum* (Boston: Little, Brown, 1973).

9 Anonymous reviews quoted in Louis D. Silveri, "The Singing of the Fisk Jubilee Singers: 1871–1874," in *Feel the Spirit: Studies in Nineteenth-Century Afro-American Music*, ed. George R. Keck and Sherrill V. Martin (Westport, Conn.: Greenwood Press, 1988), p. 106.

10 Quoted in Marsh, *The Story of the Jubilee Singers*, p. 30.

11 Quoted in ibid., p. 121.

12 Quoted in Gustavus D. Pike, *The Jubilee Singers and Their Campaign for Twenty Thousand Dollars* (Boston: Lee and Shephard, 1873), p. 118. According to Thomas Higginson, the abolition of slavery offered a counterweight to the spirituals' pain and made the sublime songs pleasurable to hear: "By these they could sing themselves, as had their fathers before them, out of the contemplation of their own low estate, into the sublime scenery of the Apocalypse. I remember that this

minor-keyed pathos used to seem to me almost too sad too dwell upon, while slavery seemed destined to last for generations; but now that their patience has had its perfect work, history cannot afford to lose this portion of its record. There is no parallel instance of an oppressed race thus sustained by the religious senti-ment alone. These songs are but the vocal expression of the simplicity of their faith and the sublimity of their long resignation." Thomas Wentworth Higgin-son, *Army Life in a Black Regiment* [1870] (East Lansing: Michigan State Univer-sity Press, 1960), p. 173.

13 I am indebted to the interpretation of music and the "slave sublime" in Paul Gil-roy's *The Black Atlantic* (Cambridge, Mass.: Harvard University Press, 1993).

14 Radano, "Denoting Difference," p. 519.

15 Quoted in Silveri, "The Singing of the Fisk Jubilee Singers," p. 109.

16 Marsh, *The Story of the Jubilee Singers*, p. 53.

17 Gilroy, *The Black Atlantic*, p. 90.

18 Quoted in Marsh, *The Story of the Jubilee Singers*, p. 67.

19 Brown also authored the introduction for the first British edition of the tran-scribed *Slave Songs of the Fisk Jubilee Singers* in 1874.

20 Quoted in Marsh, *The Story of the Jubilee Singers*, p. 95.

21 Quoted in ibid., p. 100.

22 On Herder and cosmopolitanism, see Michael Morton, *Herder and the Poetics of Thought: Unity and Diversity in "On Diligence in Several Learned Languages"* (University Park: Pennsylvania State University Press, 1989).

23 Johann Gottfried von Herder, "Music, An Art of Humanity" (1802), trans. Ed-ward A. Lippman, in *German Essays on Music*, ed. Jost Hermand and Michael Gil-bert (New York: Continuum, 1994), p. 43.

24 Johann Gottfried von Herder, *Outlines of a Philosophy of the History of Man*, vol. I [1784], trans. T. Churchhill (London: Luke Hanford, 1803), p. 348.

25 Herder's lasting influence rests in his case for the primacy of native language and native literature—crystallized in his notion of a *Sprachgeist*—in the cultural foun-dations of modern nationalism, an argument made in his *On the New German Literature: Fragments*. Music, for Herder, was instead "among the most unculti-vated nations . . . the first of the fine arts." See Du Bois, "The Negro in Literature and Art" [1914], in *W. E. B. Du Bois: Writings*, pp. 862–67. Du Bois writes: "The time has not yet come for the great development of American Negro literature. The economic stress is too great and the racial persecution too bitter to allow the leisure and the poise for which literature calls. On the other hand, never in the world has a richer mass of material been accumulated by a people than that which the Negroes possess today are becoming conscious of" (p. 866).

26 Quoted in David Levering Lewis, *W. E. B. Du Bois: Biography of a Race, 1868–1919* (New York: Henry Holt, 1993), p. 77. Du Bois later critiqued his college self as "blithely European and imperialist in outlook." W. E. B. Du Bois, *Dusk of Dawn* (New York: Harcourt, Brace, 1940), p. 32.

27 Du Bois, *Dusk of Dawn*, p. 32.

28 Arnold Rampersad, *The Art and Imagination of W. E. B. Du Bois* (Cambridge, Mass.: Harvard University Press, 1976), p. 74.

29 Georg W. F. Hegel, *The Philosophy of History*, trans. J. Sibree (Buffalo, N.Y.: Prometheus Books, 1991), p. 63.

30 W. E. B. Du Bois, "The Spirit of Modern Europe" (1900?), in *Against Racism: Unpublished Essays, Papers, Addresses, 1887–1961*, ed. Herbert Aptheker (Amherst: University of Massachusetts Press, 1985), p. 51.

31 For critiques of Du Bois's essentialist notions of racial difference, see Kwame Anthony Appiah, "The Uncompleted Argument: Du Bois and the Illusion of Race," in *'Race,' Writing, and Difference*, ed. Henry Louis Gates Jr. (Chicago: University of Chicago Press, 1986), pp. 21–37, and "Illusions of Race," in Appiah, *In My Father's House*, pp. 28–46. For a response, see Houston A. Baker Jr., "Caliban's Triple Play," in *'Race,' Writing, and Difference*, pp. 381–95.

32 Du Bois, "The Spirit of Modern Europe," pp. 56, 57, 58.

33 Ibid., pp. 60, 61.

34 Ibid., pp. 52, 53, 54.

35 Ibid., p. 62.

36 W. E. B. Du Bois, "The Conservation of Races," in *W. E. B. Du Bois on Sociology and the Black Community*, ed. Dan S. Green and Edwin D. Driver (Chicago: University of Chicago Press, 1978), p. 245.

37 Du Bois, "The Spirit of Modern Europe," pp. 62, 63, 64.

38 Wilson Moses, *Afrotopia: The Roots of African American Popular History* (Cambridge: Cambridge University Press, 1998), p. 152.

39 Du Bois, *The Souls of Black Folk*, p. 180. On "unisonance" and national identity, see Benedict Anderson, *Imagined Communities: Reflections on the Origin and Spread of Nationalism*, rev. ed. (London: Verso, 1991). See also Du Bois's salute to Samuel Coleridge-Taylor in *Darkwater* (1920). The black British composer visited the United States and quickly "turned to the sorrow songs." He used that folk influence to respond "to his own people—to the sad sweetness of their voices, their inborn sense of music, their broken, half-articulate voices." "We know in America how to discourage, choke, and murder ability when it so far forgets itself as to choose a dark skin. England, thank God, is slightly more civilized than her colonies." Du Bois, *Darkwater*, in *The Oxford W. E. B. Du Bois Reader*, ed. Eric J. Sundquist (New York: Oxford University Press, 1996), p. 584.

40 James Weldon Johnson, *Along This Way* [1933] (New York: Penguin Books, 1990), p. 203.

41 For a sympathetic account of New Negro concert music that uses *The Autobiography of an Ex-Colored Man* as a guiding text, see Jon Michael Spencer, *The New Negroes and Their Music: The Success of the Harlem Renaissance* (Knoxville: University of Tennessee Press, 1997).

42 Robert B. Stepto, *From Behind the Veil: A Study of Afro-American Narrative* (Urbana: University of Illinois Press, 1979), pp. 126–27.

43 Du Bois, *The Souls of Black Folk*, p. 14.

44 Ibid., p. 180.

45 Eric J. Sundquist, *To Wake the Nations: Race in the Making of American Literature* (Cambridge, Mass.: Harvard University Press, 1993), p. 466.

46 Gilroy, *The Black Atlantic*, pp. 119–20.

47 Du Bois, *The Souls of Black Folk*, p. 182.

48 Ibid., pp. 181, 184.

49 Ronald Radano, "Soul Texts and the Blackness of Folk," *Modernism/Modernity* 2, no. 1 (1995): 74.

50 Du Bois, "The Religion of the American Negro" (1900), in *W. E. B. Du Bois on Sociology and the Black Community*, p. 216.

51 Du Bois, *The Souls of Black Folk*, pp. 187, 182, 185.

52 Ibid., p. 182.

53 Moses, *Afrotopia*, pp. 137–48.

54 Du Bois, *The Souls of Black Folk*, p. 188.

55 Consider the criticism of Cornel West: "As a highly educated Western black intellectual, Du Bois himself often scorns the 'barbarisms' (sometimes confused with Africanisms) shot through Afro-American culture. In fact, I count eighteen allusions to the 'backwardness' of black folk." Cornel West, *The American Evasion of Philosophy* (Madison: University of Wisconsin Press, 1989), p. 143.

56 Du Bois, *The Souls of Black Folk*, p. 144.

57 Ibid., p. 137.

58 I am indebted to Homi Bhabha's observation that celebrations of cultural diversity too often depend upon a "radical rhetoric of the separation of totalized cultures that lived unsullied by the intertextuality of their historical locations, safe in the Utopianism of mythic memory of a unique collective identity." Homi K. Bhabha, *The Location of Culture* (London: Routledge, 1994), p. 34.

59 Du Bois, *The Souls of Black Folk*, pp. 170–71.

60 Houston A. Baker Jr. "The Black Man of Culture: W. E. B. Du Bois and *The Souls of Black Folk*," in *Long Black Song: Essays in Black American Literature and Culture* (Charlottesville: University Press of Virginia, 1972), pp. 96–108. For an essay that focuses more on Du Bois's black nationalism, see Baker's *Modernism and the Harlem Renaissance* (Chicago: University of Chicago Press, 1987), pp. 53–69.

61 Rampersad, *The Art and Imagination of W. E. B. Du Bois*, p. 76.

62 W. E. B. Du Bois, "Forum of Fact and Opinion," *Pittsburgh Courier*, October 31, 1936, in *Newspaper Columns by W. E. B. Du Bois*, vol. 1, *1883–1944*, ed. Herbert Aptheker (White Plains, N.Y.: Kraus-Thomson Organization, 1986), p. 130. The centrality of the Holy Grail in Lohengrin makes an appearance in Du Bois's *Dark Princess* (1928). As he prepares to hear his criminal sentence, Matthew Townes—"a man of education and culture," as the judge puts it—imagines that the dramatic scene incomplete. "There should have been music, Matthew thought, some slow beat like the Saul death march or the pulse of the Holy Grail." *Dark Princess* (New York: Harcourt, Brace, 1928), pp. 100–101. For the musical and cultural contexts of Wagner's reception in the United States and an interpretation of Wagnerism as an American musical ideology, see Joseph Horowitz, *Wagner Nights: An American History* (Berkeley: University of California Press, 1994). Du Bois's Wagnerism deserves more attention than it has hitherto received. See Wilson Moses, *Afrotopia*, p. 67.

63 Du Bois, *The Souls of Black Folk*, pp. 8–9.

64 See M. H. Abrams, *Natural Supernaturalism* (New York: Norton, 1971), for an

exposition of Hegel's influence on European romanticism. The best-known interpretation of black alienation and disalienation indebted to Hegelianism appears in Frantz Fanon, *White Skin, Black Masks*, trans. Charles Lam Markmann (New York: Grove Press, 1967). For the intellectual context of Fanon's dialectical formulations, see *The Surreptitious Speech: Présence Africaine and the Politics of Otherness, 1947–1987*, ed. V. Y. Mudimbe (Chicago: University of Chicago Press, 1992).

65 On Du Bois and Hegelianism, see esp. Shamoon Zamir, *Dark Voices: W. E. B. Du Bois and American Thought, 1888–1903* (Chicago: University of Chicago Press, 1995). Zamir contrasts Du Bois's Hegelianism against the alternative influence of Jamesian pragmatism. For a subtle interpretation that reconciles Du Bois's creative adaptations of Hegelianism and Jamesian pragmatism, see Ross Posnock, *Color and Culture: Black Writers and the Making of the Modern Intellectual* (Cambridge, Mass.: Harvard University Press, 1998), esp. pp. 111–45. For a powerful critique of assorted canonizing appropriations of "double-consciousness," including Hegelian interpretations, see Adolph L. Reed, Jr., *W. E. B. Du Bois and American Political Thought* (New York: Oxford University Press, 1997), especially pp. 91–125, 219–31.

66 On the gendered politics of Du Boisian black nationalism, see Hazel Carby, *Race Men: The Body and Soul of Race, Nation, and Masculinity* (Cambridge, Mass.: Harvard University Press, 1998).

67 Josiah Royce, *Lectures on Modern Idealism* (New Haven, Conn.: Yale University Press, 1919), p. 182.

68 For a related analysis, see Zamir, *Dark Voices*, p. 144.

69 Du Bois, *The Souls of Black Folk*, p. 134.

70 Posnock, *Color and Culture*, p. 135.

71 Du Bois, *The Souls of Black Folk*, p. 15.

72 Ibid., p. 8.

73 On Du Bois and Emersonian individualism, see Brian A. Bremen, "Du Bois, Emerson, and the 'Fate' of Black Folk," *American Literary Realism, 1870–1910* (Spring 1992): 80–88.

74 Stanley Cavell, *The Pitch of Philosophy* (Cambridge, Mass.: Harvard University Press, 1994), pp. 141–42.

75 Du Bois, *The Souls of Black Folk*, p. 9.

76 Friedrich Nietzsche, *"The Birth of Tragedy" and "The Case of Wagner,"* trans. Walter Kaufmann (New York: Vintage, 1967), pp. 160, 178.

77 Du Bois, *Dusk of Dawn*, p. 45.

78 Du Bois, "Forum of Fact and Opinion," *Pittsburgh Courier*, October 17, 1936, in *Newspaper Columns*, vol. 1, p. 124.

79 Du Bois, "Forum of Fact and Opinion," *Pittsburgh Courier*, December 19, 1936, in *Newspaper Columns*, vol. 1, p. 148.

80 Ibid., p. 126.

81 Du Bois, "Forum of Fact and Opinion," *Pittsburgh Courier*, October 31, 1936, in *Newspaper Columns*, vol. 1, p. 129.

82 Gary Tomlinson, *Metaphysical Song* (Princeton, N.J.: Princeton University Press, 1999), p. 81.

83 Du Bois, "Forum and Fact of Opinion," *Pittsburgh Courier*, October 31, 1936, in *Newspaper Columns*, vol. 1, p. 131.

84 On American racial classification and cultural stratification at the turn of the twentieth century, see Lawrence Levine, *Highbrow/Lowbrow: The Emergence of Cultural Hierarchy in America* (Cambridge, Mass.: Harvard University Press, 1988).

85 Sundquist, *To Wake the Nations*, p. 465.

86 Ibid., p. 468.

87 Consider the following from *The Souls of Black Folk*: "I sit with Shakespeare and he winces not. Across the color line I move arm in arm with Balzac and Dumas, where smiling men and welcoming women glide in gilded halls. . . . I summon Aristotle and Aurelius and what soul I will, and they come all graciously with no scorn nor condescension. So, wed with Truth, I dwell above the Veil. Is this the life you grudge us, O knightly America?" (p. 82).

88 I am indebted to the critical history of folklore studies outlined in Roger D. Abrahams, "Phantoms of Romantic Nationalism in Folkloristics," *Journal of American Folklore* (winter 1993): 3–37.

89 Consider the following passage from the late 1890s: "Not in evil, not in idleness, not in sensuality, comes the real fulness of life; pedantry is not learning, extravagance is not art, and yelling is not religion—but all life is one striving toward the Eternally Beautiful." W. E. B. Du Bois, "The Art and Art Galleries of Modern Europe," in *Against Racism*, p. 43.

90 Du Bois, *The Souls of Black Folk*, p. 182.

91 Du Bois, "The Problem of Amusement" (1897), p. 231. On Du Bois's readings in German idealism at the University of Berlin, see David Levering Lewis, *W. E. B. Du Bois: Biography of a Race, 1868–1919* (New York: Holt, 1993), p. 139.

92 Du Bois, "The Problem of Amusement," pp. 230, 235.

93 For a classic critique of the restricted economy and work ethic in Hegelian dialectics, see Jacques Derrida, "From Restricted to General Economy: A Hegelianism without Reserve," in *Writing and Difference*, trans. Alan Bass (Chicago: University of Chicago Press, 1978), pp. 251–77.

94 Du Bois, "The Problem of Amusement," p. 237.

95 Claudia Tate, *Psychoanalysis and Black Novels: Desire and the Protocols of Race* (New York: Oxford University Press, 1998), p. 80. For Tate's analysis of how textual eruptions of "surplus passion" reveal the more personal motivations behind Du Bois's political activism and his posture of Olympian detachment, see pp. 47–85.

96 Du Bois, *Dark Princess*, pp. 303, 305.

97 Du Bois, *The Souls of Black Folk*, p. 134.

98 For connections between ethnography and the "Negro vogue" in 1920s Parisian culture, see James Clifford, "Ethnographic Surrealism," in *The Predicament of Culture* (Cambridge, Mass.: Harvard University Press, 1988), pp. 118–46.

99 W. E. B. Du Bois, *Crisis*, December 1926, p. 81. Du Bois was attempting to demystify white fascination with a certain image of blackness as sublime. Consider the perspective of Slavoj Žižek in *The Sublime Object of Ideology* (London: Verso, 1989): "The sublime object is an object which cannot be approached but too closely: if we get too near it, it loses its sublime features and becomes an ordinary vulgar object—it can persist only in an interspace, in an intermediate state, viewed from a certain perspective, half-seen. If we want to see it in the light of day, it changes into an everyday object, it dissipates itself, precisely because in itself it is nothing at all" (p. 170).

100 Michael A. North, *The Dialect of Modernism: Race, Language, and Twentieth-Century Literature* (New York: Oxford University Press, 1994), p. 27.

101 This sentence paraphrases a conclusion from Thomas Crow, "Modernism and Mass Culture in the Visual Arts," in *Modernism and Modernity: The Vancouver Conference Papers*, eds. Benjamin H. D. Buchloh, Serge Guilbaut, and David Solkin (Halifax: Press of the Nova Scotia School of Art and Design, 1983), pp. 215–64.

102 W. E. B. Du Bois, "The Social Origins of American Negro Art," in *Modern Quarterly* (October–December 1925): 54–55.

103 W. E. B. Du Bois, "Negro Art (1921), in *The Emerging Thought of W. E. B. Du Bois*, ed. Henry Lee Moon (New York: Simon & Schuster, 1972), p. 355.

104 Du Bois, *Crisis*, January 1926, 141.

105 W. E. B. Du Bois, "The Position of the Negro in the American Social Order: Where Do We Go From Here?" *Journal of Negro Education* (July 1939): 562. On the essay, see Bernard W. Bell, "W. E. B. Du Bois's Struggle to Reconcile Folk and High Art," in *Critical Essays on W. E. B. Du Bois*, ed. William L. Andrews (Boston: G. K. Hall, 1985), pp. 119–20. Bell reads the 1939 statement in contrast with the "kingdom of culture" of *The Souls of Black Folk*. The 1903 text, Bell argues, expressed an integrationist sentiment Du Bois would later regard as premature. Jazz music suggested to Locke, at least by 1939, that the color line could be effectively and influentially challenged at strata other than the most elite ones; "Comparable strides took Negro popular music on an upswing of popularity and influence, carrying the occasionally successful 'rag-time composer' to the assured dominance of Negro dance and music in the jazz period. Here, too, was a collaboration and interchange of talent and effort,—perhaps the closest of all the cultural collaborations to date, and one profoundly influential on public opinion as well as upon the professional circles immediately involved." Alain Locke, "The Negro's Contribution to American Culture" [1939], in *The Critical Temper of Alain Locke: A Selection of His Essays on Art and Culture*, ed. Jeffrey C. Stewart (New York: Garland, 1983), pp. 455–56.

106 Consider the judgment of the narrator of Du Bois's late historical work, *The Black Flame*. The narrator/Du Bois asked: "Where is the outburst of literature which we began a generation ago—the poetry and music, the dance and drama? In the last decade we have not produced a poem or a novel, a history or play of stature—nothing but gamblers, prizefighters and jazz. . . . Once we could hear Shakespeare in Harlem[.]" *Worlds of Color* (New York: Mainstream, 1961), III,

pp. 345–46. Passage is quoted in Rampersad, *The Art and Imagination of W. E. B. Du Bois*, p. 274.

107 Le Roi Jones (Amiri Baraka), "The Changing Same," in *Black Music* (New York: William Morrow, 1967), pp. 193, 194. Consider Baraka's estimate of Albert Ayler's approach to the spirituals: "He says he's not interested in note; he wants to play past note and get, then, purely into sound. Into the basic element, the clear emotional thing, freed absolutely from anti-emotional concept. The records have been beautiful, at first frightening, because they tear so completely away, are not at all 'reasonable.'" "Apple Cores #3" (1966), in *Black Music*, p. 126. For analyses of Baraka's aesthetic thought, see esp. Kimberly W. Benston, *Baraka: The Renegade and the Mask* (New Haven, Conn.: Yale University Press, 1976) and Nathaniel Mackey, *Discrepant Engagement: Dissonance, Cross-Culturality, and Experimental Writing* (Cambridge: Cambridge University Press, 1993), pp. 22–48.

108 W. E. B. Du Bois, "Criteria of Negro Art," *Crisis*, October 1926, p. 292.

109 Joseph Collins, "The Dance 'Mania,'" *Vanity Fair*, February 1926, pp. 68, 84.

110 W. E. B. Du Bois, "The Art and Art Galleries of Modern Europe," in *Against Racism*, p. 35.

TWO *Swan Songs and Art Songs: The Spirituals and the "New Negro" in the 1920s*

1 Jean Toomer, "Music" (1937), in *A Jean Toomer Reader: Selected Unpublished Writings*, ed. Frederik L. Rusch (New York: Oxford University Press, 1993), p. 276.

2 Joseph Roach, *Cities of the Dead: Circum-Atlantic Performance* (New York: Columbia University Press, 1996), p. 33.

3 Jean Toomer to Lola Ridge, December 1922, in *A Jean Toomer Reader: Selected Unpublished Writings*, p. 17.

4 Quoted in Henry Louis Gates Jr., *Figures in Black* (New York: Oxford University Press, 1987), p. 198.

5 W. S. Braithwaite, "The Negro in Literature," *Crisis*, September 1924, p. 210.

6 On Harry Burleigh, see Roland Lewis Allison, "Classification of the Vocal Works of Harry T. Burleigh (1866–1949) and Some Suggestions for Their Use in Teaching Diction in Singing" (Ph.D. diss., Indiana University, 1965), and Anne Key Simpson, *Hard Trials: The Life and Music of Harry T. Burleigh* (Metuchen, N.J.: Scarecrow Press, 1990).

7 MacKinley Helm, *Angel Mo' and Her Son, Roland Hayes* (Boston: Little, Brown, 1942), pp. 106–7.

8 Ibid., pp. 107–8.

9 On Hayes's career, see Helm, *Angel Mo' and Her Son, Roland Hayes*. See also F. W. Woolsey, "Conversation with . . . Roland Hayes" [1967], *Black Perspective in Music* (fall 1974): 179–85. Warren Marr II, "Roland Hayes," *Black Perspective in Music* (fall 1974): 186–89.

10 Helm, *Angel Mo' and Her Son, Roland Hayes*, p. 189.

11 Roland Hayes, as told to Laura Haddock, "'My Song is Nothing!' Roland Hayes Calls His Voice the Tool of a More Important Mission—Racial Harmony" (1947), *Black Perspective in Music* (fall 1977): 191.

12 Anonymous editorial, "Lyrus Africanus," *Opportunity*, November 1925, p. 323.

13 Carl Van Vechten, "Paul Robeson and Lawrence Brown" [recital program notes, May 1, 1925], in *Keep A-Inchin' Along: Selected Writings of Carl Van Vechten About Black Art and Culture*, ed. Bruce Kellner (Westport, Conn.: Greenwood Press, 1979), p. 158.

14 Helm, *Angel Mo' and Her Son, Roland Hayes*, pp. 124–25.

15 The "swan song" comment appears in Jean Toomer, "On Being an American," from "Outline of an Autobiography" [c. 1931–32], in *The Wayward and the Seeking: A Collection of Writings by Jean Toomer*, ed. Darwin T. Turner (Washington, D.C.: Howard University Press, 1980), p. 123. On entropic modernity and related literary tropes, I am especially indebted to James Clifford, *The Predicament of Culture: Twentieth-Century Ethnography, Literature, and Art* (Cambridge, Mass.: Harvard University Press, 1988).

16 Alain Locke, *The Negro and His Music* [1936] (Port Washington, N.Y.: Kennikat Press, 1968), p. 18.

17 Jean Toomer, "Song of the Son," from *Cane* by Jean Toomer. Copyright 1923 by Boni & Liveright, renewed 1951 by Jean Toomer. Used by permission of Liveright Publishing Association. Edition used was *Cane*, ed. Darwin T. Turner (New York: W. W. Norton, 1988), p. 14.

18 On the modernist elegy in English poetry as a critique of the deritualization of death and burial, see Jahan Ramazani, *Poetry of Mourning: The Modern Elegy from Hardy to Heaney* (Chicago: University of Chicago Press, 1994), p. 14.

19 Nathaniel Mackey, "Sound and Sentiment, Sound and Symbol," in *The Jazz Cadence of America*, ed. Robert G. O'Meally (New York: Columbia University Press, 1998), p. 608.

20 Toomer, *Cane*, p. 83.

21 Ibid., p. 85.

22 Ibid., p. 98.

23 Ibid., p. 112.

24 Houston A. Baker Jr., *Blues, Ideology, and Afro-American Literature* (Chicago: University of Chicago Press, 1984), pp. 152, 154.

25 Toomer, *Cane*, p. 113.

26 Ibid., pp. 116–17.

27 Ibid., p. 117.

28 Ibid., p. 111.

29 David Levering Lewis, *When Harlem Was in Vogue* (New York: Oxford University Press, 1989), pp. 64–65.

30 Toomer to Waldo Frank, n.d., in *A Jean Toomer Reader*, p. 25.

31 Houston A, Baker Jr., *Afro-American Poetics: Revisions of Harlem and the Black Aesthetic* (Madison: University of Wisconsin Press, 1988), pp. 102–3.

32 Henry Louis Gates Jr., "The Same Difference: Reading Jean Toomer, 1923–1982," *Figures in Black*, p. 221.

33 Toomer, "On Being an American," from "Outline of an Autobiography" [c. 1931–32], in *The Wayward and the Seeking*, p. 123.

34 Michael A. North, *The Dialect of Modernism: Race, Language, and Twentieth-Century Literature* (New York: Oxford University Press, 1994), p. 147.

35 Toomer to Waldo Frank, n.d., in *A Jean Toomer Reader*, p. 24.

36 Claudia Tate, *Psychoanalysis and Black Novels: Desire and the Protocols of Race* (New York: Oxford University Press, 1998), p. 5.

37 W. E. B. Du Bois, "The Younger Literary Movement" [1924], in *W. E. B. Du Bois: Writings*, ed. Nathan Huggins (New York: Library of America, 1986), p. 1210.

38 Toomer, "Outline of an Autobiography," in *The Wayward and the Seeking*, p. 129.

39 Alain Locke, "From *Native Son* to *Invisible Man*: A Review of the Literature of the Negro for 1952," *Phylon* (first quarter, 1953): 34. On Du Bois's objections to the aestheticism of Renaissance publicists like Locke and Charles S. Johnson (editor of *Opportunity*), see Manning Marable, *W. E. B. Du Bois: Black Radical Democrat* (Boston: Twayne, 1986), pp. 128–36; Arnold Rampersad, *The Art and Imagination of W. E. B. Du Bois* (New York: Schocken Books, 1990), pp. 184–201.

40 Toomer to Waldo Frank, n.d., in *Cane*, p. 151.

41 Toomer, "Outline of an Autobiography," in *The Wayward and the Seeking*, pp. 132–33. Toomer also tells of his bad experience with anthologies of "Negro literature" in "Fighting the Vice" [1932], in *A Jean Toomer Reader*, pp. 102–3.

42 North, *The Dialect of Modernism*, p. 166.

43 Jean Toomer, *Essentials* [1931], ed. Rudolph P. Byrd (Athens: University of Georgia Press, 1991), sec. xxiv, [no pagination]. See also Cynthia Earl Kerman and Richard Eldridge, *The Lives of Jean Toomer: A Hunger for Wholeness* (Baton Rouge: Louisiana State University Press, 1987).

44 Henry Louis Gates Jr., "The Same Difference: Reading Jean Toomer, 1923–1982," in *Figures in Black*, p. 210.

45 W. E. B. Du Bois, *The Souls of Black Folk* (New York: Library of America, 1990), p. 9.

46 Toomer, "Remember and Return" in *The Wayward and the Seeking*, p. 437. Between 1931 and 1938, Toomer prepared a 400-page manuscript, "Remember and Return," that no publisher would accept.

47 W. E. B. Du Bois, "John Work: Martyr and Singer," *Crisis*, May 1926, p. 33.

48 Eileen Southern, *The Music of Black Americans: A History* (New York: W. W. Norton, 1983), p. 228.

49 Michael W. Harris, *The Rise of Gospel Blues: The Music of Thomas Andrew Dorsey in the Urban Church* (New York: Oxford University Press, 1992), pp. 69, 112.

50 John W. Work, "Negro Folk Song," *Opportunity*, October 1923, p. 294.

51 Jon Michael Spencer, *The New Negroes and Their Music: The Success of the Harlem Renaissance*, p. 64. On Dett, see also Anne Key Simpson, *Follow Me: The Life and Music of R. Nathaniel Dett* (Metuchen, N.J.: Scarecrow Press, 1993).

52 Harris, *The Rise of Gospel Blues*, pp. 123–24.

53 William N. Colson, "Phases of Du Bois," in *The Messenger Reader*, ed. Sondra Kathryn Wilson (New York: Modern Library, 2000), p. 215.

54 W. E. B. Du Bois, "John Work: Martyr and Singer," *Crisis*, May 1926, p. 32.

55 Helm, *Angel Mo' and Her Son, Roland Hayes*, pp. 89, 90.

56 Ibid., p. 110.

57 F. W. Woolsey, "Conversation with . . . Roland Hayes," p. 183.

58 Locke, *The Negro and His Music*, p. 19.

59 Locke, "The Negro Spirituals," in *The New Negro*, p. 201.

60 Henry Louis Gates Jr., "The Trope of a New Negro and the Reconstruction of the Image of the Black," in *The New American Studies*, ed. Philip Fisher (Berkeley: University of California Press, 1991), p. 338.

61 See esp. Lewis, *When Harlem Was in Vogue*; Nathan Huggins, *Harlem Renaissance* (New York: Oxford University Press, 1971); Harold Cruse, *The Crisis of the Negro Intellectual* (New York: Quill, 1984).

62 Houston A. Baker Jr., *Modernism and the Harlem Renaissance* (Chicago: University of Chicago Press, 1987), p. 33.

63 Spencer, *The New Negroes and Their Music*, pp. 23, 37.

64 Kevin K. Gaines, *Uplifting the Race: Black Leadership, Politics, and Culture in the Twentieth Century* (Chapel Hill: University of North Carolina Press, 1996), p. 248.

65 Ibid., p. 4.

66 Baker, *Modernism and the Harlem Renaissance*, p. 12.

67 Du Bois, *The Souls of Black Folk*, p. 148.

68 Peter Bürger, *Theory of the Avant-Garde*, trans. Michael Shaw (Minneapolis: University of Minnesota Press, 1984), p. 50.

69 One need only compare Du Bois's praise for Wagnerian opera with Adorno's denunciations of political reaction and psychic regressivity in the same music: "The eternity of Wagnerian music, like that of the poem of the *Ring*, is one which proclaims that nothing has happened; it is a state of immutability that refutes all history by confronting it with the silence of nature. . . . The forces that are unleashed end up sustaining the state of immutability and hence the powers that be—the very powers they had set out to overthrow." Theodor Adorno, *In Search of Wagner*, trans. Rodney Livingstone (London: Verso, 1981), p. 40. For Du Bois, by contrast, Wagner's music did *not* block the critical imagination through the phantasmagoria of mythic immutability.

70 William Pickens, "Art and Propaganda," in *The Messenger Reader*, pp. 275–76, 274.

71 Alain Locke, "Roland Hayes: An Appreciation," *Opportunity*, December 1923, p. 358.

72 Carl Van Vechten, "The Folksongs of the American Negro," *Vanity Fair*, July 1925, p. 52.

73 Helm, *Angel Mo' and Her Son, Roland Hayes*, p. 189.

74 Ibid., pp. 283–84. Hayes remembered his 1928 trip to Moscow in the following way: "According to the critic Braudo, I had introduced my audience to an 'active co-experience' in the tragedy of an exploited race; I had proved, he said, that the American Negroes were ready to take their part in the international struggle for freedom. I was not a little surprised by this political interpretation of my singing, until I discovered that in the Russian translations printed in my programs the

spirituals had been put through a secular revision which made propaganda out of the original evangelical texts. . . . and 'Deep River,' a song of religious aspiration if ever there was one, had become, in proletarian hands, a dreary narrative about Negroes picnicking on the banks of the Jordan River." Ibid., pp. 250–51.

75 Hayes, " 'My Song is Nothing!' " p. 191.

76 Roland Hayes to Alain Locke, October 4, 1924, Alain Locke Papers, Moorland Spingarn Research Center, Howard University [henceforth MSRC], box 164-35, folder 28.

77 Helm, *Angel Mo' and Her Son, Roland Hayes*, p. 171.

78 Locke, "Roland Hayes," pp. 356–57.

79 Ibid., p. 358.

80 Roach, *Cities of the Dead*, p. 2.

81 Alain Locke, "The Negro Spirituals," in *The New Negro*, pp. 207, 208.

82 Alain Locke, "Toward a Critique of Negro Music," *Opportunity*, November 1934, p. 328.

83 Locke quotes from the *New Age*, May 5, 1921, in "Roland Hayes," p. 358.

84 See Martin Bauml Duberman, *Paul Robeson* (New York: Random House, 1989), pp. 68–70.

85 Locke, "The Negro Spirituals," p. 208.

86 Marr, "Roland Hayes," p. 188.

87 Sterling Brown, "Roland Hayes," *Opportunity*, June 1925, p. 173.

88 Ibid., p. 174.

89 W. E. B. Du Bois, "Hayes," *Crisis*, January 1927, p. 129.

90 Edward David Caffee, "Roland Hayes," *Crisis*, January 1925, p. 109. See also Dorothy Burgess, "For Roland Hayes," *Opportunity*, December 1926, p. 387. Burgess's poem begins: "The dark flower of your voice unfolds, petal and leaf, / A very rose for joy, a piercing thorn for grief."

91 Carl Van Vechten to Alain Locke, October 13, 1925, Alain Locke Papers, MSRC, Box 164-90, Folder 58.

92 Van Vechten, "The Folksongs of the American Negro," p. 92.

93 Carl Van Vechten, *Music and Bad Manners* (New York: Alfred A. Knopf, 1916), p. 180.

94 Hans Ulrich Gumbrecht, *In 1926: Living at the Edge of Time* (Cambridge, Mass.: Harvard University Press, 1997), p. 372.

95 Van Vechten, *Music and Bad Manners*, pp. 179, 104, 224.

96 Carl Van Vechten, "Prescription for the Negro Theatre," *Vanity Fair*, October 1925, pp. 92, 98. Van Vechten found his "Prescription" appropriate for the special issue Locke edited for the periodical *Survey Graphic* that provided the basis for *The New Negro* anthology. "You might, I think, have had 'A Prescription for the Negro Theatre' for your anthology, but I understood that you wanted me to write on a set subject." Carl Van Vechten to Alain Locke, October 13, 1925, Alain Locke Papers, MSRC, Box 164-90, Folder 58. Compare the anti-exoticizing prescriptions of Alain Locke, "Steps Toward The Negro Theatre," *Crisis*, December 1922, p. 66.

97 Duberman, *Paul Robeson*, p. 100.

98 Manning Marable, *W. E. B. Du Bois: Black Radical Democrat* (Boston: G. K. Hall, 1986), p. 129.

99 Paul Robeson, *Chicago Defender*, May 19, 1934, p. 10, quoted in Doris Evans McGinty and Wayne Shirley, "Paul Robeson, Musician," in *Paul Robeson: Artist and Citizen*, ed. with intro. by Jeffrey C. Stewart (New Brunswick, N.J.: Rutgers University Press, 1998), p. 111.

100 Hayes quoted in Locke, "Roland Hayes," p. 358.

101 "H. L. Mencken, "The Music of the American Negro" (1925), in *H. L. Mencken on Music*, ed. Louis Cheslock (New York: Alfred A. Knopf, 1961), p. 151.

102 Sandburg quoted in Duberman, *Paul Robeson*, p. 81.

103 Paul Robeson, "An Actor's Wanderings and Hopes," in *The Messenger Reader*, p. 293.

104 For Robeson's stage, screen, and musical careers and the cultural politics of racial exoticism, see the essays in Stewart, ed., *Paul Robeson: Artist and Citizen*.

105 Van Vechten, "Paul Robeson and Lawrence Brown," p. 157.

106 Paul Robeson, "Reflections on O'Neill's Plays," *Opportunity*, December 1924, p. 369.

107 Carl Van Vechten, " 'Moanin' Wid a Sword In Ma Han,' " *Vanity Fair*, February 1926, p. 61. The quotation regarding Robeson comes from a photographic caption accompanying Van Vechten's "The Folksongs of the American Negro," p. 52.

108 Van Vechten, "The Folksongs of the American Negro," p. 92.

109 See Carl Van Vechten, "George Gershwin," *Vanity Fair*, March 1925, p. 40.

110 Carl Van Vechten, "Negro 'Blues' Singers," *Vanity Fair*, March 1926, pp. 67, 106. See also Carl Van Vechten, "The Black Blues," *Vanity Fair*, August 1925, pp. 57, 86, 92.

111 Carl Van Vechten to H. L. Mencken, May 29, 1925, in *Letters of Carl Van Vechten*, ed. Bruce Kellner (New Haven, Conn.: Yale University Press, 1987), p. 78.

112 Carl Van Vechten, to Arthur Davison Ficke, August 3, 1925, in *Letters of Carl Van Vechten*, p. 80. When Langston Hughes published a defense of Van Vechten and *Nigger Heaven*, Van Vechten wrote back "thanks a lot for what you say about me. . . . The situation is *easy* to explain: You and I are the only coloured people who really love *niggers*." Carl Van Vechten to Langston Hughes, March 25, 1927, ibid., p. 95. Van Vechten's racial liberalism was learned in the home of his parents. As he later wrote, "ME, I guess I would rather bathe with servants . . . than with most of the rich people I know. As a matter of fact I was brought up to bathe with servants and as my father always saw to it that any servants we had had all the pleasures and minor luxuries we had; some day I'll tell you about some of these. And he taught me to respect colored people. My father indeed was mostly responsible for founding a school for colored people." Van Vechten to Anna Marble Pollock, c. January–March 1945, in *Letters of Carl Van Vechten*, p. 210.

113 Van Vechten, " 'Moanin' Wid a Sword In Ma Han," pp. 100, 102.

114 For contrasting views on Van Vechten and interracialism, see George Schuyler,

"The Van Vechten Revolution," *Phylon* (December 1950): 368, and Hugh Gloster, "The Van Vechten Vogue," *Phylon* (1945): 310–14.

115 Arthur Huff Fauset, "Homage to Sterling Brown," *Sterling A. Brown: A UMUM Tribute*, ed. Black History Museum Committee (Philadelphia: Black History Museum UMUM Publishers, 1982), p. 2.

116 Charles H. Rowell, "'Let Me Be with Ole Jazzbo': An Interview with Sterling A. Brown," *Callaloo* 14 (1991): 805.

117 "Zora Neale Hurston: A Personality Sketch" [1960], in *Letters of Carl Van Vechten*, p. 276.

118 See esp. Sterling Brown, "The Blues as Folk Poetry" [1930], in *The Book of Negro Folklore*, ed. Langston Hughes and Arna Bontemps (New York: Dodd, Mead, 1958), pp. 371–86; "Negro Folk Expression: Spirituals, Seculars, Ballads and Work Songs," *Phylon* 14 (Winter 1953): 45–61; "The Spirituals," *The Book of Negro Folklore*, pp. 279–89; "'Portrait of a Jazz Giant: Jelly Roll Morton," *Black World*, February 1974, pp. 28–48; "Ragtime and the Blues," *Sterling A. Brown: A UMUM Tribute*, pp. 76–88.

119 Gates, "Songs of a Racial Self: On Sterling A. Brown," *Figures in Black*, pp. 226–27.

120 See Joanne V. Gabbin, *Sterling A. Brown: Building the Black Aesthetic Tradition* (Westport, Conn.: Greenwood Press, 1985); Lorenzo Thomas, "Authenticity and Elevation: Sterling Brown's Theory of the Blues," *African American Review* 31, no. 3 (1997): 409–16; John S. Wright, "The New Negro Poet and the Nachal Man: Sterling Brown's Folk Odyssey," *Black American Literature Forum* (spring 1989): 95–105.

121 Alain Locke, "Sterling Brown: The New Negro Folk-Poet," in *Negro: An Anthology* [1934], ed. Nancy Cunard, abridged reissue ed. Hugh Ford (New York: Frederick Ungar, 1970), p. 92.

122 Rowell, "Let Me Be with Ole Jazzbo," p. 804.

123 Quoted in Walter F. White, "The Tenth Spingarn Medal," *Crisis*, June 1925, p. 69.

124 Helm, *Angel Mo' and Her Son, Roland Hayes*, p. 197.

125 Alain Locke, "Apropos of Africa," *Opportunity*, February 1924, p. 38.

126 A. Philip Randolph, "Reply to Marcus Garvey," in *The Messenger Reader*, p. 357.

127 Paul Guillaume, "African Art at the Barnes Foundation," *Opportunity*, May 1924, p. 141.

128 "It was long customary to think of this [African] art first as imitation, secondly as inexpressibly crude and funny; but to-day more recent interpretations show that the primitive art of Africa is one of the greatest expressions of the human soul in all time, 'the black men invented art as they invented fire,' that they spread their ideas among their white neighbors, and that their earliest expressions had an originality and fidelity of purpose that the primitive world never surpassed." W. E. B. Du Bois, "What Is Civilization?" (1926), in *The Oxford W. E. B. Du Bois Reader*, ed. Eric Sundquist (New York: Oxford University Press, 1996), p. 651. See also *Crisis*, June 1924, p. 79; *Crisis*, May 1925, p. 39.

129 Albert C. Barnes, "The Temple," *Opportunity*, May 1924, p. 140.

130 George Hutchinson, *The Harlem Renaissance in Black and White* (Cambridge, Mass.: Harvard University Press, 1995), p. 45.

131 On Barnes, the Spingarn family, Van Vechten, and Charlotte Osgood Mason, see Bruce Kellner, " 'Refined Racism': White Patronage in the Harlem Renaissance," *The Harlem Renaissance Re-examined* (New York: AMS Press, 1987), pp. 93–106.

132 Paul Guillaume, "African Art at the Barnes Foundation," *Opportunity*, May 1924, p. 140. See also Paul Guillaume, "The Triumph of Ancient Negro Art," *Opportunity*, May 1926, pp. 146–47. For Barnes's contributions to discussions of African art in *Opportunity*, see Albert C. Barnes, "The Temple," *Opportunity*, May 1924, pp. 138–40; "Primitive Negro Sculpture and Its Influence on Modern Civilization," *Opportunity*, May 1928, pp. 139–40; "Negro Art, Past and Present," *Opportunity*, May 1926, pp. 148–49, 168, 169.

133 Guillaume, "African Art at the Barnes Foundation," p. 141.

134 Clifford, *The Predicament of Culture*, p. 202.

135 Christopher B. Steiner, *African Art in Transit* (Cambridge: Cambridge University Press, 1994), pp. 100–164.

136 Clifford, *The Predicament of Culture*, p. 136.

137 Alain Locke, "Apropos of Africa," p. 37.

138 Alain Locke, "A Note on African Art," *Opportunity*, May 1924, p. 134.

139 Alain Locke, "The Legacy of the Ancestral Arts," in *The New Negro*, pp. 254–55.

140 Hutchinson, *The Harlem Renaissance in Black and White*, p. 428.

141 Locke, "The Legacy of the Ancestral Arts," p. 256.

142 Albert C. Barnes, "Negro Art and America," in *The New Negro*, pp. 21, 20.

143 Ibid., pp. 24–25.

144 Locke, "A Note on African Art," p. 135.

145 Locke, "The Legacy of the Ancestral Arts," p. 262.

146 Ibid., p. 262.

147 Locke, "A Note on African Art," p. 136.

148 Alain Locke, "The Negro's Contribution to American Culture" [1939], in *The Critical Temper of Alain Locke*, p. 456.

149 Langston Hughes, *The Big Sea* (New York: Hill and Wang, 1964), p. 316.

150 Charlotte Osgood Mason to Alain Locke, December 1, 1928. Alain Locke Papers, MRSC, box 164-68, folder 24.

151 Spencer, *The New Negroes and Their Music*, p. 13.

THREE   *"The Twilight of Aestheticism": Locke on Cosmopolitanism and Musical Evolution*

1 Alain Locke, *The Negro and His Music* [1936] (Port Washington, N.Y.: Kennikat, 1968), p. 12.

2 Walter Pater, *The Renaissance: Studies in Art and Poetry*, in *Walter Pater: Three Major Texts*, ed. William E. Buckler (New York: New York University Press, 1986), p. 156.

3 Locke, *The Negro and His Music*, p. 20.

4 W. E. B. Du Bois, review of *The Book of American Negro Spirituals*, *Crisis*, November 1925, p. 31.

5 In addition to the Johnsons' *The Book of American Negro Spirituals* (New York: Knopf, 1925), see, for example, Samuel Coleridge-Taylor, *Twenty-Four Negro Melodies: Transcribed for Piano* (Boston: Oliver Ditson, 1905); Harry Burleigh, *Negro Minstrel Melodies* (New York: G. Schirmer, 1909); John W. Work, *Folk Songs of the American Negro* (Nashville, Tenn.: Work Brothers & Hart, 1907); R. Nathaniel Dett, *Religious Folk Songs of the Negro* (Hampton, Va.: Hampton Institute Press, 1927).

6 Slavoj Žižek, *For They Know Not What They Do: Enjoyment as a Political Factor* (London: Verso, 1991), p. 20.

7 Alain Locke, "The New Negro," in *The New Negro* [1925], ed. Alain Locke (New York: Atheneum, 1968), p. 3.

8 Quoted in Horace Kallen, "Alain Locke and Cultural Pluralism," *Journal of Philosophy* 54 (February 28, 1957): 121–22. Locke's autobiographical statement was originally published in *American Philosophy Today and Tomorrow*, ed. Sidney Hook and Horace M. Kallen (New York: Lee Furman, 1935).

9 Leonard Harris privileges Locke's philosophical texts as sources of a "master code" for a "deconstructive project" and interprets the cultural texts in a secondary manner in terms of a "subterranean integration." See Leonard Harris, "Rendering the Subtext," in *The Philosophy of Alain Locke*, ed. Leonard Harris (Philadelphia: Temple University Press, 1989), pp. 279–89. Russell J. Linnemann stresses the unity of Locke's thought. "[W]hen one steps back and tries to bring the quintessential Locke into focus," Linneman writes, "there is a remarkable sense of unity to the composite body of his thought, both in a temporal and in a multidisciplinary sense." See Russell J. Linneman, "Introduction," in *Alain Locke: Reflections on a Modern Renaissance Man*, ed. Russell J. Linnemann (Baton Rouge: Louisiana State University Press, 1982), p. xv. This chapter follows Jeffrey Stewart's suggestion that it is the "tensions in Locke's thought [which] make him interesting today." Jeffrey C. Stewart, "Introduction," in *The Critical Temper of Alain Locke: A Selection of His Essays on Art and Culture*, ed. Jeffrey C. Stewart (New York: Garland, 1983), p. 101.

10 On the impact of Herder's *Volksgeist* (spirit of a people) thesis and folk nationalism on nineteenth-century European art music, see Carl Dahlhaus, *Between Romanticism and Modernism*, trans. Mary Whittall (Berkeley: University of California Press, 1980), pp. 79–101, and Dahlhaus, *Nineteenth-Century Music*, trans. J. Bradford Robinson (Berkeley: University of California Pres, 1989), pp. 302–11.

11 Locke, *The Negro and His Music*, p. 23. The comments about Downes and Du Bois appear on p. 24.

12 Jeffrey C. Stewart, "A Black Aesthete at Oxford," *Massachusetts Review* 34, no. 3 (autumn 1993): 419, 418, 413.

13 Ross Posnock, *Color and Culture: Black Writers and the Making of the Modern Intellectual* (Cambridge, Mass.: Harvard University Press, 1998), p. 195.

14 Alain Locke, "Cosmopolitanism," hand-written draft of paper read to Cosmopolitan Club, Oxford University, June 9, 1908, Alain Locke Papers, MSRC, box

164-159, folder 8; quotation from unnumbered page [all subsequent quotations from unnumbered pages will be marked by "n.p."]. All subsequent quotations from "Cosmopolitanism" are from this draft.

15 Ibid., n.p.

16 Ibid., pp. 5, 6.

17 Ibid., p. 8.

18 Locke reflected on these topics at length in his editorial contributions to *When Peoples Meet: A Study in Race and Culture Contacts*, ed. Alain Locke and Bernhard J. Stern (New York: Progressive Education Association, 1942).

19 Locke, "Cosmopolitanism," pp. 10–11.

20 Ibid., p. 18.

21 Alain Locke, "Beauty Instead of Ashes," *Nation*, April 18, 1928, p. 434.

22 Locke, "Cosmopolitanism," p. 17.

23 Rutledge M. Dennis, "Relativism and Pluralism in the Social Thought of Alain Locke," in *Alain Locke: Reflections on a Modern Renaissance Man*, pp. 40–41.

24 For a spirited survey of the social and political valences of Western European aesthetic thought (esp. that inflected by German idealism) since the Enlightenment, see Terry Eagleton, *The Ideology of the Aesthetic* (Oxford: Basil Blackwell, 1990).

25 Alain Locke, "The Ethics of Culture" [1923], in *The Critical Temper of Alain Locke*, p. 416.

26 Pater, *The Renaissance*, pp. 72–73.

27 Locke, "The Ethics of Culture," p. 417.

28 David Levering Lewis, *When Harlem Was in Vogue* (New York: Oxford University Press, 1989), pp. 149, 117.

29 Cary D. Wintz, *Black Culture and the Harlem Renaissance* (Houston: Rice University Press, 1988), p. 116.

30 W. E. B. Du Bois to Jesse Moorland, May 5, 1927, Alain Locke Papers, MSRC, box 164-26, folder 8.

31 Jeffrey C. Stewart, "Introduction," in Alain Locke, *Race Contacts and Interracial Relations: Lectures on the Theory and Practice of Race*, ed. Jeffrey C. Stewart (Washington, D.C.: Howard University Press, 1992), p. xlii.

32 Locke, "Frontiers of Culture," in *The Philosophy of Alain Locke*, p. 231.

33 Locke, "Santayana" [review of *Domination and Powers*], in *The Philosophy of Alain Locke*, pp. 140, 141.

34 David A. Hollinger, "Ethnic Diversity, Cosmopolitanism, and the Emergence of the American Liberal Intelligentsia," *In the American Province* (Baltimore: Johns Hopkins University Press, 1985), p. 59. Hollinger further elaborates the difference between assorted models of cosmopolitanism and cultural pluralism in *Postethnic America: Beyond Multiculturalism* (New York: Basic Books, 1995), esp. pp. 79–104.

35 Consider the following *Nation* reader's reaction to Kallen's essay: "As touching Mr. Kallen's very interesting commentary on the populations of our part of North America, it may be well to cite the earlier essay. . . . 'What is an American?' asks Crevecoeur; very often he had no country before coming to America. . . .'

Here [in America] individuals of all nations are melted into a new race of men, whose labours and posterity will one day cause great changes in the world. . . . We have come out of the old kidnapping, transporting, slave-trading time . . . and we have somehow got into our heads the idea of a general liberty. Let us keep the idea there, and not bother greatly about what part of Europe (not to speak of other stricken continents) we took our origins from." A. J. M., letter to the editor, "What Is an American?" *Nation*, March 18, 1915, p. 305.

36 Horace Kallen, "Democracy Versus the Melting Pot," *Nation*, February 25, 1915, p. 220.

37 Philip Gleason, *Speaking of Diversity: Language and Ethnicity in Twentieth-Century America* (Baltimore: Johns Hopkins University Press, 1992), p. 18.

38 Consider Kallen's passing comments on civilization and ethnic identity in the American South: "South of the Mason and Dixon's line the cities exhibit a greater homogeneity. Outside of certain regions of Texas the descendants of the native white stock, often degenerate and backward, prevail among the whites, but the whites as a whole constitute a relatively weaker proportion of the population. They live among nine million negroes, whose own mode of living tends, by its mere massiveness, to standardize the 'mind' of the proletarian South in speech, manner, and the other values of social organization." Horace Kallen, "Democracy Versus the Melting Pot," *Nation*, February 18, 1915, p. 192.

39 Ibid., p. 194. Such passages inform Walter Benn Michaels's conclusion that cultural pluralism "is an oxymoron; its commitment to culture is contradicted by its commitment to pluralism." Using Kallen's argument as a template for cultural pluralism, Michaels notes: "Instead of who we are being constituted by what we do [culture], what we do is justified by who we are [pluralism]." Thus, identity essentialism lies at the root of cultural pluralist thought. Walter Benn Michaels, *Our America* (Durham, N.C.: Duke University Press, 1995), pp. 139, 140.

40 Hollinger, "Ethnic Diversity, Cosmopolitanism, and the Emergence of the American Liberal Intelligentsia," p. 65.

41 Kallen, "Democracy Versus the Melting Pot," *Nation*, February 25, 1915, pp. 218–19.

42 John Higham, *Send These to Me: Jews and Other Immigrants in Urban America* (New York: Atheneum, 1975), p. 198.

43 Correspondence quoted in Werner Sollors, "A Critique of Pure Pluralism," in *Reconstructing American Literary Identity*, ed. Sacvan Bercovitch (Cambridge, Mass.: Harvard University Press, 1986), pp. 269–73.

44 Ibid., p. 272.

45 Kallen, "Alain Locke and Cultural Pluralism," p. 120. Kallen's essay was based on his remarks at the meeting of the Alain Locke Memorial Committee, Saturday, October 29, 1955, at New York University.

46 Ibid., p. 123.

47 Rutledge M. Dennis, "Relativism and Pluralism in the Social Thought of Alain Locke," p. 42.

48 Posnock, *Color and Culture*, p. 192. For an account of Locke's pluralism that addresses the influence of Josiah Royce's more idealistic theories of "wholesome

provincialism" and "absolute pragmatism," see Hutchinson, *The Harlem Renaissance in Black and White*, pp. 78–93. Hutchinson notes that "Locke had wanted to do his graduate work under Royce but was unable to because Royce died before Locke returned to Harvard for his Ph.D." (p. 82).

49 Locke, "The New Negro," p. 12.

50 Consider Locke's view: "Beliefs in the unassimilability of these [minority] groups and of their fundamental cultural differences are, thus, the crux of all our racial minority problems. Majority stereotypes of this character impede even the recognition of the substantial amount of integration that may have taken place. . . . No minority group, in fact, can be in a sound position when cultural difference connotes inferiority. . . . The more disadvantaged minority elements are experiencing more rapid cultural change under American conditions than the older majority stocks. This means for them not only enhanced assimilation, but greater impetus toward original and exceptional adjustments and creativeness. Their unusual stress and strain brings in this way considerable dividends of positive benefit both to themselves and to the general culture. The cultural changes, particularly of the urban community, are leveling off the provincialisms of the native-born population more markedly than they are melting down the cultural distinctiveness of the minorities and the foreign-born." *When Peoples Meet*, pp. 687–88. According to the introduction to *When Peoples Meet*, Locke was responsible for the otherwise uncredited editorial commentaries.

51 Alain Locke, "The Contribution of Race to Culture" [1950], in *The Philosophy of Alain Locke*, pp. 201, 202.

52 Horace Kallen, *Cultural Pluralism and the American Idea* (Philadelphia: University of Pennsylvania Press, 1956), p. 110. On Kallen's motivation to preserve the distinctive identities of recent European immigrants, see ibid., esp. pp. 96–100. John Higham details how "the pluralist thesis from the outset was encapsulated in white ethnocentrism" in *Send These to Me*, pp. 205–15 (quotation from p. 210).

53 Locke, "Values and Imperatives" [1935], in *The Philosophy of Alain Locke*, p. 34.

54 Alain Locke, "Pluralism and Intellectual Democracy," in *Science, Philosophy and Religion: Second Symposium* (New York: Conference on Science, Philosophy and Religion in Their Relation to the Democratic Way of Life, 1942), p. 204.

55 Ibid., pp. 205–6.

56 Ibid., pp. 198–99.

57 Ibid, p. 200. The comments of one of Locke's respondents at the conference deserve mention. This commentator suggested that the philosophy of pluralism "is satisfactory to no one, or to very few, as an ultimate philosophy. Certainly Professor Locke is peering behind and beyond it as steadily, as wistfully, as any idealist. He proposes it, and I enthusiastically support it, precisely for what it is—a way of uniting for action in a world of conflict and ignorance." Edwin R. Goodenough, in "Appendix," *Science, Philosophy and Religion: Second Symposium*, p. 211.

58 Alain Locke, "Unity Through Diversity: A Baha'i Principle," *Baha'i World* 4 (1930): 373.

59 Kallen sometimes expressed similar ideas: "Actually, the more 'culture' any of them has acquired, the more liberal or general his education has been, the fuller

is his awareness of the values of the *Out-groups*, the freer are his powers to avail himself of them, and the more abundant are his means wherewith to comprehend and enjoy them. His equipment constitutes his cultural mobility; it renders him, mind and body, a cosmopolitan, literally a citizen of the world. Without ever losing his commitment to his home base, his citizenship, and his original culture, he is now also no stranger in any different country or culture. Moreover, his mobility between different cultures is an extension of his mobility within his cultural home base." Horace Kallen, "Concerning Varieties of Pluralism," in *Cultural Pluralism and the American Idea*, p. 53.

60 For a related analysis of paradox and cosmopolitanism, see Posnock, *Color and Culture*, p. 185.

61 Locke, *The Negro and His Music*, p. 36.

62 Ibid., p. 40.

63 Consider this comment by the American modernist critic, Paul Rosenfeld, one of jazz's many cultured despisers (his essay on jazz begins: "American music is not jazz. Jazz is not music."): "The belief that the Negro spirituals and the songs of the Appalachian mountaineers constitute an authentic folk music, like the English, the Russian, and the Magyar, flatters our vanities. But there is little realism to it. . . . As we know it, the Negro spiritual is an obviously sophisticated arrangement of some more primitive song. Its harmonizations are, unquestionably, the results of the contact of an inferior with a superior musical culture. . . . The characteristic syncopation, the short note on a strong beat followed immediately by a longer note on a weak beat, is found throughout the folk music of the West African Negroes and the Hottentots. Again, the characteristic intervals of the fourth and the fifth are significantly those of the Scotch folk song, are even called the Scotch intervals. In view of these facts, we can scarcely call them autochthonous. They are perhaps adaptations of the folk songs of other nations to American conditions, perhaps even superior to their original. But, purely American they most certainly are not." Jazz quotation from "Jazz and Music: Music in America," in Paul Rosenfeld, *Musical Impressions: Selections from Paul Rosenfeld's Criticism*, ed. Herbert A. Leibowitz (New York: Hill and Wang, 1969), p. 221. The quotation on spirituals from Paul Rosenfeld, "Beginnings of American Music," *Musical Impressions*, pp. 228–29. Both essays originally appeared in Rosenfeld's volume *An Hour with American Music* (Philadelphia: J. B. Lippincott, 1929). The primary literature by white writers on the African American spirituals and folk nationalist ideals in music is vast. For some of the best-known interpretations, see George Pullen Jackson, *White Spirituals in the Southern Uplands* (Chapel Hill: University of North Carolina Press, 1933); Henry E. Krehbiel, *Afro-American Folk-Songs: A Study in Racial and National Music* (New York: G. Schirmer, 1914); Daniel Gregory Mason, "The Dilemma of American Music," in *The Dilemma of American Music and Other Essays* (New York: Macmillan, 1928), pp. 1–27; Howard W. Odum and Guy B. Jackson, *Negro Workaday Songs* (Chapel Hill: University of North Carolina Press, 1926); Newman I. White, *American Negro Folk-Songs* (Cambridge, Mass.: Harvard University Press, 1928).

64 Locke, *The Negro and His Music*, p. 41.

65 Charles Taylor, "The Politics of Recognition," in *Multiculturalism: Examining the Politics of Recognition*, ed. Amy Gutmann (Princeton, N.J.: Princeton University Press, 1994), p. 25.

66 Robert Cantwell, *When We Were Good: The Folk Revival* (Cambridge, Mass.: Harvard University Press, 1996), p. 34.

67 J. B. T. Marsh, *The Story of the Jubilee Singers* (London: Hodder and Stoughton, 1885), pp. 121–22.

68 Locke, *The Negro and His Music*, p. 9.

69 Carl Dahlhaus, *The Idea of Absolute Music*, trans. Roger Lustig (Chicago: University of Chicago Press, 1989), p. 104.

70 Johann Herder, "Fourth Grove of Criticism" (1769), quoted in ibid.

71 Henry Louis Gates Jr., "Dis and Dat: Dialect and the Descent," *Figures in Black: Words, Signs, and the "Racial" Self* (New York: Oxford University Press, 1987), p. 182.

72 Alain Locke, "Spirituals," transcription from a recording, AFS 6092-6095, in Archive of Folk Song at Library of Congress, Washington, D.C., in *The Critical Temper of Alain Locke*, p. 124.

73 Zora Neale Hurston, "Spirituals and Neo-Spirituals" [1934], in Zora Neale Hurston, *The Sanctified Church*, ed. Toni Cade Bambara, pp. 80–81.

74 Lewis, *When Harlem Was in Vogue*, p. 117.

75 Locke, *The Negro and His Music*, p. 12.

76 Eugene C. Holmes observed that "Locke was more strongly attracted to Santayana's aestheticism, philosophical poetry, and naturalism, than to Royce's idealism, though he subscribed to the Roycean World Community and philosophical pacificism. He appreciated the psychological values of Jamesian pragmatism, but rejected the solipsistic implications of the Jamesian truth theory." Holmes, "Alain Leroy Locke: A Sketch," *Phylon* 20 (spring 1959): 83.

77 Alain Locke, "Our Little Renaissance," *Ebony and Topaz*, ed. Charles Johnson (New York: National Urban League, 1927), pp. 117, 118.

78 Pater, *The Renaissance*, pp. 103, 74, 141.

79 Perry Meisel, "The Chemistry of the Crystal," in *Walter Pater*, ed. Harold Bloom (New York: Chelsea House, 1985), pp. 122, 123, 127.

80 Locke, *The Negro and His Music*, pp. 12–13.

81 Alain Locke, "Beauty Instead of Ashes," *Nation*, April 18, 1928, p. 434.

82 Alain Locke, "This Year of Grace: Outstanding Books of the Year in Negro Literature," *Opportunity*, February 1931, p. 48.

83 Alain Locke, "*Color*: A Review," *Opportunity*, January 1926, pp. 14, 15.

84 Pater, *The Renaissance*, p. 156.

85 Ibid., pp. 153–54, 177, 156, 143, 73.

86 Walter Pater, "Style," from *Appreciations*, in *Walter Pater: Three Major Texts*, p. 402.

87 Ibid., p. 413. J. Hillis Miller writes that for Pater "each form of art attempts to transcend itself, to sublimate the matter in which it is forced to work by that striving to be other than itself whereby each form of art borrows from others. . . . The condition of music is pure form, the spiritualization of the material substratum

so that no referential dimension is left. . . . In the condition of music, matter has become form, or the form is the matter. . . . Nevertheless, insofar as the Andersstreben [the striving to become something other] remains an aspiration, not an achievement, as Pater implies it does, some element of unspiritualized matter remains." J. Hillis Miller, "Walter Pater: A Partial Portrait," in Bloom, ed., *Walter Pater*, pp. 88–89.

88 Roger Fry, "Negro Sculpture," in *Vision and Design*, ed. J. B. Bullen (Mineola, N.Y.: Dover, 1998), p. 71. Locke did not quote Fry's final comment on African sculpture: "It is curious that a people who produced such great artists did not produce also a culture in our sense of the word. This shows that two factors are necessary to produce the cultures which distinguish civilised peoples. There must be, of course, the creative artist, but there must also be the power of conscious critical appreciation and comparison. . . . It is for want of a conscious critical sense and the intellectual powers of comparison and classification that the negro has failed to create one of the great cultures of the world, and not from any lack of the creative aesthetic impulse, nor from lack of the most exquisite sensibility and the finest taste." Ibid., pp. 72–73.

89 For the contexts of "Negro Sculpture" and *Vision and Design*, see *A Roger Fry Reader*, ed. with introductory essays by Christopher Reed (Chicago: University of Chicago Press, 1996); *Art Made Modern: Roger Fry's Vision of Art*, ed. Christopher Green (London: Merrell Holberton, 1999).

90 Bullen, ed., *Vision and Design*, p. xxii.

91 This comment on Congo sculpture suggest Locke's preference: "Particularly surprising in view of prevalent conceptions is the subtle, placid tone and smooth flow of surface, and the austere economy of decorative elements. One of the head cups might pass as early Buddhist in its quality of austerity and mystic restraint. Clearly they belong to a seasoned and classic tradition . . . an apparent aristocratic strain in Congo art, with a characteristic refinement and subtlety." Locke, "A Collection of Congo Art" [1927], in *The Critical Temper of Alain Locke*, p. 144.

92 Alain Locke, *Negro Art: Past and Present* [1936] (New York: Arno Press, 1969), pp. 112–13.

93 Pater, "Style," pp. 411, 413.

94 Alain Locke, "We Turn to Prose: A Retrospective Review of the Literature of the Negro for 1931," *Opportunity*, February 1932, p. 43; Locke, "Black Truth and Black Beauty: A Retrospective Review of the Literature of the Negro for 1932," *Opportunity*, January 1933, p. 14.

95 Alain Locke, " 'Native Son' to 'Invisible Man': A Review of the Literature of the Negro for 1952," *Phylon* 14 (first quarter, 1953): 37.

96 Alain Locke, "The Negro: 'New' or Newer: A Retrospective Review of the Literature of the Negro for 1938, part II," *Opportunity*, February 1939, p. 39.

97 Alain Locke, "The Eleventh Hour of Nordicism: Retrospective Review of the Literature of the Negro for 1934," *Opportunity*, January 1935, p. 11.

98 George Chauncey, *Gay New York* (New York: BasicBooks, 1994), p. 264. For an incisive account of the American reception of British aestheticism between 1870 and 1920, see Jonathan Freedman, *Professions of Taste: Henry James, British Aes-*

theticism, and Commodity Culture (Stanford, Calif: Stanford University Press, 1990), esp. pp. 79–132.

99 Alain Locke, "Art or Propaganda?," *Harlem* 1 (November 1928): 12.

100 On resonances between Locke's writings and the pragmatist aesthetic thought of William James and John Dewey, see esp. Hutchinson, *The Harlem Renaissance in Black and White*; Posnock, *Color and Culture*; and the essays in *The Critical Pragmatism of Alain Locke*, ed. Leonard Harris.

101 Locke, *Negro Art: Past and Present*, p. 65.

102 Locke, "The Negro: 'New' or Newer," p. 36.

103 Locke, "Up Till Now" (1945), in *The Critical Temper of Alain Locke*, p. 193.

104 Alain Locke, "Deep River: Deeper Sea," *Opportunity*, January 1936, pp. 6, 7.

105 Locke, *The Negro and His Music*, 129.

106 Ibid., p. 88.

107 Ibid., p. 82.

108 Alain Locke, "Toward a Critique of Negro Music," part 1, *Opportunity*, November 1934, p. 328.

109 George Santayana, *The Sense of Beauty* (New York: Charles Scribner's Sons, 1896), p. 96.

110 Ibid., pp. 36–37.

111 Alain Locke, "Beauty Instead of Ashes," *Nation*, April 18, 1928, p. 433.

112 Locke, *The Negro and His Music*, p. 87.

113 Alain Locke, "Freedom Through Art," *Crisis*, July 1938, p. 228.

114 Alain Locke to Bernhard Stern, December 4, 1938, Bernhard Stern–Alain Locke Collection, Schomburg Center, New York Public Library, box 1, folder 1.

115 Locke, "Freedom Through Art," p. 228.

116 Ibid.

117 Alain Locke to Charlotte Osgood Mason, September 11, 1936, Alain Locke Papers, MSRC, box 164-71; folder 11, pp. 3–4.

118 Ibid., p. 6.

119 Alain Locke, "Resume of Talk and Discussion: Sunday Afternoon Session, National Negro Congress" (typescript, c. 1937), Alain Locke Collection, Moorland Spingarn Research Collection, Howard University, box 163-126, folder 2, pp. 1–2.

120 Alain Locke, in *When Peoples Meet*, p. 654. By contrast, Horace Kallen wrapped his model of cultural pluralism into the cause of a passionate American exceptionalism. Locke followed the model of Santayana in picturing himself "a dubious and doubting sort of American," while Kallen emphasized the Soviet repression of heterodoxy as the totalitarian inversion of American individualism. "The individual, the different, the foreign, the novel, are suppressed" in the Soviet Union, Kallen wrote in 1933. Kallen, *Individualism: An American Way of Life* (New York: Liveright, 1933), p. 138.

121 Eugene C. Holmes, "Alain Leroy Locke: A Sketch," *Phylon* 20 (Spring 1959): 87. For analyses of Locke's political statements, esp. in the 1930s, see A. Gilbert Belles, "The Politics of Alain Locke," in *Alain Locke: Reflections on a Modern Re-*

naissance Man, ed. Russell J. Linnemann, pp. 50–62; Manning Marable, "Alain Locke, W. E. B. Du Bois, and the Crisis of Black Education During the Great Depression," ibid., pp. 63–76. For a sketch of Locke's political activities while a visiting professor at the University of Wisconsin in 1946, see Beth J. Singer, "Alain Locke Remembered," in *The Critical Pragmatism of Alain Locke*, pp. 327–33.

122 W. E. B. Du Bois, *Dusk of Dawn* (New York: Harcourt, Brace, 1940), p. 321.

123 Alain Locke to W. E. B. Du Bois, May 30, 1936, *The Correspondence of W. E. B. Du Bois*, vol. 2, *Selections, 1934–1944*, ed. Herbert Aptheker (Amherst: University of Massachusetts Press, 1976), pp. 84, 85. Sterling Brown published two short volumes in Locke's Bronze Booklet Series for the Associates in Negro Folk Education, *Negro Poetry and Drama* and *The Negro in American Fiction*. Brown complained of Locke's heavy-handed editorial style: "He would change many things that I said, and I would change them right back." Rowell, " 'Let Me Be With Ole Jazzbo': An Interview with Sterling A. Brown,' " p. 804.

124 Locke, *The Negro and His Music*, p. 72.

125 Alain Locke, "We Turn to Prose: A Retrospective Review of the Literature of the Negro for 1931," *Opportunity*, February 1932, p. 42.

126 Locke, *The Negro and His Music*, p. 129.

127 Ibid., pp. 83, 73.

128 Ibid., 78.

129 Locke, "Toward a Critique of Negro Music," part 1, p. 329.

130 Locke, *The Negro and His Music*, p. 86.

131 Ibid., p. 113.

132 Van Vechten wrote in 1925 that it was in 1917 that he "outlined the reasons for my belief that it was out of American popular music that American art music would grow, just as the idiosyncratic national line of so much European art music has evolved from the national folksongs. Nearly seven years passed before my prophecy was realized, but on February 24, 1924 . . . George Gershwin's *Rhapsody in Blue* was performed for the first time by Paul Whiteman's Orchestra with the composer at the piano. . . . I am just as certain that the *Rhapsody* came out of the jazz movement in America as I am that Weber's *Der Freischutz* came out of the German folksong. Negro spirituals, Broadway, and jazz are Gershwin's musical godparents." Carl Van Vechten, "George Gershwin," *Vanity Fair*, March 1925, pp. 40, 84. See also Paul Whiteman, "The Progress of Jazz," *Vanity Fair*, January 1926, pp. 52, 98.

133 Locke, *The Negro and His Music*, p. 4.

134 Ibid., p. 86.

135 Rowell, " 'Let Me Be with Ole Jazzbo': An Interview with Sterling A. Brown," p. 805.

136 Roland Hayes to Alain Locke, October 4, 1924, Alain Locke Papers, MSRC, box 164-35; folder 28.

137 Carl Van Vechten to Alain Locke, 8 May 1937, Alain Locke Papers, MSRC, box 164-90; folder 58.

138 Alain Locke, "God Save Reality!: Part I," *Opportunity*, January 1937, p. 12.

FOUR   *"Beneath the Seeming Informality": Hughes,*
Hurston, and the Politics of Form

1   Nathaniel Mackey, "Sound and Sentiment, Sound and Symbol," in *The Jazz Cadence of American Culture*, ed. Robert G. O'Meally (New York: Columbia University Press, 1998), p. 603.
2   Zora Neale Hurston, *Dust Tracks on a Road* (New York: Harper Perennial, 1991), p. 225.
3   Alain Locke, "Beauty and the Provinces" [1929], in *The Critical Temper of Alain Locke*, ed. Jeffrey C. Stewart (New York: Garland, 1983), p. 30.
4   Alain Locke, "Propaganda—or Poetry?" [1936], in *The Critical Temper of Alain Locke*, p. 35.
5   Richard K. Barksdale, *Praisesong of Survival: Lectures and Essays, 1957–1989* (Urbana: University of Illinois Press, 1992), p. 183. For an overview of critical reactions to *The Weary Blues* and *Fine Clothes to the Jew*, see ibid., pp. 187–93.
6   For a detailed comparison of the editorial agendas of *Opportunity* and *Crisis* in the 1920s, see George Hutchinson, *The Harlem Renaissance in Black and White* (Cambridge, Mass.: Harvard University Press, 1994), esp. pp. 125–208.
7   Alain Locke, "Review of 'The Weary Blues'" [1926], in *The Critical Temper of Alain Locke*, p. 41.
8   Ibid., p. 41. Locke often showed discomfort at the use of black dialect in literature. Even with the beloved folk spirituals, he found it necessary to distance himself from lyrics in dialect. Thus in one analysis he wrote that "finally there is the music itself—that great literacy of musical speech towering up over the dialect and broken, sometimes feeble words to make an instinctive welding of all this into an amalgam of music that shades every meaning and evokes a mood almost independently of the words." Alain Locke, "Spirituals," in *The Critical Temper of Alain Locke*, p. 124. Compare Sterling Brown on the matter: "Negro dialect, however, as recorded by the most talented of our observers today, such as Julia Peterkin, Howard Odum, and Langston Hughes, has shown itself capable of much more than the 'limited two stops, pathos and humor.' . . . There is nothing 'degraded' about dialect. Dialectical peculiarities are universal. There is something about Negro dialect, in the idiom, the turn of the phrase, the music of the vowels and consonants that is worth treasuring. Are we to descend to the level of the lady who wanted Swing Low Sweet Chariot metamorphosed into 'Descend, welcome vehicle, approaching for the purpose of conveying me to my residence?'" Sterling Brown, "Our Literary Audience," *Opportunity*, February 1930, pp. 44, 45. Locke subsequently heralded Brown's dialect writing in *Southern Road* (1932) as a new dawn for African American writing.
9   Arnold Rampersad offers a revealing anecdote about Hughes's first public reading from *The Weary Blues* after its January 1926 publication. "With Alain Locke in the chair, and an admission charge of one dollar, Hughes read on January 15 at the Playhouse . . . in Washington. In a daring move, he had selected a Seventh Street bluesman, funky and unfettered, to howl during the intermission. Locke,

however, had thought of all the respectable black folk and the whites who would come, then sneaked in—to Hughes's intense annoyance—a housebroken Negro. The man played, according to Langston, "nice music, but nothing grotesque and sad at the same time, nothing primitive, and nothing very 'different.'" Rampersad, *The Life of Langston Hughes*, vol. 1, *1902–1941* (New York: Oxford University Press, 1986), p. 123.

10 Alain Locke, "Review of *Fine Clothes to the Jew*," *Saturday Review*, April 3, 1927, p. 712.

11 Zora Neale Hurston, "Concert" [c. 1942], appendix to *Dust Tracks on a Road*, in *Zora Neale Hurston: Folklore, Memoirs, and Other Writings*, ed. Cheryl A. Wall (New York: Library of America, 1995), p. 805.

12 Hurston, "Spirituals and Neo-Spirituals," in *Zora Neale Hurston: Folklore, Memoirs, and Other Writings*, p. 873. All subsequent references to Hurston's essay will be to this edition.

13 Langston Hughes, "The Negro Artist and the Racial Mountain," *Nation*, June 23, 1926, p. 692. See also Hughes's bitterly humorous critique of the pretensions of African-American "society" in Washington, D.C. "Our Wonderful Society: Washington," *Opportunity*, August 1927, pp. 226–27. For a defense of Washington "society" against Hughes's cynicism, see Brenda Ray Moryck, "I, Too, Have Lived in Washington," *Opportunity*, August 1927, pp. 228–31, 243.

14 On whiteness and class, see David R. Roediger, "Introduction: From the Social Construction of Race to the Abolition of Whiteness," in *Toward the Abolition of Whiteness* (London: Verso, 1994).

15 George S. Schuyler, "The Negro-Art Hokum," *Nation*, June 16, 1926, p. 662. Schuyler's comment on music deserves quotation: "True, from dark-skinned sources have come those slave songs based on Protestant hymns and biblical texts known as the spirituals, work songs and secular songs of sorrow and tough luck known as the blues that outgrowth of ragtime known as jazz (in the development of which whites have assisted. . . . But these are contributions of a caste in a certain section of the country. They are foreign to Northern Negroes, West Indian Negroes, and African Negroes. They are no more expressive or characteristic of the Negro race than the music and dancing of the Appalachian highlanders . . . are expressive or characteristic of the Caucasian race. If one wishes to speak of the musical contributions of the peasantry of the South, very well. Any group under similar circumstances would have produced something similar. It is merely a coincidence that this peasant class happens to be of a darker hue than the other inhabitants of the land." Ibid., p. 662. For an overview of the debate, see Onwuchekwa Jemie, *Langston Hughes: An Introduction to the Poetry* (New York: Columbia University Press, 1976), pp. 3–12.

16 Hutchinson, *The Harlem Renaissance in Black and White*, p. 221.

17 Consider this comment from Ralph Ellison about the 1920s: "Even though few recognized it, such artists as Ellington and Louis Armstrong were the stewards of our vaunted American optimism and guardians against the creeping irrationality which ever plagues our form of society. *They created great entertainment, but for them (ironically) and for us (unconsciously) their music was a rejection of that chaos and*

license which characterized the so-called jazz age associated with F. Scott Fitzgerald. . . . Place Ellington with Hemingway, they are both larger than life, both masters of that which is most enduring in the human enterprise: the power of man to define himself against the ravages of time through artistic style." Ellison, "Homage to Duke Ellington on His Birthday," in *Going to the Territory* (New York: Random House, 1986), p. 219 (italics added).

18 Hughes, "The Negro Artist and the Racial Mountain," p. 694.

19 Ibid., p. 694.

20 Carl Van Vechten to Langston Hughes, 25 March 1927, *Letters of Carl Van Vechten*, ed. Bruce Kellner (New Haven, Conn.: Yale University Press, 1987), p. 95.

21 Langston Hughes, "Our Wonderful Society," *Opportunity*, August 1927, p. 226.

22 Melvin Tolson, "His Life," in *Critical Essays on Langston Hughes*, ed. Edward J. Mullen (Boston: G. K. Hall, 1986), p. 120.

23 Jessie Fauset, "Our Book Shelf," *Crisis*, March 1926, p. 239.

24 Langston Hughes, *Fine Clothes to the Jew* (New York: Alfred A. Knopf, 1927), p. xiii.

25 Langston Hughes, review of *Blues* by W. C. Handy, *Opportunity*, August 1926, p. 258.

26 Ibid., p. 258.

27 Langston Hughes, "Songs Called the Blues," *Phylon* (second quarter 1941): 143–44, 145.

28 Sherley Anne Williams, "The Blues Roots of Contemporary Afro-American Poetry," in *Afro-American Literature: The Reconstruction of Instruction*, ed. Dexter Fisher and Robert B. Stepto (New York: Modern Language Press Association of America, 1978), p. 75.

29 Ibid.

30 Among Albert Murray's many articulations of the blues aesthetic, see esp. *The Hero and the Blues* (Columbia: The University of Missouri Press, 1973) and *Stomping the Blues* (New York: Doubleday, 1976). For a related approach, see Ralph Ellison, *Shadow and Act* (New York: Random House, 1964). Amiri Baraka argues against Murray and jazz neoclassicists that the term "'Blues Aesthetic' . . . is useful only if it is not depoliticization of reference. . . . Without the dissent, the struggle, the outside of the inside, the aesthetic is neither genuinely Black nor Blue—but the aesthetic of submission—whether for pay or out of ignorance or ideological turpitude." Baraka, "The 'Blues Aesthetic' and the 'Black Aesthetic': Aesthetics as the Continuing Political History of a Culture," *Black Music Research Journal* 11 (fall 1991): 101, 109. See esp. Le Roi Jones [Amiri Baraka] *Blues People: Negro Music in White America* (New York: William Morrow, 1963); *Black Music* (New York: William Morrow, 1967); and *The Music: Reflections on Jazz and Blues* (New York: William Morrow, 1987).

31 Hughes, review of *Blues* by W. C. Handy, p. 258.

32 Langston Hughes, quoted in Rampersad, *The Life of Langston Hughes*, vol. 1, *1902–1941*, p. 111.

33 Locke, "Spirituals," in *The Critical Temper of Alain Locke*, p. 123.

34 Locke, *The Negro and His Music*, p. 32.

35 Jahan Ramazani, *Poetry of Mourning* (Chicago: University of Chicago Press, 1994), p. 142.

36 Roediger, *Toward the Abolition of Whiteness*, p. 13.

37 Sherwood Anderson, review of *The Ways of White Folks*, *Nation*, July 11, 1934, in *Langston Hughes: Critical Perspectives Past and Present*, ed. Henry Louis Gates Jr. and Kwame Anthony Appiah (New York: Amistad, 1993), p. 19.

38 E. C. Holmes, review of *The Ways of White Folks*, *Opportunity*, September 1934, p. 284.

39 For Hughes's role in the "proletarian literature" movement, see Michael Denning, *The Cultural Front* (London: Verso, 1996), esp. pp. 200–229.

40 Langston Hughes, "The Blues I'm Playing," in *The Ways of White Folks* [1934] (New York: Alfred A. Knopf, 1944), p. 100. All subsequent references to the short story will be to this edition.

41 Ibid., pp. 96, 103.

42 Ibid., pp. 107, 108.

43 Ibid., p. 109.

44 Sigmund Freud, *Three Essays on Sexuality*, in *The Standard Edition of the Complete Psychological Works of Sigmund Freud* (vol. 7), trans. James Strachey (London: Hogarth Press, 1953), p. 238.

45 Johnson, quoted in Spencer, *The New Negroes and Their Music*, p. 29.

46 Barksdale, *Praisesong of Survival*, p. 210.

47 Holmes, review of *The Ways of White Folks*, p. 284.

48 Langston Hughes, "The Blues I'm Playing," in *The Ways of White Folks*, pp. 109, 108, 103, 117.

49 Ibid., p. 111.

50 Ibid., pp. 110, 111.

51 Ibid., p. 119.

52 Ibid., p. 115.

53 See Langston Hughes, "The Weary Blues," in *The Langston Hughes Reader* (New York: George Braziller, 1958), pp. 87–88.

54 Ramazani, *Poetry of Mourning*, pp. 144–45. For analyses of "The Weary Blues" and Hughes's other blues and blues-related poems, see Steven C. Tracey, *Langston Hughes and the Blues* (Urbana: University of Illinois Press, 1988), esp. pp. 141–251.

55 Ramazani, *Poetry of Mourning*, p. 148.

56 For distinctions between the more specific and short-lived Popular Front and a more general "cultural front," see Denning, *The Cultural Front*.

57 Alain Locke, review of *The Ways of White Folks*, *Survey Graphic*, November 23, 1934, p. 565.

58 Hughes, "The Blues I'm Playing," in *The Ways of White Folks*, pp. 108, 107.

59 Langston Hughes, "Too Much of Race," *Crisis*, September 1937, p. 272.

60 On Hughes' initial contacts with Mason, see Rampersad, *The Life of Langston Hughes: 1902–1941*, pp. 147–49.

61 Zora Neale Hurston, "Appendix," *Dust Tracks on a Road*, ed. Robert Hemenway (Urbana: University of Illinois Press, 1984), p. 309.

62 Alain Locke, "Toward a Critique of Negro Music," *Opportunity*, December 1934, p. 367.

63 Alain Locke, "Toward A Critique of Negro Music," *Opportunity*, November 1934, p. 330. In the same text Locke turns from his usual focus on the spirituals to suggest that "perhaps there is more vital originality and power in our secular folk music than even in our religious folk music. It remains for real constructive genius to develop both in the direction which Dvorak clairvoyantly saw." Ibid., p. 330.

64 Locke, "Toward a Critique of Negro Music," p. 329.

65 Locke, *The Negro and His Music*, p. 4.

66 Ibid., p. 118.

67 Zora Neale Hurston, "Characteristics of Negro Expression," in *The Sanctified Church* (Berkeley, Calif.: Turtle Island, 1982), pp. 58–59. Subsequent references to the essay will be to this edition.

68 Henry Louis Gates Jr., *The Signifying Monkey* (New York: Oxford University Press, 1988), p. 118. Gates writes in the book's introduction that "Free of the white person's gaze, black people created their own unique vernacular structures and relished in the double play that these forms bore to white forms. Repetition and revision are fundamental to black artistic forms, from painting to sculpture to music and language use. I decided to analyze the nature and function of Signifyin(g) precisely because it *is* repetition and revision, or repetition with a signal difference. Whatever is black about black American literature is to be found in this identifiable black Signifyin(g) difference." Ibid., p. xxiv.

69 Hurston, "Spirituals and Neo-Spirituals," pp. 869, 870.

70 Hurston, "The Sanctified Church," in *Zora Neale Hurston: Folklore, Memoirs, and Other Writings*, p. 902.

71 Hurston, "Spirituals and Neo-Spirituals," p. 870.

72 Hurston, "How It Feels to Be Colored Me," in *Zora Neale Hurston: Folklore, Memoirs, and Other Writings*, p. 826.

73 Hurston, "Spirituals and Neo-Spirituals," p. 870.

74 Ibid., p. 873.

75 Hurston, *Dust Tracks on a Road*, p. 274.

76 Hurston, "Spirituals and Neo-Spirituals," p. 871.

77 Hemenway, *Zora Neale Hurston*, p. 126.

78 Ibid., p. 101.

79 Zora Neale Hurston, *Mules and Men* [1935] (New York: Harper & Row, 1990), p. 1.

80 Hemenway, *Zora Neale Hurston*, pp. 81, 214–25.

81 Hurston, "Characteristics of Negro Expression," pp. 53–54.

82 Hurston, "Stories of Conflict," in *Zora Neale Hurston: Folklore, Memoirs, and Other Writings*, p. 913.

83 For Brown's criticisms, see Hemenway, *Zora Neale Hurston*, p. 219.

84 See Tate, *Psychoanalysis and Black Novels*, pp. 148–177. Tate makes a strong case for how Hurston's youthful devotion to a career as an ethnographer (and later as a

novelist) "would be more than a devotion; it would be a means of mourning and reparation." Ibid., p. 160.

85 Françoise Lionnet, "Autoethnography: The An-Archic Style of *Dust Tracks on a Road*," in *The Bounds of Race*, ed. Dominick LaCapra (Ithaca, N.Y.: Cornell University Press, 1991), p. 185.

86 Hazel V. Carby, "The Politics of Fiction, Anthropology, and the Folk: Zora Neale Hurston," in *New Essays on "Their Eyes Were Watching God,"* ed. Michael Awkward (Cambridge: Cambridge University Press, 1990), pp. 75, 76.

87 Zora Neale Hurston, "Works-in-Progress for *The Florida Negro*," in *Zora Neale Hurston: Folklore, Memoirs, and Other Writings*, p. 875.

88 Zora Neale Hurston, "Concert," appendix to *Dust Tracks on a Road*, in *Zora Neale Hurston: Folklore, Memoirs, and Other Writings*, pp. 804, 805, 808.

89 Hurston, *Dust Tracks on a Road*, p. 194.

90 Locke, *The Negro and His Music*, p. 135.

91 Ibid., p. 15.

92 Ibid., p. 97.

93 Alain Locke, "Negro Music Goes to Par," *Opportunity*, July 17, 1939, pp. 197–98.

94 Hurston, "Characteristics of Negro Expression," p. 55.

95 James A. Snead, "Repetition as a Figure of Black Culture," in *Black Literature and Literary Theory*, ed. Henry Louis Gates Jr. (New York: Methuen, 1984), p. 67.

96 Hurston, "What White Publishers Won't Print," in *Zora Neale Hurston: Folklore, Memoirs, and Other Writings*, p. 955. Compare Hurston's stated naturalism with Du Bois's future-oriented idealism in which both art and nature "strive toward one vast Ideal, the infinite beauty of the other world." I emphasize the dialectical cast of Du Bois's thoughts on music and art, but readers should recognize his distance from Theodor Adorno, one of the most prominent European dialecticians of a younger generation. (See also chapter 2, note 69.) The contrast is relevant because Snead's defense of nonregressive repetition in "black culture" and his critique of Eurocentric Hegelianism might be read as a postmodernist's riposte to Adorno's influential criticism. There is no evidence that Du Bois was especially fond of middle-period Beethoven, with its dialectical emphasis on dynamic motivic development in the relation of part to whole (as Adorno famously theorized). Although Du Bois's reflections on the matter are brief, he did not seem to approach unvarying musical repetition as necessarily regressive and contrary to future-oriented utopianism. He clearly believed that great music (whether the "sorrow-songs" or Wagnerian opera) had a special capacity for inspiring extramusical notions of social transformation and moral perfectionism through a critique of the present.

97 Paul Gilroy, *The Black Atlantic* (Cambridge, Mass.: Harvard University Press, 1993), pp. 124, 38.

98 Ingrid Monson, "Doubleness, Irony, and Jazz Improvisation: Irony, Parody, and Ethnomusicology," *Critical Inquiry* 20 (winter 1994): 283–313. See also Ingrid Monson, *Saying Something: Jazz Improvisation and Interaction* (Chicago: University of Chicago Press, 1996), esp. pp. 73–132.

99 Shamoon Zamir, *Dark Voices: W. E. B. Du Bois and American Thought, 1888–1903* (Chicago: University of Chicago Press, 1996), p. 213.

100 Monson, "Doubleness, Irony, and Jazz Improvisation," p. 299.

101 Samuel A. Floyd Jr., *The Power of Black Music* (New York: Oxford University Press, 1995), pp. 8, 10.

102 Leon Forrest, *The Furious Voice of Freedom* (Wakefield, R. I.: Asphodel Press, 1994), p. 364.

103 Ibid., 350.

104 Compare the perspective of Roland Barthes on Walter Fisher-Dieskau in his essay, "The Grain of the Voice": "everything in the (semantic and lyrical) structure is respected and yet nothing seduces, nothing sways us to *jouissance*. His art . . . never exceeds culture: here is it the soul which accompanies the song, not the body . . . the whole of musical pedagogy teaches not the culture of the 'grain' of the voice but the emotive modes of its delivery—the myth of respiration. . . . The breath is the *pneuma*, the soul swelling or breaking, and any exclusive art of breathing is likely to be a secretly mystical art. . . . The lung, a stupid organ, . . . swells but gets no erection; it is in the throat, place where the phonic metal hardens and is segmented, in the mask that *signifiance* explodes, bringing not the soul but *jouissance*. With FD, I seem only to hear the lungs, never the tongue, the glottis, the teeth, the mucous membranes, the nose." Roland Barthes, "The Grain of the Voice," in *Image-Text-Music*, trans. Stephen Heath (New York: Hill and Wang, 1977), p. 183. In the case of most African American music the traditional attentiveness to the embodied voice and its throaty "grain" does not "exceed culture"—or at least does not exceed Barthes' implied European norm of "culture"—but rather exemplifies it. For a relevant discussion of how "Hurston links performance and the performative, acting out and action," see Michael Norton, *The Dialect of Modernism*, p. 185.

105 Forrest, *The Furious Voice of Freedom*, p. 345.

FIVE "Saving Jazz from Its Friends": The Predicament of Jazz Criticism in the Swing Era

1 Robert Cantwell, *When We Were Good: The Folk Revival* (Cambridge, Mass.: Harvard University Press, 1996), p. 38.

2 John Hammond, "Basie Makes Chi Debut—Field's Flops in N.Y. 'Satchelmo's' Book Reveals Boastful Artist," *Down Beat*, November 1936, p. 3.

3 Ted Gioia, *The History of Jazz* (New York: Oxford University Press, 1997), p. 7.

4 For the cultish search for authenticity and the real jazz among British jazz fans in the 1930s and 1940s, see Simon Frith, "Playing with Real Feeling: Making Sense of Jazz in Britain," *New Formations* 4 (spring 1988): 7–24.

5 For analyses of decline narratives in jazz criticism and historiography see esp. Scott De Veaux, "Constructing the Jazz Tradition: Jazz Historiography," *Black American Literature Forum* 25 (fall 1991): 525–59; John Gennari, "Jazz Criticism: Its Development and Ideologies," *Black American Literature Forum* 25 (fall 1991): 449–533; Bernard Gendron, " 'Moldy Figs' and Modernists: Jazz at War

(1942–1946)," in *Jazz Among the Discourses*, ed. Krin Gabbard (Durham, N.C.: Duke University Press, 1995), pp. 31–56; Bernard Gendron, "A Short Stay in the Sun: The Reception of Bebop (1944–1950)," *Library Chronicle* 24 (1994): 137–59.

6   For the critical reception of New Orleans jazz, see esp. Bruce Boyd Raeburn, "New Orleans Style" (Ph.D. diss., Tulane University, 1991). I am indebted to Raeburn, director of the Hogan Jazz Archive at Tulane University, for sharing his time and expertise during extensive conversations.

7   Art Hodes, "The Jazz Band Today," *Jazz Record*, April 1943, p. 3.

8   Roger Pryor Dodge, "Consider the Critics," in *Jazzmen*, ed. Frederic Ramsey Jr. and Charles Edward Smith (New York: Harcourt Brace, 1939), pp. 340–41. For an overview of early jazz magazines, see Ronald G. Welburn, "American Jazz Criticism, 1914–1940" (Ph.D. diss., New York University, 1983), esp. pp. 79–103.

9   Regarding the production and critical reception of "Black, Brown and Beige," see esp. *The Duke Ellington Reader*, ed. Mark Tucker (New York: Oxford University Press, 1993), pp. 153–204; Mark Tucker, "The Genesis of *Black, Brown and Beige*," *Black Music Research Journal* 13 (fall 1993): 67–86, and Scott De Veaux, "*Black, Brown and Beige* and the Critics," *Black Music Research Journal* 13 (fall 1993): 125–46.

10   Jake Trussell Jr., "Why Fusion?" *Jazz Music*, September 1943, p. 4.

11   Duke Ellington, "The Duke Steps Out" [1931], in *The Duke Ellington Reader*, p. 49.

12   John Hammond, "Is the Duke Deserting Jazz?" *Jazz Record*, February 15, 1943, p. 5.

13   Richard Gehman, "A Triumph of Enthusiasm," *Esquire*, January 1959, p. 79.

14   Alan Pomerance, *Repeal of the Blues* (Secaucus, N.J.: Citadel Press, 1988), p. 21.

15   Roger Pryor Dodge, "Negro Jazz" [1929], in Roger Pryor Dodge, *Hot Jazz and Jazz Dance*, ed. Pryor Dodge (New York: Oxford University Press, 1995), p. 3.

16   Duke Ellington, "Duke Says Swing Is Stagnant" [1939], in *The Duke Ellington Reader*, p. 135.

17   John Hammond and Irving Townsend, *John Hammond on Record* (New York: Ridge Press, 1977), p. 199.

18   John Hammond, "Random Notes on the Spirituals to Swing Recordings" (liner notes), *Spirituals to Swing: The Legendary Carnegie Hall Concerts of 1938–9*, Vanguard: VSD, 47/48.

19   Irving Kolodin, "Number One Swing Man," *Harper's*, September 1939, p. 431.

20   John Hammond, "An Experience in Jazz History," *Black Music in Our Culture*, ed. Dominique Rene de Lerma (Kent, Ohio: Kent State University Press, 1970), p. 44.

21   Eileen Southern, *The Music of Black Americans: A History* (New York: W. W. Norton, 1988), p. 428.

22   Hammond, "An Experience in Jazz History," p. 44.

23   Kolodin, "Number One Swing Man," p. 435.

24   David Ware Stowe, *Swing Changes: Big Band Jazz in New Deal America* (Cambridge, Mass.: Harvard University Press, 1994), p. 83.

25   Kolodin, "Number One Swing Man," p. 435.

26 John Hammond, "Many New Faces In New York Swing Spots," *Down Beat*, October 1936, p. 3.

27 The friendship of Hammond and Goodman eventually frayed, even though Goodman married into Hammond's family. Their autobiographies give conflicting accounts of Hammond's role in Goodman's success. For a helpful attempt at untangling their complex relationship, see James Lincoln Collier, *Benny Goodman and the Swing Era* (New York: Oxford University Press, 1989), esp. pp. 93–109.

28 Benny Goodman and Irving Kolodin, *The Kingdom of Swing* [1939] (New York: Frederick Ungar, 1961), p. 124.

29 Ibid., pp. 129, 133, 157.

30 Gary Giddins, *Visions of Jazz* (New York: Oxford University Press, 1998), p. 156.

31 Scott De Veaux, *The Birth of Bebop* (Berkeley: University of California Press, 1997), pp. 125–26.

32 Stowe, *Swing Changes*, p. 55.

33 John Hammond, "Benny Goodman's Carnegie Hall Concert," *Tempo*, February 1938, p. 8.

34 For the history of Swing Era jazz concerts, see Scott De Veaux, "The Emergence of the Jazz Concert, 1935–1945," *American Music* 7 (1989): 6–29.

35 Gerald Early, "Pulp and Circumstance," in *The Culture of Bruising: Essays on Prizefighting, Literature, and Modern American Culture* (Hopewell, N.J.: Ecco Press, 1994), p. 199.

36 On the Clef Club and related concerts in Carnegie Hall, see "Black Music Concerts in Carnegie Hall, 1912–1915," *Black Perspective in Music* (spring 1978): 71–88; R. Reid Badger, "James Reese Europe and the Prehistory of Jazz," in *Jazz in Mind*, ed. Reginald T. Buckner and Steven Weiland (Detroit: Wayne State University Press, 1991), pp. 19–37.

37 Southern, *The Music of Black Americans*, p. 438.

38 Paul Whiteman and Margaret McBridge, *Jazz* (New York: J. H. Sears, 1926), n.p., quoted in Roger Pryor Dodge, "Consider the Critics," in Ramsey and Smith, eds., *Jazzmen*, p. 322.

39 Olin Downes, [review], *New York Times*, February 13, 1924, p. 16.

40 Carl Van Vechten, "George Gershwin," *Vanity Fair*, March 1925, pp. 40, 78, 84.

41 Quoted in Gioia, *The History of Jazz*, p. 89.

42 John Hammond, "An Experience in Jazz History," in de Lerma, ed., *Black Music in Our Culture*, p. 47.

43 Marshall Stearns, "Swing Moves from New Orleans to Chicago," *Down Beat*, August 1936, p. 6.

44 Early, "Pulp and Circumstance," p. 182.

45 See Eric Lott, *Love and Theft: Blackface Minstrelsy and the American Working Class* (New York: Oxford University Press, 1993).

46 For a discussion of "black art in whiteface" in the early careers of Irving Berlin, Al Jolson, Fred Astaire, and Paul Whiteman, see Ann Douglas, *Terrible Honesty: Mongrel Manhattan in the 1920s* (New York: Farrar, Straus and Giroux, 1995), esp. pp. 346–86. For a more critical view, see Michael Rogin, *Black Face, White Nose:*

Jewish Immigrants in the Hollywood Melting Pot (Berkeley: University of California Press, 1996), esp. pp. 73–120.

47 Early, "Pulp and Circumstance," p. 181.

48 Frederic Ramsey Jr., "Jazz on Stage," *Jazz Forum* 2 (September 1946): 14.

49 James Dugan and John Hammond, "The Music Nobody Knows" (program notes, "From Spirituals to Swing," December 23, 1938), reprinted in *Black Perspective in Music* (fall 1974): 196.

50 John Hammond quoted in "Interview with John Hammond," in Ronald G. Welburn, "American Jazz Criticism, 1914–1940" (Ph.D. diss., New York University, 1983), p. 214.

51 *New Masses*, November 15, 1938, p. 21.

52 An advertisement for Hammond's concert began: "American Negro music as it was invented, developed, sung, played and heard by the Negro himself—the true, untainted folk song, spirituals, work songs, songs of protest, chain gang songs, Holy Roller chants, shouts, blues, minstrel music, honky-tonk piano, early jazz, and finally, the contemporary swing of Count Basie, presented by the greatest living artists from the South, the Southwest, and Negro communities in the North." *New Masses*, November 22, 1938, p. 23.

53 "Between Ourselves," *New Masses*, November 8, 1938, p. 2.

54 John Hammond, "Jim-Crow Blues," *New Masses*, 13 December 1939, p. 27. See Lawrence Gellert, "Negro Songs of Protest," in Cunard, ed., *Negro: An Anthology*, pp. 226–37. On the political uses of folk music, see Robert Cantwell, *When We Were Good: The Folk Revival* (Cambridge, Mass: Harvard University Press, 1996); Michael Denning, *The Cultural Front* (New York: Verso, 1995); R. Serge Denisoff, *Great Day Coming: Folk Music and the American Left* (Urbana: University of Illinois Press, 1971); Robbie Lieberman, *My Song Is My Weapon: People's Songs, American Communism, and the Politics of Culture, 1930–1950* (Urbana: University of Illinois Press, 1989).

55 Hammond quoted in Denning, *The Cultural Front*, p. 325.

56 James Higgins quoted, "Between Ourselves," *New Masses*, November 29, 1938, p. 2.

57 "Between Ourselves," *New Masses*, November 15, 1938, p. 2.

58 Dugan and Hammond, "The Music Nobody Knows," p. 195.

59 "Boogie-Woogie," *New Yorker*, December 31, 1938, p. 13.

60 Dugan and Hammond, "The Music Nobody Knows," p. 205.

61 John Hammond, "John Hammond Says," *Tempo*, November 1937, p. 2.

62 John Sebastian, "Music in North Carolina," *New Masses*, December 27, 1938, p. 27.

63 John Hammond, "'Boogie-Woogie' and Beethoven Inspire Wilson Record," *Down Beat*, June 1936, p. 10.

64 H. Howard Taubman, "Negro Music Given at Carnegie Hall," *New York Times*, December 24, 1938, p. 13.

65 John Hammond, "Kansas City a Hot-Bed for Fine Swing Musicians," *Down Beat*, September 1936, pp. 1, 9.

66 John Hammond, "Basie Makes Chi Debut—Field's Flops in N.Y. 'Satchelmo's' Book Reveals Boastful Artist," *Down Beat*, November 1936, p. 3.

67 John Hammond, "NY Swing Concert Proved Headache—Too Hard to Commercialize on Jam Music," *Down Beat*, June 1936, p. 6.

68 Pomerance, *Repeal of the Blues*, p. 45.

69 Donald Clarke, *Wishing on the Moon* (London: Viking Press, 1994), p. 134.

70 Ibid., p. 139.

71 Hammond and Townsend, *John Hammond on Record*, p. 206.

72 Taubman, "Negro Music Given at Carnegie Hall," p. 13. New York's *Amsterdam News* covered the event with a personality profile of the singer Ruby Smith, the niece of Bessie Smith. Hammond dedicated the event to the memory of Bessie Smith, who had died the year before under questionable circumstances (Hammond and other's blamed racial indifference) in a Southern hospital. "Spirituals to Swing," *Amsterdam News* (New York), December 24, 1938, p. 20.

73 F. D. P., "Swing Rhythms Sway Audience at Carnegie Hall," *New York Herald Tribune*, December 24, 1938, p. 10.

74 Hammond, "Basie Makes Chi Debut," p. 3.

75 Hughes Panassié, "Self-Defense," *Record Changer*, April 1946, p. 28.

76 "Many people complain, too, that he [Hammond] is full of racial prejudice. He claims to be impartial on this score, but when he makes sweeping statements like 'The best of the white folk still cannot compare to the really good Negroes in relaxed, unpretentious dance music,' a lot of the white folk consider him clearly intolerant." E. J. Kahn Jr., "Young Man with a Viola," *New Yorker*, July 29, 1939, p. 22. A profile of Hammond by Otis Ferguson, a *New Republic* contributor, made the point about reverse Jim Crow: "He's dedicated to the cause of the Negro. Fine. . . . And when he goes around saying 'white musician' the way you'd use the term greaseball, he not only confuses his readers and upsets his own standards but starts the Jim Crow car all over again, in reverse. Some will tell you that you're not doing much to eliminate a color line by drawing it all over the place yourself, and certainly something ought to be done among those of Mother Hammond's Chickens who have been led into believing that criticism consists in saying: Which is better, black or white? and raising all that hell." Ferguson, "John Hammond," *HRS Rag*, September 1938, pp. 5–6.

77 Jake Trussell Jr., "Jim Crow—Upside Down," *Jazz Record*, April 1944, p. 4.

78 Kolodin, "Number One Swing Man," pp. 432, 433.

79 Stowe, *Swing Changes*, pp. 122–23, 125. See also Irving Kolodin, "The Dance Band Business: A Study in Black and White," *Harper's*, June 1941, pp. 72–82.

80 John Hammond, "John Hammond Says," *Tempo*, July 1937, p. 2.

81 Hammond and Townsend, *John Hammond on Record*, p. 326.

82 For a superb development of this topic, see DeVeaux, *The Birth of Bebop*.

83 Roger Pryor Dodge, "From Spirituals to Swing," *HRS Rag*, January 1939, n.p.

84 Roger Pryor Dodge, "Consider the Critics," in Ramsey and Smith, eds., *Jazzmen*, pp. 333–34.

85 Roger Pryor Dodge, "Negro Jazz," in Pryor Dodge, ed., *Hot Jazz and Jazz Dance* (New York: Oxford University Press, 1995), pp. 14, 4.

86 Ibid., p. 5.

87 Ibid.

88 Ibid.

89 Roger Pryor Dodge, [review], *Record Changer*, November 1945, p. 27.

90 Alma Huber, "Must Jazz Be Progressive?," *Jazz Record*, April 1944, p. 9.

91 For a relevant defense of "riff" styles and a critique of New Orleans purism, see Hugues Panassié, review of *A Critic Looks at Jazz*, *Record Changer*, December 1946, p. 19.

92 Roger Pryor Dodge, "On the Labels," *Record Changer*, November 1945, pp. 27, 26.

93 Dodge, "Negro Jazz," pp. 6, 7.

94 Roger Pryor Dodge, "Negro Jazz as Folk Material for Our Modern Dance" (address to National Dance Congress, 1936), in *Hot Jazz and Jazz Dance*, p. 30.

95 Dodge, "Negro Jazz," p. 7.

96 On French composers and jazz, see Bernard Gendron, "Jamming at Le Boeuf: Jazz and the Paris Avant-Garde," *Discourse* 12 (fall–winter 1989–90): 3–27.

97 Dodge, "Negro Jazz," p. 8.

98 Roger Pryor Dodge, "Harpsichords and Jazz Trumpets," *Hound & Horn* (July–September 1934): 596, 590.

99 For the guild consciousness of jazz musicians in the 1920s, see Burton W. Peretti, *The Creation of Jazz: Music, Race, and Culture in Urban America* (Urbana: University of Illinois Press, 1992), p. 215.

100 Dodge, "Harpsichords and Jazz Trumpets," p. 593.

101 Dodge, "Negro Jazz," p. 5.

102 Roger Pryor Dodge, "Jazz in the Twenties" [1942], in *Hot Jazz and Jazz Dance*, p. 105.

103 Roger Pryor Dodge, "Duke Ellington" [1943], in *Hot Jazz and Jazz Dance*, p. 108.

104 Dodge, "Harpsichords and Jazz Trumpets," p. 600.

105 Roger Pryor Dodge, "Consider the Critics," in Ramsey and Smith, eds., *Jazzmen*, p. 341.

106 Roger Pryor Dodge, "Hot Jazz: Notes on the Future," *HRS Rag*, January–February 1941, p. 14.

107 Roger Pryor Dodge, "Categorical Terms in Jazz," *Record Changer*, June 1945, p. 38.

108 Roger Pryor Dodge, "Jazz: Its Rise and Decline" [1955], in *Hot Jazz and Jazz Dance*, pp. 208, 215.

EPILOGUE

1 W. E. B. Du Bois, *The Souls of Black Folk* (New York: Vintage, 1990), p. 190.

2 Duke Ellington, "Duke Says Swing Is Stagnant" (originally published in *Down Beat*, February 1939), in *The Duke Ellington Reader*, ed. Mark Tucker (New York: Oxford University Press, 1993), pp. 134, 133.

3 Benny Goodman, "Now Take the Jitterbug," *Collier's*, February 25, 1939, p. 60.

4   Gary Giddins, *Visions of Jazz* (New York: Oxford University Press, 1998), p. 154.

5   Theodor Adorno, *Minima Moralia*, trans. E. F. N. Jephcott (London: Verso, 1978), p. 50.

6   Quoted in Richard Gehman, "A Triumph of Enthusiasm," *Esquire*, January 1959, p. 80.

7   Benny Goodman and Irving Kolodin, *The Kingdom of Swing* (New York: Frederick Ungar, 1961), p. 236.

8   Gerald Early, "On *Good Morning Blues: The Autobiography of Count Basie*," in *Tuxedo Junction: Essays on American Culture* (Hopewell, N.J.: Ecco Press, 1994), p. 278. For reflections on Basie and Ellington that lead to conclusions similar to Hammond's, see Eric Hobsbawm, *The Jazz Scene* (New York: Pantheon, 1993), pp. 291–301, 312–25.

9   Duke Ellington, "Duke Says Swing Is Stagnant," in *The Duke Ellington Reader*, p. 135.

10   James Dugan and John Hammond, "The Music Nobody Knows," p. 191.

11   Mark Tucker, "The Renaissance Education of Duke Ellington," in *Black Music in the Harlem Renaissance*, ed. Samuel A. Floyd Jr. (Westport, Conn.: Greenwood Press, 1990), p. 123.

12   Duke Ellington, *Music Is My Mistress* (Garden City, N.Y.: Doubleday, 1973), p. 17.

13   Harlem Renaissance leaders' skepticism about jazz and blues, according to Samuel Floyd, was a dilemma that "would resolve itself in time" (but not during the 1920s). "Black Music in the Harlem Renaissance: An Overview," in *Black Music in the Harlem Renaissance*, p. 5. The acceptance of Ellington's symphonic jazz played a key role in the dilemma's resolution.

14   Duke Ellington, "The Duke Steps Out" (1931), in *The Duke Ellington Reader*, p. 49.

15   Ibid., p. 49.

16   R. D. Darrell, "Black Beauty" (1932), in *The Duke Ellington Reader*, pp. 59–60.

17   Helen Oakley, "Stuff and Nonsense," *Down Beat*, June 1936, p. 5. Oakley, president of the Chicago Hot Club, hosted a successful Ellington performance for Chicago musicians. She was offered a New York job under Ellington's manager, Irving Mills, who fully appreciated the economic value of publicizing Ellington's distinctive image as a sophisticated composer.

18   Ellington, quoted in Carl Cons, "A Black Genius in a White Man's World," *Down Beat*, July 1936, p. 6.

19   Paul Eduard Miller, "Are Colored Musicians Superior to Whites?" *Down Beat*, October 1936, p. 5.

20   Paul Eduard Miller, "Symphonic Sweet and Hot Jazz Need Real Standards of Comparison," *Down Beat*, September 1936, p. 2.

21   For further considerations on this episode in the Hammond-Ellington relationship, see Paul A. Anderson, "Ellington, Rap Music, and Cultural Difference," *Musical Quarterly* (spring 1995): 172–206.

22   Alain Locke, *The Negro and His Music* (Port Washington, N.Y.: Kennikat Press, 1968), p. 4.

23 Alain Locke, "Toward a Critique of Negro Music," *Opportunity*, December 1934, pp. 365–66.

24 Alain Locke wrote that "the Carnegie Hall concert . . . under John Hammond's direction, assembled an historical sequence of authentic folk music played by relatively genuine, unspoiled folk musicians. There were slightly contaminating elements of 'jitterbug exhibitionism' about this concert, and also of that hieratic snobbery too frequent with faddist patrons of rising causes, but in spite of all that, the concert was a high-water mark in the annals of Negro music." Locke, "Negro Music Goes to Par," *Opportunity*, July 1939, p. 199.

25 Duke Ellington, " 'Situation Between the Critics and Musicians Is Laughable'— Ellington," *Down Beat*, April 1939, in *The Duke Ellington Reader*, p. 137.

26 Alain Locke to Duke Ellington, undated [October 1939], Alain Locke Papers, MSRC, box 164-27; folder 23.

27 Ellington, *Music Is My Mistress*, p. 103.

28 Bill Chase, *Amsterdam* (New York) *News*, December 31, 1938, p. 17.

29 Gama Gilbert, "Capacity Crowd Hears Whiteman," *New York Times*, December 26, 1938, p. 28.

30 Ellington, *Music Is My Mistress*, p. 182. The 1943 Carnegie Hall concert inaugurated an annual Ellington tradition of concerts that were, in Ellington's words "really a series of social-significance thrusts." Within a few years "a 'major' work was expected of us at every Carnegie Hall concert." Ibid., pp. 183, 184.

31 Ellington quoted in Helen Oakley, "Ellington to Offer 'Tone Parallel,' " *Down Beat*, January 15, 1943, p. 13. "Unlike the Goodman offering and those of others in the dance field who have advanced on Carnegie, the Ellington performance will be a serious program hailing the attention of Carnegie's customary patrons." Ibid., p. 13.

32 Gary Tomlinson, "Cultural Dialogics and Jazz: A White Historian Signifies," *Black Music Research Journal* (fall 1991): 248.

33 Scott DeVeaux, "Constructing the Jazz Tradition," *Black American Literature Forum* (fall 1991): 553.

34 Wynton Marsalis, in conversation with Cornel West. See West, *Restoring Hope: Conversations on the Future of Black America*, ed. Kelvin Shawn Sealey (Boston: Beacon Press, 1997), p. 127.

SELECTED BIBLIOGRAPHY

Abrahams, Roger D. "Phantoms of Romantic Nationalism in Folkloristics." *Journal of American Folklore* (winter 1993): 3–37.

Abrams, M. H. *Natural Supernaturalism*. New York: W. W. Norton, 1971.

Adorno, Theodor. *In Search of Wagner*, trans. Rodney Livingstone. London: Verso, 1981.

———. *Philosophy of Modern Music*, trans. Anne G. Mitchell and Wesley V. Blomster. New York: Continuum 1973.

Allison, Roland Lewis. "Classification of the Vocal Works of Harry T. Burleigh (1866–1949) and Some Suggestions for Their Use in Teaching Diction in Singing." Ph.D. diss., Indiana University, 1965.

Anderson, Benedict. *Imagined Communities: Reflections on the Origin and Spread of Nationalism*. London: Verso, 1991.

Anderson, Paul A. "Ellington, Rap Music, and Cultural Difference." *Musical Quarterly* (spring 1995): 172–206.

Appiah, Kwame Anthony. "The Conservation of 'Race.'" *Black American Literature Forum* 23 (spring 1989): 37–60.

———. *In My Father's House: Africa in the Philosophy of Culture*. New York: Oxford University Press, 1992.

———. "The Uncompleted Argument: Du Bois and the Illusion of Race." In *'Race,' Writing, and Difference*, ed. Henry Louis Gates Jr. Chicago: University of Chicago Press, 1986.

Baker, Houston A., Jr. *Afro-American Poetics: Revisions of Harlem and the Black Aesthetic*. Madison: University of Wisconsin Press, 1988.

———. *Blues, Ideology, and Afro-American Literature: A Vernacular Theory*. Chicago: University of Chicago Press, 1984.

———. "Caliban's Triple Play." In *'Race,' Writing, and Difference*, ed. Henry Louis Gates Jr. Chicago: University of Chicago Press, 1984.

——. *Long Black Song: Essays in Black American Literature and Culture*. Charlottesville: University Press of Virginia, 1972.

——. *Modernism and the Harlem Renaissance*. Chicago: University of Chicago Press, 1987.

Baraka, Amiri (LeRoi Jones). *Black Music*. New York: William Morrow, 1967.

——. "The 'Blues Aesthetic' and the 'Black Aesthetic': Aesthetics as the Continuing Political History of a Culture." *Black Music Research Journal* 11 (fall 1991): 101–10.

——. *Blues People: Negro Music in White America*. New York: William Morrow, 1963.

——. "In the Tradition (Not a White Shadow but Black People Will Be Victorious)." In *Moment's Notice: Jazz in Poetry & Prose*, ed. Art Lange and Nathaniel Mackey. Minneapolis: Coffee House Press, 1993.

Barksdale, Richard K. *Praisesong of Survival: Lectures and Essays, 1957–1989*. Urbana: University of Illinois Press, 1992.

Barnard, F. M. *Herder's Social and Political Thought*. Oxford: Oxford University Press, 1965.

Barnes, Albert. "Negro Art, Past and Present." *Opportunity*, May 1926, pp. 148–49, 168–69.

——. "Primitive Negro Sculpture and Its Influence on Modern Civilization." *Opportunity*, May 1928, pp. 139–40, 147.

——. "The Temple." *Opportunity*, May 1924, pp. 138–40.

Barthes, Roland. *Image-Text-Music*, trans. Stephen Heath. New York: Hill and Wang, 1977.

Bell, Bernard W. "W. E. B. Du Bois's Struggle to Reconcile Folk and High Art." In *Critical Essays on W. E. B. Du Bois*, ed. William L. Andrews. Boston: G. K. Hall, 1985.

Benston, Kimberly W. *Baraka: The Renegade and the Mask*. New Haven, Conn.: Yale University Press, 1976.

——. "Late Coltrane: A Re-Membering of Orpheus." *Massachusetts Review* (winter 1977).

——. "Performing Blackness: Re/Placing Afro-American Poetry." In *Afro-American Literary Study in the 1990s*, ed. Houston A. Baker Jr. and Patricia Redmond. Chicago: University of Chicago Press, 1989.

Bhabha, Homi K. *The Location of Culture*. London: Routledge, 1994.

Bluestein, Gene. *The Voice of the Folk: Folklore and American Literary Theory*. Amherst: University of Massachusetts Press, 1972.

Bremen, Brian A. "Du Bois, Emerson, and the 'Fate' of Black Folk." *American Literary Realism, 1870–1910* (spring 1992): 80–88.

Brown, Sterling. "The Blues as Folk Poetry." In *The Book of Negro Folklore*, ed. Langston Hughes and Arna Bontemps. New York: Dodd, Mead, 1958.

——. "Negro Folk Expression: Spirituals, Seculars, Ballads and Work Songs." *Phylon* (winter 1953): 45–61.

——. "The New Negro In Literature (1925–1955)." In *The New Negro Thirty Years Afterward*. Washington, D.C.: Howard University Press, 1955: 57–71.

——. "Our Literary Audience." *Opportunity*, February 1930, pp. 42–46, 61.

———. "Portrait of a Jazz Giant: 'Jelly Roll' Morton." *Black World* (February 1974): 28–48.

———. "Ragtime and the Blues." *Sterling A. Brown: A UMUM Tribute*, ed. Black History Museum Committee. Philadelphia: Black History Museum UMUM Publishers, 1982.

———. "Roland Hayes." *Opportunity*, June 1925, pp. 173–74.

———. "The Spirituals." In *The Book of Negro Folklore*, ed. Langston Hughes and Arna Bontemps. New York: Dodd, Mead, 1958.

Bürger, Peter. *Theory of the Avant-Garde*, trans. Michael Shaw. Minneapolis: University of Minnesota Press, 1984.

Burleigh, Harry. *Negro Minstrel Melodies*. New York: G. Schirmer, 1909.

Cantwell, Robert. *When We Were Good: The Folk Revival*. Cambridge, Mass.: Harvard University Press, 1996.

Carby, Hazel V. "The Politics of Fiction, Anthropology, and the Folk: Zora Neale Hurston." In *New Essays on "Their Eyes Were Watching God,"* ed. Michael Awkward. Cambridge: Cambridge University Press, 1990.

———. *Race Men: The Body and Soul of Race, Nation, and Masculinity*. Cambridge, Mass.: Harvard University Press, 1998.

Cavell, Stanley. *The Pitch of Philosophy*. Cambridge, Mass.: Harvard University Press, 1994.

Chauncey, George. *Gay New York*. New York: BasicBooks, 1994.

Clarke, Donald. *Wishing on the Moon*. London: Viking Press, 1994.

Clifford, James. *The Predicament of Culture: Twentieth-Century Ethnography, Literature, and Art*. Cambridge, Mass.: Harvard University Press, 1988.

Collier, James Lincoln. *Benny Goodman and the Swing Era*. New York: Oxford University Press, 1989.

Collins, Joseph. "The Dance 'Mania,'" *Vanity Fair*, February 1926, pp. 68, 84.

Colson, William N. "Phases of Du Bois." In *The Messenger Reader*, ed. Sondra Kathryn Wilson. New York: Modern Library, 2000.

Cone, James H. *The Spirituals and the Blues: An Interpretation*. Maryknoll, N.Y.: Orbis Books, 1972.

Crow, Thomas. "Modernism and Mass Culture in the Visual Arts." In *Modernism and Modernity: The Vancouver Conference Papers*, ed. Benjamin H. D. Buchloh, Serge Guilbaut, and David Solkin. Halifax: Press of the Nova Scotia School of Art and Design, 1983: 215–64.

Cruse, Harold. *The Crisis of the Negro Intellectual*. New York: Quill, 1984.

Cunard, Nancy, ed. *Negro: An Anthology*. New York: Frederick Ungar, 1970.

Dahlhaus, Carl. *Between Romanticism and Modernism*, trans. Mary Whittall. Berkeley: University of California Press, 1980.

———. *The Idea of Absolute Music*, trans. Roger Lustig. Chicago: University of Chicago Press, 1989.

———. *Nineteenth-Century Music*, trans. J. Bradford Robinson. Berkeley: University of California Press, 1989.

Denning, Michael. *The Cultural Front*. London: Verso, 1996.

Dennis, Rutledge M. "Relativism and Pluralism in the Social Thought of Alain

Locke." In *Alain Locke: Reflections on a Modern Renaissance Man*, ed. Russell J. Linnemann. Baton Rouge: Louisiana State University Press, 1982.

Denisoff, R. Serge. *Great Day Coming: Folk Music and the American Left*. Urbana: University of Illinois Press, 1971.

Derrida, Jacques. *Writing and Difference*, trans. Alan Bass. Chicago: University of Chicago Press, 1978.

DeVeaux, Scott. *The Birth of Bebop*. Berkeley: University of California Press, 1997.

———. "*Black, Brown and Beige* and the Critics." *Black Music Research Journal* 13 (fall 1993): 125–46.

———. "Constructing the Jazz Tradition: Jazz Historiography." *Black American Literature Forum* 25 (fall 1991): 525–60.

———. "The Emergence of the Jazz Concert, 1933–1945." *American Music* 7 (spring 1989): 6–29.

Dodge, Roger Pryor. "Consider the Critics." In *Jazzmen*, ed. Frederic Ramsey Jr. and Charles Edward Smith. New York: Harcourt, Brace, 1939.

———. "Harpsichords and Jazz Trumpets." *Hound & Horn* (July–September 1934): 587–608.

———. *Hot Jazz and Jazz Dance*, ed. Pryor Dodge. New York: Oxford University Press, 1995.

Douglas, Ann. *Terrible Honesty: Mongrel Manhattan in the 1920s*. New York: Farrar, Straus and Giroux, 1995.

Duberman, Martin Bauml. *Paul Robeson*. New York: Random House, 1989.

Du Bois, W. E. B. *Against Racism: Unpublished Essays, Papers, Addresses, 1887–1961*, ed. Herbert Aptheker. Amherst: University of Massachusetts Press, 1985.

———. *The Autobiography of W. E. B. Du Bois: A Soliloquy on Viewing My Life from the Last Decade of Its First Century*. New York: International Publishers, 1968.

———. "Criteria of Negro Art." *Crisis*, October 1926, pp. 290, 292, 294, 296–97.

———. *Darkwater*. In *The Oxford W. E. B. Du Bois Reader*, ed. Eric J. Sundquist. New York: Oxford University Press, 1996.

———. *Dark Princess*. New York: Harcourt, Brace, 1928.

———. *Dusk of Dawn*. New York: Harcourt, Brace, 1940.

———. *The Emerging Thought of W. E. B. Du Bois*, ed. Henry Lee Moon. New York: Simon & Schuster, 1972.

———. *Newspaper Columns by W. E. B. Du Bois*, vol. 1, *1883–1944*, ed. Herbert Aptheker. White Plains, N.Y.: Kraus-Thomson Organization, 1986.

———. Review of *The Book of American Negro Spirituals*. *Crisis*, November 1925, p. 31.

———. Review of *The New Negro*. *Crisis*, January 1926, pp. 140–41.

———. Review of *Nigger Heaven*. *Crisis*, December 1926, pp. 81–82.

———. "The Social Origins of American Negro Art." In *Modern Quarterly* (October–December 1925): 53–56.

———. *The Souls of Black Folk*. New York: Library of America, 1990.

———. *W. E. B. Du Bois on Sociology and the Black Community*, ed. Dan S. Green and Edwin D. Driver. Chicago: University of Chicago Press, 1978.

———. *W. E. B. Du Bois: Writings*, ed. Nathan Huggins. New York: Library of America, 1986.

Du Bois, W. E. B., Ralph Bunche, et al. "The Passing of Alain Leroy Locke." *Phylon* 15 (3rd quarter 1954): 243–42.

Du Bois, W. E. B., and Alain Locke. "The Younger Literary Movement." *Crisis*, February 1924, pp. 161–63.

Eagleton, Terry. *The Ideology of the Aesthetic*. Oxford: Basil Blackwell, 1990.

Early, Gerald. *The Culture of Bruising: Essays on Prizefighting, Literature, and Modern American Culture*. Hopewell, N.J.: Ecco Press, 1994.

———. *Tuxedo Junction: Essays on American Culture*. Hopewell, N.J.: Ecco Press, 1994.

———, ed. *Lure and Loathing: Essays on Race, Identity and the Ambivalence of Assimilation*. Allen Lane, Eng.: Penguin, 1993.

Ellington, Duke. *Music Is My Mistress*. Garden City, N.Y.: Doubleday, 1973.

Ellison, Ralph. *The Collected Essays of Ralph Ellison*, ed. John F. Callahan. New York: Modern Library, 1995.

———. *Going to the Territory*. New York: Random House, 1986.

———. *Shadow and Act*. New York: Random House, 1964.

Erenberg, Lewis A. "Things to Come: Swing Bands, Bebop, and the Rise of a Postwar Jazz Scene." In *Recasting America*, ed. Lary May. Chicago: University of Chicago Press, 1989.

Fabre, Genevieve, and Robert O'Meally. *History and Memory in African-American Culture*. New York: Oxford University Press, 1994.

Floyd, Samuel A., Jr., ed. *Black Music in the Harlem Renaissance*. Westport, Conn.: Greenwood Press, 1990.

———. *The Power of Black Music*. New York: Oxford University Press, 1995.

Foley, Barbara. *Radical Representations: Politics and Form in U.S. Proletarian Fiction, 1929–1941*. Durham, N.C.: Duke University Press, 1993.

Forrest, Leon. "A Solo Long-Song: For Lady Day." *Callaloo* 16 (spring 1993): 332–67.

———. *The Furious Voice of Freedom*. Wakefield, R.I.: Asphodel Press, 1994.

Freedman, Jonathan. *Professions of Taste: Henry James, British Aestheticism, and Commodity Culture*. Stanford, Calif.: Stanford University Press, 1990.

Freud, Sigmund. *Three Essays on Sexuality*. In *The Standard Edition of the Complete Psychological Works of Sigmund Freud*, vol. 7, trans. James Strachey. London: Hogarth Press, 1953.

Frith, Simon. "Playing with Real Feeling: Making Sense of Jazz in Britain." *New Formations* 4 (spring 1988): 7–24.

Fry, Roger. *A Roger Fry Reader*, ed. Christopher Reed. Chicago: University of Chicago Press, 1996.

———. *Vision and Design*, ed. J. B. Bullen. Mineola, N.Y.: Dover, 1998.

Gabbard, Krin, ed. *Jazz Among the Discourses*. Durham, N.C.: Duke University Press, 1995.

Gabbin, Joanne V. *Sterling A. Brown: Building the Black Aesthetic Tradition*. Westport, Conn.: Greenwood Press, 1985.

Gaines, Kevin K. *Uplifting the Race: Black Leadership, Politics, and Culture in the Twentieth Century*. Chapel Hill: University of North Carolina Press, 1996.

Gates, Henry Louis, Jr. *Figures in Black: Words, Signs, and the "Racial Self."* New York: Oxford University Press, 1987.

———. *The Signifying Monkey: A Theory of African-American Literary Criticism*. New York: Oxford University Press, 1988.

———. "The Trope of a New Negro and the Reconstruction of the Image of the Black." In *The New American Studies*, ed. Philip Fisher. Berkeley: University of California Press, 1991.

Gates, Henry Louis, Jr., and Kwame Anthony Appiah, eds. *Langston Hughes: Critical Perspectives Past and Present*. New York: Amistad, 1993.

Gendron, Bernard. "Jamming at Le Boeuf: Jazz and the Paris Avant-Garde." *Discourse* 12 (fall–winter 1989–90): 3–27.

———. "'Moldy Figs' and Modernists: Jazz at War (1942–1946)." In *Jazz Among the Discourses*, ed. Krin Gabbard. Durham, N.C.: Duke University Press, 1995.

———. "A Short Stay in the Sun: The Reception of Bebop (1944–1950)." *Library Chronicle* 24 (1994): 137–59.

Gennari, John. "Jazz Criticism: Its Development and Ideologies." *Black American Literature Forum* (fall 1991): 449–523.

Giddens, Gary. *Visions of Jazz*. New York: Oxford University Press, 1998.

Gilroy, Paul. *The Black Atlantic: Modernity and Double Consciousness*. Cambridge, Mass.: Harvard University Press, 1993.

———. "One Nation Under a Groove: The Cultural Politics of 'Race' and Racism in Britain." In *Anatomy of Racism*, ed. David Theo Goldberg. Minneapolis: University of Minnesota Press, 1990: 263–82.

———. *Small Acts: Thoughts on the Politics of Black Cultures*. London: Serpent's Tail, 1993.

Gioia, Ted. *The History of Jazz*. New York: Oxford University Press, 1997.

Gleason, Philip. *Speaking of Diversity: Language and Ethnicity in Twentieth-Century America*. Baltimore: Johns Hopkins University Press, 1992.

Goodman, Benny, and Irving Kolodin. *The Kingdom of Swing*. New York: Frederick Ungar, 1961.

Green, Christopher, ed. *Art Made Modern: Roger Fry's Vision of Art*. London: Merrell Holberton, 1999.

Guillaume, Paul. "African Art at the Barnes Foundation." *Opportunity*, May 1924, pp. 140–42.

———. "The Triumph of Ancient Negro Art." *Opportunity*, May 1926, pp. 146–47.

Gumbrecht, Hans Ulrich. *In 1926: Living at the Edge of Time*. Cambridge, Mass.: Harvard University Press, 1997.

Gutmann, Amy, ed. *Multiculturalism: Examining the Politics of Recognition*. Princeton, N.J.: Princeton University Press, 1994.

Hammond, John. "An Experience in Jazz History." In *Black Music in Our Culture*, ed. Dominique Rene de Lerma. Kent, Ohio: Kent State University Press, 1970.

———. "Jim-Crow Blues." *New Masses*, December 13, 1938, pp. 27–28.

———. "King of Swing." *Crisis*, April 1937, pp. 110–11, 123–24.

———. "Random Notes on the Spirituals to Swing Recordings" (liner notes). *Spirituals to Swing: The Legendary Carnegie Hall Concerts of 1938–9*, Vanguard: VSD, 47/48.

Hammond, John, and Irving Townsend. *John Hammond on Record*. New York: Ridge Press, 1977.

Harris, Leonard. "Rendering the Subtext." In *The Philosophy of Alain Locke: Harlem Renaissance and Beyond*, ed. Leonard Harris. Philadelphia: Temple University Press, 1989.

———, ed. *The Critical Pragmatism of Alain Locke*. Lanham, Md.: Rowman & Littlefield, 1999.

Harris, Michael W. *The Rise of Gospel Blues: The Music of Thomas Andrew Dorsey in the Urban Church*. New York: Oxford University Press, 1992.

Harris, Neil. *Humbug: The Art of P. T. Barnum*. Boston: Little, Brown, 1973.

Hasse, John Edward. *Beyond Category: The Life and Genius of Duke Ellington*. New York: Simon & Schuster, 1993.

Hegel, Georg W. F. *The Philosophy of History*, trans. J. Sibree. Buffalo, N.Y.: Prometheus Books, 1991.

Helm, MacKinley. *Angel Mo' and Her Son, Roland Hayes*. Boston: Little, Brown, 1942.

Hemenway, Robert E. *Zora Neale Hurston: A Literary Biography*. Urbana: University of Illinois Press, 1980.

Herder, Johann Gottfried von. "Music, An Art of Humanity," trans. Edward A. Lippman. In *German Essays on Music*, ed. Jost Hermand and Michael Gilbert. New York: Continuum: 1994.

———. *Outlines of a Philosophy of the History of Man*, vol. 1, trans. T. Churchill. London: Luke Hanford, 1803.

Higginson, Thomas Wentworth. *Army Life in a Black Regiment*. East Lansing: Michigan State University Press, 1960.

Higham, John. *Send These To Me: Jews and Other Immigrants in Urban America*. New York: Atheneum, 1975.

Hobsbawm, Eric. *The Jazz Scene*. New York: Pantheon, 1993.

Hollinger, David A. *In the American Province*. Baltimore: Johns Hopkins University Press, 1985.

———. *Postethnic America: Beyond Multiculturalism*. New York: Basic Books, 1995.

Holmes, E. C. "Alain LeRoy Locke: A Sketch." *Phylon* 20 (spring 1959): 82–89.

———. Review of *The Ways of White Folks*. *Opportunity*, September 1934, pp. 283–84.

Horowitz, Joseph. *Wagner Nights*. Berkeley: University of California Press, 1994.

Huggins, Nathan Irvin. *Harlem Renaissance*. New York: Oxford University Press, 1971.

Hughes, Langston. *The Big Sea*. New York: Hill and Wang, 1964.

———. *Fine Clothes to the Jew*. New York: Alfred A. Knopf, 1927.

———. *Langston Hughes Reader*. New York: George Braziller, 1958.

———. "The Negro Artist and the Racial Mountain." *Nation*, June 23, 1926, pp. 692–94.

———. "Our Wonderful Society." *Opportunity*, August 1927, pp. 226–27.

———. Review of *Blues* by W. C. Handy. *Opportunity*, August 1926, p. 258.

———. "Songs Called the Blues." *Phylon* (second quarter 1941): 143–45.

——. *The Ways of White Folks*. New York: Alfred A. Knopf, 1944.

Hurston, Zora Neale. *Dust Tracks on a Road*, ed. Robert Hemenway. Urbana: University of Illinois Press, 1984.

——. *Zora Neale Hurston: Folklore, Memoirs, and Other Writings*, ed. Cheryl A. Wall. New York: Library of America, 1995.

——. *Mules and Men*. New York: Harper & Row, 1990.

——. *The Sanctified Church*, ed. Toni Cade Bambara. Berkeley: Turtle Island, 1983.

Hutchinson, George. *The Harlem Renaissance in Black and White*. Cambridge, Mass.: Harvard University Press, 1995.

Jackson, Walter A. "Melville Herskovits and the Search for Afro-American Culture." *History of Anthropology* 4 (1986): 78–86.

Jemie, Onwuchekwa. *Langston Hughes: An Introduction to the Poetry*. New York: Columbia University Press, 1976.

Johnson, Charles S., ed. *Ebony and Topaz: A Collectanea*. New York: National Urban League, 1927.

Johnson, James Weldon. *Along This Way*. New York: Penguin Books, 1990.

Johnson, James Weldon, and J. Rosamond Johnson, eds. *The Book of American Negro Spirituals*. New York: Viking Press, 1925.

Kallen, Horace. "Alain Locke and Cultural Pluralism." *Journal of Philosophy* 54 (February 28, 1957): 119–27.

——. *Cultural Pluralism and the American Idea*. Philadelphia: University of Pennsylvania Press, 1956.

——. "Democracy Versus the Melting Pot." *Nation*, February 18, 1915; February 25, 1915.

——. *Individualism: An American Way of Life*. New York: Liveright, 1933.

——. "Pluralism and Culture." In *The New Negro Thirty Years Afterward*. Washington, D.C.: Howard University Press, 1995: 41–47.

Kellner, Bruce. " 'Refined Racism': White Patronage in the Harlem Renaissance," *The Harlem Renaissance Re-Examined*. New York: AMS Press, 1987.

Kerman, Cynthia Earl, and Richard Eldridge. *The Lives of Jean Toomer: A Hunger for Wholeness*. Baton Rouge: Louisiana State University Press, 1987.

Kojeve, Alexander. *Introduction to the Reading of Hegel*, trans. James H. Nichols Jr. Ithaca, N.Y.: Cornell University Press, 1969.

Kolodin, Irving. "The Dance Band Business: A Study in Black and White." *Harper's*, June 1941, pp. 72–82.

——. "Number One Swing Man." *Harper's*, September 1939, pp. 431–40.

Kramer, Victor A., ed. *The Harlem Renaissance Re-Examined*. New York: AMS Press, 1987.

Levine, Lawrence. *Black Culture and Black Consciousness: Afro-American Folk Thought from Slavery to Freedom*. New York: Oxford University Press, 1977.

——. *Highbrow/Lowbrow: The Emergence of Cultural Hierarchy in America*. Cambridge, Mass.: Harvard University Press, 1988.

Lewis, David Levering. *W. E. B. Du Bois: Biography of a Race, 1868–1919*. New York: Henry Holt, 1993.

——. *When Harlem Was in Vogue*. New York: Oxford University Press, 1989.

Linnemann, Russell J., ed. *Alain Locke: Reflections on a Modern Renaissance Man*. Baton Rouge: Louisiana State University Press, 1982.

Lionnet, Françoise. "Autoethnography: The An-Archic Style of *Dust Tracks on a Road*." In *The Bounds of Race*, ed. Dominick LaCapra. Ithaca, N.Y.: Cornell University Press, 1991: 164–95.

Locke, Alain. "Apropos of Africa." *Opportunity*, February 1924, pp. 37–40, 58.

——. "Beauty Instead of Ashes." *Nation*, April 18, 1928, pp. 432–34.

——. *The Critical Temper of Alain Locke: A Selection of His Essays on Art and Culture*, ed. Jeffrey C. Stewart. New York: Garland, 1983.

——. "Freedom Through Art." *Crisis*, July 1938, pp. 227–29.

——. *The Negro and His Music*. Port Washington, N.Y.: Kennikat, 1968.

——. *Negro Art: Past and Present*. New York: Arno Press, 1969.

——. "A Note on African Art." *Opportunity*, May 1924, pp. 134–38.

——. "Our Little Renaissance." In *Ebony and Topaz*, ed. Charles Johnson. New York: National Urban League, 1927: 117–18.

——. *The Philosophy of Alain Locke: Harlem Renaissance and Beyond*, ed. Leonard Harris. Philadelphia: Temple University Press, 1989.

——. *Race Contacts and Interracial Relations: Lectures on the Theory and Practice of Race*, ed. Jeffrey C. Stewart. Washington, D.C.: Howard University Press, 1992.

——. "Roland Hayes: An Appreciation." *Opportunity* (December 1923): 356–58.

——. "Steps Toward the Negro Theatre." *Crisis*, December 1922, pp. 66–68.

——. "Toward a Critique of Negro Music." *Opportunity*, November 1934, pp. 328–31; *Opportunity*, December 1934, pp. 365–67, 385.

——, ed. *A Decade of Negro Expression*. Charlottsville, Va.: Michie, 1928.

——, ed. *The New Negro*. New York: Atheneum, 1968.

Locke, Alain, and Bernhard J. Stern, eds. *When Peoples Meet: A Study in Race and Culture Contacts*. New York: Progressive Education Association, 1942.

Lott, Eric. *Love and Theft: Blackface Minstrelsy and the American Working Class*. New York: Oxford University Press, 1993.

Lovell, John, Jr. *Black Song: The Forge and the Flame*. New York: Macmillan, 1972.

Lutz, Tom. "Curing the Blues: W. E. B. Du Bois, Fashionable Diseases, and Degraded Music." *Black Music Research Journal* 11 (fall 1991): 137–56.

Mackey, Nathaniel. *Bedouin Hornbook*. Charlottesville: Callaloo Fiction Series/University Press of Virginia, 1986.

——. *Discrepant Engagement: Dissonance, Cross-Culturality, and Experimental Writing*. New York: Cambridge University Press, 1994.

——. "Sound and Sentiment, Sound and Symbol." In *The Jazz Cadence of America*, ed. Robert G. O'Meally. New York: Columbia University Press, 1998: 602–28.

Marable, Manning. *W. E. B. Du Bois: Black Radical Democrat*. Boston: G. K. Hall, 1986.

Marcuse, Herbert. *The Aesthetic Dimension: Toward a Critique of Marxist Aesthetics*. Boston: Beacon Press, 1978.

Marr, II, Warren. "Roland Hayes." *Black Perspective in Music* (fall 1974): 186–89.

Marsh, J. B. T. *The Story of the Jubilee Singers: With Their Songs*. Boston: Houghton, Osgood, 1880.

McGinty, Doris Evans, and Wayne Shirley. "Paul Robeson: Musician." In *Paul Robeson: Artist and Citizen*, ed. Jeffrey C. Stewart. New Brunswick, N.J.: Rutgers University Press, 1998: 105–20.

McGrath, F. C. *The Sensible Spirit: Walter Pater and the Modernist Paradigm*. Tampa: University of South Florida Press, 1986.

Meisel, Perry. "The Chemistry of the Crystal." In *Walter Pater*, ed. Harold Bloom. New York: Chelsea House, 1985.

Mencken, H. L. *H. L. Mencken on Music*, ed. Louis Cheslock. New York: Alfred A. Knopf, 1961.

Michaels, Walter Benn. *Our America: Nativism, Modernism, and Pluralism*. Durham, N.C.: Duke University Press, 1995.

Miller, J. Hillis. "Walter Pater: A Partial Portrait." In *Walter Pater*, ed. Harold Bloom. New York: Chelsea House, 1985.

Monson, Ingrid. "Doubleness, Irony, and Jazz Improvisation: Irony, Parody, and Ethnomusicology." *Critical Inquiry* 20 (winter 1994): 283–313.

——. *Saying Something: Jazz Improvisation and Interaction*. Chicago: University of Chicago Press, 1996.

Morton, Michael. *Herder and the Poetics of Thought: Unity and Diversity in "On Diligence in Several Learned Languages."* University Park: Pennsylvania State University Press, 1989.

Moses, Wilson. *Afrotopia: The Roots of African American Popular History*. Cambridge: Cambridge University Press, 1998.

Mullen, Edward J., ed. *Critical Essays on Langston Hughes*. Boston: G. K. Hall, 1986.

Murray, Albert. *The Hero and the Blues*. Columbia: University of Missouri Press, 1973.

——. *Omni-Americans*. New York: Da Capo, 1970.

——. *Stomping the Blues*. New York: McGraw-Hill, 1976.

Nancy, Jean-Luc. "The Sublime Offering." In *Of the Sublime: Presence in Question*, trans. Jeffrey S. Librett. Albany: State University of New York Press, 1993.

Nietzsche, Friedrich. *"The Birth of Tragedy" and "The Case of Wagner,"* trans. Walter Kaufmann. New York: Vintage, 1967.

North, Michael A. *The Dialect of Modernism: Race, Language, and Twentieth-Century Literature*. New York: Oxford University Press, 1994.

Ogren, Kathy J. *The Jazz Revolution: Twenties America and the Meaning of Jazz*. New York: Oxford University Press, 1989.

Pater, Walter. *The Renaissance: Studies in Art and Poetry*. New York: Macmillan, 1909.

——. *Walter Pater: Three Major Texts*, ed. William E. Buckler. New York: New York University Press, 1986.

Peretti, Burton W. *The Creation of Jazz: Music, Race, and Culture in Urban America*. Urbana: University of Illinois Press, 1992.

Poirier, Richard. *Poetry and Pragmatism*. Cambridge, Mass.: Harvard University Press, 1992.

Pomerance, Alan. *Repeal of the Blues*. Secaucus, N.J.: Citadel Press, 1988.

Posnock, Ross. *Color and Culture: Black Writers and the Making of the Modern Intellectual*. Cambridge, Mass.: Harvard University Press, 1998.

Radano, Ronald. "Denoting Difference: The Writing of the Slave Spirituals." *Critical Inquiry* 22 (spring 1996): 506–44.

———. "Soul Texts and the Blackness of Folk." *Modernism/Modernity* 2, no. 1 (1995): 71–95.

Raeburn, Bruce Boyd. "New Orleans Style." Ph.D. diss., Tulane University, 1991.

Ramazani, Jahan. *The Poetry of Mourning: The Modern Elegy from Hardy to Heaney*. Chicago: University of Chicago Press, 1994.

Rampersad, Arnold. *The Art and Imagination of W. E. B. Du Bois*. New York: Schocken Books, 1990.

———. *The Life of Langston Hughes*, vol. 1, *1902–1941*. New York: Oxford University Press, 1986.

Ramsey, Frederic, Jr., and Charles Edward Smith, eds. *Jazzmen*. New York: Harcourt, Brace, 1939.

Randolph, A. Philip. "Reply to Marcus Garvey." In *The Messenger Reader*, ed. Sondra Kathryn Wilson. New York: Modern Library, 2000: 348–57.

Reed, Jr., Adolph L. *W. E. B. Du Bois and American Political Thought: Fabianism and the Color Line*. New York: Oxford University Press, 1997.

Reeve, Charles. "The Ethics of Anglo-American Formalism." Ph.D. diss., Cornell University, 1999.

Roach, Joseph. *Cities of the Dead: Circum-Atlantic Performance*. New York: Columbia University Press, 1996.

Robeson, Paul. "An Actor's Wanderings and Hopes." In *The Messenger Reader*, ed. Sondra Kathryn Wilson. New York: Modern Library, 2000: 292–93.

Roediger, David R. *Toward the Abolition of Whiteness*. London: Verso, 1994.

———. *The Wages of Whiteness: Race and the Making of the American Working Class*. London: Verso, 1991.

Rogin, Michael. *Blackface, White Noise: Jewish Immigrants in the Hollywood Melting Pot*. Berkeley: University of California Press, 1998.

Rosenfeld, Paul. *Musical Impressions: Selections from Paul Rosenfeld's Criticism*, ed. Herbert A. Leibowitz. New York: Hill and Wang, 1969.

Rowell, Charles H. "Let Me Be with Ole Jazzbo: An Interview with Sterling A. Brown." *Callaloo* 14 (1991): 795–815.

Royce, Josiah. *Lectures on Modern Idealism*. New Haven, Conn.: Yale University Press, 1919.

Santayana, George. *The Sense of Beauty*. New York: Charles Scribner's Sons, 1896.

Schuyler, George S. "The Negro-Art Hokum," *Nation*, June 16, 1926, pp. 662–63.

———. "Phylon Profile, XXII: Carl Van Vechten." *Phylon* (4th quarter 1950): 362–73.

Shirley, Wayne D. "The Coming of 'Deep River.'" *American Music* (winter 1997): 493–534.

Silveri, Louis D. "The Singing of the Fisk Jubilee Singers: 1871–1874." In *Feel the Spirit: Studies in Nineteenth-Century Afro-American Music*, ed. George R. Keck and Sherrill V. Martin. Westport, Conn.: Greenwood Press, 1988.

Simpson, Anne Key. *Hard Trials: The Life and Music of Harry T. Burleigh*. Metuchen, N.J.: Scarecrow Press, 1990.

Snead, James A. "Repetition as a Figure of Black Culture." In *Black Literature and Literary Theory*, ed. Henry Louis Gates Jr. New York: Methuen, 1984.

Sollors, Werner. "A Critique of Pure Pluralism." In *Reconstructing American Literary History*, ed. Sacvan Bercovitch. Cambridge, Mass.: Harvard University Press, 1986.

Southern, Eileen. *The Music of Black Americans*. New York: W. W. Norton, 1983.

Spencer, Jon Michael. *The New Negroes and Their Music*. Knoxville: University of Tennessee Press, 1997.

Steiner, Christopher B. *African Art in Transit*. Cambridge: Cambridge University Press, 1994.

Stepto, Robert B. *From Behind the Veil: A Study of Afro-American Narrative*. Urbana: University of Illinois Press, 1979.

Stewart, Jeffrey C. "A Black Aesthete at Oxford." *Massachusetts Review* 34 (autumn 1993): 411–28.

———. "Introduction." In Alain Locke, *Race Contacts and Interracial Relations: Lectures on the Theory and Practice of Race*. Washington, D.C.: Howard University Press, 1992.

———, ed. *The Critical Temper of Alain Locke: A Selection of His Essays on Art and Culture*. New York: Garland, 1983.

Stowe, David Ware. *Swing Changes: Big Band Jazz in New Deal America*. Cambridge, Mass.: Harvard University Press, 1994.

Sundquist, Eric. *To Wake the Nations: Race in the Making of American Literature*. Cambridge, Mass.: Harvard University Press, 1993.

Tate, Claudia. *Psychoanalysis and Black Novels: Desire and the Protocols of Race*. New York: Oxford University Press, 1998.

Taylor, Charles. "The Politics of Recognition." In *Multiculturalism: Examining the Politics of Recognition*, ed. Amy Gutmann. Princeton, N.J.: Princeton University Press, 1994.

Thurman, Howard. *Deep River: Reflections on the Religious Insights of Certain of the Negro Spirituals*. Port Washington, N.Y.: Kennikat Press, 1969.

Tomlinson, Gary. "Cultural Dialogics and Jazz: A White Historian Signifies." *Black Music Research Journal* 11 (fall 1991), 229–64.

———. *Metaphysical Song*. Princeton, N.J.: Princeton University Press, 1999.

Toomer, Jean. *Cane*, ed. Darwin T. Turner. New York: W. W. Norton, 1988.

———. *A Jean Toomer Reader: Selected Unpublished Writings*, ed. Frederik L. Rusch. New York: Oxford University Press, 1993.

———. *Essentials*, ed. Rudolph P. Boyd. Athens: University of Georgia Press, 1991.

———. *The Wayward and the Seeking: A Collection of Writings by Jean Toomer*, ed. Darwin T. Turner. Washington, D.C.: Howard University Press, 1980.

Tracey, Steven C. *Langston Hughes and the Blues*. Urbana: University of Illinois Press, 1988.

Tucker, Mark, ed. *The Duke Ellington Reader*. New York: Oxford University Press, 1993.

———. "The Genesis of *Black, Brown and Beige*." *Black Music Research Journal* 13 (fall 1993): 67–86.

———. "The Renaissance Education of Duke Ellington." In *Black Music in the Harlem Renaissance*, ed. Samuel A. Floyd Jr. Westport, Conn.: Greenwood Press, 1990.

Van Vechten, Carl. "The Black Blues." *Vanity Fair*, August 1925, pp. 57, 86.

———. "The Folksongs of the American Negro." *Vanity Fair*, July 1925, pp. 52, 92.

———. "George Gershwin." *Vanity Fair*, March 1925, pp. 40, 78, 84.

———. *Keep A-Inchin' Along: Selected Writings of Carl Van Vechten about Black Art and Culture*, ed. Bruce Kellner. Westport, Conn.: Greenwood Press, 1979.

———. *Letters of Carl Van Vechten*, ed. Bruce Kellner. New Haven, Conn.: Yale University Press, 1987.

———. "'Moanin' Wid a Sword In Ma Hand.'" *Vanity Fair*, February 1926, pp. 61, 100, 102.

———. *Music and Bad Manners*. New York: Alfred A. Knopf, 1916.

———. "Negro 'Blues' Singers." *Vanity Fair*, March 1926, pp. 67, 106, 108.

———. "Prescription for the Negro Theatre." *Vanity Fair*, October 1925, pp. 46, 92, 98.

———. "Religious Folk Songs of the American Negro—A Review." *Opportunity*, November 1925, pp. 330–31.

Watts, Jerry Gafio. *Heroism and the Black Intellectual: Ralph Ellison, Politics, and Afro-American Intellectual Life*. Chapel Hill: University of North Carolina Press, 1994.

Weiskel, Thomas. *The Romantic Sublime: Studies in the Structure and Psychology of Transcendence*. Baltimore: Johns Hopkins University Press, 1976.

Welburn, Ronald G. "American Jazz Criticism, 1914–1940." Ph.D. diss., New York University, 1983.

Werner, Craig Hansen. *Playing the Changes: From Afro-Modernism to the Jazz Impulse*. Urbana: University of Illinois Press, 1994.

West, Cornel. *The American Evasion of Philosophy: A Genealogy of Pragmatism*. Madison: University of Wisconsin Press, 1989.

———. *Restoring Hope: Conversations on the Future of Black America*, ed. Kelvin Shawn Sealey. Boston: Beacon Press, 1997.

Whiteman, Paul. "The Progress of Jazz." *Vanity Fair*, January 1926, pp. 52, 98.

Williams, Sherley Anne. "The Blues Roots of Contemporary Afro-American Poetry." In *Afro-American Literature: The Reconstruction of Instruction*, ed. Dexter Fisher and Robert B. Stepto. New York: Modern Language Press Association of America, 1978.

Wintz, Cary D. *Black Culture and the Harlem Renaissance*. Houston: Rice University Press, 1988.

Woolsey, F. W. "Conversation with . . . Roland Hayes." *Black Perspectives in Music* (fall 1974): 179–85.

Work, John W. "Negro Folk Song." *Opportunity*, October 1923, pp. 292–94.

Wright, John S. "The New Negro Poet and the Nachal Man: Sterling Brown's Folk Odyssey." *Black American Literature Forum* 23 (spring 1989): 95–105.

Zamir, Shamoon. *Dark Voices: W. E. B. Du Bois and American Thought, 1888–1903*. Chicago: University of Chicago Press, 1996.

Žižek, Slavoj. *For They Know Not What They Do: Enjoyment as a Political Factor*. London: Verso, 1991.

———. *The Sublime Object of Ideology*. London: Verso, 1989.

INDEX

97, 157–58, 233–35, 237, 239–41, 246–
47, 250, 252–53, 262–63. *See also* aesthetics; concert spirituals; jazz
criticism
Autobiography of an Ex-Colored Man
(Johnson), 29–30

Baker, Houston A., 39, 69, 71, 83–84
Baraka, Amiri, 53, 279 n.107, 298 n.30
Barksdale, Richard, 170, 190
Barnes, Albert, 104–5, 108–9
Barthes, Roland, 302 n.104
Basie, Count, 231, 241, 244, 250–51, 257–
58, 263
"Beauty Instead of Ashes" (Locke), 123,
148–49, 153, 158–59
Bechet, Sidney, 226, 241
Beecher, Henry Ward, 18–19
Bhabha, Homi, 275 n.58
Bismarck, Otto von, 24, 27
Black, Brown and Beige (Ellington), 223,
247, 255, 264, 266–67
Black Music (Baraka), 53, 279 n.107
black nationalism, 25–29, 66, 114–15, 138–
39, 153; and W. E. B. Du Bois, 24–29,
32–33, 47, 53, 104, 114–15, 123, 143; and
Marcus Garvey, 104; and Alain
Locke, 123, 138, 142–43, 165; and music, 79–80, 138, 166, 259–60
Bledsoe, Jules, 97
blues, 179–94, 238; and artifice and authenticity, 181–83; and blues aesthetic, 181–82, 186, 298 n.30; and classic blues of the 1920s, 99, 177, 185; and
Langston Hughes's fiction, 186–94;
and Langston Hughes's poetry, 9,
170–71, 179–86, 193; and Albert Murray, 182; and Sherley Anne Williams,
181–82
"Blues I'm Playing, The" (Hughes),
186–94
"Blues Roots of Contemporary Afro-
American Poetry, The" (Williams),
181–82
Boas, Franz, 135–36, 204–5

Book of American Negro Poetry (John-
son), 76
Book of American Negro Spirituals (John-
son), 97, 100
Bourne, Randolph, 127
Braithwaite, William Stanley, 60
Brown, Colin, 21–22, 99
Brown, Lawrence, 63, 96
Brown, Sterling, 90–93, 101–3; and Ro-
land Hayes, 90–93, 102; and Zora
Neale Hurston, 206; and Alain
Locke, 101–3, 161–62, 165; and Negro
Renaissance, 101–2, 142–43, 161, 296
n.8; and popular music, 91, 102, 165,
242; and post-Renaissance influence,
102; *Southern Road*, 102; and Jean
Toomer, 90–91; and Carl Van Vech-
ten, 96, 101
Bürger, Peter, 85
Burleigh, Harry, 14, 60, 62, 79–81, 83,
86, 97, 99

Cane (Toomer), 6, 60, 65–73. *See also*
Jean Toomer
canonization, 220–21, 232–33, 259–61,
251–56, 267–69; and African American literature, 198; and notions of the
jazz tradition, 251–56, 267–69; and
problem of genre definition in music, 220–21, 228, 232–33, 246–47, 259–
61. *See also* jazz criticism
Cantwell, Robert, 140, 219, 228
Carby, Hazel, 206–7
Cavell, Stanley, 43
"Characteristics of Negro Expression"
(Hurston), 10, 197–98, 202, 204–5,
210–11
Chauncey, George, 154
Christianity, 35–36, 113–14, 167, 174, 201–3
classicism, 105–9, 150–53, 157–58, 248–56,
293 n.91. *See also* aesthetics; jazz criti-
cism; Alain Locke
Clifford, James, 106
Coleridge, Samuel Taylor, 79, 274 n.39
Colson, William, 80

Douglas, Ann, 51
Downes, Olin, 13–14, 49, 118–19, 195, 232
Duberman, Martin, 96
Du Bois, William Edward Burghardt
    (W. E. B.), 4–6, 13–17, 24–57, 85–86,
    114–15, 153–54; and aesthetic ideal-
    ism, 5, 37, 43–44, 47, 51, 53, 55, 73, 85,
    124, 301 n.96; and black nationalism,
    24, 26, 28–29, 32–33, 47, 53, 104, 114–
    15, 123, 143; and cosmopolitanism,
    27–28, 42, 44, 52–53; and "Criteria of
    Negro Art, The," 54–55, 212; and
    cultural evolution, 46, 114; and *Dark
    Princess*, 47–48, 75, 275 n.62; and dia-
    lectical thought, 25, 40–41, 45–46, 85,
    115, 212–13; and *Dusk of Dawn*, 162;
    and Fisk Jubilee Singers, 24, 29, 33–
    35, 37, 77, 139–40; and Fisk Univer-
    sity, 30, 77–80; and folk romanti-
    cism, 5, 16, 24, 36–37, 55, 66, 114–15;
    and Germany, 26, 43–44, 47; and
    Roland Hayes, 62, 92; and Langston
    Hughes, 171, 180, 183, 186; and jazz
    music, 48–49; and the "kingdom of
    culture," 29–31, 40, 43–44; and Alain
    Locke, 29, 52, 113–14, 118–19, 123, 126,
    139–40, 153, 162, 195; and the NAACP,
    52; and politics, 24, 52, 162; and pro-
    paganda, 85–86, 153–54, 162, 212; and
    religion, 35–36; and slavery, 34, 36;
    and socialism, 44, 162; and the "sor-
    row songs," 28–32, 34–37, 45, 74, 78,
    114–15, 139, 212; and *Souls of Black
    Folk, The*, 5–6, 16, 24–25, 28–49, 54,
    212; and Jean Toomer, 66, 69–70, 73–
    74; and utopianism, 92, 212; and Carl
    Van Vechten, 50, 100, 176; and Rich-
    ard Wagner, 37, 39–41, 43–44; and
    Booker T. Washington, 27, 31; and
    John W. Work, 79–80
Dusk of Dawn (Du Bois), 162
Dust Tracks on a Road (Hurston), 204,
    206
Dvořák, Antonin, 60, 79, 164–65, 264

Early, Gerald, 231, 233–35, 258
Eliot, T. S., 67, 72
elitism, 78–85, 101–2, 126
Ellington, Duke, 11, 223–25, 254–68;
    and *Black, Brown and Beige*, 11, 223,
    255, 264, 266–67; and black national-
    ism, 259–60; and genre labels in mu-
    sic, 259, 261, 264, 267–68; and John
    Hammond, 11, 223–25, 247, 255–56,
    259, 262–65; and jazz critics, 11, 223–
    25, 247, 254–57, 261–68; and Alain
    Locke, 166, 264–65; and modern
    jazz, 267–68; and New Negro im-
    agery, 223, 225, 259–61, 264–67; and
    "Reminiscing in Tempo," 262–64;
    and Paul Whiteman, 205, 259–60,
    263–66
Ellison, Ralph, 74, 182, 297–98 n.17
Emperor Jones (O'Neill), 62, 98
"Ethics of Culture" (Locke), 125

"failure" of Harlem Renaissance, 82–85
Fauset, Arthur Huff, 101
Fauset, Jessie, 178–79
Fine Clothes to the Jew (Hughes), 168, 171,
    179–80
Fisk Jubilee Singers, 17–24, 29–31, 33–35,
    49, 60, 77–81, 139–40
Fisk University, 13–14, 17, 30, 60, 77–80;
    university choir, 13–14, 118–19
Floyd, Samuel A., Jr., 3, 214
folk nationalism, 114–15, 138–40, 143, 157,
    172. *See also* black nationalism
formalism, 141, 145–55, 158. *See also* aes-
    thetics; Roger Fry; Alain Locke;
    Walter Pater
Forrest, Leon, 215–16
Frank, Waldo, 70, 72, 75–76, 236
Frazier, E. Franklin, 90
Freud, Sigmund, 55, 71, 185, 189
"From Spirituals to Swing" (concert),
    10–11, 225, 235–43, 264–65
Fry, Roger, 150–52, 293 n.88. *See also* for-
    malism

Neale Hurston, 101; and Alain Locke, 89, 93, 160, 165–66; "Moanin' Wid a Sword in Ma Hand," 99–101; *Nigger Heaven*, 50, 96, 100–101; "Prescription for the Negro Theatre," 95–96, 283 n.96; and racial exoticism, 50–51, 95–96, 98–99, 101, 160; and Paul Robeson, 62–63, 96–99; and spirituals, 62–63, 86, 89, 93, 95–98, 100–101

Vision and Design (Fry), 151–52. *See also* African sculpture; formalism; Roger Fry; Alain Locke

Wagner, Richard, 38–39, 41, 43–45, 48, 75, 282 n.69
Washington, Booker T., 27, 30–31, 42, 60, 62, 64, 83, 87, 123
Washington, D.C., 162, 259–60
Waste Land, The (Eliot), 67, 72
Ways of White Folk, The (Hughes), 186–87, 194. *See also* "Blues I'm Playing, The" (Hughes); Langston Hughes
Weary Blues, The (Hughes), 168, 170–71, 178–79, 193
Wendell, Barrett, 132–33
West, Cornel, 274 n.55
When Harlem Was in Vogue (Lewis), 125–26, 144–45. *See also* Harlem Renaissance
White, George, 18, 21
White, Walter, 236
Whiteman, Paul, 164–65, 197, 205, 226, 229, 233–35, 246, 259–60, 263–66
Williams, Sherley Anne, 181–82
Woodson, Carter G., 54
Work, John W., 78–81
Wright, Richard, 74, 206

Zamir, Shamoon, 213
Žižek, Slavoj, 114–15, 172, 278 n.99

PAUL ALLEN ANDERSON is Assistant Professor
of American Culture and African American Studies
at the University of Michigan.

Library of Congress Cataloging-in-Publication Data
Anderson, Paul Allen.
Deep river : music and memory in Harlem
Renaissance thought / Paul Allen Anderson.
p. cm. — (New Americanists)
Includes bibliographical references (p.) and index.
ISBN 0-8223-2577-2 (cloth : alk. paper)
ISBN 0-8223-2591-8 (pbk. : alk. paper)
1. African Americans—New York (State)
—New York—Music—History and criticism.
2. Harlem (New York, N.Y.)—Intellectual life—20th
century. 3. Harlem Renaissance. I. Title II. Series.
ML3556.A53 2001
780'.89'9607307471—dc21   2001018750